Big Dipper

stories, poems, songs and activities for young children

edited by: June Epstein
June Factor
Gwendda McKay
Dorothy Rickards
music by: June Epstein
designed by: Dorothy Rickards
illustrated by: Alison Lester

Melbourne
OXFORD UNIVERSITY PRESS
Oxford Wellington New York

Contents   ■ Stories   □ Poetry   ● Music   ▼ 'Ideas'   ○ Riddles

You and me
- □ Me — *Nola Wood* — 4
- □ My Feet — *Joanne Wallis* — 4
- □ Hair — *Dorothy Mills* — 4
- □ Different — *Carmel Brennan* — 5
- ○□ If I Were You — *Debra Alway* — 5
- □ Everybody — *June Factor* — 5

Families
- ● Our House — *Gwendda McKay & June Epstein* — 6
- ■ Grandmother's Birthday — *Dorothy Rickards* — 8
- ▼□ My Granny — *Julia Norman* — 9
- □ Our Family — *Joan M. Shilton* — 10
- □ Relations — *Dorothy Rickards* — 10
- ▼ Finger Family — *Dorothy Rickards* — 11

Brothers and sisters
- ▼●■ Jonathan's Singing Day — *June Epstein* — 12
- □ Little Brother — *Karen Dowel* — 16
- □ Sons — *Colleen Clancy* — 16
- □ In the Middle — *Leonne Leslie* — 16
- □ Older Brothers — *Alison Lawrie* — 17
- □ Older Sister — *Gwendda McKay* — 17

Night-time
- ▼■ Night in Brick Road — *Chris Wallace-Crabbe* — 18
- □ Teddy — *Annette Maloney* — 20
- □ Bedtime — *Annette Maloney* — 20
- □ Night Rider — *Margaret McCarthy* — 21

Day-time
- □ Sunday — *Susan Uhe* — 22
- ■□ Wake Up! — *Dorothy Rickards* — 22
- ○□ Where Is It? — *Joanne Wallis* — 23
- ○□ Socks — *Elizabeth Cockerell* — 23

Hungry-time
- □ Peas — *Joanne Wallis* — 24
- □ Fish Fancies — *Colleen Clancy* — 24
- □ Dessert — *Joan M. Shilton* — 24
- ■ The Snitcher Snatch — *Dorothy Mills* — 25
- ○□ Will I Really Truly Burst? — *Joan M. Shilton* — 29

Play-time
- ▼■ The Good Ship *Play* — *June Epstein* — 30
- □ Bubbles — *Barbara Cork* — 32
- □ The Ball — *Iola Tilley* — 32
- ▼□ The New Phone — *Anne LeRoy* — 32

Rainy days
- □ Splish! Splosh! — *Nola Wood* — 33
- □ Mr Rainman — *Sue Killeen* — 33
- □ Safety Yellow — *Isobel Pratt* — 33
- ○□ Rain — *Teresa Hoy* — 33
- ▼●■ Wet Saturday — *June Epstein* — 34

Good and bad days
- □ Cleaning Up Day — *Joan M. Shilton* — 37
- □ Mum's Right — *Nola Wood* — 37
- □ Tom — *Mary Roberts* — 38
- □ Measles — *Kim Hadden* — 39
- □ Catching Things — *Elizabeth Cockerell* — 40
- □ Stay At Home Day — *Joan M. Shilton* — 40

Where do you live?
- ▼□ Poor Mrs Duck — *Kathryn Taylor* — 41
- □ Living-places — *Julia Norman* — 42

In the city
- □ Chimneys — *Alison Lawrie* — 43
- ●□ City Song — *Dorothy Rickards* — 43
- ■ Window in the Sky — *Anita Lucas* — 44
- ▼□ City Scene — *Beverley Hannaker* — 45
- □ I Live Up There — *Jane Bradley* — 46
- ○▼□ Traffic Lights — *Gwendda McKay* — 47
- ■ Bob's Pup — *Mary Roberts* — 48

In the country
- ▼● The Aboriginal Boy — *June Epstein* — 50
- □ Newborn — *Gayle Sweeney* — 51
- □ Farmyard — *Gail Gregory* — 51
- □ In the Bush — *Anne LeRoy* — 51

On the move
- □ Trains — *Jo-Anne Steven* — 52
- ○□ Travelling — *Dorothy Rickards* — 52

Seasons
- □ Eucalypt Year — *June Epstein* — 53
- □ Winter and Summer — *Julie Black* — 53

Contents

Seasons
- Let Me Wonder — Susan Uhe — 54
- Spring — Mills McKay — 55
- Summer — Dorothy Mills — 55
- Autumn — Dorothy Mills — 55
- Winter — Roger Pelletier — 55

Wind ways
- Mrs Ippendippidy's Washing — Sue Bailes — 56
- A Dream — Anne LeRoy & June Epstein — 58
- Wild Wind — Dorothy Mills — 59
- Where the Wind Blows — Valerie Havard — 59
- Where? — Isobel Pratt — 60

Sky ways
- Clouds — Jenny Bryant — 61
- Blue — Dorothy Mills — 61
- A Cloud Game — Annette Nolan — 62

Big and small
- Small — Robyn Curnow — 64
- Seeing — Barbara Cork — 64
- The Competition — June Epstein — 65

Big animals
- What Am I? — Merron Looney — 66
- Tromp! Tromp! — Kathryn Taylor — 68
- Elephant — Sonya Higgs — 68
- Hippo — Jo-Anne Steven — 68
- Yaks' Gnus — Lee Andrews — 69

Small animals
- The Ears of Mandy — June Epstein — 70
- Slide-Swim-Fly — Sue Cochrane — 72
- Snake — Dorothy Mills — 72
- Egg — Joanne Wallis — 73
- Don't Call Him That — Anne LeRoy — 73
- Picnic Day — Laurel Hoffrichter — 74

Very small animals
- Caterpillar Lunch — Kathryn Taylor — 77
- Caterpillar — Janette Jenkins — 77
- Metamorphosis — Anne LeRoy & June Epstein — 78
- Snail — Teresa O'Halloran — 80
- Big Black Spider — Angela Stubbs — 80
- A Visitor — Joan M. Shilton — 80
- Little Fleas — Lee Andrews — 80
- Cheek! — Sonya Higgs — 80

Imaginary animals
- The Marmadin — Lee Andrews — 81
- The Higglebump — Virgina Brown — 81
- Puggly Beasts — Henry Parker — 82
- Fat Horace — Linda Davison — 83
- Dragons are Imaginary? — Bronwyn Williams — 85

Magic
- Katharine's Magic Horse — June Epstein — 86
- The Power of Five — Judith Howard — 88
- Llewellyn the Witch — Colleen Clancy — 89
- John's Task — Mary Roberts — 90

Let's pretend
- Tracks in the Dirt — Joanne Wallis — 93
- Kings and Queens — Anne LeRoy & June Epstein — 94

Special days
- Red Letter Days — Dorothy Rickards — 96
- The Bells — June Epstein — 97
- Bottle Bell Tunes — arr: June Epstein — 98
- Day at the Beach — Barbara Prictor — 99
- The Show — Sue Berry — 100
- Splashalong and the Melbourne Cup — Terry Duff — 101

Birthdays
- Off to the Party — Robyn Cordes — 102
- Birthday — Dorothy Mills — 102
- The Instant Party — June Epstein — 103

Festivals
- Chinese New Year — Dorothy Rickards — 106
- Easter Buns — Gwendda McKay — 107
- Christmas — Dorothy Mills — 108
- A Christmas Riddle — Judy Hocking — 108
- Parcels — Dorothy Mills — 109
- Christmas Eve — Dorothy Rickards — 110

Index — 111

You and me

Hair

There's
Curly hair
Straight hair
Fine hair
Strong.
Black hair
Blonde hair
Short hair
Long.
Who cares
If my hair's
Every sort of wrong?
Hair!
Wash it
Dry it
Brush it
Part it
Comb it
Plait it—

     There!

Dorothy Mills

My Feet

When I sit upon *that* seat
The carpet talks up to my feet,
They chat about the time of day
Until I have to walk away.

When I sit upon *this* chair
My feet and the lino floor just stare,
They silently wait until I go—
They're not the best of friends, you know!

BUT—

When I sit out on my swing
The lush green grass and my feet sing.

Joanne Wallis

Me

I look in the mirror
And what do I see?
I see myself
Looking at me!

Nola Wood

You and me

Different

Are we different?
   Yes, we are,
Just as different as 'near' and 'far'.
Are we different?
   Yes, you see,
     For you are YOU
     And I am ME.

Carmel Brennan

Everybody

Girls grow into women
Boys grow into men.

Women can be mothers
Men can be fathers.

Girls and boys
Women and men
Mothers and fathers.
What can they do?

A girl can build a tower of blocks
A boy can cuddle a baby doll.

A woman can be a farmer
A man can be a dressmaker.

A mother can drive a taxi
A father can cook the spaghetti.

Girls and boys
Women and men
Mothers and fathers.

When you grow up
What will you be?
What will you do?

June Factor

If I Were You

If I were you and you were me,
Think of all the fun there'd be.
You'd have red hair, I'd have gold,
I'd be young and you'd be old.
You'd have less legs, I'd have more,
Because you'd have two and I'd have four.
And you'd be in bed at night when it's dark,
But I'd stay awake in the yard and bark!

Debra Alway

Families

Families

Some-bo-dy look-ing, some-bo-dy cook-ing, Some-bo-dy feed-ing, some-bo-dy read-ing, Some-bo-dy play-ing, some-bo-dy say-ing:

Slowly and very loudly indeed

'When can we have some peace?'

Slowly and very softly indeed

'When can we have some peace?'

Families

Grandmother's Birthday

Dominic and his family lived on the sixteenth floor of a tall building in the city.

Grandmother looked after Dominic and his baby sister, while Mother and Father went to work. Every morning, when Grandmother took Dominic to school, the three of them—Grandmother, Dominic and Toula—went down, down, down in the lift.

Every afternoon they went up, up, up when school was over.

When Dominic hurt his leg and had to stay home from school and rest it for a whole week, Grandmother and baby Toula stayed up on the sixteenth floor with him every day.

Grandmother told him stories about the country where she was born.

Dominic told Grandmother stories he had learned at school.

Toula listened a little bit to both of them, but mostly she played with her blocks and her cuddly bear.

It was a happy week, until Friday. Then Dominic was very quiet and sad. At last he told Grandmother what was the matter—it was the day he was to bring home the present he had made at school for her birthday. He had drawn a picture of a beautiful grey and yellow spider, and over it he had carefully stitched a web of fine wool. But Grandmother's birthday was on Saturday, and his present was down, down, down in the lift and across the road, at school.

It was meant to be a surprise.

Grandmother told Dominic she would look forward to the surprise when his leg was better. She kissed him, and began to cook the evening meal.

When Dominic looked out at the rain-clouds racing across the sky, he noticed a spider outside on the corner of the window. He thought it must be a very tired spider to have climbed up sixteen floors, and he hoped it would stay on his window-sill to have a rest.

Grandmother was pleased to see the little live creature when she came to open Dominic's window a little, before he went to sleep. She and Dominic watched it as it busily began to spin a fine web of silk across the corner of the closed window.

'Please don't open the window tonight,' said Dominic.

'All right, we won't disturb the spider,' agreed Grandmother.

In the night it rained again, and Dominic worried about the

Families

spider. But the next morning it was a beautiful day of sunshine for Grandmother's birthday.

Dominic looked to see if the spider had been washed away. Then he shouted with surprise, 'Grandmother! Grandmother! Look! Look at the diamonds and pearls on our window-sill!'

Grandmother hurried to the window and saw that the raindrops on the spider's web were like jewels in the sunshine.

'Thank you, Dominic,' she said. 'If you hadn't noticed the spider and stopped me from opening the window last night, I wouldn't have had this beautiful birthday present!'

Dorothy Rickards

My Granny

Daddy's Mum's my Granny,
And I'm very glad she's mine.
She tells me lots of stories
Of things about the time
When Daddy was quite little
And did the things I do.
She always smells of perfume
And she's fashionable too.
She beats me playing Rummy,
But at Snap I am the winner;
Her cooking is delicious,
Especially roast dinner.
My Granny has her photos
All about the place.
(In photographs of Daddy
I find it's just my face!)
Round her neck her glasses
On a chain get in the way
When suddenly I hug her
Ten times or more a day.
She takes me driving sometimes
In her car that's shiny-new.
I do so love my Granny!
Do you love your Granny, too?

Julia Norman

Families

Our Family

Baby cannot feed herself,
She slops her food about,
She gets it in her little spoon
But cannot find her mouth.

Annette is untidy,
She never shuts the doors,
She leaves the cupboards open
And pulls out all the drawers.

David is a fuss-pot,
He puts EVERYTHING away!
So when we want to find things
We have to search all day.

Mummy likes things spic 'n' span,
At times I must agree,
But I can never find things
If they're not right there to see.

Dad keeps his tool-shed tidy
With its nails and bolts and locks,
But almost every morning
We hear, 'Mum, where are my socks?'

Joan M. Shilton

Relations

My father's brothers are my uncles,
And his sister is my aunt;
All the children are my cousins,
Cousins by the tens and dozens—
Can I count them? No, I can't!

Then there are the sisters, brothers,
Parents, cousins of my Mum,
And all their children, nephews, nieces,
When I try to count the pieces
There's another baby come.

When brothers, sisters, wives and husbands
Bring their families home for tea,
Bruno (bigger), Gina (smaller),
And tall Sebastiano, all are
Older than their uncle—ME!

Dorothy Rickards

Brothers and sisters

Jonathan's Singing Day

One day Jonathan woke up and thought, 'This is my Singing Day.' So when his father came to see if he had been to the bathroom, and if he had dressed himself, he sang:

Good morning, good morning, I've been to the bathroom, I've washed my face, I've put on my shirt and I've put on my socks but I can't tie up my shoes.

That was because they were new shoes, with laces. He had tied the bows all by himself, but they felt very loose and he did not want to trip. His father showed him how to tie them more tightly, and they went to breakfast.

Jonathan's mother was in hospital. She was having a new baby.

'Do you want cheese or jam on your toast?' asked his father.

Jonathan sang:

Cheese is very good and jam is very nice but honey is best of all.

His father gave him the honey and he spread it himself.

After breakfast, Jonathan went to the gate to wait for his friend the postman. It was a long time before the postman came, so Jonathan rode his tricycle up and down the driveway.

As the wheels went round and round he rang his bell and sang:

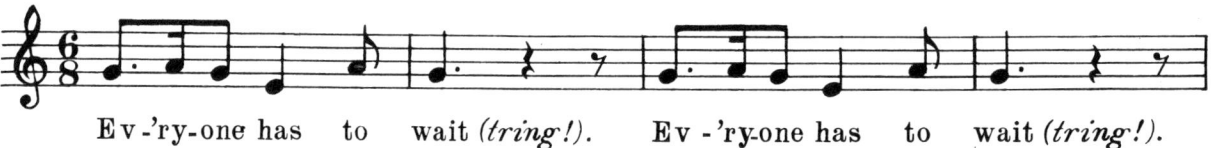

Ev-'ry-one has to wait *(tring!)*. Ev-'ry-one has to wait *(tring!)*.

Brothers and sisters

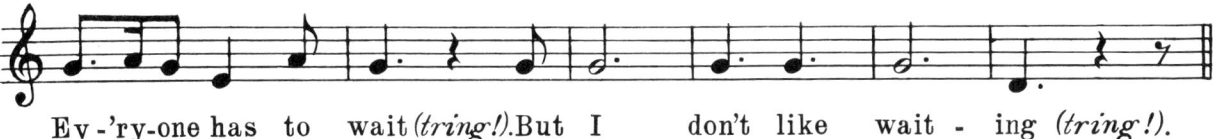
Ev-'ry-one has to wait *(tring!)*. But I don't like wait-ing *(tring!)*.

At last the postman came. He propped his bike against the fence and gave Jonathan four postcards, three parcels and some letters.
Jonathan sang:

It must be Christ-mas, mer-ry, mer-ry Christ-mas. Hoo-ray!

'It's the wrong time of the year for Christmas,' said the postman. 'The cards and parcels are for your new baby brother Roger. Sorry you're disappointed.'
Jonathan sang:

I'm dis-ap-point-ed, I'm dis-ap-point-ed, I'm dis-ap-point-ed.

'I remember when *you* were born,' said the postman. 'There were so many cards and letters for you that I could hardly carry them.'
Jonathan sang:

I don't re-mem-ber that at all.

The postman laughed. 'Of course you wouldn't,' he said. 'You were much too small.' He rode away down the street.

Jonathan took the cards and parcels and letters into the house. His father put them on the table and said, 'We have to go to the hospital soon to bring Mummy and Roger home. Would you like to draw a Welcome Home picture?'
Jonathan sang:

Wel-come, wel-come, I'm ve-ry glad to see you.
Wel-come, wel-come, I'm ve-ry glad to see you.

Brothers and sisters

Then he sat down and drew a picture of himself eating his toast and honey, because his mother had said, 'While I'm in hospital having the baby, be a good boy, wash your face and hands, clean your teeth, and sit nicely at the table for your meals.'

His father said, 'That's a beautiful picture,' and fastened it to the door of the fridge with a little magnet shaped like a beetle. Then they went to get Mummy and the baby.

Jonathan's mother was so pleased to see him that she hugged him tightly and he sang his welcome song again.

His mother said, 'That's a beautiful song. Soon you'll be able to sing duets with Roger.'

But Roger was asleep. He was small and pink, as much as Jonathan could see inside the shawl.

'He will wake up when he is hungry,' said his mother.

Jonathan waited, and soon the baby opened his mouth wide. He had no teeth. 'Waaaaaaaah! Waaaaaaaah! Waaaaaaaah!' he cried. 'Waaaaaaaah! Waaaaaaaah! Waaaaaaah!'

Brothers and sisters

He cried till he was fed.
He cried till his nappy was changed.
He cried till he was fed again.
Then he went to sleep.
'I don't call that singing,' said Jonathan. He tried it himself.

Wa-aa-aa-aa-aa-ah! Wa-aa-aa-aa-aa-ah! Wa-aa-aa-aa-aa-ah!

Jonathan laughed and everyone else laughed too.
'Wait till he is older,' said his mother.
Jonathan sang:

Ev-'ry-one has to wait *(clap).* Ev-'ry-one has to wait *(clap).*

Next day Jonathan woke up and jumped out of bed. His father came in and sang:

Good morn-ing, good morn-ing. I hope you had a ve-ry good sleep.

(His voice was very much lower than Jonathan's.)
'Yes, thank you,' said Jonathan.
'No singing today?' asked his father.
Jonathan shook his head. 'Today is my *Jumping* Day,' he said. He jumped all the way to the bathroom, he jumped back to his bedroom, he jumped to breakfast, and he jumped all the way down the path to meet his friend the postman.
'It isn't Christmas and you aren't a new baby,' said the postman, 'but I see that your Auntie in Perth has sent two parcels. One is for Roger, and the other one is for *you.*'
And Jonathan jumped for joy.

June Epstein

Brothers and sisters

Little Brother

I have a little brother,
He's my mummy's baby boy,
And I've heard my mummy saying
That he's Daddy's pride and joy.
I have a little brother,
But I'll tell you what I'll do—
If you like I'll wrap him up
      And give him to you.

Karen Dowel

Sons

A grumpy old woman named Rita
Had four naughty boys
All called Peter.
I once heard her say,
'Peter, please run away
And take Peter
And Peter
And Peter!'

Colleen Clancy

In the Middle

Older brother, younger sister—
I'm always in between.
I'm always in the middle,
Don't you think it's mean?

Why couldn't I be the eldest
And stay up till half-past nine?
Why couldn't I be the youngest?
That would be just fine.

Why am I in the middle?
Neither the bottom nor the top,
Never the oldest, never the youngest—
Why can't somebody swap?

Leonne Leslie

Brothers and sisters

Older Brothers

Older brothers—
  play ball
  grow tall
    ride bikes
    like hikes
      play rough
      act tough
        slam doors
        slide on floors
          throw sticks
          play tricks
            eat lots
            get spots
              have fun
              make me run . . .
Older brothers!

Alison Lawrie

Older Sister

Older sister—
  hogs phone
  when home
    likes to dress
    make-up mess
      comes home late
      watches weight
        foils me
        spoils me
          fusses me
          bosses me
            shuts me out
            when I shout—
Older sister!

Gwendda McKay

Night-time

Night in Brick Road

Pavlos lived in Brick Road with his father in a small grey house. The house had a small back yard. It had a very, very small front yard.

Pavlos liked animals. He would have liked to have a horse. He would have liked a dog. Or a cat. Or even an elephant.

'Dad,' said Pavlos one day, 'could I have a dog?'

His father looked up from the paper. 'No,' he said.

'Could I have a horse? Or a cat?' Pavlos asked.

'No,' said his father. 'This house is too small for animals.'

Pavlos saw very few animals, ever. Except for the animals on TV. On TV he saw dogs and cats playing. He saw horses racing. He saw elephants and other wild animals. But they were only on TV. They were just pictures. They were not animals he could touch or talk to.

One day his friend, Jimmy, went to the zoo. The zoo was full of all kinds of animals. It was very exciting, Jimmy said. Jimmy told Pavlos about all the different kinds of animals.

'Dad,' said Pavlos, 'could we go to the zoo?'

'No,' said his father. 'The zoo is too far away.'

'Couldn't we go, please?' Pavlos asked.

'No,' said his father. 'I am too tired from working so hard.'

Pavlos dreamed of animals. He dreamed about them often. He dreamed about elephants and kangaroos and dogs and horses. His dreams were very exciting. But they were only dreams. They were just pictures. He wished the animals were real.

One night he was having a great dream. It was a dream of horses. They were galloping down the road. Their hooves went clippety-cloppety-clop on the road.

Suddenly he woke up. Hooves were still clippety-clopping on the road! He could hear them clearly. He really could.

Pavlos got out of bed. He went to the front of the house. He opened a window and looked out. The street lights were still on.

There, coming down Brick Road, was a horse. A big, white horse it was, pulling a white cart. There was a thin man getting out of the cart. He was carrying milk-bottles. He was the milkman.

Pavlos was so excited that he called out, 'Hullo! Hullo!'

The milkman turned around. 'Hullo, sonny,' he said, with a smile.

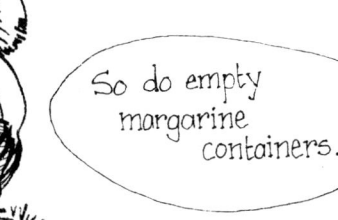

Night-time

The white horse just went on walking beside him. It was very big indeed. It was a beautiful horse.

When the horse went around the corner, Pavlos went back to bed.

The next night he woke again when he heard the hooves. He got out of bed and opened the front window. There was the big, white horse.

'Hullo, sonny,' said the milkman. 'Can't sleep, eh?'

'I just wanted to see your beautiful horse,' said Pavlos.

'Good on you, sonny,' said the milkman, smiling. 'Not many horses left on the job these days.'

After that, Pavlos woke up early very often. He had a big white horse to see.

Chris Wallace-Crabbe

Night-time

Teddy

Sometimes my teddy is silly,
He tells me he's scared of the night.
So I cuddle him under the blankets,
But he whispers, 'Please leave on the light'.

Annette Maloney

Bedtime

Time for bed.
Do I have to go?
Just ten minutes more,
I'm nearly six you know!

Annette Moloney

Night-time

Night Rider

I have a flying horse named Ned,
    And often when I'm put to bed
I wait till all is quiet, and then
    I put my track-suit on again.
Out of the window, off we go.
    We soar up high, we swoop down low,
We speed across the velvet sky,
    A Jumbo Jet goes roaring by.
A spacecraft slips between the stars,
    Brimful of green-skinned men from Mars.
We hope maybe that one day soon
    We'll get as far as Old Man Moon.
But we must hurry home, you see,
    In case my family misses me.

Margaret McCarthy

Day-time

Sunday

Sunday
  Fun day
    So-much-to-be-done day.

A jolly day
  A holiday
    An icecream-and-lolly day.

A gay day
  A play day
    Hip-hip-hooray!

Oh, please stay,
  Sunday!
    Don't go away!

But soon it will be Monday.

Susan Uhe

Wake Up!

In the morning, very early, the sun came up into the sky and shone
so brightly that it woke the birds.

The birds woke up and began to sing and chirp and chatter
so loudly that they woke
Margaret.

Margaret shouted 'Good morning!'
so happily that she woke
Danny.

Danny jumped out of bed and stamped his feet
so noisily that he woke
Dad.

Dad made a cup of coffee and some toast, and it smelt
so good that it woke
Mum.

Mum looked at the sunshine and opened the back door to let it in,
and woke
Tigger-Dog.

Tigger-Dog barked a big, happy 'Woof, woof!'

But—it DIDN'T wake Moggie-Cat.

Moggie-Cat just went on sleeping in the clothes basket
on the back verandah.

Dorothy Rickards

Day-time

Where Is It?

I know that sock was in my drawer,
But I can't find it any more.

I've looked in the wardrobe,
  and under the chair,
I just can't find it anywhere.

I've looked under my bed
  and on top of my shelf.
A sock can't go wandering off by itself!

I've looked everywhere
  and searched high and low,
Everywhere possible socks might go.

Oh! it wouldn't be there—
  though I should take a look.
It's been there all the time,
    TIGHTLY SNUGGLING MY FOOT!

Joanne Wallis

Socks

I hate socks—
I can never find a pair,
they say I've got to wear them
and that's not fair.

Sometimes I get a stripey one,
and choose the other plain,
and then I put my long boots on
and play out in the rain.

It's harder when I wear shoes,
for then my mum can tell
if I pick out a pair of socks
that don't match very well.

When I've finished growing up
I'll make the strictest law
that no-one has to wear socks
until they're eighty-four!

Elizabeth Cockerell

Hungry-time

Peas

If I wanted my peas
  I would eat them all up.
But I DON'T like my peas
  and I think they're YUK!

  So I WON'T eat my peas
    and I don't really care
  If I'm never allowed
    to get off this chair!

Joanne Wallis

Fish Fancies

If I were a fish
My favourite dish
Would be
Caramel coral and clams,
Or baked turtle eggs
And toasted prawn legs
Fish custard, trifle
And jam!

Colleen Clancy

Dessert

Pete likes apple dumpling,
Mum likes pumpkin pie,
Dad likes fruit and custard
And fritters you can fry.
I like cream and jelly,
We just can't agree,
When it's time for pudding
We're a mixed up family!

Joan M. Shilton

Hungry-time

The Snitcher Snatch

One day at milk and fruit time at the kindergarten, something very strange happened. Sue was in the back row. With one eye she watched Mrs Roland telling a story and with the other eye she watched Sally's mum putting out glasses of milk and bowls of apples. The cold milk and crisp apples looked lovely. Sue could hardly wait. But—

>just when Mrs Roland said 'Go to the bathroom
>to wash your hands'
>just when Sally's mum went back to the kitchen
>just when Mrs Graham, the assistant, turned her back

>Sue thought she saw something—

>something creep-creeping
>something black and busy
>something gulp-gulping.

>But she was not quite sure.

The children went to the tables. The bowls and glasses were all empty. Sally's mum looked very surprised. Then she went pale. 'It must have been stolen,' she said.

Mrs Graham, the assistant, ran out of the washroom. 'Quick, ring the police, we have been attacked by—

>the Snitcher Snatch
>with the big Black Patch
>who steathily steals
>everyone's meals.'

When the police came they poked, prodded and peered. They shook their heads. 'The Snitcher Snatch has left no trace.'

That day the children went home very hungry and thirsty.

Two nights later at dinner time, another strange thing happened.

Sue's mother had just finished cooking a beautiful baked dinner. It was Sue's favourite meal, roast leg of lamb, golden baked potatoes and green peas with mint sauce. Sue's mother put it on the table. It looked good and it smelled good. Sue could hardly wait. But—

>just when her mother went to call her father
>just before her father came
>just as Sue turned to the tap to wash her hands

Hungry-time

Sue thought she saw something—

something creep-creeping
something black and busy
something gulp-gulping.

But she was not quite sure.

When Sue's father came to the table, he could *smell* the dinner, but he could not *see* any dinner. All the plates were empty.
He looked very surprised. 'Why did you call me? Isn't it ready yet?'
Sue's mother went pale. 'It must have been stolen, we have been attacked by—

the Snitcher Snatch
with the big Black Patch
who stealthily steals
everyone's meals.

I'll ring the police.'
But the police were too busy. Everyone was complaining.
That night Sue's family had only milk for dinner. They went to bed very hungry.
The next week the Snitcher Snatch went too far. The mayor of the city had very important visitors and he had thirty chefs cooking a very special meal for them. They had cooked roast lamb, roast chicken and roast pork. Fried fish, baked fish, grilled fish. Green vegetables, white vegetables and yellow vegetables. Baked vegetables, boiled vegetables, fried vegetables. Salads, savouries and sweets. Cheese cakes, sponge cakes and fruit cakes.
The chefs had just finished setting everything out. It looked good and it smelled good. But—

just when the chefs returned to the kitchen
just before the mayor and the important visitors came in

something came creep-creeping
something black and busy
something gulp-gulping.

When the mayor and the visitors came into the room they could *smell* the food, but they could not *see* any food. All the plates were empty.
The mayor went pale. 'We have been attacked by—

Hungry-time

the Snitcher Snatch
with the big Black Patch
who stealthily steals
everyone's meals.'

The mayor and his visitors had to go home very hungry. The mayor was very angry.

He called the police. 'Everyone in the city has to help to catch the Snitcher Snatch.'

He and the police talked all night and they made a plan.

This was the plan.

The city carpenters would make a big Snitcher Snatch cage in the

Hungry-time

gardens. The mayor would have a big butterfly net especially made. Everyone in the city would prepare a most enticing picnic meal. When the food was ready they would all hide behind bushes in a circle. They would all wait very quietly for the Snitcher Snatch.

The picnic day came. Some of the fathers cooked sausages, chops, steaks and rissoles at the barbecues. Some of the mothers spread out the food. They had made their very best cheese cakes and pavlovas. It looked good and it smelled good.

Then they made a big circle. They hid behind the bushes and were very quiet. They waited for the Snitcher Snatch.

The mayor waited too—holding his big net ready. And—

>just when the meat was nearly cooked
>just when everyone had hidden

>Sue thought she saw something—

>something creep-creeping
>something black and busy.

>And she was *quite* sure.

The Snitcher Snatch crept closer to the food. The mayor made a signal and everyone in the circle crept closer to the Snitcher Snatch. The mayor raised his net and crept forward.

>The Snitcher Snatch crept closer and closer to the food.
>The mayor crept closer and closer to the Snitcher Snatch.
>Sue and the circle of people all holding hands crept closer and closer to both of them.

>Just before the Snitcher Snatch had time to gulp—

Hungry-time

the mayor rushed forward with the net, and put it over him! Everyone cheered! Now they could enjoy their meals in peace! The Snitcher Snatch was caught!

Sue's city was the only city in the world with a real live Snitcher Snatch in a cage in their city gardens. The Snitcher Snatch was happy now. People from all over the world came to feed him, and they brought him all sorts of strange food. Over his cage was written:

> 'Snitcher Snatch
> With the big Black Patch
> Now he never steals
> Anyone's meals.'

Dorothy Mills

Will I Really Truly Burst?

When we had finished tea tonight
I had an awful thirst,
Mum said, 'Now don't you drink too much
Or you will surely burst!'

I've only got a little skin
And it fits so perfectly,
I wonder if I eat too much
Will it still stretch right round me?

If my insides grow bigger
Will my skin still get there first?
If I keep on eating dinner
Will I really truly burst?

Joan M. Shilton

Play-time

In the good ship *Play* on a summer day
We sailed across the sea.
With a broom for a mast we went very, very fast
And the wind blew merrily.
The sails were a skirt and an old red shirt,
And the First Mate was a Cat.
A Cat (miaow miaow), a Cat, (miaow miaow),
The First Mate was a Cat.
A Cat (miaow miaow), a Cat (miaow miaow)
The First Mate was a Cat.

In the good ship *Play* on a summer day
It was a terrible sight,
For the First Mate bit the Captain's tail
And began a terrible fight.
With a growling and a howling and a miaowing and a barking
They jumped into the sea,
Woof woof! miaow miaow! woof woof! miaow miaow!
There was no-one left but me.
Woof woof! miaow miaow! woof woof! miaow miaow!
There was no-one left but me.

Play-time

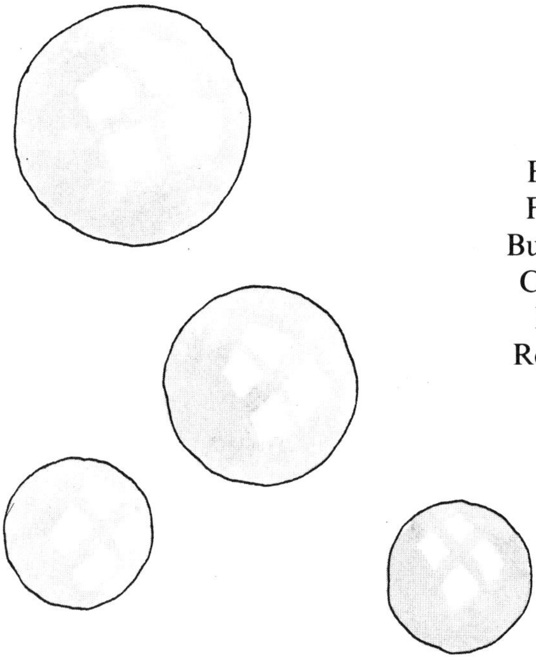

Bubbles

Blowing bubbles,
Floating bubbles,
Bubbles everywhere.
Coloured bubbles,
Round bubbles,
Resting in my hair.

Barbara Cork

The Ball

The coloured ball rolled down the hill,
And as it rolled it seemed
That all its colours were as one
With nothing in between.

Iola Tilley

The New Phone

We've got this new green phone, you see,
And all day long my friends call me,
And I just can't get on with things
Because it rings and rings and rings.

Anne LeRoy

Rainy days

Splish! Splosh!

Splish! Splosh!
Mackintosh.
Raindrops on my head.

Oh what fun,
Without the sun
Raindrops fall instead.

Nola Wood

Mr Rainman

Old Mr Rainman
Turn on your dripping taps,
Gush down the drain pipes
And start that pit-a-pat.
Dance on the roof tops
And run down the panes;
Then Mr Rainman
Turn off your taps again!

Sue Killeen

Safety Yellow

I've a little yellow raincoat,
And a little yellow hat,
I've little yellow gumboots,
I keep them by the mat.

I wear my 'Safety Yellow'
When I'm walking in the rain,
Then everyone can see me
And I come home safe again.

Isobel Pratt

Rain

Splishy, splashy drops of rain
Trickling down the window pane.

Splishing, splashing on the street,
While splitter, splatter go my feet.

Home at last and still I hear
Gurgling water flowing near.

It's water swooshing in the lane
And swirling quickly down the drain.

Teresa Hoy

Rainy days

Wet Saturday

One Saturday afternoon Belinda, Philip, Manuela and Jonathan were playing at Ahmed's house. It was raining so hard that they could not go outside, so they spent the time making musical instruments. Ahmed's father helped them. They made sticks, shakers, drums, rattles, and then they played a game about machines.

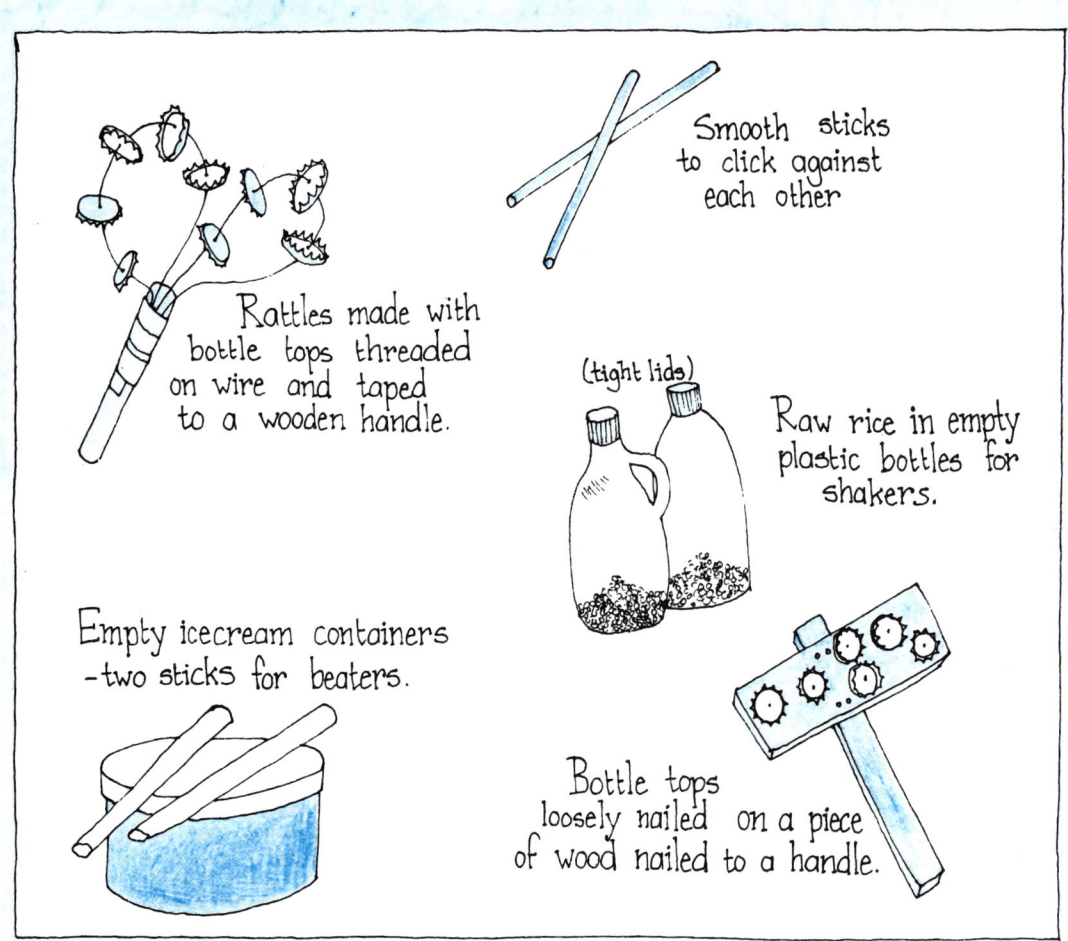

Ahmed pretended to be the foreman of a factory and the other children were the machines. Each child had to make the noise of a machine with a musical instrument. The foreman stood in front and told them when to start playing softly, one at a time, and when to play together. He had to count 'ONE, TWO, THREE, FOUR,' loudly and steadily, and beat time with his hands to keep them all together. He was really like the conductor of a band or orchestra.

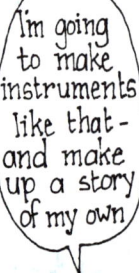

Rainy days

Ahmed's father wrote out a big chart for the different instruments.

```
CHART FOR THE MACHINE GAME
                                    'o' means no noise at all.
First Machine: STICKS
 1  | 2 | 3 | 4 |  1  | 2 | 3 | 4
click| o | o | o |click| o | o | o     keep on going like that

Second Machine: DRUMS
 1  | 2 | 3  | 4 |  1  | 2 | 3  | 4
boom| o |boom| o |boom | o |boom| o    keep on going like that

Third Machine: SHAKERS
 1 |  2  | 3 |  4   | 1 |  2  | 3 |  4
 o |shake| o |shake | o |shake| o |shake   keep on going like that

Fourth Machine: RATTLES
  1   | 2  | 3  |  4  |  1   | 2  | 3  |  4
rattle|all |the |time |rattle|all |the |time   keep on going like that
```

When all the machines were going together, Ahmed told them to get louder and quicker. Whenever he felt like it he said 'STOP!' and there was a sudden silence. Sometimes he told the machines to start all together and sometimes he told them to stop playing one at a time.

After a while he changed over and gave someone else a turn at being the foreman.

After *Machines*, the children made up a sound game called *The Storm*. There was no counting in this one, but there was a story teller—that was Manuela.

Rainy days

Manuela's Storm Story

The story part	*What everyone did to make it sound like a real storm.*
It was a quiet, hot day until the wind began to blow.	*Everyone made noises like the wind: Aaaaaaaaaaaaaaah! Eeeeeeeeeeeeeeeh!*
The leaves fell from the trees.	*Philip was holding the shakers, and he made soft shaking noises like falling leaves.*
There were a few drops of rain.	*Ahmed clicked the sticks together to sound like raindrops.*
Then the wind became stronger and stronger.	*Everyone made loud noises like The wind: Eeeeeeeeeeeeeeeh! Aaaaaaaaaaaaaaah! Oooooooooooh!*
In the house the windows rattled,	*Belinda used the rattle to sound like rattling windows.*
and a door slammed.	*That was done by Jonathan with the drum.*
Suddenly there was a big peal of thunder.	*The drum and the rattle were played together, getting louder and louder like thunder, and then dying away.*
Down came the rain.	*Ahmed made rain sounds with the sticks, and kept on going.*
There was more thunder.	*Belinda and Jonathan made thunder noises with the drum and rattle, as they did before.*
And all the people ran into their houses.	*Everybody made running noises with their feet.*

After *The Storm* game, the children made a procession and marched around the room playing their instruments.

It was a good idea for a wet Saturday afternoon.

June Epstein

Good and bad days

Cleaning Up Day

'Get in and clean your room up!'
It's a job I hate to do,
But things are in a horrid mess
And I can't find one black shoe.

The socks are strewn around the floor,
My runners can't be found,
My schoolbag's simply disappeared—
It's just gone 'underground'!

The bed-clothes are all tangled—
Beauty! There's my shoe!
And there's the pair of runners—
Great! My schoolbag, too!

I really don't quite understand
How things can get this way
When I only sleep in here at night
And I'm at school all day!

Joan M. Shilton

Mum's Right

Mum's right, I guess—
My room's a mess.
But that's the way I like it!

Nola Wood

Good and bad days

Tom

Tom, put on your trousers,
Tom, put on your shirt,
Tom, put on your shoes and socks,
And don't go in the dirt.

    I'll throw away my trousers,
    I'll trample on my shirt,
    I'll bury both my shoes and socks
    And roll in all the dirt.

How nice to see you Granny,
A chockie cake for tea,
A pity Tom's a-monstering,
The more for you and me.

    Mum, I've put on my trousers,
    Mum, I've put on my shirt,
    Mum, I've put on my shoes and socks,
    I hate the sight of dirt.

Mary Roberts

Good and bad days

Measles

I woke up one morning and there were some spots.
And there were some whats?
Spots! Spots! Red spots on my face!
'Measles,' Mum said, 'they're measles, you know.'
I don't like these measles. I want them to go!

'You can't go to school with those spots on your face.
You'd be sure to spread measles all over the place.'
These spots aren't so bad, these spots are just fine.
I don't mind these spots, I'm glad they are mine.

Then my skin became itchy, I started to scratch.
These measles aren't really a good thing to catch.

My friends cannot come to my house after school;
I wish that they could, but that is the rule.
And I feel very hot. 'It's a fever,' Mum said.
'The right thing to do is to stay in your bed.'
But I don't like staying in bed all the day—
You never can have any fun that way.

Then Mum said, 'Cheer up! For one thing is plain,
Now you've had measles they won't come again.'

Kim Hadden

Good and bad days

Catching Things

I played outside
  the other day,
I caught a ball
  then threw it away.
I went to a party
  the other day,
I caught a balloon
  and tossed it away.
I had soapy water
  the other day,
I caught some bubbles
  and blew them away.
I got very wet
  the other day,
I caught a cold,
    Couldn't throw it away,
    Couldn't toss it away,
    Couldn't blow it away.
I went to bed
  the other day.

Elizabeth Cockerell

Stay At Home Day

It's doo bad whed you have to sday
Ad hobe, and lie id bed
Because you ache all over
Ad you're stuvved ub in the head.

It's doo bad whed you've lods of books
Ad lods of tibe as well,
Ad you card be bothered readig
Ad your nose has lost id's sbell.

For food, the odly stuff you have
Is pedicillin mixture,
Ad twedty-seven big white pills
Which they idsist will fix you.

Joan M. Shilton

Where do you live?

Poor Mrs Duck

Poor Mrs Duck!
Whatever will she do?
She built her nest
In a worn-out shoe.

Poor Mrs Duck!
Whatever will she say?
The dustbin-man
Moved the shoe away.

Poor Mrs Duck!
She flew far and fast
And found her nest
In the shoe at last.

There's Mrs Duck,
With her baby, Pip,
Living on top
Of a rubbish tip!

Kathryn Taylor

I live in the bush where my kind of food grows. Where does everybody else live?

I like the sea-side, but I often go to town where there's food to be picked up.

We penguins like living close to one another — low-rise flats, you might say.

Kangaroo's off to the country.

—near the sea.

I'm from the desert — just down here for a visit.

I'm at home anywhere.

Mind your own business, Koala — my place is well-hidden under the river bank.

Where do you live?

Living-Places

Where do you live?

> The whole world over
> People live in different places—
> Up on a mountain, down by a river,
> In crowded cities, or open spaces,
> In houses, in flats, in tents, or trailers,
> Underground, on the ground, high in the air,
> Where it's hot, where it's cold, where it's dry or raining.

Millions of people live everywhere.

Julia Norman

In the city

Chimneys

Short ones
Fat ones
Narrow and high,
Lots of different chimneys
Decorate the sky.

Have you seen a factory one
With letters down the side?
Or a garden-burner one
That's short and fat and wide?

Some blow white smoke,
Others have black,
Some have lots of steam
Coming from their stack.

If I were a chimney
It would be a funny joke
To lift my hat to all my friends
And blow a puff of smoke!

Alison Lawrie

City Song

Balancing birds on telegraph wires
Look like the music of my city song—
    City noises, honking, hooting,
    Scraping feet and taxis tooting,
    Ringing bells and voices speaking,
    Rattling tins and tram wheels shrieking—
All make music for my city song.

Dorothy Rickards

In the city

Window in the Sky

Jamie lived with his mother on the nineteenth floor of a high-rise block of flats near the city.

From his window he could see the long lines of traffic moving in the streets below. They looked just like toy cars and buses coming and going. There were so many that Jamie was never quick enough to count them all. There must be millions and trillions of cars in the city, he often thought. At night he couldn't see the shapes of the cars, but rows of headlights shining brightly into the darkness told him the roads were still busy.

When the shops far below were lit up with coloured lights, it was like gazing into fairyland.

On the days when there was no smog to lie thick and heavy like a grey blanket over the roof tops, Jamie could see right across the city to the sea. He liked to watch the large ships slowly moving towards the docks, bringing passengers and cargo from the other side of the world. The sea, which looked so calm and flat on a good day, changed into tossing, heaving foam when the weather was bad. It reminded Jamie of the thick, white suds that raced around inside the washing machines at the laundrette.

Sometimes it was a bit frightening living so high up, especially when the wind blew very hard, and the building made strange creaking noises. Often a bird would hit against the window pane with a loud bang.

A friend of Jamie's mother had lent them a telescope, and Jamie loved to watch the workmen on the building sites in the city. They looked so tiny and far away, until he peered through the telescope, and then it was as if the men were inside the room with him.

Sometimes the workmen rode to the top of the building sites on steel girders. They held on tightly, as large cranes slowly pulled the girders higher and higher. Jamie said it would be very handy to have one of those on top of their building, for when the lifts broke down, but his mother said she'd rather walk the nineteen flights of stairs, thank you very much!

Jamie liked watching out of the window much more than he liked doing anything else. His mother was always complaining that he needed to get more fresh air and exercise.

In the city

One afternoon, when he arrived home from school, his mother seemed to be very happy. She sang softly as she poured Jamie a glass of milk and put butter and cheese on some biscuits. Then she sat down at the kitchen table and grinned at him.

'I've found a house for us to live in! It's small, and quite old, but it's away from the city, which means you'll have lots of space to run around in. And what's best of all, we'll have a garden of our own. There's even a large tree with a cubby house in it. You have to climb a ladder to get to it.'

Jamie's eyes grew wide with amazement. A house, a garden, and a tree house! He wanted to go, but part of him wanted to stay.

A sea gull, which had strayed too far, leisurely glided past the window.

'Well?' said his mother. 'Aren't you pleased?'

'It sounds terrific,' he said, 'but we won't be able to look out of the window and see the men working on the buildings, or the ships coming and going. I'll feel a little bit sad when we leave this place. Won't you be a bit sad too, Mum?'

'No way!' said his mother. 'I'll always remember the bad things about living here.'

But Jamie looked out of the window and thought, 'Even when I'm sitting in my tree house, in my very own garden, I'm going to remember the good times I've had living way up in the sky.'

Anita Lucas

City Scene

See-saw sky-scraper,
pocked with holes like
a nutmeg grater.

Beverley Hannaker

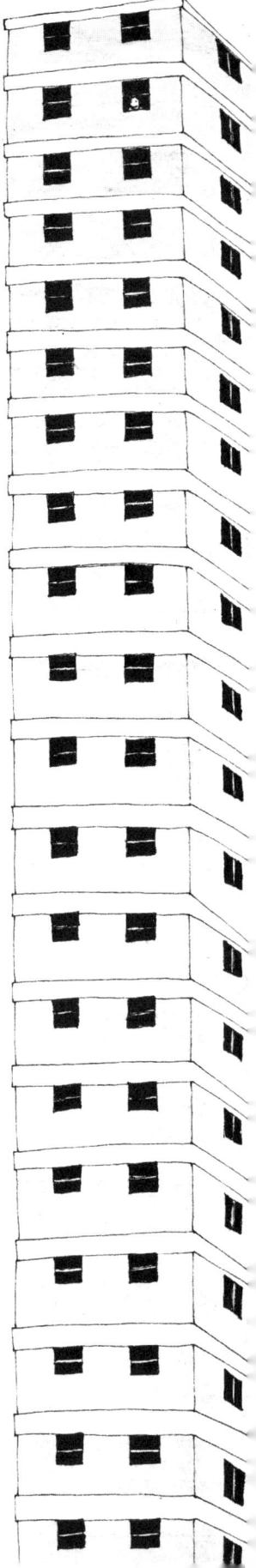

I can't see why it's called a flat....

There are other names, like <u>apartment</u>, or <u>unit</u>...

What's flat about high-rise living?

In the city

I Live Up There

You see those flats?
I live up there.
Mine's the blue window
Up in the air.

There's lifts and stairs
And doors and doors,
And twenty-seven
Identical floors.

The swings outside
Are too far away,
So we sit up here
With Mum all day.

It's good when it's cold
Up here all warm;
You can watch all the people
Out in the storm.

But if it's sunny and warm outside,
And I'm sick of TV, or I want a ride,
When Dad comes home from the early shift
He takes me down in the silver lift.

Jane Bradley

In the city

Traffic Lights

Green eye, yellow eye, red eye,
Watch at the intersection,
Never asleep at their post up high,
So—behave with circumspection.

    Green eye, green eye, shining bright,
    That's the walk-over-carefully light.
    Yellow eye shining warns 'beware!'
    Signals the change for red eye to stare.
    Red eye, red eye shining bright,
    That's the nobody-walk-across light.

Green eye, yellow eye, red eye,
Watch at the intersection.

Gwendda McKay

In the city

Bob's Pup

'Mum, d'you know what I'd like for my birthday?' Bob said one bedtime.

'What?'

'I'd really love to have a pup.'

'Oh Bob, we can't promise. We'd love you to have your own pet. But you're not quite six. And pups cost a lot to buy and feed. And here in the city the roads are dangerous with all the traffic.'

Bob's face fell.

'I'll talk to Dad,' Mum said. 'But don't be disappointed if we say no.'

The day before Bob's birthday, Dad came home early and told him he might be lucky. There was a place out of town where stray bitches were sent to have their pups and people could go and get one for a small price. Bob was very excited. He would have a pup after all!

They went in the car to a house where there were many kennels and pens and pups everywhere—brown fluffy ones like balls of fur, black and white ones, all kinds. How could they choose?

'Hey, look there,' said Dad. In one pen was a black Labrador with four puppies playing around her.

'Yes, they're the best of all,' said the man in charge. 'Well-bred those pups are. Not bitsers. Come into the pen, Bob.'

The pups were strong and black. Their paws looked too big for their legs. One pup came and looked at Bob with his head on one side and then tried to pull his shoelace off. Bob laughed. 'I'd love this one, Dad.'

So Banjo became Bob's pup.

And the house became very different. Banjo loved to chew socks and slippers, pull towels off the bathroom rail, cushions off chairs, eat rubber balls, dig holes in the garden. He made puddles on the carpet and Mum said they'd never train him. But Bob loved Banjo.

One day Bob went to kick the footie on the nature strip with Harry and Margie from next door. When it bounced on the road they all looked both ways before they ran to get it. Margie kicked the ball to Bob. He missed it. It hit the kerb and shot onto the road. Banjo ran out after it. There was a screech of brakes, a horrible thud.

Banjo was dead.

In the city

Bob did not know he had so many tears inside him. His face was puffed up; his heart hurt all the time. Everyone was very, very sad. Dad had to dig a big hole and bury Banjo. Mum sat with Bob until at last he fell asleep. Next day she walked to school with him and told Miss Mathers about Banjo, and all day Miss Mathers tried to help Bob not to think about it.

'Later we'll get another dog—a grown-up one,' said Dad, 'and we'll teach him about traffic.'

But Bob said, 'I only want Banjo.'

One winter night Mum asked Bob to put out the rubbish tin. He heard a noise: miaow, miaow. He looked around. Out of the shelter of a bush came a kitten. It was such a sad sight. Its orangey fur was matted. It was so thin that its sides were almost touching. When Bob went to pick it up, it cringed as if it expected to be hit. He took it inside.

'Oh, the poor thing,' Mum said. 'It's been left to live in the streets. How can people be so cruel?'

She got a bowl of milk. The kitten pushed its nose in and lapped up every drop. It trembled all over. Bob gave it a bit of meat.

'Listen,' said Bob, 'she's purring.'

The kitten looked up and blinked her eyes. Then she sat down and washed herself all over. Her fur became smooth and shiny.

'She's really pretty,' said Dad. 'D'you want to keep her, Bob?'

Bob nodded. 'Gee, thanks Dad!'

That night Bob felt something creeping very quietly on his bed. He put out his hand. He felt a bony little head and back. A rough little tongue licked his hand. Then the kitten curled up beside him and purred and purred.

Bob thought of Banjo. The nasty feeling had gone. 'But I'll always love you, Banjo,' he thought.

Mary Roberts

In the country

The Aboriginal Boy

Kanbi was an Aboriginal boy whose people lived in the bush. Sometimes he came to stay with friends in the city. He played with the children and told them stories about his people.

Sometimes he sang and played the rhythm sticks. The children joined in with rhythm sticks, too.

June Epstein

words and music: June Epstein **Song of the Aboriginal Boy**

Long years ago, before the white man came, My tribe knew the bush, the sun-light and the rain. They hunt-ed and fished and they camped a-round a fire, Their old men were wise and their young men were brave. Ma-ny chil-dren share now the sun-light and the rain, And I shall tell them all of the wise men of my tribe.

I'm beating the rhythm with my tail.

My webbed feet can clap out that rhythm very well!

Clapping, rapping, tapping - even finger-snapping - its all rhythm!

In the country

Newborn

Down behind the thistles
In the gully, near the creek,
Lies something wet and shining,
Something very weak.

Its legs are rather wobbly,
It's very, very shy,
It's nuzzling for its first meal,
Though it's not yet dry.
It's got a velvet nose,
But a rough little tongue.
It's a newborn calf
With its proud cow-mum.

Gayle Sweeney

In the Bush

In the bush
you might see
koalas dozing in a tree.
In the bush
you might hear
kangaroos thumping
very near,
lizards scuttling
through dry grass,
noisy parrots
flying past.
In the bush
tread with care—
you never know
what's hiding there!

Anne LeRoy

Farmyard

Little hen
feathered and red
pecking round for scraps of bread.

Little goat
fierce and white
thinks his rope is much too tight.

Little calf
soft and shy
peeking out with one brown eye.

Little cat
black and lean
crouching so he won't be seen.

Little pig
muddy and stout
trying hard to wriggle out.

Gail Gregory

On the move

Trains

Big trains, little trains,
Old trains and new.
Shiny trains and dirty trains
To carry me and you.

> Blue trains, red trains,
> And silver trains that gleam.
> People trains and goods trains,
> Electric trains and steam.

I'd love to be a driver
Of a great big train.
I'd drive my train all round the world
And not come home again.

Jo-Anne Steven

Travelling

Walk every day—
it's not far away
   to school.

There's a bus to catch
to the footy match
   as a rule.

Get a tram that stops
at the city shops—
   what a crush!

Drive in a car
to a farm—not far
   in the bush.

Sleeping's great
travelling interstate
   on a train.

Across the world
be quickly whirled
   in a plane.

But, whatever the way,
I'm happy to say:
   'Home again!'

Dorothy Rickards

Seasons

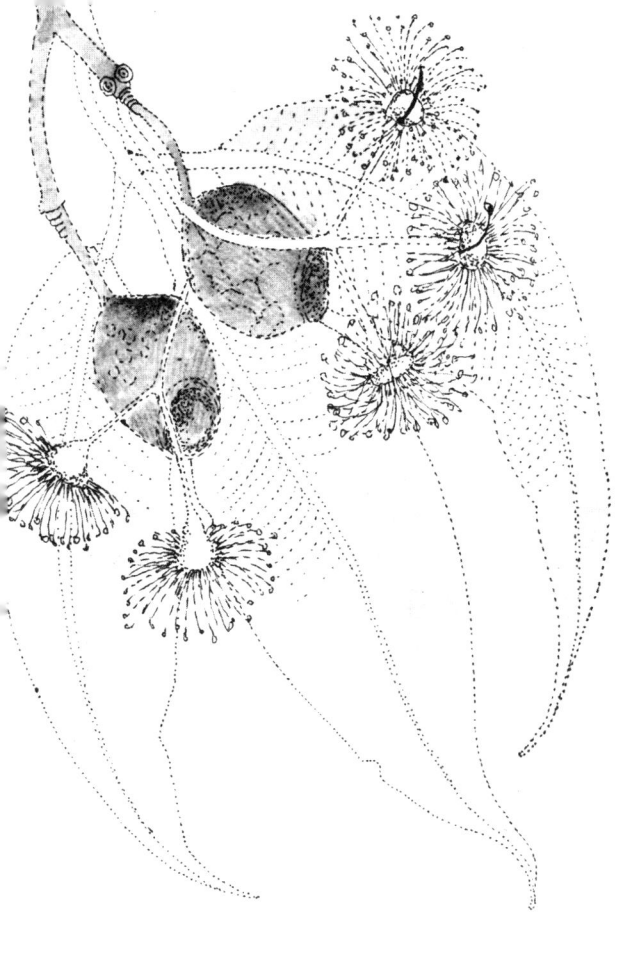

Eucalypt Year

He made a pattern with grey-green leaves
On paper, stuck with paste.

He chewed the reddish new gum tips
For eucalyptus taste.

He pulled at blossoms like ballet skirts
Till tickling ants fell down.

But gumnuts were his favourite things,
Pot-bellied, rough and brown.

June Epstein

Winter and Summer

Sniffle and sneeze,
Cough and wheeze—
 Oh, winter, disappear!

Sea and sun,
Sand and fun—
 I think that summer's here.

Julie Black

Here's a riddle for you, penguin. Why did the seagull fly over the sea?

Because he couldn't fly under it, of course.

Does anyone know any good riddles?

Seasons

Let Me Wonder

I wonder why the grass is green,
I wonder where the wind has been.

I wonder why some trees grow tall
And in winter have no leaves at all.

I wonder how it feels to fly
Across the endless, cloudless sky.

Just let me sit beneath the sun
And wonder and wonder until I'm done.

Susan Uhe

Seasons

Spring

In spring there's a warming
That blows in the air.
In spring there's a greening
Of elms that were bare.
In spring there's a reddening
On tips of gum trees.
In spring there's a showing
  Of wild flowers growing,
    There's a flowering, a showering,
      A breezing, a sneezing,
        A blowing, a growing,
For spring's in the air.

Mills McKay

Autumn

Autumn days
Smoky haze
Bright coloured trees
Rustly leaves
March to May
Autumn days.

The days are cool
The birds have gone,
There's one red leaf
Just hanging on.

One red leaf left till last
Fluttering like a flag on a mast.
One lonely leaf, flying high,
Bright, bright red against the sky.
One red leaf, just hanging on,
One last gust,
  and then—
    it's
      gone.

Dorothy Mills

Summer

Lazy days, heat-hazy days,
Six weeks summer holidays.

Lying around keeping cool,
Swimming at the local pool,
Long, cool drinks at people's places,
Cool cream put on sunburnt faces,
Warm brown earth on bare brown toes,
Pink zinc plastered on my nose.

Lazy days, heat-hazy days,
Six weeks summer holidays.

Dorothy Mills

Winter

Runny nose,
cold toes,
Walking in the rain.

  Sniff, snort!
  I've caught
  Another cold again.

    Freezing air,
    Wet hair,
    Fingers dropping off.

      Damp coat,
      Sore throat,
      Listen to my cough.

Roger Pelletier

Wind ways

Mrs Ippendippidy's Washing

It was a hot, blustery day. Mrs Ippendippidy had just finished hanging out her washing. There on the clothes-line hung Mr Ippendippidy's two new shirts, Sarah Ippendippidy's bright red jumper, little Martin Ippendippidy's old blue jeans and a pretty green dress belonging to Mrs Ippendippidy herself.

As Mrs Ippendippidy turned to pick up her wash-basket, the strong North Wind whipped her washing from the line and carried it away.

'My washing!' cried Mrs Ippendippidy, but by then her washing had disappeared over her neighbour's fence. Mrs Ippendippidy went inside to tell the sad tale to her husband.

Meanwhile, North Wind had carried Mrs Ippendippidy's clothes over eight rows of houses and dropped them neatly on the top of a tall gum tree.

Mrs Ippendippidy went outside and sang out at the top of her voice,

'North Wind, you have taken my washing away with you but Mr Ippendippidy needs his new blue shirts to wear to work, and Sarah wants her bright red jumper and little Martin has got all his other jeans dirty and I did like that pretty green dress. Please can you bring them back to me?'

North Wind replied, 'Mrs Ippendippidy, I can pick your clothes up again if I want to, but I cannot bring them back to you as I am from the North and I must keep travelling on.'

Mrs Ippendippidy sighed, 'I need my clothes.'

The next day Mrs Ippendippidy went outside again. This time there was a slight breeze blowing from the East.

'East Wind,' cried Mrs Ippendippidy, 'North Wind has carried my washing away and cannot bring it back. Can you please bring it back to me?'

'Alas,' East Wind replied. 'I am travelling off around the world. I must keep blowing from the East. I cannot bring your clothes back here but I could take them around the world with me!'

'Oh, no!' shouted Mrs Ippendippidy. 'I need my clothes back here!'

The next morning there was a strong wind blowing from the West. Mrs Ippendippidy rushed outside and pleaded with West Wind.

Wind ways

'West Wind, West Wind—North Wind has carried all my washing away and cannot bring it back. Please can you bring it back to me?'

West Wind howled back at Mrs Ippendippidy.

'I am West Wind, blowing from the West. How can I bring your clothes back to you, when they have been blown South? You must wait for South Wind. He will bring your washing back.' Then he blew away in an angry hurry.

Mrs Ippendippidy rushed inside to tell her husband.

'Of course,' said Mr Ippendippidy. 'We should have thought of it before. If North Wind took the washing away, South Wind is the only one who can bring it back.'

So Mr and Mrs Ippendippidy waited for South Wind. Each day they looked at the weather vane to see which way the wind was blowing, but it was a whole week before South Wind came.

Mrs Ippendippidy rushed outside waving her arms and shouting to the wind, 'South Wind, South Wind, I am so glad you have arrived. I have been waiting for you for a whole week. Last week North Wind took my washing from the clothes line and carried it away. There were two new shirts belonging to Mr Ippendippidy, Sarah's bright red jumper, little Martin's old blue jeans and my favourite pretty green dress. Please, South Wind, will you bring them back to me?'

South Wind stirred the leaves on the trees in Mrs Ippendippidy's backyard and replied, 'Of course, Mrs Ippendippidy.' Then, as Mrs Ippendippidy watched, all the trees began to bend, and papers and leaves were whipped into the sky, and there, over her neighbour's fence, came all Mrs Ippendippidy's washing, nicely dried and aired.

'Thank you, oh thank you!' cried Mrs Ippendippidy, gathering up her washing. 'Thank you so much, South Wind.'

South Wind blew softly over Mrs Ippendippidy's house, drying her next lot of washing. But Mrs Ippendippidy kept a watchful eye on it all day long.

Sue Bailes

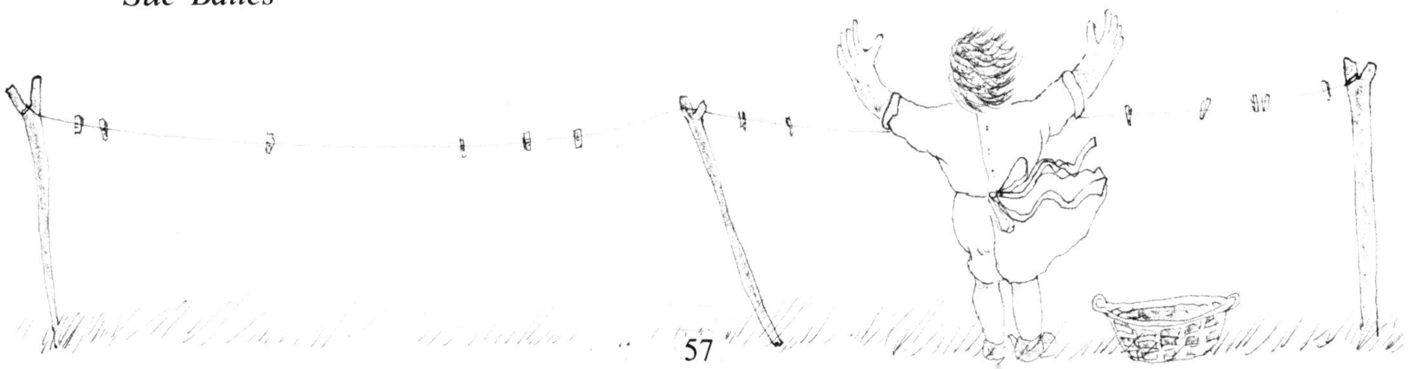

Wind ways

A Dream

words: Anne LeRoy
music: June Epstein

I dreamt that the stars in the sky all came tum-bling down, They cov-ered road and hill and plain, they cov-ered all the town. And then an an-gry storm blew up and whipped the wind on high, It gath-ered up those twink-ling stars and blew them, and blew them, and blew them to the sky.

Wind ways

Wild Wind

Wild wind,
Screaming high,
Chasing clouds
Across the sky,
Rattling, shaking,
Blowing, breaking,
Wild wind.

Dorothy Mills

Where the Wind Blows

The wind is creeping through the trees,
It swirls and twirls where no-one sees,
Then out it comes to have some fun
And washing dances in the sun.

It creeps behind a little girl,
Tugs her skirt and flips a curl,
Then like a bird it flies away
To make the tree-tops toss and sway.

At night the wind begins to howl,
Ruffles the fur of cats that prowl
While hunting birds or tasty mice,
Or any other food that's nice.

When tired of playing in the town
The wind slips off and rushes down
Over the beach and out to sea,
Wild as the waves, and flying free.

Valerie Havard

Wind ways

Where?

I can hear the wind blowing,
I can feel its cold breath,
I can see the trees tossing.
Now it's gone! Where?

Isobel Pratt

"I can use this wind to fly on like a glider."

"Feel that wind on my face! It's moving my tree! Thanks, wind — I like this."

"Listen to the wind, platypus! It's like a song...."

"What a strong wind! That shirt looks like a piece of Mrs Ippendippidy's washing — all the way from page 57."

"I'm looking at the grass moving, kangaroo. The wind's doing that, too."

"You're a busy-body, wind! And I don't like the taste of dust in my mouth down here."

Sky ways

Clouds

Clouds are fluffy,
   Friendly,
      Free.
Sun is shining through at me.

Clouds are heavy,
   Angry,
      Grey.
Rain is pouring down all day.

Jenny Bryant

Blue

Bright blue, light blue,
Sky-when-it's-only-just-light blue,
Sea-when-the-water's-just-right blue,
Sky-when-it's-nearly-night blue.
Bright blue, light blue.

Dorothy Mills

Lovely smells you're bringing my way, wind!

Sky ways

A Cloud Game

Shaun stared out of the car window. Trees and more trees, sheep and more sheep, were all he could see.

'How much longer till we get there, Dad?'

'About another hour, mate.'

'Oh, that takes forever.'

'Well, how about singing some more songs?' Mum suggested. But Shaun was tired of singing, especially when no-one else knew the words and he had to sing by himself.

Then Dad said, 'How about playing *Clouds?*' and that cheered Shaun instantly. Dad was good at thinking up new games.

'All you have to do,' Dad explained, 'is to look at the clouds and think of animals or people or toys or pictures from the shapes they make. Then you tell us what you can see.'

Shaun was already looking out at the clouds even before Dad had finished talking. He wanted to be the first to spot a picture cloud. But Mum was so fast, he didn't have a chance.

'Look!' she called, 'I can see a gorilla chasing a butterfly.'

'Where? Where?' Shaun wanted to know.

'See those two clouds right up there? The small cloud in front has two little feelers poking out at the top like a butterfly, and the one behind has hairy arms like a fat gorilla when he's scratching himself.'

Shaun could see the butterfly cloud easily, but Mum had to do a bit more talking and explaining before he could imagine the other one to be a fat, hairy gorilla. Then he began to laugh because that very cloud was slowly changing shape and it looked to Shaun as if the gorilla was curling into a ball to practise his somersaults.

'He's doing somersaults.'

'I think he's trying to clean his toenails,' said Dad.

The next cloud picture was one Shaun spotted.

'Hey, look, there's a kangaroo in the sky,' he yelled. He didn't have to point out the kangaroo to Dad, because Dad was just about to say the same thing.

'Maybe we'll see a joey,' said Mum.

Sky ways

Each of them looked all over the sky. Dad had to make sure he watched where he was driving, too, so he couldn't search as carefully as Shaun or Mum. Those two watched the clouds very closely. Shaun even squirmed around in his seat to look out of the back window. But there was no joey-kangaroo to be seen anywhere. In fact none of the clouds looked like animals any more. They didn't look like anything except clouds. For a moment Shaun thought he saw a train, but it wasn't really long enough and besides, there was only one wheel.

'What do we do now, Dad?' he asked. 'The sky isn't drawing any more picture clouds.'

'It's just as well the clouds have blown away,' said Dad. 'It means we'll have fine, sunny weather for our picnic. Who's hungry?'

Annette Nolan

Big and small

Seeing

I see a bear,
a great big bear.

I see a mouse,
a tiny little mouse.

One so big,
the other so small—

I wonder if the bear
can see the mouse at all?

Barbara Cork

Small

It's been a hard day,
I thought to myself.
Shopping with Mummy
Is bad for my health.
I am so little
That people don't see
That what they are standing on
Really is me.
'Look out!' they cry,
'Get out of the way!'
Oh! How I would like
To be big for a day!
I am a person
Just like them all,
It isn't my fault
That I'm not quite as tall.
And if I were big
I could just hear them say,
'Excuse me, I'm sorry
I got in your way.'
But because I'm down here
And they're right up there,
They shove me and push me,
They don't seem to care.
One day, perhaps,
I'll know what to do—
I'll gather my friends,
They'll come along too.
We'll go to the market,
I'll give a big speech,
And this time it won't be
The children we'll teach.
I'll talk to the big folk
And tell them out loud
That we really don't like
Being pushed in the crowd.

Robyn Curnow

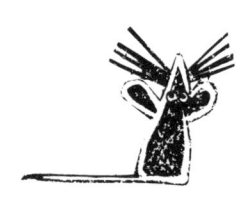

Big and small

The Competition

Words and music: June Epstein

Introduction to each verse

Plink - a! Plonk - a! Plink - a! Plonk - a! Plink - a! Plonk - a!
Plink - a! Plonk! The Flea and the Frog and the Kang - a - roo Were
ar - gu - ing one day at the Zoo. Said the 'Roo, 'I can make the
high - est jump', And he gave his tail a whack - et - y thump.

After the last verse

Plink - a! Plonk - a! Plink - a! Plonk - a! Plink! Plonk!

The Frog said, 'Ah, but you must confess
That I can go higher, for I weigh less.'
Said the Flea, who was nimble but very small,
'I bet I can go the highest of all.'

The other two laughed at the tiny Flea,
And each said, 'What! Go higher than me?'
'Yes,' said the Flea, 'I will prove it too,
If Frog will sit on the back of Roo.'

So Kangaroo took Frog on his head,
And Flea jumped up on Frog and said,
'If you will jump right over that wall,
I will be the highest of all.'

The Kangaroo said, 'You're a clever one,'
And the Frog croaked, 'Yes, the Flea has won.'
So all three jumped right out of the Zoo,
The Flea and the Frog and the Kangaroo.

Big animals

What Am I?

Something was there! The bushes rustled, the ground shook, and with a tremendous crash a beast burst out of the undergrowth. His face was worried, his eyes were thoughtful and he was muttering in a very low voice to himself,

'I don't know what I am,
It's a problem you see,
I don't know what I'm called,
But I know that I'm me.'

The beast looked up. There was a brightly-coloured bird twittering and fluttering, swooping and gliding in and out of the bushes. The beast called to the bird,

'My friend in the tree,
Would you please look and see
What you think I can be?
I don't know what I'm called,
But I know that I'm me.'

The bird looked at the beast. He thought for a few moments and then he replied,

'I don't know a lot,
But I'll tell you what's what—
You're big like a house,
Which is something I'm not.'

Then the little bird darted off to another part of the forest. The beast thought,

'I'm not quite so sure
I'm a house and no more,
But what can there be
That is me—just me?'

The animal twitched his grey hide and strolled away in search of someone else who could tell him what he was.

Presently he met a deer, nibbling the leaves and flicking her dainty slender ears. The beast coughed and said,

'Can you tell me, my friend,
What you think I can be?
I don't know what I'm called,
But I know that I'm me.'

'Well,' said the deer,

'I don't know a lot,
But I'll tell you what's what—
Those legs look like tree-trunks,
And I'm glad mine do not.'

'Tree trunks?' said the beast, 'Tree trunks?' He looked at his legs, then at a tree trunk, then back at his legs.

Big animals

Yes, they were similar. His legs were thick and rough and coarse, but he had no leaves. He thought,

    'I'm not quite convinced
    I'm entirely a tree,
    But what can it be
    That is me—just me?'

So he flapped his huge ears and set off to find out.
He saw a bee busying himself with some red and yellow flowers.
'Ah,' said the beast eagerly,

    'Can you tell me my friend
    What you think I can be?
    I don't know what I'm called,
    But I know that I'm me.'

'Oh,' said the bee,

    'I don't know a lot,
    But I'll tell you what's what—
    You're as strong as a tractor,
    And I'm sorry I'm not.'

And he buzzed away to find another flower.

The beast thought about this and, as he was thinking, he walked across to the edge of the river and sat in the shade. He thought and he thought and he thought.

    'I don't feel like a tree,
    Nor yet like a house,
    Though I'm big, and as strong as a tractor.
    But what really is me—
    The real, real me,
    Must lie in some hidden factor.
    Perhaps it is true
    That I am something new—
    Hold on! It's as plain as can be!
    I'm a tree-tractor-house,
    No! A tractor-hee-trouse,
    No! A tractor-tree-house—
    THAT IS ME!'

The tractor-tree-house was very happy. His great house body raised itself on his tree trunk legs and with all his tractor strength, he threw back his head, lifted his long, wrinkly trunk and trumpeted as long and as loudly as he could.

While the forest was still trembling with the happy noise of the tractor-tree-house, a tiny ant voice could be heard from the ground.

'Silly old elephant,' it said.

Merron Looney

Big animals

Elephant

Have you ever seen an elephant
Sitting down to dinner?
If you saw how much he eats
You'd know why he's not thinner.

Sonya Higgs

Hippo

The big fat hippopotamus
Lying in the river.
He'd been there for seven years,
When he began to shiver.
'Oh dear,' he said, 'I've caught a cold.
I'm really such a fool.'
So now he lives in luxury
In a heated swimming pool.

Jo-Anne Steven

Tromp! Tromp!

The elephant has such BIG FEET,
He really is a wonder!
    Through the jungle, up and down,
    The animals for miles around
    Hear the TROMP-TROMP elephant sound
And think it must be thunder!
    TROMP!
      TROMP!
        TROMP!

Kathryn Taylor

What time was it when the elephant sat on the gate?

Time to get a new gate.

Are you putting that in your riddle book?

In a word, yes!

Big animals

Yaks' Gnus

YAKS yodel youthfully,
Along the mountain trail.
Yaks yodel youthfully,
Though some may think they wail!

YAKS yodel youthfully,
And think they are so fine,
While neighbouring gnus just mutter
'Yaks don't yodel, they just whine!'

    GNUS natter needlessly
    And gossip and tell lies,
    Gnus natter needlessly
    And like to moralise.

    GNUS natter needlessly
    Which makes the yaks disgusted,
    And leads those yaks to all conclude
    That gnus cannot be trusted.

The gnus consider that the yaks
Would natter till they're blue,
If yaks were half as well-informed
And knew news as gnus do.

And if the yaks should meet the gnus
I'm certain that they'd say:
'The trouble with you nattering gnus
Is that you 'yak' all day!'

Lee Andrews

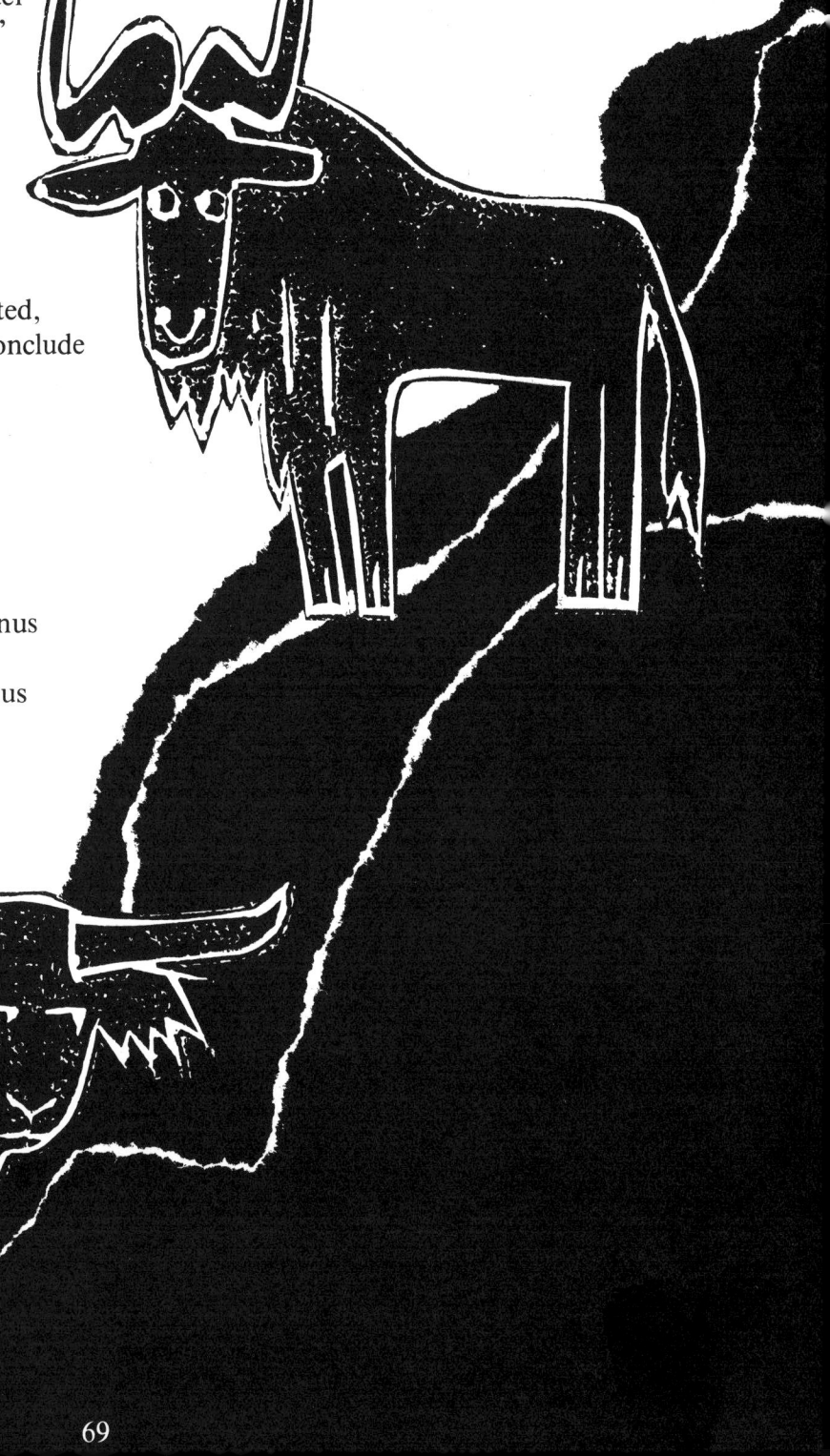

Small animals

The Ears of Mandy

There was a fat grey cat who was so old that none of the children in his house could remember when he was a kitten. He was old before they were born.

He was called Mandy because someone mistook him for a girl cat, and by the time they found out he wasn't, it was too late.

He spent most of the day lying on the window seat in the living-room, or on a cushion on the back verandah. He was too old to be active, and his eyes were so bad that he could hardly see at all. But his whiskers twitched a lot.

And his ears!

That cat could hear anything and everything. You might say he lived through his ears.

His ears told him when the day started, because he heard the birds begin to sing. Then he heard the *tring tring* of the alarm,

the *creak creak* of the bed,

the *patter patter* of small feet

and the *slap slap* of Somebody's slippers.

Click went the latch of the back door, *eek eek* went its hinges, and Somebody said, 'Outside, Mandy!' And out he went.

When he was ready to come in again he gave one *miaow* at the back door.

Chink chink went the cups and saucers.

Guggle guggle went the milk as it was poured into his own special dish.

Purr purr, went Mandy when he had finished his breakfast and wanted to say 'thank you'. He snuggled against Somebody's pyjama leg and a big warm hand stroked his fur, and he heard Somebody's voice say, 'Good puss.'

That was how Mandy's day always began.

But one morning a terrible thing happened.

He heard the birds begin to sing while it was still dark.

He waited for the alarm. There was no *tring tring*.

He waited for the bed. There was no *creak creak*.

He listened for the *patter patter* of small feet and the *slap slap* of Somebody's slippers, but *nothing happened*.

All was quiet for a very long time. Then he heard footsteps on the path outside the back door. *Click* went the door, *eek eek* went the hinges, and a voice said, 'Outside Mandy!' Only it wasn't

Small animals

Somebody's voice. Mandy knew it belonged to the boy-next-door.

Mandy would have refused to go outside. But he needed to go.

When he was ready for breakfast there was another unpleasant surprise. His special dish of milk had been placed on the back verandah instead of on the kitchen floor. 'Miaow,' said Mandy at the back door. But nobody opened it.

Mandy was insulted. He would have refused to drink the milk. But he was thirsty.

That was a terrible day. He could not hear his family at all. They had gone away. He could not get inside the house. He had to sleep all day on the cushion on the verandah.

Mandy would have refused to sleep. But he was old and tired.

At tea-time, the boy-next-door gave him some choice meat, and later he let him into the house for a while. He even said, 'Good puss,' and tried to stroke him. But his hand was so different from Somebody's that it made Mandy cross. In fact he would have scratched the boy-next-door if he had not been a well-trained cat who knew his manners. Besides he was very old.

The next day was just as bad, and the next, and the next.

On the next day after that, Mandy was lying on his cushion listening to the cars swishing along the road and the people tramping along the footpath. Suddenly something wonderful happened.

Small animals

From all the different sounds in the street, Mandy's ears picked out one particular sound. His whiskers began to twitch. It was the special *vrrrm vrrrm* that he knew came only from the engine of one special car. It was Somebody's car.

Mandy listened. *Beep beep* went a horn, *slam* went a car door, *cling clang* went the gate. *Vrrrrm, vrrrrm* went the car along the drive, *slam slam slam* went the car doors, *chatter chatter* went the voices. And he knew his family had come home.

Next day, Mandy woke early on his window seat in the living-room. He did not wait to hear the birds, or the alarm, or the bed or the feet or the slippers. He forgot he was old and fat and slow. He went quickly *pit-pat pit-pat* into the bedroom, jumped onto Somebody's bed and snuggled down on the blankets. A big warm hand stroked his fur and Somebody's sleepy voice said, 'Good puss!'

Then Mandy made his own loudest, happiest special purring noise, and it was everybody else's turn to listen.

June Epstein

Slide-Swim-Fly

Snake slide slip slither
Over dry hard clay.
Snake slide slip slither
Hot hot day.

    Fish swim swish sway
    Through the murky way.
    Fish swim swish sway
    Deep deep bay.

Bird fly flutter flit
Through the open sky.
Bird fly flutter flit
Blue blue sky.

Sue Cochrane

Snake

Sleeping snake
Curled up tight.

    Waking snake
    Starts in fright.

        Slithering snake
        Quickly glides

            Out of sight.

Dorothy Mills

Small animals

Egg

I'm watching an egg, and I've just heard a shpink!
There is something inside that egg, I think.
It's wobbling and turbling, and now there's a crack!
There is something inside that egg, for a fact.

It's rolling and rombling and tombling about,
I wonder what frobulous thing will come out?

The egg has split open as wide as can be,
And now there's an eye that is looking at me!
The rest of its body pops out with a flick,
And there stands before me—
                a new little chick!

Joanne Wallis

Don't Call Him That

If you should meet a little creature
With spines upon his back,
Four little feet, a long thin snout,
Eyes small and beady and black,
Don't call him porcupine or hedgehog
Because that's just not true.
His proper name's Echidna—
Spiny ant-eater will do.

Anne Le Roy

Small animals

Picnic Day

Once upon a time there was a frog who lived with his friend Mouse in a small house with a red door, under the largest tree in the bush. Frog was a very fat frog, a very green frog. Mouse, on the other hand, was very, very thin, and he had the longest tail of any mouse that Frog had ever seen.

One day, when they were shopping at the market place, they saw a notice pinned to a tree.

Mouse cleared his throat and read it in a loud voice:

'*A picnic will be held under the large gum tree near the river at 3 o'clock this afternoon. All welcome. Join the fun. Prizes given to the winners of games and competitions. Signed OWL.*'

'That sounds like fun,' said Frog. 'Will we go, Mouse?'

'Of course we'll go, Frog, we might win some prizes.'

Frog jumped for joy. He jumped so much that he landed once or twice on Mouse's tail!

'Ouch!' cried Mouse. 'Do be careful!'

Frog looked very embarrassed. 'I'm so sorry, Mouse, did I hurt you very much?'

'Just a little, Frog,' said Mouse, trying to be brave.

Frog picked up Mouse's tail gently. 'It seems to have a bend in it, Mouse. Do you think it will be all right?'

'Yes, yes,' Mouse replied, recovering quite well. 'Let's get our shopping done so we can go home and get ready for the picnic.'

So home they went with Mouse's tail dragging, a little bent, behind them.

When they arrived at the picnic, quite a few people were already there. Water-rat was looking very smart in a red waistcoat, with a gold stop-watch attached.

'He must be going to time the races,' said Mouse excitedly.

'Dear friends,' said Owl, 'gather around. I would like four contestants for the cheese-eating contest.'

Mouse put his paw up straight away. He loved cheese. Frog didn't, so he said he'd wait for another competition.

Small animals

Mouse lined up at the table with Rat, Possum and Field-mouse. When Owl said 'Go!' they had to eat all the cheese on their plates before the whistle went.

Mouse ate and ate and ate. He had so much in his mouth he could hardly chew. He even had cheese on his whiskers.

Suddenly the whistle blew. 'STOP!' cried Owl. He looked to see how much cheese each contestant had eaten.

'The winner is Rat,' said Owl, and gave him an enormous piece of cheese as a prize. Frog noticed Mouse was a little sad when he didn't win, and said, 'Don't worry, Mouse, think of all the delicious cheese you ate. There are lots more competitions to win.'

The next event was a sack race. Frog and Mouse both joined in. Frog had a lot of trouble getting into his sack because he was so fat. He had to wriggle around so that he would fit. Mouse didn't have any trouble because he was very thin.

'When I say "GO!" jump up to the large stump near the river and back to the starting line,' said Owl.

The animals hopped as fast as they could in their sacks. Poor Frog tripped over because he didn't have much room to jump in his sack. Mouse did quite well. He would have come second, but his tail popped out and tripped him up, just as he was about to cross the finishing line. Mouse was very cross with his tail.

'It's not much fun having a long tail when it trips you up,' he said to Frog.

'No,' said Frog, 'and it's much less fun being so fat you can hardly fit into a sack.'

The next competition was for the longest tail. Four mice entered the competition. When all the tails were measured, Mouse's was nearly twice as long as anyone else's, even if it did have a slight bend in it. Mouse was delighted when Owl gave him the prize, a soft brush for his fur.

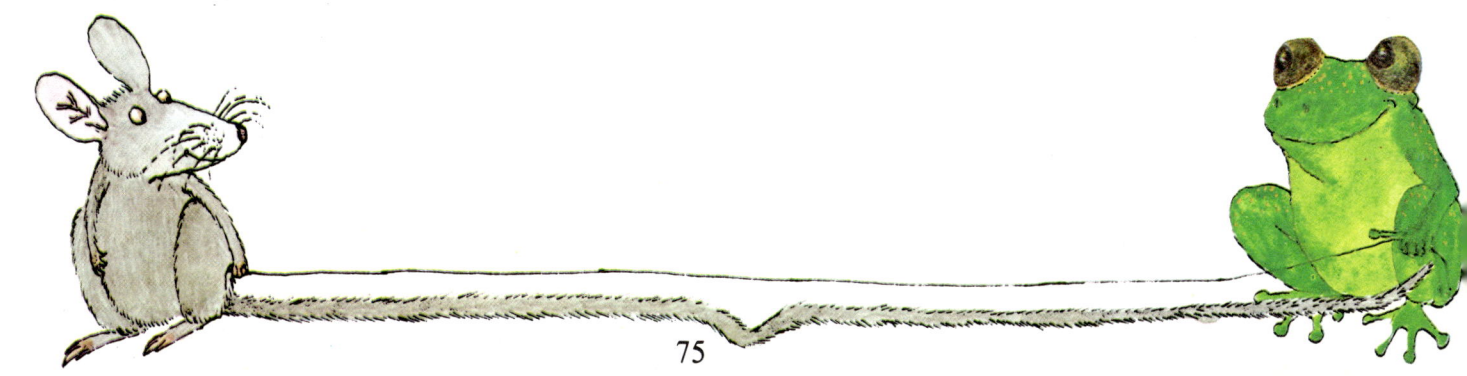

Small animals

Frog was very happy when Mouse won, but he still wanted to win something himself. Then Owl said there was going to be a swimming race.

'I'm very good at swimming, even if I am fat,' said Frog. He lined up with Toad and Bullfrog, and when Owl said 'GO!' he swam across the river and back as fast as he could go. He won quite easily, and was very proud now that he too had a prize. It was a scrubbing brush for washing his back in the bath. It was just what he needed because, being fat, he found it hard to wash his own back.

That was the end of the picnic, and as they went off home Frog and Mouse thanked Owl for such a lovely day.

Laurel Hoffrichter

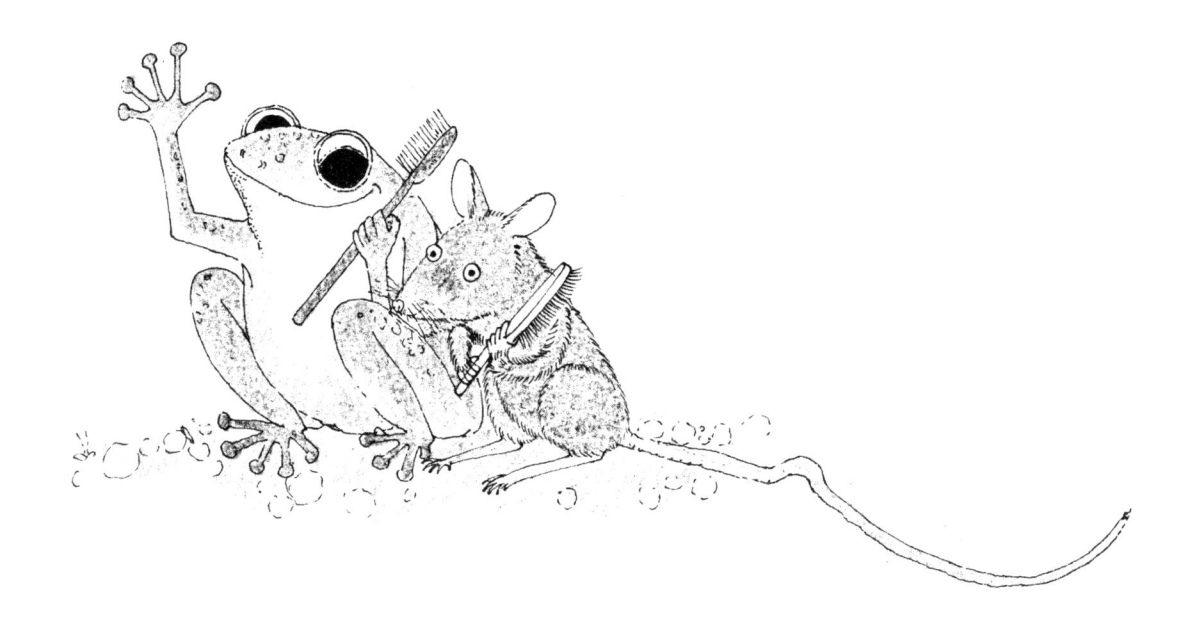

Very small animals

Caterpillar Lunch

Here comes Mr Caterpillar
    Munch! Munch! Munch!
        Nibbling through
            A leaf or two
                For caterpillar lunch.

Kathryn Taylor

Caterpillar

Caterpillar, Caterpillar, why are you so thick?
I ate all the cabbage and I'm going to be sick!

Janette Jenkins

Very small animals

words: Anne LeRoy **Metamorphosis** music: June Epstein

Kit-tens look like cats, and pup-pies look like dogs, So why don't lit-tle tad-poles look like lit-tle frogs?

Bear cubs look like bears, and lit-tle sloths like sloths, So why don't cat-er-pil-lars look like lit-tle moths?

What's a sloth?

Take a look on page 72

What are you doing, Hopping Mouse?

I'm playing metamorphosis. I'm asleep, and deciding what I'll turn into when I wake up.

You can't fool me! I know that a small hopping mouse grows into a big hopping mouse. It doesn't become a different animal.

A BIG hopping mou...

Very small animals

Kit-tens, pup-pies and o-ther things don't need a spe-cial pro-cess, But cat-er-pil-lars and tad-poles do. They go through me-ta-mor-phos-is!

I like this game. I've just changed into a flying beetle! Bzzz!

You know, all insects grow by changing themselves — that's metamorphosis!

So do frogs and toads and... er.... such like creatures.

Well, I hatched out of an egg, so there!

COCOON DO NOT DISTURB

Very small animals

Big Black Spider

A big black spider is on my wall.
I can see him creep, I can see him crawl.
He's hairy and scarey and lives on flies,
And he's got eight legs, and two small eyes.
It looks as though he's here to stay,
But I really wish he'd go away.

Angela Stubbs

Snail

Slithery slide,
   I must hide
Under a tree
   For no-one to see.

One foot, two,
   Beware! A shoe!
Slithery slide,
   I must hide.

Teresa O'Halloran

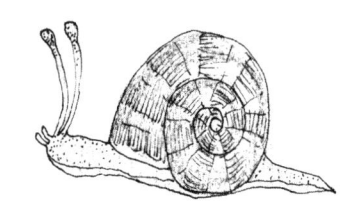

A Visitor

We had an unexpected
Visitor today,
She came in on the silver-beet
And was nearly washed away.

We found her struggling in the sink
And when her wings were dry,
Ladybird, quick as a wink,
Flew off into the sky.

Joan M. Shilton

Little Fleas

Do little fleas have hairy knees?
Wear knee-high socks and brogues?
And do they wear Bermuda shorts,
The stylish little rogues?

Do little fleas wear running shoes
By Adidas and Co?
And tight blue jeans and denim shirts—
Well, do they? Yes or no?

Lee Andrews

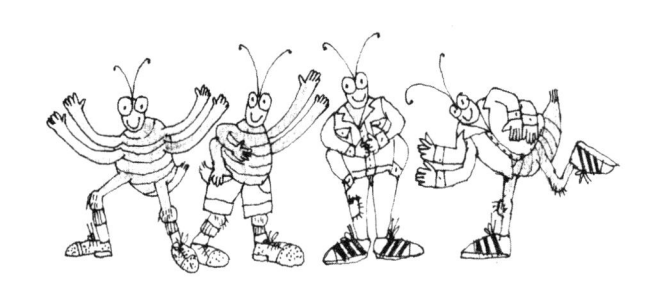

Cheek!

Today I saw little ant
Climb upon our sofa.
He lay right down and had a sleep,
The lazy little loafer!

Sonya Higgs

Imaginary animals

The Marmadin

The Marmadin, the Marmadin
Has one arm out and one arm in.
He glumps and gloozes up and down,
And frightens creatures all around.
His voice is cackle tremulous,
His fangs, both sharp and venomous,
His coat is scaled and barnacled,
He was, they say, once manacled,
But no strong chains can keep him in—
They cannot hold a Marmadin.

His eyes are crimson, black and blue,
Of various and stunning hue.
His claws are not desirable,
You'd not find him admirable.
His mane is slimy slithery,
He'll beckon you—'Come hithery!'
But do not listen—don't give in—
No! Never to a Marmadin.

Lee Andrews

The Higglebump

We haven't got a puppy,
   They make my sister wheeze,
And we haven't got a kitten,
   They make my daddy sneeze,
But I *have* got a Something,
   That lives down in the shed,
And I call him Mr Higglebump,
   Because of his big head.
He's a little bit of everything
   That's soft and warm and cuddly,
But he isn't very clever,
   His brain is very muddly.
He's like a sort of pussy,
   With a curly tail and paws,
But a little bit unusual,
   For he hasn't any claws.
His ears are like an elephant's
   And he doesn't like to fight
For his mouth is made for eating things
   He never tries to bite.
He likes the things that I like,
   And never is a grump,
And when I need a Something,
   There's Mr Higglebump.

Virginia Brown

Imaginary animals

Puggly Beasts

This Puggly Beast keeps opening doors
   When cold, wet winds are blowing;
When draughts go whistling round the floors
   He wishes it was snowing.

Now, this one steals the marmalade
   From off the breakfast table,
And wipes it on the door-handles
   Whenever he is able.

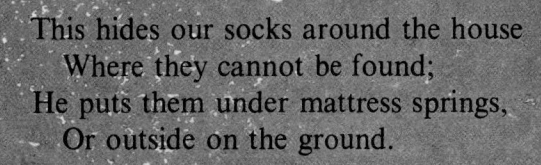

This hides our socks around the house
   Where they cannot be found;
He puts them under mattress springs,
   Or outside on the ground.

And this brings mud from out-of-doors
   And stamps it on the mat.
It always makes him laugh and laugh
   When YOU get blamed for that.

Henry Parker

Imaginary animals

Fat Horace

Once upon a time there was a very fierce dragon who lived in a cave at the top of a high mountain. The dragon's name was Horace, and all the people who lived down in the valley below were afraid of him. His tail was long and spiked. His claws were sharp. His teeth were strong and white, and his fiery breath was very, very hot.

Every morning, Horace would fly from his cave down into the valley, and snatch five sleek cows to take home for breakfast. And when he had finished eating them, Horace would settle down for an after-breakfast nap.

Every day, when he woke up from his nap, Horace would fly into the valley and grab ten woolly lambs for his lunch. And by the time he had finished eating, it was time for his after-lunch snooze.

Every evening, when he woke from his snooze, Horace would fly into the valley and seize twenty fat pigs. And after eating the pigs for tea, Horace would curl up in his cave and go to sleep for the night.

Now Horace was not only very fierce, but with all this eating, he was also getting very fat. Horace didn't notice this until he started to have trouble squeezing through the entrance of his cave.

Then he discovered that his fiery breath was getting cooler and cooler, until one morning, the best he could manage was a puff of smoke.

Finally, Horace was so fat that he couldn't get off the ground when he wanted to fly into the valley one day, and he had to walk all the way instead. That was when Horace decided that it was time he lost some weight.

First, he tried doing special exercises in front of his mirror each morning, but ... his stomach got in the way when he tried to touch his toes, so he gave up.

Then Horace tried Yoga and Meditation before lunch every day, but ... his stomach rumbled so much, he couldn't remember to concentrate, so he gave that up too.

He even tried jogging every evening before tea, but ... that made him so hungry that he ate more than ever, and got even fatter.

Finally, in desperation, Horace put an advertisement in the newspaper. The advertisement read:

'URGENT!
OVERWEIGHT DRAGON NEEDS HELP
TO LOSE WEIGHT. ENQUIRE AT
DRAGON'S CAVE.'

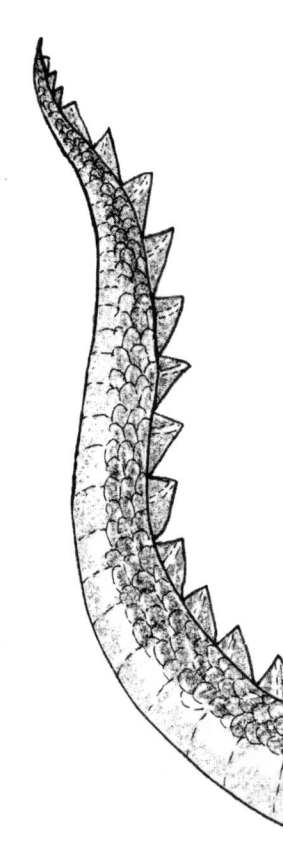

Imaginary animals

Unfortunately for Horace, the people in the valley were too frightened of him to want to help, so for a long time he just kept getting fatter and fatter.

Then one day a little girl appeared at the entrance to Horace's cave. Her name was Sarah, and she said that she had come to help him to lose weight. Horace didn't think she would have much luck, but he invited her into the cave anyway.

'Thank you,' said Sarah. 'We'll start tomorrow.'

Next morning, Horace got up and started squeezing out through the entrance of the cave, when Sarah appeared and asked him where he was going.

'I'm just going to snatch a few cows for breakfast,' said Horace.

'But I've already got your breakfast,' said Sarah, and she set a steaming bowl of porridge on the table.

Horace ate that in a trice, but before he could ask for more, Sarah said, 'Now it's time for our after-breakfast walk.'

So together they went for a long walk on the mountain and when they got back, it was time for lunch.

Horace was just setting off down the mountain when Sarah asked him where he was going.

'I'm just going to get a few sheep for lunch,' he said.

'But I've already got your lunch,' said Sarah, and she brought out a big plate of salad.

Horace ate that as quick as you please, but before he had time to ask for more, Sarah said, 'Now it's time for a game of chess.' They finished their game and it was time for tea.

Before Horace had time even to think about seizing a few pigs for tea, Sarah had dished up a large bowl of soup. As soon as he had finished it, Sarah said, 'Now there is just enough time for a story before you go to bed.' So she told him a wonderful tale about a far-off land where there are lots of dragons and not many people, until Horace was fast asleep.

Sarah stayed with Horace for quite a long time, and Horace gradually got thinner and thinner. Although he was eating much less than he used to, Horace was so busy going for walks, and playing chess, and listening to stories, he had no time to feel hungry.

Then one day Sarah said that it was time for her to go back to her home and her family. At first Horace was sad, for he had grown

Imaginary animals

very fond of Sarah, but she said, 'Horace, you're thin again now. You don't need me any more. You can fit easily through the cave entrance, and your fiery breath is getting hotter every day. I'm sure you could even fly again if you tried to.'

Horace knew she was right, but he didn't want to live by himself again.

'Sarah,' he said, 'I've decided that it is time I was leaving too. I am going to fly away to the far-off land where there are lots of dragons and not many people.'

'I'll miss you, Horace,' said Sarah, giving him a big hug.

'I'll miss you too,' said Horace. 'Goodbye, Sarah. I'll write to you.' And he sprang into the air and flew away.

'Goodbye, goodbye,' called Sarah. She watched him until he was quite out of sight, and then she turned and walked down the mountain back to her home.

Linda Davison

Dragons are Imaginary?

My mum says dragons are imaginary,
And I know she thinks she's right,
But she's never in my room
When they visit me at night.

Dad says there are no fairies,
That they're not really there,
But he's never in the garden
When their laughter fills the air.

And me, I don't say anything,
I know that they're quite wrong,
Because my secret friends and I
Play together all day long.

Bronwyn Williams

Magic

Katharine's Magic Horse

Katharine had a little wooden horse. Her aunt had sent it to her from Sweden. Every night when Katharine went to bed she put the horse under her pillow, and as soon as the light was turned out she wriggled her hand under the pillow to feel it. It was a very special horse. Katharine and the horse had a very special secret.

words and music: June Epstein

Galloping along

I ride him on Sunday, I ride him on Monday, I ride him on Tuesday, Wednesday, Thursday, Friday, Saturday too. We ride over roof tops, And jump over tree tops, And we can go right above the clouds and up into the

Magic

blue. Wher-ev-er I want to be, (And it can be an-y-where) I don't have to tell him, I know he will take me there. And no-one can see us, And no-bo-dy guess-es, For no-bo-dy knows my lit-tle horse is mag-ic.

Magic

The Power of Five

'Can you reach the stars?' he said.
'Of course I can, of course I can.'
'And can you float around the moon
Holding tight to a red balloon
Sweeping stars up with a broom?'
'Of course I can, of course,' she said.

'Can you make it snow?' he said.
'Of course I can, of course I can.'
'Can you calm a stormy sea,
Teach the fish to jump with glee
And make the sun shine now for me?'
'Of course I can, of course,' she said.

'I think you're wonderful!' he said.
'Of course I am, of course I am!'
'You are so clever, you're always right,
I'm only four—do you think I might
Be as clever when I am five?'
'Of course you will, of course,' said she.

Judith Howard

Magic

Llewellyn the Witch

Abra-Ka-Dabra
Llewellyn the witch
Can put you in orbit
with one little twitch.

She'll curse and she'll grumble
Her belly will rumble
Then zippety-wham!
You're a frog!

Colleen Clancy

What's worse than a bad riddle?

Two bad riddles!

Magic

John's Task

A poor farmer fell into debt to a wealthy land-owner. He trembled lest he be thrown into prison and not be able to work his small-holding. He felt even worse when the land-owner visited him.

'You deserve to go to prison,' the land-owner said. 'But I am not an unjust man. See here, I will give you and your family a chance. Seven of my fields are badly overgrown with thistles. They must be cut.'

'Certainly, sir. At once, sir. I'll clear your fields this very day.'

'Not you, you fool. You are already becoming slow and stiff. Lend me your son. If he can clear my fields in seven days, I will forgive you your debt. If not, the boy can remain as my servant for life.'

John, the boy, was dearly loved by his parents and already a great help to his father. He insisted on going with the farmer.

'Don't you see, Father, what a good chance this is to free our farm from debt? I am young and strong. Only one field a day. Just lend me your scythe and your stone and I'll be gone. Look out for me in a week's time. And have something special in the pot for our supper, Mother.'

It was high summer, and even before sunrise next day John was up, had eaten the meagre breakfast of bread and milk left on the landlord's kitchen table, filled his leather bottle with water and put a hunk of bread inside his shirt for lunch. He put the scythe over his shoulder and strode out over the dewy grass. The field was choked and purple with thistles. They nodded their fluffy heads and raised

Magic

their cruel thorny fingers as if to mock him, but John bent to his task with a will. At every stroke the proud purple heads bowed and fell.

Larks rose, singing in the clear air, the sun strode over the sky. The day grew hotter and hotter. Soon John was bathed in sweat. Dust and flying downy seeds choked his nose and throat. His head felt about to burst.

'Slow down, you fool,' he told himself, 'slow and steady wins the race.'

But even though he took more time and worked rhythmically, as the day wore on he grew sick with the blistering heat and his legs trembled beneath him.

By evening the field was clear—all but a small patch near the gate. John was glad to bolt down a poor meal of thin stew and bread and then throw himself on his hard bed to sleep.

Next day he was stiff and his hands blistered, but he worked on grimly. A hawk hovered overhead, waiting to swoop on field mice John disturbed from their thistle homes. Crows mocked him from the hedges. By nightfall, the second field was only three-quarters cleared and the land-owner sneered as he came to inspect the work.

'You'll need to smarten yourself up, lad, at this rate. And mind you cut all the thistles. Look over there, you've missed a patch. Big thistles from little thistles grow, you know.'

Poor John. Struggle as he might, strive all he could, each day he

Magic

found the task becoming too great. Although now he had wisely learned to lie in the shade at noon and his body was accustomed to the rhythm of the scythe, he knew the last three fields were even larger than the first four. 'To work for this man for ever, how could I bear it?' he thought.

On the fifth day, the hawk lazily circling overhead suddenly dropped, and in one swift movement caught up in its great claws a baby rabbit. John shouted and whirled the scythe over his head. Startled, the hawk dropped his prey. The baby rabbit lay stunned and John put his hand over it to protect it. He saw the cruel, tawny eyes of the hawk as it circled low once more and then flew slowly away.

'You poor little fellow,' said John, uncovering the rabbit whose eyes were bulging with terror. He gently put him down in the grass. With a sudden bound the rabbit was gone.

On the last night of the week John hardly slept. Every time he closed his eyes he saw row after row of thistles pushing closer and closer, thistles that refused the bite of steel and remained upright and defiant. His cruel master was up early and gloated as he watched the boy trudge stubbornly out to work. One day left and two whole fields to cut.

'I'll just have to work like a demon, even if it kills me,' John told himself as he pushed open the rough gate in the stone wall.

He stopped, gasped and rubbed his eyes. The field was bare of thistles. Each one lay wilting among the thick grass. John ran to the last field. It, too, was clear, but under the gate were squeezing dozens and dozens of rabbits—big old bucks, fat does, soft-eyed babies. Their white scuts bobbed in the grass. They were gone.

John stayed all day in the fields, trimming every furrow so that not one purple top could be seen. At nightfall he called the landowner who was angry and puzzled, yet kept his bargain.

And in later years, when John farmed his own land, no rabbits were ever trapped and no thistles ever grew.

Mary Roberts

Let's pretend

Tracks in the Dirt

Tracks in the dirt
   and they lead to a tree,
But I'm not going to follow them—
   NO! NOT ME!

It might be a Tigerbird
   with wings like a plane,
Or maybe a Rhinobear
   as large as a train.

There are tracks in the dirt
   and they lead to a tree,
But I'm not going to follow them—
   NO! NOT ME!

Joanne Wallis

When I'm at the beach I sometimes play detectives — I try to work out what sort of creatures make the tracks I find in the sand.

Look out, kangaroo! You're walking backwards.

What a big kangaroo!

Well, seagull, can you work out who made the tracks all over this clean page?

When I go to the beach I like to race with the waves and see how many tracks I can make before they're washed away!

Race? You must be joking!

Let's pretend

If All the Queens Should Come to Dine

words: Anne Le Roy

music: June Epstein

Slowly, with royal dignity

JONATHAN: If all the Queens should come to dine, You'd

BELINDA: need a dinner set so fine. If all the Queens should

JONATHAN: come to dine, You'd need a dinner set so fine. A

plain white one would never do, A plain white one

JONATHAN AND BELINDA: would never do. If all the Queens should come to dine, It

must be gold and royal blue. La, la, la, la, la,

Let's pretend

la, la, la, la, la, la, la, la, la, la, la.

Kings and Queens

Jonathan and his friend Belinda played Kings and Queens. They had paper crowns and cloaks made from curtains. They put a tea-set on a box with some biscuits and apples and had a royal feast.

Then they sang a song about all the Queens coming to dine.

Jonathan sang the first part, then Belinda sang. They sang the last part together, and walked slowly about in a Royal Procession.

After the Royal Procession, Jonathan made a bow and Belinda made a deep curtsey.

Belinda cut her crown out of a piece of white paper. She glued the ends together and stuck on pieces of red paper for jewels. Jonathan's crown was cut from a red and blue and white paper bag which just fitted his head.

Belinda painted some white cardboard party plates with blue patterns. They looked so fine that Jonathan painted a plate for each person in the family. He made beautiful patterns in all colours, and everybody used the plates that evening for tea.

June Epstein

Special days

CALENDAR
- with the compliments of Boothby's Butcher Shops -

"Sausages worth fighting for!"

NOVEMBER

SUN	MON	TUES	WED	THUR	FRI	SAT
30						1
2	3	4	5	6	7	8
9	10	11	12	13	14	15
16	17	18	19	20	21	22
23	24	25	26	27	28	29

Bill arrives! (2) · Melbourne Cup (4) · Circus (7) · My birthday (17)

Melbourne Cup - 4th

DECEMBER

SUN	MON	TUES	WED	THUR	FRI	SAT
	1	2	3	4	5	6
7	8	9	10	11	12	13
14	15	16	17	18	19	20
21	22	23	24	25	26	27
28	29	30	31			

Mum's birthday (1) · School finishes (18) · Going to Zoo (13) · New Years Eve party at Zonro's (31)

Christmas Day - 25th   Boxing Day - 26th

Red Letter Days

Red Letter Days are Special Days,
Days on the calendar marked in red:
    Christmas and Fete days,
    Birthdays, great days,
    Circus and Zoo days,
    Year-when-it's-new days,
Days that you feel are like holidays,
Those are the ones in red.

Dorothy Rickards

How many rabbits did you see on page 90 and page 91?

What rabbits? I didn't see any rabbits.

Have another look – count the ears and divide by two.

Special days

The Bells

One day Jonathan was out walking with his grandmother when he heard a wonderful sound.

Ding-dong- ding-dong - ding-dong - ding-dong! Clash! Crash! Clash!

He stopped to listen.

'They are bells,' said his Grandmother. 'It must be a special day for someone. Probably a wedding.'

'Could we see it?' asked Jonathan.

'We'll try,' said Grandmother. 'We'll follow the sound of the bells.'

They hurried around the corner, along one side street and down another, with the bells sounding louder all the time, until they came to a church. It *was* a wedding. There were the bride and bridegroom standing outside smiling, while people took photographs of them. The bride wore a white dress and carried flowers. The groom had a white rose in his buttonhole. Their friends were throwing pink, blue and yellow confetti over them.

'Where are the bells?' asked Jonathan. He had to shout now because they were so loud.

'I expect they are in the church tower. They are so big and heavy that people have to pull them with ropes to make them sound,' said grandmother.

On the way home, Jonathan's ears felt as if they were ringing, too, from the noise.

'I wish I could ring bells like that,' he said.

'When we get home I will show you how to make bottle bells,' promised Grandmother. 'They won't be like church bells but you'll have fun with them.'

Jonathan began to skip, and he sang the names of all the different bells he knew. 'Big bells, *little* bells, church bells, *door* bells, school bells, *bicycle* bells, fire bells, *telephone* bells ...'

As soon as they were home, they went to the kitchen cupboard and found some empty bottles. They poured different amounts of water into them and stood them on the table. Jonathan found that by striking them *gently* with a fork handle he could make musical sounds. He pretended he was playing church bells for a wedding.

'I'll show you how to play tunes,' said Grandmother, 'but first we must collect eight bottles all the same size. That may take a few days.'

Special days

When they had the eight bottles, they put a broomstick between two chairs and tied the bottles so that they were hanging from the broomstick. Next they carefully poured water into each bottle, less and less water each time. Jonathan found that the less water in a bottle, the higher was the sound he could make with it. He put some colour into the water to make it easier to see. Very soon he was able to make a musical scale with the bottles, like the scale Grandmother played on her piano.

'Thanks, Grandma,' he said. 'Now I'll try to play tunes like those wedding bells.'

June Epstein

SOME TUNES TO PLAY ON BOTTLE BELLS

arr: June Epstein

Grandfather's Clock

Good King Wenceslas

The First Noël

Why is a fish a good musician?

Because he knows his scales!

Hey! That's my lunch! And it's not that kind of scale in music

A scale is a row musical n

Special days

Day at the Beach

Warm sun   fine sand   dogs run   seagulls land

tiny shells   big balls   digging wells   building walls

sparkling seas   rolling waves   bent trees   rocky caves.

Barbara Prictor

Special days

The Show

Hurry up Mum, come on let's go
Or we'll be late for the Royal Show.
Look, there's the wheel! Quick, in at the gate!
Let's buy a ticket before it's too late.

There are so many rides and so much to see,
Oh, look at that monster—hey, wait for me!
Can I have a show-bag and something to eat?
A hot-dog, or doughnut—that's really a treat.

The animal nursery—Gosh, what a jam!
There are chickens all colours, and even a lamb.
Can I have a kitten or maybe a pup
Or a little white rabbit who won't play up?

There's baa-baa black sheep, and look at that goat—
He's trying to eat somebody's coat!
Come, see the dogs, don't they look fine
With rosettes and ribbons! I wish one was mine.

The tractors, the cars, the cakes and the flowers,
To see all the things will really take hours.
You look at them, Mum, while I have a ride
And we'll meet up again round the other side.

Home again now, our money all spent,
Mum says it's hard to see where it went.
The rides, the show-bags, wasn't it great?
I'll be back next year—I can hardly wait!

Sue Berry

Special days

Splashalong and the Melbourne Cup

Charlie's father owned a lot of race-horses. His favourite horse, Fizzer, was going to race in the Melbourne Cup.

Charlie's father had given Charlie a race-horse named Splashalong. Charlie wanted Splashalong to race in the Melbourne Cup too.

He asked his father if he could race Splashalong. His father laughed. 'Splashalong can only run fast enough when it rains, and it doesn't look like raining.' He laughed again. 'Besides, Splashalong has flat feet. Enter him if you like, Charlie, but he can't win.'

Charlie ran into the stable and told Splashalong. Fizzer was in the next stall. He began to laugh. 'Look at your flat feet. You couldn't win the Melbourne Cup.'

Splashalong just held his head high and said, 'At least I can try.'

Every day, Charlie took Splashalong for a practice gallop around the race-track. All the jockeys laughed and said, 'Look at your flat feet. You couldn't win the Melbourne Cup.' Splashalong just held his head high and said, 'At least I can try,' and he wished it would rain on Melbourne Cup Day.

Melbourne Cup Day came. It was a beautiful day without clouds in the sky.

Some races were run before the Melbourne Cup race. Big black clouds began to gather in the sky. Charlie said, 'I think it might rain.' Splashalong wished it would rain.

The horses lined up for the Melbourne Cup race. The race started.

The horses were off down the track with Fizzer out in front and Splashalong last. Galloping, galloping, faster and faster, the horses rounded the first bend. Thunder rumbled in the sky. Lightning flashed and heavy drops of rain started to fall.

Round the second bend the horses raced neck and neck. Splashalong felt the rain beat on his back. He felt the rain drip down his legs and he felt the mud between his hooves. He didn't slip and slide like the other horses because he had flat feet.

Splashalong galloped past the horse in front. He galloped past another horse and he galloped past Fizzer.

Splashalong had galloped past all the horses and he galloped past the Finishing Post. He had won the race.

Charlie hugged him. Splashalong smiled. He had tried and he had won, and it rained and rained and rained.

Terry Duff

Birthdays

Off to the Party

'Watch out!' said Mum,
'That you mind your manners.'

'Be careful,' said Dad,
'That you don't get wet.'

'Make sure,' said Sue,
'That you don't gulp your tea.'

'Have fun!' said Gran,
The best advice yet!

Robyn Cordes

Birthday

Birthday
Balloon day
Cut-the-cake-soon day.
Present day
Candle day
Stay-up-to-see-the-moon day.
Friends to play
Friends to stay
Come-to-my-party
HOORAY!!

Dorothy Mills

Birthdays

The Instant Party

Mr Benvenuto lived in a little house near the bus-stop, opposite a block of flats. Whenever the children from the flats were waiting to catch the red bus they would see Mr Benvenuto digging in his garden or sitting on the verandah with a grey cat on his knees. Some of them would call out, 'Buenos dias!', or 'Gunaydin!'

Mr Benvenuto knew that was their way of saying 'Hello' in different languages because they came from different countries. Although he spoke English very well he answered, 'Buon giorno,' because a long time ago he too had come from another country, Italy.

He often gave them a flower or a tomato from his garden, and when it rained he invited them to keep dry on his verandah. He was a kind man.

Mr Benvenuto's hair was white, so the children thought he must be very old.

'I think he is twenty,' said Manuela.

'I think he is forty,' said Ahmed.

'I think he is a hundred,' said Giorgio.

Philip, who was the youngest, asked him straight out, 'How old are you, Mr Benvenuto?'

His big sister said, 'Sh! That's not polite.'

But Mr Benvenuto smiled and said, 'I shall be seventy-two on Saturday.'

Birthdays

'Then it will be your birthday,' said Philip. 'Will your family give you lots of presents?'

'I shouldn't think so,' said Mr Benvenuto. 'I haven't really got any family, except for Puss here.'

The children thought this was very sad. They went away to talk about it, and soon they had an idea.

On Saturday, Mr Benvenuto was making himself a cup of instant coffee when he heard a slight noise. Then suddenly there was a knock at the front door and some people started to sing a song he knew. It was 'Happy Birthday'. It was sung in several languages.

Mr Benvenuto hurried to open the door. There stood the children from the flats, and every one was holding out a present.

'We made them ourselves,' they said (in several languages at the same time).

Manuela's present was a duster cut out of some bright red cloth.

Philip's was a crayon drawing of Puss, with a gold drawing pin to fasten it up.

Ahmed's was a box of chocolate crackles.

Emma's was a plastic mat to put under Puss's saucer of milk, to keep the floor clean. She had cut a fringe all round it.

The other children had helped to make a birthday cake. It was covered with white icing and coloured candles.

Mr Benvenuto was surprised and pleased.

'We must have an instant party,' he said. 'Come in, come in!'

'What's instant?' asked Philip.

'It means straight away,' said Mr Benvenuto.

So everyone went into the house and Mr Benvenuto lit the candles and blew them out and wished. Then they ate the cake and the chocolate crackles, and Mr Benvenuto opened a packet of potato crisps and some bottles of lemonade. After that they pushed back the table and chairs and played a singing game.

Everyone stood in a circle and sang the questions. The person who was answering the questions stood in the middle and sang what everyone was to do in the *tra-la-la* part. Manuela was first. She sang in her own language, 'I come from Spain,' and she chose to dance. At the end of the verse she picked the next person to stand in the middle. The game went on like that until everyone had a turn.

It was a wonderful party.

June Epstein

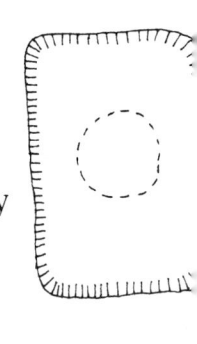

Birthdays

Mr Benvenuto's Singing Game

1. Manuela's turn: *Words and music: June Epstein*

EVERYONE: Where do you come from?
MANUELA: Yo vengo de España. *(I come from Spain.)*
EVERYONE: What do they do in Spain?
MANUELA: Toda la gente baila. *(Ev'ryone dances together.)*
EVERYONE (dancing): Tra la la la, Tra la la la, Tra la la la la la la la, Tra la la la, Tra la la la, Tra la la la la la la.

2. *Philip's turn:*   Where do you come from?
                    ΕΙΜΑΙ ΕΛΛΗΝΑΣ*   ** I am Greek*
                    (I come from Greece.)
                    What do they do in Greece?
(clapping):   ΟΛΟΙ ΜΑΖΙ ΠΑΛΑΜΑΚΙΑ
                    (Everyone claps together.)
                    Tra la la la etc.

3. *Emma's turn:*   Where do you come from?
                    I come from Australia.
                    What do they do in Australia?
                    Everyone hops together.
(hopping):   Tra la la la etc.

Let's try that game!

I only speak Australian. How would I know what to do in the tra la la la bit?

The person in the middle does it as well as sings it, of course.

Festivals

Chinese New Year

Snick, snack, clatter and clack!
Picketty, pocketty, pow!
Let's all wake the dragon up,
Make a mighty row!

Happiness and prosperity
Are yours the whole year through—
Let the dragon on his way
Take a gift from you.

Tick, tack! Firecrackers smack!
Old hundred-legs is here.
Wham and bang! and clash and clang!
Happy, happy New Year!

Dorothy Rickards

Festivals

Easter Buns

I love Easter buns
    They are shiny and sweet,
I love Easter buns
    They are spicey to eat.
        Spicey buns
        Nicey buns
    Sticky and hot
        Sticky buns
        Licky buns
    Let's eat the lot!

Gwendda McKay

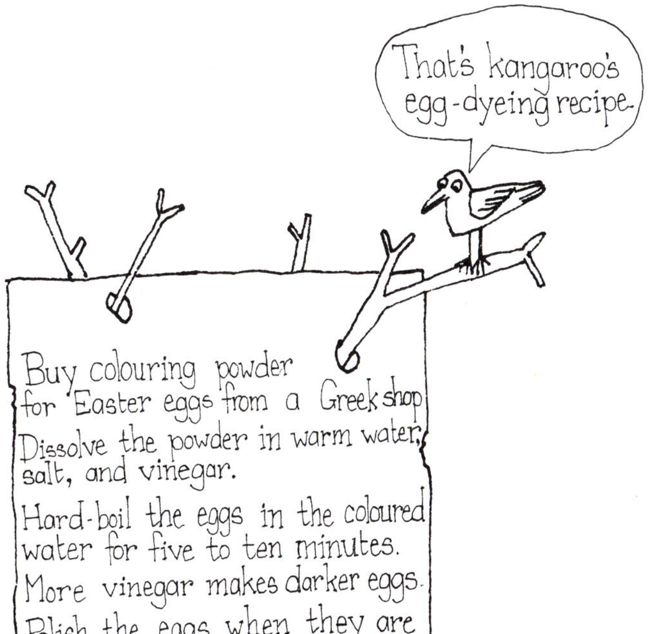

Festivals

Christmas

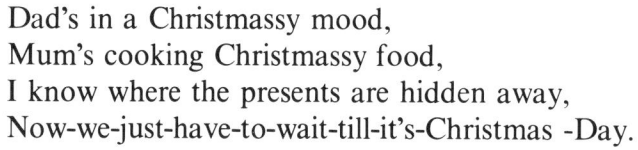

Dad's in a Christmassy mood,
Mum's cooking Christmassy food,
I know where the presents are hidden away,
Now-we-just-have-to-wait-till-it's-Christmas -Day.

Dorothy Mills

A Christmas Riddle

I am green
and packed in a box
for most of the year.
I come out
in December.
Children dress me
with stars and streamers,
and coloured lights
that flicker on and off.
I stand proudly,
showing off
near a window,
waiting for toys
to be placed
in my branches.
When fully clothed,
I am laden
and heavy.
It is a happy time.
But I am glad
to rest
back in my box
until next year.
What am I?

Judy Hocking

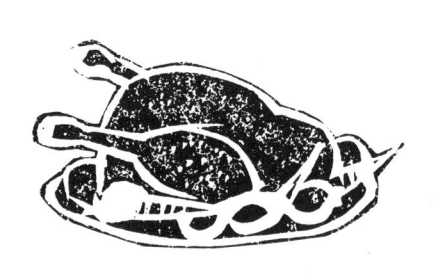

Festivals

Parcels

Mysterious parcels
Are under the tree,
I've put some there,
And some are for me.
I've felt them all,
   What can they BE?

Dorothy Mills

Everyone's disappeared! We're playing hide and seek, I can't find anybody!

You'll find kangaroo, platypus, hopping mouse, seagull, and two penguins looking out of that Christmas tree if you search hard enough.

Festivals

Christmas Eve

Stars caught in trees on summer nights
Flicker and gleam like little lights.
There's a story I've heard of a star hung high
In Bethlehem in a wintry sky;
But here it is hot, and the nights are mild,
When we remember the birth of a child.

Dorothy Rickards

Index

Aboriginal Boy, The, 50
aeroplanes, 21, 52
animals, 5, 8-9, 18-19, 21, 22, 24, 41, 48-9, 51, 59, 62-87, 90-2, 100
  baby animals, 41, 48-9, 51, 73, 78-9, 100
ants, 53, 67, 80
Autumn, 55
aunts, 10, 66-7

babies, 10, 12-15
Ball, The, 32
beach, 59, 93, 99
bears, 64, 78
bed, 20, 21, 39-40
Bedtime, 20
bee, 67
Bells, The, 97-8
Big Black Spider, 80
birds, 22, 43, 44, 55, 59, 66, 72, 92
Birthday, 102
birthdays, 8-9, 51, 96, 102, 103-5
Blue, 61
Bob's Pup, 48-9
bottle bells, 97-8
boys, 5, 6, 16
brothers, 6, 10, 16-17
Bubbles, 32
buses, 44, 52
bush, 50, 51, 52
butterflies, 62, 77-9

calf, 51
cars, 9, 44, 52, 62-3
Catching Things, 40
Caterpillar, 77
Caterpillar Lunch, 77
cats, 18, 22, 30-1, 48-9, 51, 59, 70-1, 78-9, 104
Cheek!, 80
chicks, 73, 100
Chimneys, 43
Chinese New Year, 106
Christmas, 108
Christmas Eve, 110
Christmas Riddle, A, 108
city, 8-9, 42, 43-9, 52
City Scene, 45
City Song, 43
Cleaning Up Day, 37
clothes, 10, 23, 33, 37-8, 56-7, 80
Cloud Game, A, 62-3
Clouds, 61
clouds, 59, 61-3, 86
cocoon, 27
colours, 32, 33, 47, 61, 94-5
Competition, The, 65
cooking, 5, 9, 24, 25-8
cousins, 10
cows, 51, 84
crowds, 64
curtsey, 95

dad, 5, 6, 10, 12-15, 16, 22, 24, 25-8, 46, 48-9, 62-3, 85, 102, 108
Day at the Beach, 99
death, 48-9
deer, 66
Different, 5
dogs, 5, 18, 22, 30-1, 48-9, 78, 100
Don't Call Him That, 73

dragons, 83-5, 106
Dragons Are Imaginary?, 85
Dream, A, 58
dreams, 18, 58
dressing, 12, 23, 38
dressmaker, 5
drinking, 29
duck, 41

Ears of Mandy, The, 70
Easter Buns, 107
eating, *see* food
echidna, 73
Egg, 73
eggs, 73, 79
  dyeing, 107
elephants, 18, 66-8
Eucalypt Year, 52
Everybody, 5

factories, 34-5, 43
fairies, 85
families, 6-11, 21, 24
father, *see* dad
farm, 51, 52, 90-2
farmer, 5, 90-2
Farmyard, 51
Fat Horace, 83-5
fingers, 11, 55
First Noel, The, 98
fish, 24, 27, 72
Fish Fancies, 24
flats, living in, 8-9, 44-6, 103
fleas, 65, 80
flying, 21, 52, 54, 83-5, 86-7
food, 10, 12, 24-9, 68, 74-6, 77, 83-5, 94-5, 100, 104, 106, 107
footprints, 93
frogs, 65, 74-6, 78-9, 89

girls, 5, 11, 59
gnus, 69
goats, 51, 100
Good King Wenceslas, 98
Good Ship Play, The, 30
gorilla, 62
Grandfather's Clock, 98
grandmothers, 8-9, 38, 97-8, 102
Grandmother's Birthday, 8-9
grass, 4, 54
Greece, 103-5
growing up, 5, 23

Hair, 4
hen, 51
Higglebump, The, 81
hippopotamus, 68
holidays, 22, 55, 96
home, 6-7, 41-2, 44-5, 52 *see also* houses
hornpipe, 30
horses, 18-19, 86-7, 101
  flying horses, 21, 86-7
hospital, 12-14
houses, 6-7, 18, 42, 45, 66-7
husbands, 10

If All the Queens Should Come to Dine, 94-5
If I Were You, 5
I Live Up There, 46

ill, 8-9, 39-40, 53, 55
insects, 8-9, 53, 65, 67, 77-80
Instant Party, The, 103
In the Middle, 16
Italy, 103-5

jet plane, 21, 52
John's Task, 90-2
Jonathan's Singing Day, 12
jumping, 15, 65
jungle, 66-8

kangaroos, 18, 51, 62-3, 65
Katharine's Magic Horse, 86-7
kindergarten, 25
kings, 94-5
kittens, 48-9, 78-9
koalas, 51

ladybird, 80
leaves, 53-5
Let Me Wonder, 53
letters, 12-15
Little Brother, 16
Little Fleas, 80
Living Places, 42
lizard, 51
Llewellyn the Witch, 89

Machine Game, The, 35
machines, 34-5, 44
Manuela's Storm Story, 36
Marmadin, The, 81
mayor, 26-8
Me, 4
Measles, 39
medicine, 40
Melbourne Cup, 101
men, 5
Metamorphosis, 77-9
milkman, 18-19
mirror, 4
mischief, 82
Monday, 22
monsters, 25-8, 81-2, 93, 100
moon, 21, 88
moths, 77-9
mother, *see* mum
Mr Benvenuto's Singing Game, 105
Mr Rainman, 33
Mrs Ippendippidy's Washing, 55
mum, 5, 6, 10, 12-15, 16, 22, 23, 24, 25-9, 37, 39, 46, 48-9, 62-3, 64, 85, 100, 102, 108
Mum's Right, 37
musical instruments, 34-6
My Family, 11
My Feet, 4
My Granny, 9

nephews, 10
Newborn, 51
New Phone, The, 32
nieces, 10
Night in Brick Road, 18
noises, 6-7, 12-15, 34-6, 43, 70-1, 66-9, 97-8

Older Brothers, 17
Older Sisters, 17

111

Index

Our Family, 10
Our House, 6
owl, 74-6

parcels, 12-15, 109
parrots, 51
parties, 102-5
Peas, 24
Picnic Day, 74-6
pig, 51
police, 25-8
Poor Mrs Duck, 41
postman, 12-15
Power of Five, The, 88
presents, 8-9, 13, 103-4, 109
Puggly Beasts, 82
pupa, 77
puppets, 11
puppies, 48-9, 78-9, 100

queens, 94-5

rabbits, 92, 100
Rain, 33
rain, 8-9, 33-6, 50, 55, 61, 101
Red Letter Day, 96
Relations, 10

Safety Yellow, 33
school, 8, 39, 52
sea, 44, 53, 93, 99
Seeing, 64
sheep, 62, 84, 100
ships, 30-1, 44
shoes, 12, 23, 37, 101
Show, The, 100

sisters, 6, 10, 16-17
skin, 29
sky, 21, 44-5, 54, 55, 56-63, 86-7
sky-scrapers, 8-9, 44-6
Slide-Swim-Fly, 72
sloths, 72, 78
Snail, 80
Snake, 72
Snitcher Snatch, The, 25
Socks, 23
socks, 10, 12, 23, 37-8, 82
spacecraft, 21
Spain, 103-5
spiders, 8-9, 80
Splashalong and the Melbourne Cup, 101
Splish! Splosh!, 33
Spring, 55
stars, 21, 58, 88, 110
Stay At Home Day, 40
storm, 36, 58
Summer, 53, 55
sunburn, 55
Sunday, 22

tadpoles, 78-9
taxis, 5, 43
Teddy, 20
telephone, 32
telescope, 44
tidiness, 10, 37
toes, 11, 55
Tom, 38
Tracks in the Dirt, 93
Trains, 52
traffic, 44, 48-9

traffic lights, 47
trams, 43, 52
transport, 52
Travelling, 52
trees, 53, 54, 55, 56-60, 66-7, 108
tricycle, 12
Tromp! Tromp!, 68

uncles, 10
untidiness, 10, 23, 37

Visitor, A, 80

Wake Up!, 22
washing, 4, 12
 clothes, 56-7, 59, 60
Wet Saturday, 34-6
What Am I?, 66
Where?, 60
Where Is It?, 23
Where the Wind Blows, 59
Wild Wind, 59
Will I Really Truly Burst?, 29
wind, 54, 55, 56-60
Window in the Sky, 44-5
Winter, 55
Winter and Summer, 53
witch, 89
wives, 10
women, 5
work, 5, 90-2

Yaks' Gnus, 69

zoo, 18, 65, 96

Oxford University Press
OXFORD LONDON GLASGOW NEW YORK TORONTO
MELBOURNE WELLINGTON KUALA LUMPUR SINGAPORE
HONG KONG TOKYO DELHI BOMBAY CALCUTTA MADRAS
KARACHI NAIROBI DAR ES SALAAM CAPE TOWN

This book is copyright. Apart from any fair dealing for the purposes of private study, research, criticism or review, as permitted under the Copyright Act, no part may be reproduced by any process without written permission. Inquiries should be made to the publishers.

© *Text June Epstein, June Factor, Gwendda McKay, Dorothy Rickards.*
© *Illustrations Alison Lester*

First published 1980

NATIONAL LIBRARY OF AUSTRALIA CATALOGUING IN PUBLICATION DATA

Big dipper.

   Index
   For children
   ISBN 0 19 554289 4

   1. Children's literature, Australian.
   I. Epstein, June.

A820'.08003

TYPESET BY DAVEY LITHO GRAPHICS PTY. LTD.
PRINTED IN HONG KONG BY HING YIP PRINTING CO.
PUBLISHED BY OXFORD UNIVERSITY PRESS, 7 BOWEN CRESCENT, MELBOURNE

Accounting Fundamentals
7e

MICHAEL G. CURRAN, JR.
Rider University

McGraw-Hill Irwin

Boston   Burr Ridge, IL   Dubuque, IA   Madison, WI   New York   San Francisco   St. Louis
Bangkok   Bogotá   Caracas   Kuala Lumpur   Lisbon   London   Madrid   Mexico City
Milan   Montreal   New Delhi   Santiago   Seoul   Singapore   Sydney   Taipei   Toronto

McGraw-Hill Irwin

ACCOUNTING FUNDAMENTALS

Published by McGraw-Hill/Irwin, a business unit of The McGraw-Hill Companies, Inc., 1221 Avenue of the Americas, New York, NY, 10020. Copyright © 2006 by The McGraw-Hill Companies, Inc. All rights reserved. No part of this publication may be reproduced or distributed in any form or by any means, or stored in a database or retrieval system, without the prior written consent of The McGraw-Hill Companies, Inc., including, but not limited to, in any network or other electronic storage or transmission, or broadcast for distance learning.

Some ancillaries, including electronic and print components, may not be available to customers outside the United States.

This book is printed on acid-free paper.

1 2 3 4 5 6 7 8 9 0 WCK/WCK 0 9 8 7 6 5

ISBN 0-07-301460-5

Editorial director: *Brent Gordon*

Publisher: *Stewart Mattson*
Sponsoring editor: *Steve Schuetz*
Senior developmental editor: *Kimberly D. Hooker*
Marketing manager: *Richard Kolasa*
Media producer: *Greg Bates*
Project manager: *Trina Hauger*
Production supervisor: *Gina Hangos*
Lead designer: *Pam Verros*
Senior photo research coordinator: *Jeremy Cheshareck*
Senior media project manager: *Susan Lombardi*
Developer, Media technology: *Brian Nacik*
Cover design: *Allison Traynham*
Cover image: *© PictureQuest*
Typeface: *10/12 Times Roman*
Compositor: *Cenveo*
Printer: *Quebecor World Versailles Inc.*

Library of Congress Cataloging-in-Publication Data
Curran, Michael G.
  Accounting fundamentals / Michael G. Curran, Jr.—7th ed.
    p. cm.
  Includes index
  ISBN 0-07-301460-5 (alk. paper)
  1. Accounting. I. Title.
  HF5635.C967 2006
  657—dc22

2004061137

www.mhhe.com

To my family for a lifetime of love and support:

Tricia, Michael, Christopher, Bonnie, and Becky

And to our extended family:

Dan; Kelly, Zachary, and Abigail; Niccole, and Bubba Dukes; and Guinness

ABOUT THE AUTHOR

Michael Curran earned his BS and MA in business education at Rider University and his EdD in business education at Temple University. Dr. Curran has taught accounting at Eastern Camden County High School and Delran High School in New Jersey and accounting education at Temple University.

At Rider University, Dr. Curran prepares business educators in all disciplines including accounting education.

Dr. Curran served with the New Jersey State Department of Education as a Business Education State Supervisor. He was also a manager for Vocational Education Programs and an interim Assistant Commissioner for Vocational Education.

Dr. Curran served as the president of the National Business Education Association and of the Eastern Business Education Association.

For relaxation, Dr. Curran does research in the area of accounting education—bringing the "real" world into the classroom.

Dr. Curran and his wife, Tricia, have run two marathons together, and you may pass him when he seeks solitude on the Appalachian Trail.

NOTES TO THE STUDENT

STUDYING THE TEXTBOOK

- To understand the content of the chapters, read each chapter twice. First, read the chapter quickly to get a general idea of the material it contains. Then read the chapter again—slowly and thoroughly. Study the illustrations carefully.

- After you complete your second read-through, study the chapter summary, which reinforces the important points covered. Also study the marginal notes to reinforce the important terms, concepts, rules, and procedures presented in the chapter. The World Wide Web (www) inquiries should be researched for a deeper understanding of concepts presented within the chapter.

- You should read the chapter a third time if you want to succeed on the Study Guide exercises. (See the suggestions for using the Study Guide.)

USING THE STUDY GUIDE

- Consult the Study Guide before you start each chapter of the text. Read the objectives. The objectives tell you what tasks you should be able to perform after you complete the chapter. Previewing the Study Guide will help you understand the reasons for studying the chapter.

- Read the directions for completing the chapter. Follow all the directions unless your instructor gives you other directions.

- Read each chapter in the text and be sure to do the Study Guide exercise. You can verify your work with the self-check answers at the back of the Study Guide.

- The Study Guide exercises allow you to see how well you understand the content of each chapter. If you have difficulty with the exercises or make many errors, reread the chapter in the text before you start the exercises, problems, or case studies given at the end of the chapter.

COMPLETING THE PROBLEMS

- Read all instructions before you try to complete the problem.

- Think through the steps you must take to complete the problem.

- If a problem has several parts, check off the parts in your text as you finish each one. Checking off the parts will help you avoid omitting any parts.

- Use the accounting records illustrated in the text as your model for the records you are asked to prepare in the problems.

- Carefully check your calculations.

- Prepare all accounting records neatly and legibly. Errors can easily occur if the amounts are not written clearly.

PREFACE

Accounting Fundamentals, 7th edition, offers students a brief but comprehensive introduction to accounting by providing students with an understanding of accounting theory, principles, terminology, and many of the financial records, forms, and statements used in business today. *Accounting Fundamentals* is designed to give students without any prior understanding of accounting theory, principles, and procedures a practical and straightforward understanding of accounting theory, principles, and procedures used to record, classify, summarize, and analyze financial data.

Accounting Fundamentals is especially well suited for those who want short chapters without long and elaborate discussions. It presents the essential facts in a simple and easy-to-understand manner, with numerous examples and illustrations to help students master the concepts.

This textbook contains 27 chapters, each covering a specific aspect of accounting. The chapters are organized in a logical sequence that allows students to move from the simple to the complex while constantly building upon their prior learning.

■ NEW THIS EDITION

The boxed manual and computerized text sets have been replaced with one convenient, easy-to-handle single text and CD-ROM package. All of the student and instructor supplements are now completely electronic, which allows both students and instructors to print out only the material that is needed.

In addition, QuickBooks®, which no longer distributes a free education version, has been replaced with a General Ledger software application. This custom-built general ledger software helps students master every aspect of the general ledger from recording sales to preparing financial reports for specific fiscal periods.

■ PEDAGOGY

Performance Objectives. The objectives appear at the beginning of both the student text and study guide to provide students with the guidance and purpose of the chapter. Students can quickly and easily see the specific objectives they should be able to master after completing each chapter.

Marginal Notes. These marginal notes appear throughout the text and are designed to reinforce the students' understanding of key accounting terms, rules, and procedures introduced in the chapter. Marginal notes serve as a quick and handy review device by offering brief definitions of key terms and brief statements of rules and procedures.

Also appearing in the margins are **www inquiries.** These notes encourage students to explore the Internet for supplemental information or applications relevant to the content of the chapter.

■ END-OF-CHAPTER ACTIVITIES

Exercises. These assignments are designed to provide quick reinforcement of the major concepts and procedures taught in the chapter. The exercises are short and can be used in the classroom for demonstration purposes, or they can be assigned for homework.

Problems. The problems are broader in scope than the exercises. They correlate with the chapter objectives and appear in both the text and study guide and usually involve the analysis of transactions and the preparation of financial records.

Case Studies. Case studies allow students to get beyond the mechanics of keeping financial records to asking why certain activities take place. The case studies draw on the content of each chapter and enable students to analyze accounting processes and expand their critical-thinking skills.

Projects. There are four projects through the text. They appear after Chapters 6, 10, 20, and 23 and are designed to help students integrate their knowledge and skills at four important points in the course. Each project covers the material taught in the group of chapters preceding it.

Practice Set. At the end of the course is a practice set that is the culminating activity for the course. The Practice Set takes the students through an entire accounting cycle for a retail merchandising business.

■ STUDENT SUPPLEMENTS

The following student supplements appear on the CD-ROM that is packaged FREE with the text:

- **Study Guide** that correlates with the text on a chapter-by-chapter basis. It contains performance goals for each chapter, instructions for completing the chapter, and exercises that help students evaluate their knowledge of the text material. **Self-checks** are provided at the end of the study guide. These self-checks for the study guide exercises and problem material give the students immediate feedback about the level of their knowledge and the quality of their work. This information shows students whether they need to reread the chapter or redo a problem.

- **Excel Workbook** contains all of the working papers needed to complete the exercises, problems, projects, and practice set provided in the text. Brief self-checks, which consist of one or more important elements for each problem, allow students to verify the accuracy of their work.
- **Application software** includes Excel and General Ledger Software applications. The User's Guide includes specific instructions for spreadsheet problems in Chapters 1–6, Project 1, and Chapters 11–12. Template files have been created for one or more problems in Chapters 1–6 and Project 1. Instructions are given for creating spreadsheets to calculate sales tax and discounts in Chapters 11 and 12. As the accounting transactions become more complex, General Ledger Software is introduced.

INSTRUCTOR SUPPLEMENTS

Instructors will also have the convenience of an all-in-one resource. The Instructor's Resource CD-ROM allows you to create a custom presentation from your own materials or from the following list of instructor tools included on the CD-ROM:

- **Instructors Manual and Key** offers instructors detailed information about the text, teaching suggestions for the course, suggested tests, complete solutions to the end-of-chapter assignments, end-of-text practice set, and General Ledger software problems.
- **PowerPoint presentations** accompany each chapter, illustrating the crucial chapter concepts and procedures.
- **Computerized Test Bank** offers a resource of testing assignments.

ACKNOWLEDGMENTS

The author thanks the following individuals who critiqued and assisted in the development of the text and ancillary package: Diane Sandefur, Elliott Bookkeeping School; Tina Hovermale, Thompson Institute; and Phil Malkinson.

The author received valuable feedback from the following dedicated reviewers:

Joseph S. Barbagallo, CPA, CFFA
Margolis and Company, Philadelphia

Dale Bolduc
Seacoast Career Schools

Pauline Booher
Leidy Chevrolet, Mifflintown

Tina Hovermale
Thompson Institute, Chambersburg

Shawn Kennedy
Kennedy Welding Supply, Trenton

Diane Sandefur
Elliott Bookkeeping School

Angela Seidel
Cambria-Rowe Business College

Stephen Shinham
Valley College of Technology

John Whitelock
CCBC Catonsville

The author is grateful to the contributions and efforts of the McGraw-Hill/Irwin team, including Brent Gordon, editorial director; Stewart Mattson, publisher; Steve Schuetz, sponsoring editor; Richard Kolasa, senior marketing manager; Kimberly Hooker, senior developmental editor; Gregory Bates, media producer; Susan Lombardi, senior media project manager; Trina Hauger, project manager; Pam Verros, lead designer; Gina Hangos, production supervisor; and Jeremy Cheshareck, senior photo researcher.

The author especially thanks Dr. Edward B. Brower, the epitome of an accounting education theorist and practitioner, for teaching him to be a professional educator, for showing him the value of professional involvement and accounting education research, and for demonstrating how to bring the "real" world into the classroom.

CONTENTS

NOTES TO THE STUDENT   VII
PREFACE   VIII

PART ONE
INTRODUCTION TO ACCOUNTING

1. Principles of Accounting   3
2. The Effect of Revenue and Expenses   11
3. Asset, Liability, and Owner's Equity Accounts   18
4. Revenue and Expense Accounts   26
5. The Trial Balance   33
6. Financial Statements   38

Project 1   43

PART TWO
THE ACCOUNTING CYCLE

7. The General Journal   47
8. The General Ledger   56
9. The Worksheet and the Financial Statements   66
10. Closing the Ledger   72

Project 2   80

PART THREE
RECORDING FINANCIAL DATA

11. Introduction to Merchandising Businesses: Sales   85
12. Introduction to Merchandising Businesses: Purchases   93
13. Accounting for Purchases   97
14. Accounting for Sales   104
15. The Sales Journal   116
16. The Purchases Journal   121
17. The Cash Receipts Journal   127
18. The Cash Payments Journal   137
19. The Accounts Receivable Ledger   146
20. The Accounts Payable Ledger   157

Project 3   167

PART FOUR
SUMMARIZING AND REPORTING FINANCIAL INFORMATION

21. Worksheet Adjustments   173
22. Cost of Goods Sold and Statements   184
23. Adjusting and Closing the General Ledger   193

Project 4   205

PART FIVE
ACCOUNTING FOR SPECIAL PROCEDURES

24. Banking Procedures   209
25. Petty Cash and Other Special Cash Procedures   219
26. Payroll Procedures   225
27. The Combined Journal   241

PRACTICE SET   249
GLOSSARY   253
INDEX   257

PART ONE

Introduction to Accounting

- **Chapter 1**
  Principles of Accounting
- **Chapter 2**
  The Effect of Revenue and Expenses
- **Chapter 3**
  Asset, Liability, and Owner's Equity Accounts
- **Chapter 4**
  Revenue and Expense Accounts
- **Chapter 5**
  The Trial Balance
- **Chapter 6**
  Financial Statements
- **Project 1**

Welcome to the world of business accounting. In Part One you will be introduced to the language of business in a service business. Some of the terms you will use and learn about include *assets, liabilities, owner's equity, balance sheet,* and *transaction.* Each term plays an important part in understanding how the operations of businesses work. An important concept in Part One is the use of the accounting equation that provides balance to every financial transaction a business encounters. You will learn how expenses affect revenue and how debits are different from credits. It will be interesting to see how the transactions all come together in the financial statements that are prepared at the end of an accounting period. You begin learning these concepts in Part Two. ■

Accounting Careers

Who Makes the Rules?

Have you thought about the rules that accountants follow—those rules that you are trying to learn in accounting class? Who makes up all those rules? The answer is somewhat complex. The accounting profession and the procedures it follows have evolved in response to changes in business practices. Following the stock market crash in 1929, the U.S. Congress established the Securities and Exchange Commission to protect the interests of corporate stockholders. The SEC is responsible for establishing generally accepted accounting principles, known today as GAAP. These principles are the basis for accounting study and practice. In 1973 the Financial Accounting Standards Board was formed and charged with establishing GAAP, under the direction of the SEC.

In addition, the American Institute of Certified Public Accountants (AICPA) is the national organization of CPAs with over 340,000 members who work in public accounting, business, industry, government, and education. AICPA can provide information and materials to inform you, the student, about CPA career tracks. Please view their website at www.aicpa.org.

ACTIVITY

- Find the website for the Financial Accounting Standards Board and review its activities and responsibilities.
- Prepare a short report on an accounting principle that is being studied or reviewed by the FASB.
- What are some of the career paths in accounting as described by the AICPA?

CHAPTER ONE

Principles of Accounting

OBJECTIVES

Upon completion of this chapter, you should be able to:

1. Describe the functions of accounting.
2. Complete an accounting equation.
3. Prepare a balance sheet.
4. Demonstrate the process of recording transactions in equation form.

INTRODUCTION

Accounting involves recording, classifying, and summarizing financial information and then interpreting the results to owners, managers, and other interested parties. The people who have the training necessary for accounting work are known as *bookkeepers, accounting clerks,* and *accountants.* In some businesses, these people have specialized job titles such as accounts receivable clerk, accounts payable clerk, payroll clerk, office cashier, financial analyst, and controller.

The major purpose of every private business is to make a profit. The functions of accounting are to keep track of money and other property invested in a business and to determine the gain or losses that result from the business's operations. Owners and managers need complete and accurate financial information so that they can plan and make wise decisions. ■

■ BEGINNING AN ACCOUNTING SYSTEM

When a business opens, it is important to establish and maintain a set of financial records. The *proprietor,* or owner, should make a list of the money and other property that is being used to begin the business. After operations get under way, changes will take place in the amount and nature of the money and other property. Information about these changes must be recorded as changes occur. By keeping records on a continuous basis, the owner will be able to see how profitable the activities of the business are.

Consider how an accounting system is set up for Van Lieu Creative Solutions. Rebecca Van Lieu plans to open this human resources agency on July 24. She will provide clients with career planning, résumé preparation, job testing services, and placement in all types of jobs. Before starting operations, Van Lieu transfers some of her personal property (money and furniture) to the business.

- The first item she invests is $10,000 in *cash.* Van Lieu withdraws this money from her personal bank account and deposits it in a separate bank account set up for the new business.
- The second item she invests is office *furniture* that cost $2,000. This furniture includes a desk, chairs, and bookcases.

Accounting Terminology

- Account
- Accounting
- Accounting equation
- Accounts payable
- Assets
- Balance sheet
- Business transactions
- Creditors
- Invest
- Investment
- Liabilities
- Owner's equity
- Proprietor

Accounting: Recording, classifying, and summarizing financial information; interpreting the results.

Proprietor: Owner of a business.

A business may take one of three legal forms: a sole proprietorship, a partnership, or a corporation.

Accounts: Assets, liabilities, and owner's equity are comprised of individual accounts, like cash, loans payable, and capital.

Assets: Property that a business owns.

Investment: Assets used in the business that were provided by the owner.

Thus, Van Lieu invests a total of $12,000 in the business. This investment includes two kinds of property: cash and furniture. All the property the business owns is called its *assets.* Because this property belongs to Van Lieu, the amount of her *investment* is $12,000 (the total of the assets). In accounting, Van Lieu's investment is called her *capital,* or equity, and represents her current financial interest in the business. The financial position of her human resources agency at this time is as follows:

Assets		Financial Interest	
Cash	$10,000	Rebecca Van Lieu, Capital	$12,000
Furniture and Equipment	$2,000		
Total Assets	$12,000	Total Financial Interest	$12,000

Before opening for business, Van Lieu buys additional office equipment for $5,000 on credit from Micro Systems. As a result of this transaction, the business now owns assets totaling $17,000 ($10,000 + $7,000). Until Van Lieu pays for the office equipment, Micro Systems also has a financial interest in her firm's assets.

Liabilities: Debts owed by a business.

Accounts Payable: Short-term debts owed for credit purchases.

Creditors: Companies and individuals to whom money is owed.

Such debts owned by a business are **liabilities.** Short-term debts owed for credit purchases are called **accounts payable.** Amounts owed for mortgages and loans are also liabilities. These are called *mortgages payable* and *loans payable.* Companies and individuals to whom money is owed are **creditors.** Micro Systems is a creditor of Van Lieu Creative Solutions. Because Van Lieu owes $5,000 for the office equipment, Micro Systems has an interest of $5,000 in her business.

Micro Systems' interest in the human resources agency is shown under the heading "Liabilities" in the following illustration. Van Lieu's interest appears under the heading "Owner's Equity."

Other common liabilities include notes payable, dividends payable, and salaries payable.

Assets		Financial Interest	
Cash	$10,000	Liabilities	
Furniture and Equipment	7,000	Accounts Payable	$5,000
		(Micro Systems)	
		Owner's Equity	
		Rebecca Van Lieu, Capital	12,000
Total Assets	$17,000	Total Financial Interest	$17,000

Owner's Equity: Financial interest of the owner in a business.

Owner's equity is an accounting term that indicates the financial interest of the owner in a business. *Proprietorship* and *net worth* are other terms sometimes used in place of owner's equity. The amount of the owner's equity can be calculated by subtracting the total liabilities from the total assets.

Note that the assets equal the financial interest of the creditors plus the financial interest of the owner; that is, assets equal liabilities plus the owner's equity. This equality is shown in the **accounting equation.**

Accounting Equation:
Assets = Liabilities + Owner's Equity.

Assets	=	Liabilities	+	Owner's Equity
$17,000	=	$5,000	+	$12,000

This equation is very important. It is a device used for checking the accuracy of accounting records, and it is also the basis for the formal statement of a business's financial position—the balance sheet.

■ THE BALANCE SHEET

The *balance sheet* is an itemized list of assets, liabilities, and owner's equity of a business on one particular date. The balance sheet for Van Lieu Creative Solutions, giving the firm's financial position when operations began, is shown below.

VAN LIEU CREATIVE SOLUTIONS
BALANCE SHEET
JULY 24, 20XX

Assets		Liabilities and Owner's Equity	
Cash	10,000.00	Liabilities	
Furniture and Equipment	7,000.00	Accounts Payable	5,000.00
		Owner's Equity	
		Rebecca Van Lieu, Capital	12,000.00
		Total Liabilities	
Total Assets	17,000.00	and Owner's Equity	17,000.00

> **Balance Sheet:** Itemized list of assets, liabilities, and owner's equity, showing financial position of a business on a certain date.
>
> Balance Sheet
>
> The balance sheet provides a financial snapshot of the business on a specific date.

At the top of every balance sheet is a heading that includes the name of the business, the name of the statement, and the date. This heading answers the questions: Who? What? and When? Property and financial interests are arranged on the balance sheet in the order they appeared in the accounting equation. The assets are listed on the *left side* and totaled. Cash, furniture, and equipment are the only assets of the business when it opens on July 24.

Note that liabilities are listed on the upper *right side* of the balance sheet. Van Lieu's liabilities consist only of accounts payable. Remember that accounts payable are short-term debts or sums of money owed to creditors for credit purchases. The Owner's Equity section follows the Liabilities section on the right side of the balance sheet.

The total liabilities and the amount of the owner's equity are added. The totals of both sides of the balance sheet are recorded on the same horizontal line so that the equality can be seen clearly. When the total assets equal the total of the liabilities and the owner's equity, the balance sheet is *in balance*. Quite often financial reports, like the balance sheet, are prepared using software and appear as electronic spreadsheets.

Accepted accounting practices should be followed in preparing a financial statement such as the balance sheet. The heading should be on three lines. When ruled accounting paper is used, it is customary to omit dollar signs from the amounts. A *single line* drawn across each column means that figures above the line are either added or subtracted. *Double lines* show that the work is completed. All lines should be drawn with a ruler.

> **WWW Inquiry**
> Find the URL address for JC Penney. How much did total assets increase or decrease over the last two years?

■ THE EFFECT OF BUSINESS ACTIVITIES ON THE BALANCE SHEET

Business activities such as buying, selling, receiving money, and paying bills cause continual changes in the amounts of the assets, liabilities, and owner's equity. These activities are called *business transactions*. Business transactions are the exchange of one item of value for another or a promise of value in the future.

The effect of each transaction on the assets, liabilities, and owner's equity of a business must be analyzed so that the transaction can be recorded correctly.

Transaction (a). Rebecca Van Lieu pays $800 for tables, lamps, and a cell phone for the office. As a result of this transaction, additional furniture and a phone is acquired, and cash is paid out. In accounting terms, one would say:

1. The asset Furniture and Equipment is *increased* by $800.
2. The asset Cash is *decreased* by $800.

> **Business Transactions:** Business activities involving the exchange of one item of value for another.
>
> **Transaction (A)**
> Purchase of an asset for cash. Return of an asset for a cash refund.

	Assets	=	Liabilities	+	Owner's Equity
	Cash + Furniture and Equipment	=	Accounts Payable	+	Rebecca Van Lieu, Capital
Totals	$10,000 + $7,000	=	$5,000	+	$12,000
1. Furniture acquired	+800				
2. Cash paid out	−800				
New totals	$9,200 + $7,800	=	$5,000	+	$12,000
	$17,000	=	$17,000		

This transaction, like all business transactions, affects at least two items. Cash is reduced by $800, but there is now additional furniture and a phone that cost $800. The form of the assets has changed, but their total is still $17,000. The liabilities and the owner's equity have not been affected. The accounting equation balances because each side still totals $17,000.

If Van Lieu returned the tables, lamps, and phone and received a cash refund, the form of the assets would change in a different way.

1. The asset Cash would *increase*.
2. The asset Furniture and Equipment would *decrease*.

Transaction (B)
Payment of a liability (an account payable).

Transaction (b). A notice from Micro Systems reminds Van Lieu that a monthly payment of $500 is due on the office equipment she bought on credit. She sends a check for $500.

1. The asset Cash is *decreased* by $500.
2. The liability Accounts Payable (Micro Systems) is *decreased* by $500.

	Assets	=	Liabilities	+	Owner's Equity
	Cash + Furniture and Equipment	=	Accounts Payable	+	Rebecca Van Lieu, Capital
Previous totals	$9,200 + $7,800	=	$5,000	+	$12,000
1. Cash paid out	−500				
2. Amount owed Micro Systems decreased			−500		
New totals	$8,700 + $7,800	=	$4,500	+	$12,000
	$16,500	=	$16,500		

The assets have decreased by $500 and the liabilities have also decreased by $500. Each side of the equation now totals $16,500. Thus the equation still balances.

Transaction (C)
Investment of cash by the owner.

Transaction (c). Van Lieu withdraws $2,000 from her personal bank account and deposits it in the business's account as an additional cash investment.

1. The asset Cash is *increased* by $2,000.
2. Rebecca Van Lieu, Capital is *increased* by $2,000.

	Assets		=	Liabilities	+	Owner's Equity
	Cash	+	Furniture and Equipment	=	Accounts Payable	+	Rebecca Van Lieu, Capital
Previous totals	$8,700	+	$7,800	=	$4,500	+	$12,000
1. Cash received	+2000						
2. Owner's equity increased							+2,000
New totals	$10,700	+	$7,800	=	$4,500	+	$14,000
	$18,500			=	$18,500		

Again, the form and amount of the assets have changed. Their total is now $18,500. The owner's equity has increased by $2,000, and the equation still balances.

Transaction (d). Van Lieu borrows $1,000 from the bank. The bank now has a financial interest of $1,000 in her business.

Transaction (D)
Loan from the bank.

1. The asset Cash is *increased* by $1,000.
2. The liability Loans Payable is *increased* by $1,000.

	Assets	=	Liabilities	+	Owner's Equity
	Cash	+	Furniture and Equipment	=	Loans Payable	+	Accounts Payable	+	Rebecca Van Lieu, Capital
Previous totals	$10,700	+	$7,800	=			$4,500	+	$14,000
1. Cash received	+1000								
2. Liabilities increased					+1,000				
New totals	$11,700	+	$7,800	=	$1,000	+	$4,500	+	$14,000
	$19,500			=		$19,500			

In this example, the liability Loans Payable increased by $1,000 and the owner's equity remained the same.

Transaction (e). Van Lieu buys a copier/fax machine for $2,500 from the Capital Equipment Company on credit; payment is due in 60 days.

Transaction (E)
Purchase of an asset on credit (incurring a liability—an account payable).

1. The asset Furniture and Equipment is *increased* by $2,500.
2. The liability Accounts Payable (Capital Equipment Company) is *increased* by $2,500.

	Assets	=	Liabilities	+	Owner's Equity
	Cash + Furniture and Equipment	=	Loans Payable + Accounts Payable	+	Rebecca Van Lieu, Capital
Previous totals	$11,700 + $7,800	=	$1,000 + $4,500	+	$14,000
1. New equipment acquired	+2,500				
2. New debt acquired			+2,500		
New totals	$11,700 + $10,300	=	$1,000 + $7,000	+	$14,000
	$22,000	=	$22,000		

Furniture and Equipment and Accounts Payable have each been increased by $2,500. The assets total $22,000, and the liabilities and the owner's equity also total $22,000. The financial interest in the assets of the business is now shared by the bank, by Micro Systems, and by the Capital Equipment Company as creditors and by Van Lieu as the owner.

WWW Inquiry
Find the URL address for the May Department Stores Company. List some of the different divisions for the May Company.

CHAPTER 1 SUMMARY

- Assets are the property owned by a business. Liabilities are debts owed by a business. Owner's equity is the difference between the assets and the liabilities and represents the financial interest of the owner in a business.
- Liabilities represent the claims of the creditors to the assets of a business, and owner's equity is the claim of the owner to the assets.
- The fundamental accounting equation is Assets = Liabilities + Owner's Equity. This equation serves as a basis for accounting procedures and for the balance sheet.
- The balance sheet is a statement of assets, liabilities, and owner's equity. It shows the financial position of a business on one particular date.
- Every business transaction affects at least two items. When transactions are properly analyzed and recorded in equation form, the total assets will always equal the total of the liabilities plus the owner's equity.

CHAPTER APPLICATIONS

EXERCISES

Complete the following assignments on the forms provided in your workbook.

EXERCISE 1-1

Identifying assets, liabilities, and owner's equity.

Instructions:
Classify each item that follows as an asset, a liability, or owner's equity for Kennedy Welding.

1. Cash
2. Loan payable to a bank
3. Account payable to a creditor
4. Office furniture
5. Dennis Kennedy, Capital
6. Delivery equipment
7. Mortgage payable to a bank
8. Office equipment
9. Owner's financial interest
10. Store equipment

Example: *Supplies—an asset*

EXERCISE 1-2

Completing accounting equations.

Instructions:
For each accounting equation listed, compute the missing figure.

	Assets	=	Liabilities	+	Owner's Equity
(1)	$23,000.00	=	$15,000.00	+	_____
(2)	$12,000.00	=	_____	+	$3,000.00
(3)	_____	=	$10,000.00	+	$8,000.00
(4)	$28,000.00	=	_____	+	$15,000.00
(5)	$50,000.00	=	$15,000.00	+	_____
(6)	_____	=	$18,000.00	+	$28,000.00

EXERCISE 1-3

Identifying assets, liabilities, and owner's equity and completing the accounting equation. The accounting records of Black's Video Center show the following asset, liability, and owner's equity items.

Loan Payable	$30,000	Christopher Black, Capital	$105,000
Building	70,000		
Cash	50,000	Supplies	3,000
Office Equipment	20,000	Accounts Payable	8,000
Mortgage Payable	40,000	Store Equipment	20,000
Land	20,000		

Instructions:

1. Classify each of the items as an asset, a liability, or as owner's equity.
2. Compute the total assets and the total liabilities.
3. Complete the accounting equation: Assets = Liabilities + Owner's Equity

EXERCISE 1-4

Accounting for assets, liabilities, and owner's equity.

Instructions:

1. Identify the balance sheet items that will be affected by each of the following transactions.
2. Use plus and minus signs to show whether the item has increased or decreased.

BALANCE SHEET ITEMS

Assets	Liabilities
Cash	Loan Payable
Supplies	Accounts Payable
Office Equipment	**Owner's Equity**
Delivery Equipment	Barbara Fabian, Capital

Example: *Paid cash for supplies.*
Cash −
Supplies +

1. Barbara Fabian invested cash in her business.
2. Bought a delivery truck on credit.
3. Paid cash for new office desks.
4. Purchased supplies on credit, agreeing to pay in 30 days.
5. Paid the first installment due on the delivery truck.
6. Sold used office desks for cash.
7. Returned supplies for a cash refund.
8. Purchased a computer for the office on credit.
9. Borrowed cash from the First Service Bank.
10. Returned supplies that were purchased on credit.

PROBLEMS

Complete all assigned problems on the forms provided in your workbook.

PROBLEM 1-1

Completing the accounting equation and preparing a balance sheet. Information about Wagoner Delivery Service is shown here.

Instructions:

1. Complete the accounting equation for Wagoner Delivery Service.
2. Prepare a balance sheet dated May 31 of the current year.

Cash	$ 8,000
Equipment	12,000
Delivery Trucks	30,000
Accounts Payable	22,000
Steven Wagoner, Capital	28,000

PROBLEM 1-2

Accounting for assets, liabilities, and owner's equity. The balance sheet for Pat's Beauty Salon, owned and operated by Patricia Brennan, is shown here.

PAT'S BEAUTY SALON
BALANCE SHEET
APRIL 1, 20XX

Assets		Liabilities and Owner's Equity	
Cash	$ 3,600	Liabilities	
Shop Equipment	8,600	Accounts Payable	$ 4,100
Office Equipment	2,200	Owner's Equity	
Furniture	1,200	Patricia Brennan, Capital	11,500
		Total Liabilities and	
Total Assets	$15,600	Owner's Equity	$15,600

Various business transactions that occurred at Pat's Beauty Salon during April are listed below.

Instructions:

1. Enter the balance sheet items that would be affected by these transactions.
2. Indicate whether each item would be increased or decreased.
3. Enter the amount of the transaction. The information for the first transaction is shown as an example. See Transaction (a) in the workbook.

Transactions:

a. Patricia Brennan invested an additional $3,000 in the business.
b. Paid $2,000 for new shop equipment.
c. Bought two chairs for the reception area from Skyline Furniture for $450 and agreed to pay in 60 days.
d. Paid $600 for a printer.
e. Paid $500 for a hair dryer.
f. Paid $225 to Skyline Furniture for one-half the amount owed on the two chairs.
g. Patricia Brennan invested an additional $2,000 in the business.

PROBLEM 1-3

Accounting for assets, liabilities, and owner's equity.
The balance sheet items for Tree Boy's Landscaping are given in equation form in the workbook.

Instructions:

1. Record each of the following transactions in the equation.
2. Use plus and minus signs to show the changes in the balance sheet items.
3. Record new balances after each transaction has been entered.
4. When all transactions have been recorded, total the assets and complete the equation.

Transactions:

a. Eric Rosenthal invested an additional $3,000 in the business.
b. Paid $2,000 for lawn mowing equipment.
c. Purchased office file cabinets for $600 on credit from Kimberly Distributing.
d. Sold used office equipment for $100.
e. Issued a check for $200 to Kimberly Distributing as a partial payment of the balance due for the file cabinets.

PROBLEM 1-4

Accounting for assets, liabilities, and owner's equity.
The balance sheet items for Keepfer Insurance Agency are given in equation form in the workbook.

Instructions:

1. Record each of the following transactions in the equation.
2. Use plus and minus signs to show the changes in the balance sheet items.
3. Record new balances after each transaction has been entered.
4. When all transactions have been recorded, total the assets and complete the equation.

Transactions:

a. Purchased two computers for a total of $2,000 on credit from Office Systems.
b. Jean Keepfer invested an additional $5,000 in the business.
c. Paid $300 for office supplies.
d. Paid $200 for office file cabinets.
e. Returned a damaged computer that was purchased on credit from Office Systems for $1,000.
f. Issued a check for $500 to Office Systems as a partial payment of the balance due.

CASE STUDY

Write the answer to the case study on the form provided in your workbook.

Gabriel Michaels is planning to start a landscaping business. When preparing his financial records, he decided *not* to have separate accounts of cash, lawn equipment, and office equipment. He thought it would be easier and more efficient to list them all as assets and include them in the "assets" account. When he told his accountant his plans, his accountant advised him that separate accounts would serve him better.

Critical Thinking

- *What do you suppose the accountant told Michaels about separating the accounts? What is the accepted accounting procedure when setting up a book of accounts?*

CHAPTER TWO

The Effect of Revenue and Expenses

OBJECTIVES

Upon completion of this chapter, you should be able to:

1. Analyze business transactions involving revenue and expenses.
2. Record the effects of revenue and expenses in the accounting equation.
3. Compute net income or net loss.

INTRODUCTION

Revenue and Expenses play an important role in owner's equity. The costs of operating the business decrease the owner's equity. Revenues increase owner's equity. ■

■ REVENUE, EXPENSES, AND NET INCOME

The staffing services provided by Rebecca Van Lieu will produce *revenue,* or *income.* In producing this revenue, the employment agency will incur certain business costs, which are known as *expenses.*

The revenue remaining after the expenses have been deducted is *net income* (also called *net profit*). When there is a net income, the owner's equity is increased. On the other hand, if expenses are greater than revenue, the result is a *net loss,* which decreases the owner's equity.

Transaction (f)   At the end of the first week of operations, Rebecca Van Lieu received $1,000 for résumé preparation and job placements.

1. The asset Cash is *increased* by $1,000.
2. Owner's equity is *increased* by $1,000 in revenue.

Accounting Terminology

- Accounts receivable
- Expenses
- Net income
- Net loss
- Paid on account
- Received on account
- Revenue

Revenue: Inflow of assets from business operations, usually from providing services or selling goods. Revenue increases equity.

Expenses: Costs of operating a business. Expenses decrease equity.

Net Income: The amount remaining when revenue exceeds expenses.

Net Loss: The amount remaining when expenses exceed revenue.

	Assets			=	Liabilities			+	Owner's Equity		
	Cash	+	Furniture and Equipment	=	Loans Payable	+	Accounts Payable	+	Rebecca Van Lieu, Capital	+	Revenue
Previous totals	$11,700	+	$10,300	=	$1,000	+	$7,000	+	$14,000	+	$ 0
1. Cash received	+1,000										
2. Owner's equity increased by revenue											1,000
New totals	$12,700	+	$10,300	=	$1,000	+	$7,000	+	$14,000	+	$1,000
					$8,000			+	$15,000		
	$23,000			=		$23,000					

11

Transaction (f)
Provided services for cash.

The increase in cash is recorded, as usual, under Assets. Note that a separate column has been added under Owner's Equity for recording revenue. This column will make revenue figures easily available when other financial reports are prepared. The total of the assets has increased to $23,000. Owner's equity has also increased because of the revenue. The new total of the liabilities and the owner's equity (including revenue) is $23,000 ($8,000 + $15,000).

In business, goods are often sold and services are often provided on credit. Customers who buy on credit do not pay cash immediately. Instead, they promise to pay later. The amounts that a firm's customers have promised to pay in the future are an asset known as *accounts receivable*. (Remember that the liability incurred by a business when it promises to pay its creditors is called *accounts payable*.)

Accounts Receivable:
Amounts customers have promised to pay in the future for services or goods bought on credit.

Transaction (g)
Provided services on credit.

Transaction (g) Van Lieu tests and screens job applicants for a client, Reeta Stern, and bills her for $800. Revenue is obtained in the form of an account receivable. This causes changes in the assets and in the owner's equity.

1. The asset Accounts Receivable is *increased* by $800.
2. Owner's equity is *increased* by $800 in revenue.

	Assets			=	Liabilities		+	Owner's Equity	
	Cash +	Accounts Receivable +	Furniture and Equipment	=	Loans Payable +	Accounts Payable	+	Rebecca Van Lieu, Capital +	Revenue
Previous totals	$12,700 +	$ 0 +	$10,300	=	$1,000 +	$7,000	+	$14,000 +	$1,000
1. Account receivable obtained		+800							
2. Owner's equity increased by revenue									800
New totals	$12,700 +	$800 +	$10,300	=	$1,000 +	$7,000	+	$14,000 +	$1,800
					$8,000			$15,800	
	$23,800			=				$23,800	

WWW Inquiry:
Find the URL address for General Motors. What was GM's consolidated income from continuing operations in the last available year?

Note that a separate column has been added under Assets to record accounts receivable. The total of the assets has increased to $23,800. Owner's equity has also increased through additional revenue. This new total of the liabilities and the owner's equity (including revenue) is $23,800 ($8,000 + $15,800).

Transaction (h) At the end of the first week of operations, Van Lieu pays a salary of $300 to her assistant. This expense causes changes in the assets and the owner's equity.

Transaction (h)
Payment of an expense (salaries).

1. The asset Cash is *decreased* by $300.
2. Owner's equity is *decreased* by $300 in expenses.

	Assets	=	Liabilities	+	Owner's Equity
	Cash + Accounts Receivable + Furniture and Equipment	=	Loans Payable + Accounts Payable	+	Rebecca Van Lieu, Capital + Revenue − Expenses
Previous totals	$12,700 + $800 + $10,300	=	$1,000 + $7,000	+	$14,000 + $1,800 − $ 0
1. Cash paid out	−300				
2. Owner's equity decreased by expense					300
New totals	$12,400 + $800 + $10,300	=	$1,000 + $7,000	+	$14,000 + $1,800 − $300
			$8,000		$15,500
	$23,500	=			$23,500

Note that a separate column has now been included under Owner's Equity for recording expenses. Thus the expense figures will be easily available for financial reports. The total of the assets has decreased to $23,500. Owner's equity has also decreased because of the expense for salaries. The new total of liabilities and the owner's equity accounts (including expenses) is $23,500 ($8,000 + $15,500).

When a business sells on credit, it sends bills or statements to its customers and then receives payments from the customers. The amounts from these customers are referred to as *money received on account*. Similarly, the amounts that the business pays to its creditors are referred to as the money *paid on account*.

WWW Inquiry:
Find the URL address for General Motors. What amount of interest expense was incurred by GM in the last available year?

Transaction (i) Van Lieu receives a check for $400 on account from Reeta Stern, who owes $800 for testing and screening of applicants. This is a partial payment of her bill.

Transaction (i)
Receipt of partial payment on account.

1. The asset Cash is *increased* by $400.
2. The asset Accounts Receivable is *decreased* by $400.

	Assets	=	Liabilities	+	Owner's Equity
	Cash + Accounts Receivable + Furniture and Equipment	=	Loans Payable + Accounts Payable	+	Rebecca Van Lieu, Capital + Revenue − Expenses
Previous totals	$12,400 + $800 + $10,300	=	$1,000 + $7,000	+	$14,000 + $1,800 − $300
1. Cash paid out	+400				
2. Amount owed by a customer decreased	−400				
New totals	$12,800 + $400 + $10,300	=	$1,000 + $7,000	+	$14,000 + $1,800 − $300
			$8,000		$15,500
	$23,500	=			$23,500

The total of the assets remains at $23,500 because there has merely been a substitution of one asset (cash) for another asset (accounts receivable). No change has occurred in the liabilities or the owner's equity.

Transaction (j) Van Lieu pays $100 for repairs to the copier/fax machine. The following financial changes are caused by this expense transaction.

Transaction (j)
Payment of an expense (equipment repairs).

1. The asset Cash is *decreased* by $100.
2. Owner's equity is *decreased* by $100 in expenses.

	Assets			=	Liabilities		+	Owner's Equity		
	Cash +	Accounts Receivable +	Furniture and Equipment	=	Loans Payable +	Accounts Payable	+	Rebecca Van Lieu, Capital +	Revenue −	Expenses
Previous totals	$12,800 +	$400 +	$10,300	=	$1,000 +	$7,000	+	$14,000 +	$1,800 −	$300
1. Cash paid out	−100									
2. Owner's equity decreased by expense										100
New totals	$12,700 +	$400 +	$10,300	=	$1,000 +	$7,000	+	$14,000 +	$1,800 −	$400
					$8,000		+	$15,400		
	$23,400			=				$23,400		

After the transactions involving revenue and expenses have been recorded, the accounting equation is still in balance. Each side now totals $23,400. The owner's equity is $15,400, or $1,400 more than Rebecca Van Lieu's personal investment in the business. The $1,400 is the net income from business operation (found by subtracting the expenses of $400 from the revenue of $1,800).

Compare the present balance sheet with the one prepared when the business opened on July 24. Both these balance sheets follow. Note the overall effects of the ten recorded transactions.

In the Owner's Equity section of the July 31 balance sheet, observe that Van Lieu's original investment ($12,000) has been increased by the additional cash investment of $2,000 plus the net income of $1,400 for the one-week period.

Balance Sheet Start of Business

Note:
Assets = Liabilities + Owner's Equity.

VAN LIEU CREATIVE SOLUTIONS
BALANCE SHEET
JULY 24, 20XX

Assets		Liabilities and Owner's Equity	
Cash	10,000.00	Liabilities	
Furniture and Equipment	7,000.00	Accounts Payable	5,000.00
		Owner's Equity	
		Rebecca Van Lieu, Capital	12,000.00
		Total Liabilities	
Total Assets	17,000.00	and Owner's Equity	17,000.00

VAN LIEU CREATIVE SOLUTIONS
BALANCE SHEET
JULY 31, 20XX

Balance Sheet after Transactions Have Occurred

Assets		Liabilities and Owner's Equity	
Cash	12,700.00	**Liabilities**	
Accounts Receivable	400.00	Loans Payable	1,000.00
Furniture and Equipment	10,300.00	Accounts Payable	7,000.00
		Total Liabilities	8,000.00
		Owner's Equity	
		Rebecca Van Lieu, Capital July 24, 20XX	12,000.00
		Additional Investment	2,000.00
		Net Income	1,400.00
		Rebecca Van Lieu, Capital July 31, 20XX	15,400.00
Total Assets	23,400.00	Total Liabilities and Owner's Equity	23,400.00

CHAPTER 2 SUMMARY

- The inflow of assets received from business operations—usually from providing services or selling goods—is known as *revenue*. The costs of business operations are called *expenses*.
- *Revenue* is usually obtained in the form of cash or accounts receivable.
- *Accounts receivable* are amounts that customers have promised to pay in the future for services or goods bought on credit.

- The difference between revenue and expenses is *net income* (net profit) or *net loss*.
- When revenue is greater than expenses, there is a *net income*. When expenses are greater than revenue, there is a *net loss*.
- *Net income* results in an increase in the owner's equity. Additional investments also cause an increase in the owner's equity.
- *Net loss* results in a decrease in the owner's equity.

CHAPTER APPLICATIONS

EXERCISES

Complete the following assignments on the forms provided in your workbook.

EXERCISE 2-1

Computing net income and owner's equity.
The accounting records of Elmer Mears' medical practice show the following balances on September 30.

Cash	$23,000	Accounts Payable	$ 7,000
Accounts Receivable	7,000	Elmer Mears, Capital	54,000
Office Equipment	20,000	Revenue	18,000
Medical Equipment	24,000	Expenses	5,000

Instructions:
1. Compute the net income.

2. Compute the owner's equity as of September 30.
3. Complete the accounting equation:
   Assets = Liabilities + Owner's Equity.

EXERCISE 2-2

Computing a net loss and owner's equity.
The accounting records of Farrell eBay Sales show these balances on July 31.

Cash	$16,000	Accounts Payable	$11,000
Accounts Receivable	9,000	Kelly Farrell, Capital	32,000
Supplies	3,000	Revenue	4,000
Equipment	12,000	Expenses	7,000

Instructions:
1. Compute the net loss.
2. Compute the owner's equity as of July 31.

EXERCISE 2-3

Analyzing transactions.

Instructions:

1. Determine how assets, liabilities, and owner's equity are affected by the following transactions.
2. Use plus and minus signs to show the changes.

Example: *Cash invested by owner.*
   + Assets, + Owner's Equity

1. Paid cash for office rent.
2. Provided services for cash.
3. Issued checks to pay salaries.
4. Paid cash for equipment repairs.
5. Performed services on credit.
6. Purchased equipment on credit.
7. Received cash on account from credit customers.
8. Issued a check to a creditor.
9. Paid the telephone bill.
10. Borrowed cash from the bank.

EXERCISE 2-4

Preparing a balance sheet that includes net income.
On July 31 of the current year, William Neilson's financial records show the following amounts:

Cash	$15,000	William Neilson,	
Accounts Receivable	22,000	Capital, July 1	$50,000
Equipment	40,000	Net Income	7,000
Accounts Payable	20,000		

Instructions:

1. Prepare a balance sheet for William Neilson, Psychologist, as of July 31 of the current year. (Refer to the balance sheet on page 15 to see how net income is entered in the Owner's Equity section.)

PROBLEMS

Complete all assigned problems on the forms provided in your workbook.

PROBLEM 2-1

Analyzing transactions and determining the effect of a net income. On July 1, the O'Brien Employment Agency has assets, liabilities, and owner's equity as shown in the equation in the workbook.

Instructions:

1. Analyze the following transactions and record the effects on the equation. (Use plus and minus signs to show the changes.) Enter new totals after each transaction.
2. Compute the net income for July. Then add the net income to the capital to compute the owner's equity.
3. Total the assets and complete the accounting equation.

Transactions:

a. Paid $1,800 for the month's rent.
b. Received $700 for providing employment services.
c. Paid $200 for the telephone bill.
d. Received $1,500 for providing employment services.
e. Provided services for $1,400 on credit.
f. Paid $1,000 to creditors on account.
g. Received $500 from customers on account.

PROBLEM 2-2

Analyzing transactions and determining the effect of a net loss. On June 5, Linda Neeld started Neeld's Auto Repair Service.

Instructions:

1. Use the equation form in the workbook to record the following transactions. (Use plus and minus signs to show the effects on the equation.) Enter totals after each transaction.
2. Compute the net loss for June. Then subtract the net loss from the capital to compute the owner's equity.
3. Total the assets and complete the accounting equation.

Transactions:

a. Neeld invested $60,000 in the business.
b. Paid $2,000 for June rent.
c. Purchased a used tow truck for $40,000 on credit.
d. Received $1,400 for repairing automobiles.
e. Received a bill for $600 for advertising; payment is due in 30 days.
f. Completed repair jobs for customers with charge accounts and billed the customers $1,000.
g. Issued a check for $2,000 in partial payment of the amount due for the tow truck.
h. Paid $1,800 for employees' wages.
i. Received $600 from charge customers on account.

PROBLEM 2-3

Analyzing transactions and determining the results of operations. Brenda Burg, D.D.S., opened her dental office on May 1.

Instructions:

1. Use the equation form in the workbook to record the following transactions. (Use plus and minus signs to

show the changes.) Enter totals after each transaction.

2. Compute the net income or net loss.
3. Compute the owner's equity.
4. Total the assets and complete the accounting equation.

Transactions:

a. Burg invested $50,000 in her dental practice.
b. Purchased dental equipment for $60,000 on credit.
c. Received $1,900 for providing dental services.
d. Paid $200 for the telephone bill.
e. Paid $600 for office file cabinets.
f. Provided dental services for $2,000 on credit.
g. Paid $1,700 for office rent.
h. Paid $6,000 to a creditor on account.
i. Received $2,000 on account from patients.
j. Returned a damaged file cabinet and received a refund of $200.

PROBLEM 2-4

Preparing a balance sheet. Account balances are listed below for the Global Travel Agency.

Instructions:

1. Compute the net income or net loss.
2. Prepare a balance sheet dated May 31 of the current year.

Cash	$13,000	Commissions	$14,500
Accounts Receivable	15,000	Rent Expense	2,000
Equipment	18,000	Salaries Expense	4,000
Accounts Payable	11,000	Advertising Expense	1,000
Lynne Russell,		Telephone Expense	300
Capital, May 1	28,000	Postage Expense	200

CASE STUDY

Write the answer to the case study on the form provided in your workbook.

In starting his computer consulting business, Russ Begly decided to use the following accounts:

Cash
Equipment
Accounts Payable
Russ Begly, Capital

Knowing little about setting up financial records for a business, he is wondering if these accounts are correct or if he should change them or include others.

> **Critical Thinking**
>
> ■ *What do you think?*
>
> **Hint:** Does the equipment account accurately reflect his needs for both office equipment and computer equipment?

CHAPTER THREE

Asset, Liability, and Owner's Equity Accounts

Accounting Terminology

- Account
- Account balance
- Credit
- Debit
- General ledger
- Pencil footing
- Source document

OBJECTIVES

Upon completion of this chapter, you should be able to:

1. Set up T accounts.
2. Enter opening balances in T accounts.
3. Record debits and credits in asset, liability, and owner's equity accounts.
4. Foot and balance the accounts.
5. Prove the fundamental accounting equation.

INTRODUCTION

In the first two chapters, the effects of business transactions were analyzed and recorded through the use of the basic accounting equation: Assets = Liabilities + Owner's Equity. However, keeping actual records in this way would be very difficult and time consuming. Businesses therefore use a *separate* record, known as an ***account***, for each asset, liability, and owner's equity item. ■

Account: Record showing increases and decreases in a single asset, liability, or owner's equity item.

■ THE FORM OF ACCOUNTS

The simplest form of an account looks like the letter "T" and is therefore called a ***T account***. The name of the account is written at the top of the form. The left side of the account is known as the ***debit side***. The right side is referred to as the ***credit side***.

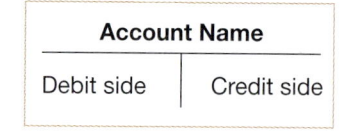

Debit Side: Left side of an account.

Credit Side: Right side of an account.

Account Name	
Debit side	Credit side

The entire group of accounts that a business uses for its assets, liabilities, and owner's equity is known as the ***general ledger***.

General Ledger: Entire group of accounts for a business's assets, liabilities, and owner's equity.

■ OPENING ACCOUNTS FOR THE BALANCE SHEET ITEMS

Look again at the beginning balance sheet for Van Lieu Creative Solutions, shown on page 5. The assets are listed on the left side of the balance sheet. Similarly, the beginning amount of each asset is entered on the left side—the debit side—of its account. The assets of Van Lieu Creative Solutions appear in the accounts as shown on page 15.

18

Cash		Furniture and Equipment	
10,000		7,000	

Liabilities are listed on the right side of the balance sheet. Similarly, the beginning amounts are recorded on the right side—the credit side—of each liability account. The amount of owner's equity, representing the owner's investment, is also listed on the right side of the balance sheet. It is therefore entered on the right side—the credit side—of the capital account. Thus the amounts for the liability Accounts Payable and the owner's equity of Van Lieu Creative Solutions appear in the accounts as shown below.

Accounts Payable		Rebecca Van Lieu, Capital	
	5,000		12,000

Entering an amount on the left side of an account is known as *debiting* the account. Entering an amount on the right side is known as *crediting* the account. The amount entered is called a *debit* or a *credit* according to the side on which it is recorded. The abbreviation accountants use for debit is *Dr.* and for credit it is *Cr.* The abbreviation *Dr.* for debit comes from the Latin word *debitor.* A debitor is one who owes. *Cr.* comes from *creditor* which, in Latin, means someone who is trusted.

Debiting: Entering an amount on the left side of an account.

Crediting: Entering an amount on the right side of an account.

The illustration below shows how the beginning amounts (opening balances) were recorded in the T accounts for Van Lieu Creative Solutions. Note that the asset accounts were debited, but the liability Accounts Payable and the owner's capital account were credited. Now that all the balance sheet accounts have been opened, the amounts on the left side of the asset accounts (debits) are equal to the amounts on the right side of the liability and owner's equity accounts (credits). The total of the debits is $17,000, and the total of the credits is also $17,000. This is the same as the total on each side of the balance sheet.

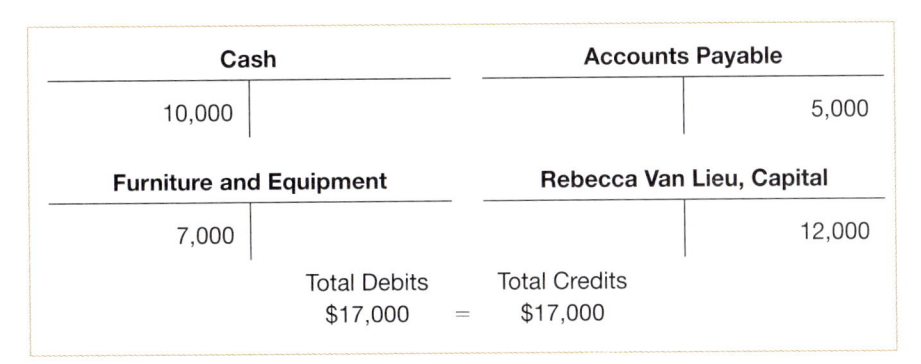

Cash		Accounts Payable	
10,000			5,000

Furniture and Equipment		Rebecca Van Lieu, Capital	
7,000			12,000

Total Debits $17,000 = Total Credits $17,000

In addition to a method for recording the opening balances, a business needs a way to record later increases and decreases in asset accounts. Increases in an asset account must be added to the opening balance. This can easily be done if each increase is recorded on the same side (the debit side) and listed just below the previous entry. Decreases in an asset account are of an opposite nature and must be kept separate from increases. Therefore, the right, or credit, side is used for decreases.

Since the opening balances of the liability account and the owner's equity account were entered on the right, or credit, side of the accounts, any increases in them must also be entered on that side. Decreases must be entered on the left, or debit, side.

The entry for a business transaction must include at least one debit and one credit. The procedure for recording each part of the transaction depends on two considerations: (1) the kind of account affected (asset, liability, or owner's equity) and (2) whether an increase or a decrease is involved.

Rules for Debiting and Crediting

Asset Accounts:
- Record increases as debits.
- Record decreases as credits.

Liability and Owner's Equity Accounts:
- Record increases as credits.
- Record decreases as debits.

DEBIT	ASSET ACCOUNTS	CREDIT
The original amount is entered on this (debit) side.		Decreases are entered on this (credit) side.
Increases are entered on this side.		

DEBIT	LIABILITY AND OWNER'S EQUITY ACCOUNTS	CREDIT
Decreases are entered on this (debit) side.		The original amount is entered on this (credit) side.
		Increases are entered on this side.

■ RECORDING CHANGES IN ACCOUNTS

To see how changes are entered in accounts, let us review the transactions of Van Lieu Creative Solutions. Remember that each transaction will affect at least two accounts.

Recording Increases and Decreases in Asset Accounts. Transaction (a) involved the purchase of additional furniture for $800. This transaction resulted in an increase in one asset (Furniture and Equipment) and a decrease in another asset (Cash).

The increase of $800 in the asset Furniture and Equipment is entered on the debit side of the Furniture and Equipment account because increases in assets are recorded as debits. The offsetting $800 decrease in the asset Cash is entered on the credit side of the Cash account because decreases in assets are recorded as credits.

Source Documents: Paper evidence of a transaction.

The paper evidence of transactions are called *source documents.* Any paperwork containing information that affects an account can be a source document. Some examples include checks, receipts, and shipping documents.

Furniture and Equipment		Cash	
7,000		10,000	(a) 800
(a) 800			

Account Balance: Difference between total debits and total credits in an account.

The $9,200 left in the Cash account (a debit of $10,000 minus a credit of $800) is known as the *balance* of the account. The balance is computed by subtracting the smaller amount ($800) from the larger amount ($10,000). Because the debit side of the Cash account is larger, this account is said to have a *debit balance.*

Recording Decreases in Liability Accounts. Transaction (b) involved the $500 check given to Micro Systems in partial payment for the office equipment. This transaction caused a decrease of $500 in the liability Accounts Payable and a decrease of $500 in the asset Cash.

The original amount of the Accounts Payable ($5,000) is on the credit side of the account. The decrease of $500 is entered on the debit side to show a decrease in the amount owed. The balance of Accounts Payable is now $4,500 (a credit of $5,000 minus a debit of $500). Note that this account has a *credit balance.*

The $500 decrease in the asset Cash is entered on the credit side of the Cash account because decreases in assets are recorded as credits. The balance of the Cash account is now $8,700 (a debit of $10,000 minus credits of $1,300).

Cash				Accounts Payable		
10,000	(a)	800		(b) 500		5,000
	(b)	500				

Recording Increases in the Owner's Equity Account.
Transaction (c) involved Rebecca Van Lieu's additional cash investment of $2,000 in the business. This transaction caused a $2,000 increase in the asset Cash and a $2,000 increase in the owner's equity Rebecca Van Lieu, Capital.

The Cash account is debited for $2,000 to record an increase. The increase of $2,000 in Rebecca Van Lieu, Capital is entered on the credit side because increases in the owner's equity are recorded as credits. After this transaction is recorded, the Cash account has a balance of $10,700 (debits of $12,000 minus credits of $1,300) and the capital account has a balance of $14,000 (credits of $12,000 and $2,000).

> **WWW Inquiry**
> Find the URL address for Coca-Cola. What is the gross profit on its income statement for the last available year?

Cash				Rebecca Van Lieu, Capital		
	10,000	(a)	800			12,000
(c)	2,000	(b)	500		(c)	2,000

Recording Increases in Liability Accounts.
In Transaction (d), Van Lieu borrowed $1,000 from the bank. This transaction caused a $1,000 increase in the asset Cash and a $1,000 increase in the new liability account, Loans Payable.

The Cash account is debited for $1,000 to record the increase in the asset. The increase of $1,000 in Loans Payable is entered on the credit side because increases in liabilities are recorded as credits.

Cash				Loans Payable		
	10,000	(a)	800		(d)	1,000
(c)	2,000	(b)	500			
(d)	1,000					

Transaction (e) also caused an increase in an asset account and an increase in a liability account. In this transaction, Van Lieu bought a copier/fax machine for $2,500 and agreed to pay for it in 60 days. As a result of the transaction, there was a $2,500 increase in the asset Furniture and Equipment and a $2,500 increase in the liability Accounts Payable.

The Furniture and Equipment account is debited for $2,500 to show the increase in this asset. The increase of $2,500 in Accounts Payable is entered on the credit side because increases in liabilities are recorded as credits.

Furniture and Equipment			Accounts Payable		
	7,000		(b)	500	5,000
(a)	800			(e)	2,500
(e)	2,500				

■ FINDING THE BALANCES OF ACCOUNTS

The balance of an account can easily be found whenever that information is needed. If there are entries on only one side of the account, the procedure for finding the balance is as follows: (1) All the amounts recorded in the account are added, and (2) the total is written in small pencil figures at the foot (bottom) of the column of amounts. Look at the Furniture and Equipment account given here. Because there are no entries on the credit side, the total of the debits ($10,300) is the account balance.

The normal balance of an account is on the increase side.

	Furniture and Equipment	
	7,000	
(a)	800	
(e)	2,500	
	10,300	

A total or balance written in small pencil figures is called a *pencil footing.* Pencil is used to set these amounts apart from the regular entries, which are written in ink. To *foot* or *pencil-foot* a column of figures means to total the figures.

Pencil Footing: Total or balance written in small pencil figures.

If there are entries on both sides of an account, additional steps are involved in computing the balance: (1) The debits and credits are each added. (2) The totals are pencil-footed on each side of the account. (3) The smaller total is subtracted from the larger total. (4) The difference—the balance—is pencil-footed on the side with the larger total.

The Accounts Payable account shown on page 21 has a credit balance of $7,000 (credits of $7,500 minus debits of $500). There is no need to pencil-foot the debit side because it contains only one amount. However, the credit side has two pencil footings—the total of the credits ($7,500) and the account balance ($7,000).

	Accounts Payable		
(b)	500		5,000
		(e)	2,500
	7,000		7,500

■ USING ACCOUNT BALANCES TO PROVE THE ACCOUNTING EQUATION

WWW Inquiry
Find the URL address for JC Penney. What amount of dividends were declared in the last year? (Hint: go to the Five Year Financial Summary)

Once the account balances have been computed, they can be used to prove the accounting equation. The balance of $11,700 in the Cash account plus the balance of $10,300 in the Furniture and Equipment account equals the total assets of $22,000. The balances of $1,000 in Loans Payable and $7,000 in Accounts Payable and the balance of $14,000 in the capital account also total $22,000. Thus the equation is in balance.

Assets	=	Liabilities	+	Owner's Equity
$22,000	=	$8,000	+	$14,000

CHAPTER 3 SUMMARY

- A separate account is kept for every asset, liability, and owner's equity item in a business. The accounts are used to record the increases and decreases caused by daily transactions. All accounts together are known as the general ledger.
- Two things must be considered when analyzing and recording each part of a business transaction: (1) the kind of account affected (asset, liability, or owner's equity) and (2) whether an increase or decrease is involved.
- The left side of an account is the debit side, and the right side is the credit side.

- The following rules apply when business transactions are analyzed and recorded.
    1. Increases in assets are recorded as debits.
    2. Decreases in assets are recorded as credits.
    3. Increases in liabilities and in owner's equity are recorded as credits.
    4. Decreases in liabilities and in owner's equity are recorded as debits.
- An account balance is the difference between the total debits and the total credits in an account.

CHAPTER APPLICATIONS

EXERCISES

Complete the following assignments on the forms provided in your workbook.

EXERCISE 3-1

Analyzing transactions in T accounts. Transactions have been entered in the T accounts shown. The debit and credit amounts for each transaction are identified by the same letter.

Instructions:
Analyze the accounts and provide an explanation for each entry.

Example: *Simmons invested $20,000 in her business.*

Cash				Equipment			
(Ex.)	20,000	(a)	400	(a)	400	(c)	400
(c)	400	(d)	500	(b)	1,000		
(e)	5,000						

Accounts Payable				Dorothy Susan Simmons, Capital			
(d)	500	(b)	1,000			(Ex.)	20,000
						(e)	5,000

EXERCISE 3-2

Computing balances and proving the account equation. This is a continuation of Exercise 3-1. Refer to the T accounts in Exercise 3-1

Instructions:
1. Compute the balance of each account.
2. Total the asset account balances and complete the equation: Assets = Liabilities + Owner's Equity.

EXERCISE 3-3

Accounting for assets, liabilities, and owner's equity.

Instructions:
1. Set up T accounts for Cash, Supplies, Office Equipment, Accounts Payable, and John Nori, Capital.
2. Analyze and record each of the following transactions in the T accounts. Identify each part of an entry by writing the letter of the transaction next to the amount.
3. Compute and enter the balance on the appropriate side of the account.
4. Total the asset account balances and complete the equation: Assets = Liabilities + Owner's Equity.

Transactions:
a. Nori invested $15,000 in his insurance business.
b. Paid $400 for office supplies.
c. Purchased office equipment for $2,000 on credit.
d. Returned damaged supplies and received a refund of $100.
e. Issued a check for $500 as a partial payment on the balance due for equipment.

EXERCISE 3-4

Accounting for assets, liabilities, and owner's equity.

Instructions:
1. Set up T accounts for Cash, Office Equipment, Delivery Equipment, Accounts Payable, and Erik Lier, Capital.
2. Analyze and record each of the following transactions in the T accounts. Identify each part of an entry by writing the letter of the transaction next to the amount.
3. Compute and enter the balance on the appropriate side of the account.
4. Total the asset account balances and complete the equation: Assets = Liabilities + Owner's Equity.

- A total or balance written in small pencil figures is called a pencil footing. Pencil is used to set these amounts apart from the regular entries, which are written in ink.
- To foot or pencil-foot a column of figures means to total the figures.

Transactions:

a. Lier invested $20,000 in his delivery business.
b. Purchased file cabinets for $400 on credit from the Gunn Equipment Company.
c. Lier gave his $15,000 truck to the business.
d. Returned a damaged file cabinet and received credit for $80 from Gunn Equipment Company.
e. Issued a check for $120 to the Gunn Equipment Company as a partial payment on the balance due for the file cabinets.

PROBLEMS

Complete all assigned problems on the forms provided in your workbook.

PROBLEM 3-1

Recording balances and transactions in T accounts.
The following accounts and opening balances are for Clean Air Control Systems, a firm that tests air quality and develops antipollution systems.

Cash	$45,000	Land	$ 20,000
Office Equipment	10,000	Accounts Payable	18,000
Testing Equipment	13,000	Niccole Hank,	
Building	50,000	Capital	120,000

Instructions:

1. Record the opening balances in the T accounts provided in the workbook.
2. Analyze and record the following transactions in the accounts. Identify each part of an entry by writing the letter of the transaction next to the amount.
3. Foot the accounts and enter the balances.
4. Total the asset account balances. Then complete the equation: Assets = Liabilities + Owner's Equity.

Transactions:

a. Paid $26,000 to purchase more land.
b. Paid $18,000 for an addition to the building.
c. Purchased testing equipment for $4,000 on credit; payment is due in 60 days.
d. Sold used office equipment and received $2,000.
e. Returned defective testing equipment and received credit for $1,500.
f. Hank invested an additional $10,000 in the business.
g. Paid $5,000 to creditors on account.

PROBLEM 3-2

Recording balances and transactions in T accounts.
The Anderson Garage provides parking facilities, towing, and repair services. Its accounts and opening balances are as follows:

Cash	$20,000	Land	$10,000
Office Equipment	5,000	Loans Payable	25,000
Towing Equipment	25,000	Accounts Payable	5,000
Building	30,000	Richard Anderson,	
		Capital	60,000

Instructions:

1. Record the opening balances in the T accounts provided in the workbook.
2. Analyze and record the following transactions in the accounts. Identify each part of an entry by writing the letter of the transaction next to the amount.
3. Foot the accounts and enter the balances.
4. Total the asset account balances, and total the liability account balances. Then complete the equation: Assets = Liabilities + Owner's Equity.

Transactions:

a. Anderson invested an additional $10,000 in the business.
b. Purchased office equipment for $2,000 on credit.
c. Borrowed an additional $6,000 from the First Service Bank.
d. Paid $8,000 for a used tow truck.
e. Returned damaged office equipment and received credit for $500.
f. Paid $4,000 for a vacant lot.
g. Paid the balance of $1,500 due on the office equipment.
h. Paid $4,000 for an addition to the building.

CASE STUDY

Write the answer to the case study on the form provided in your workbook.

When Tom Stern began his investment management consulting business, he prepared his financial records using the following accounts:

Cash

Accounts Receivable

Office Equipment

Communication Equipment

Accounts Payable

Tom Stern, Capital

He figured that since he was using only six accounts, he didn't have to worry about debits or credits. Since he was just starting, he thought there was no need for having account balances on the left or right.

Critical Thinking

- *Is Stern's assessment correct? Is there a need for keeping balances on the debit or credit side? Why?*

CHAPTER FOUR

Revenue and Expense Accounts

Accounting Terminology

- Withdrawals account
- Owner's equity accounts

OBJECTIVES

Upon completion of this chapter, you should be able to:

1. Record debits and credits in revenue, expense, and withdrawal accounts.
2. Explain the rules of debit and credit.
3. Apply the rules of debit and credit for revenue, expense, and withdrawals on owner's equity.

INTRODUCTION

Accounts must be provided for recording the receipt of revenue and the payment of expenses. As discussed in Chapter 2, if revenue is greater than expenses, there is a net income. If expenses exceed revenue, there is a net loss.

Specific accounts are used to show the kinds of revenue and expenses that are connected with the operation of a business. To see how revenue and expenses are recorded in such accounts, let us review the transactions of Van Lieu Creative Solutions that were discussed in Chapter 2. ■

■ RECORDING REVENUE

In Transaction (f), Rebecca Van Lieu received $1,000 for résumé preparation and job placements. The increase in cash is recorded as a debit to the Cash account. Because revenue has been earned, there is an increase in owner's equity. This increase must be recorded as a credit to an owner's equity account. The Rebecca Van Lieu, Capital account is not used to record this transaction. Just as a business has separate accounts for each asset and each liability, it must keep a separate account for each item of owner's equity—capital, revenue, and expenses.

The increase in the owner's equity that results from revenue is therefore recorded in a separate revenue account. The title of the revenue account usually shows the source of the revenue. In Rebecca Van Lieu's business, the title Employment Fees is used. Van Lieu credits this account for $1,000 to record the revenue she earned during the first week of operations.

Cash				Employment Fees	
	10,000	(a)	800	(f)	1,000
(c)	2,000	(b)	500		
(d)	1,000				
(f)	1,000				

In Transaction (g), Van Lieu tested and screened job applicants for $800 on credit for a client, Ellen Dete. The increase in the asset Accounts Receivable is recorded as a debit to the Accounts Receivable account. Because revenue was earned, owner's equity increased. This increase is recorded by crediting the Employment Fees account for $800.

Accounts Receivable			Employment Fees		
(g)	800			(f)	1,000
				(g)	800

In Transaction (i), Van Lieu received $400 on account from Donald Lynch. This transaction involves only an exchange of one asset (accounts receivable) for another (cash). It is recorded by debiting the Cash account to show the increase in cash and by crediting the Accounts Receivable account to show the decrease in accounts receivable. Note that the owner's equity is not affected by this transaction.

Cash				Accounts Receivable			
	10,000	(a)	800	(g)	800	(i)	400
(c)	2,000	(b)	500				
(d)	1,000						
(f)	1,000						
(i)	400						

■ RECORDING EXPENSES

In Transaction (h), Van Lieu paid a salary of $300 to her assistant. The decrease in the asset Cash is recorded as a credit to the Cash account. An expense account is used to record the decrease in the owner's equity resulting from the expense for salaries.

Just as a business needs a separate revenue account to record increases in the owner's equity from revenue, it must also have a separate expense account for each type of expense incurred. Because expenses decrease the owner's equity, the $300 that Van Lieu paid in salaries is debited to a Salaries Expense account.

WWW Inquiry
Find the URL address for Coca-Cola. What types of property, plant, and equipment does Coca-Cola list on its most recent balance sheet?

Cash				Salaries Expense	
	10,000	(a)	800	(h)	300
(c)	2,000	(b)	500		
(d)	1,000	(h)	300		
(f)	1,000				
(i)	400				

Van Lieu will need other expense accounts in addition to Salaries Expense. An account must be opened for each major expense item in a business so that the owner can easily identify the various costs of operations. In addition, when income tax returns are prepared, expenses must be itemized by certain categories. Therefore, Van Lieu opens another expense account—Repairs Expense—when she pays $100 for repairs to the copier/fax machine in Transaction (j). This expense is recorded by debiting the Repairs Expense account for $100 and by crediting the Cash account for $100.

Cash				Repairs Expense	
	10,000	(a)	800	(j) 100	
(c)	2,000	(b)	500		
(d)	1,000	(h)	300		
(f)	1,000	(j)	100		
(i)	400				

■ RECORDING THE OWNER'S WITHDRAWALS

Most owners of businesses live on money that they obtain from the firm. Thus they usually withdraw cash or other assets for their personal use on a regular basis. The business is expected to make up the resulting decrease in the owner's equity through net income.

Transaction (k)
Withdrawal of cash by the owner.

Transaction (k) Van Lieu withdraws $500 in cash from her business for her personal use. This transaction has the following effects.

1. Owner's equity is *decreased* by $500.
2. The asset Cash is *decreased* by $500.

A separate account, called a **withdrawal account** is used to record decreases in the owner's equity due to withdrawals for personal use. This account provides a complete record of the owner's withdrawals from the business. The $500 that Van Lieu withdrew is therefore debited to a new owner's equity account—Rebecca Van Lieu, Withdrawals. The Cash account is credited.

Owner's equity accounts
- Capital Account—use for changes in the owner's investment.
- Withdrawals Account—use for personal withdrawals by the owner.
- Revenue Accounts—use for revenue earned by the business.
- Expense Accounts—use for expenses incurred by the business.

Cash				Rebecca Van Lieu, Withdrawals	
	10,000	(a)	800	(k) 500	
(c)	2,000	(b)	500		
(d)	1,000	(h)	300		
(f)	1,000	(j)	100		
(i)	400	(k)	500		

■ THE RULES OF DEBIT AND CREDIT

Analyzing transactions correctly to determine the debits and credits is an essential accounting skill. The following illustration summarizes the rules for debiting and crediting the various accounts.

WWW Inquiry
Find the URL address for Coca-Cola. What types of current liabilities does Coca-Cola show on its most recent balance sheet?

GUIDE FOR DEBITING AND CREDITING

DEBIT	ASSET ACCOUNTS	CREDIT
Enter the original amount on this side. Enter increases on this side.		Enter decreases on this side.

DEBIT	LIABILITY ACCOUNTS	CREDIT
Enter decreases on this side.		Enter the original amount on this side. Enter increases on this side.

DEBIT	OWNER'S EQUITY ACCOUNTS	CREDIT
Enter decreases (e.g. withdrawals) on this side.		Enter the beginning investment on this side. Enter increases (e.g. additional investments) on this side.

DEBIT	REVENUE ACCOUNTS	CREDIT
Enter decreases in owner's equity through reduction of revenue (sales returns, allowances, and so forth) on this side.	Enter increases in owner's equity through revenue (usually from sales of goods or services) on this side.	

DEBIT	EXPENSE ACCOUNTS	CREDIT
Enter decreases in owner's equity through expenses (rent, salaries, utilities, selling expenses, administrative expenses, and so forth) on this side.	Enter increases in owner's equity through reduction of expenses on this side.	

■ THE EFFECTS OF REVENUE, EXPENSES, AND WITHDRAWALS ON OWNER'S EQUITY

Van Lieu Creative Solutions earned revenue totaling $1,800 during its first week of operations. It also had expenses totaling $400 in the period. The $1,400 difference between revenue and expenses is net income. However, Van Lieu withdrew $500 for her personal use in anticipation of the net income. Thus there is a net increase of $900 in her owner's equity for the period ($1,400 in net income minus $500 in withdrawals).

If a new balance sheet were prepared for Van Lieu Creative Solutions, the information about the owner's equity would appear as shown below.

The net changes in the owner's equity account are due to:
- Additional owner's investment.
- Net income or net loss.
- Owner's withdrawals.

Owner's Equity
Rebecca Van Lieu, Capital
    July 31, 20XX $12,000
    Additional Investment   2,000
    Total Investment   14,000
    Net Income   1,400
    Less Withdrawals   500
    Net Increase in Owner's Equity   900
    Rebecca Van Lieu, Capital
        July 31, 20XX   14,900

CHAPTER 4 SUMMARY

- Many business transactions involve earning revenue and incurring expenses.

- A separate account is opened for each major revenue and expense item. The account name describes the source of the revenue or the type of expense involved. The following rules are used for making entries in these accounts.
    1. Increases in owner's equity caused by revenue are recorded as credits to a revenue account.
    2. Decreases in owner's equity caused by expenses are recorded as debits to the appropriate expense accounts.

- A separate withdrawal account is opened to record the owner's withdrawals. Decreases in owner's equity caused by withdrawals (funds withdrawn for the owner's personal use) are debited to this account.

- At the end of the period of operations, all revenue and expenses are totaled. The total expenses are subtracted from the total revenue to find the net income, which increases the owner's equity. Withdrawals are subtracted from the net income to show the net increase in the owner's equity. If expenses are greater than revenue or if withdrawals are greater than the net income, there will be a decrease in the owner's equity.

CHAPTER APPLICATIONS

EXERCISES

Complete the following assignments on the forms provided in your workbook.

EXERCISE 4-1

Analyzing transactions in T accounts. Transactions have been entered in the T accounts shown for Robert Norman, D.D.S. The debit and credit amounts for each transaction are identified by the same letter.

Instructions:

1. Analyze the accounts and provide an explanation for each entry.

Example: *Norman invested $19,000 in his dental practice.*

Cash				Robert Norman, Capital		Dental Fees		
(Ex.) 19,000	(b)	400		(Ex.) 19,000		(a)	600
(a) 600	(d)	500				(c)	1,400
(e) 800							

Accounts Receivable		Robert Norman, Withdrawals		Salaries Expense
(c) 1,400	(e) 800	(d) 500		(b) 400

EXERCISE 4-2

Computing a net income and proving the accounting equation.

Instructions:

1. Refer to Exercise 4-1 and compute the balance of each account.
2. Use the appropriate balances to compute the net income.
3. Use the net income and the drawing account balance to compute owner's equity.
4. Total the assets and prove the accounting equation: Assets = Liabilities + Owner's Equity.

EXERCISE 4-3

Computing a net loss and proving the accounting equation. The account balances for Gerald White, Management Consultant are shown below.

Instructions:

1. Use the appropriate balances to compute the net loss and the decrease in owner's equity.
2. Complete the accounting equation: Assets = Liabilities + Owner's Equity.

Cash	$10,000	Consultation Fees	$4,500
Accounts Receivable	5,000	Rent Expense	1,500
Equipment	12,000	Salaries Expense	2,000
Accounts Payable	8,000	Telephone Expense	500
Gerald White, Capital	22,000	Professional Expense	1,200
Gerald White, Withdrawals	2,000	Office Expense	300

Save your work for use in Exercise 5-1.

EXERCISE 4-4

Accounting for revenue, expenses, and owner's equity.

Instructions:

1. Set up the T accounts listed below for Sandy Espe, Attorney at Law.

Cash	Legal Fees
Accounts Receivable	Rent Expense
Sandy Espe, Capital	Telephone Expense
Sandy Espe, Withdrawals	Professional Expense

2. Analyze and record each of the following transactions in the T accounts.
3. Identify each part of an entry by writing the letter of the transaction next to the amount.
4. Foot the accounts, and enter the balance on the appropriate side of each account.
5. Determine the net income or net loss from operations.
6. Compute owner's equity.
7. Complete the accounting equation: Assets = Liabilities + Owner's Equity.

Transactions:

a. Espe invested $20,000 in her legal practice.
b. Received $500 for providing legal services.
c. Provided legal services for $2,800 on credit.
d. Paid $1,000 for office rent.

e. Paid $200 for professional dues.
f. Espe withdrew $500 for personal use.
g. Received $2,000 on account from clients.
h. Paid $100 for the telephone bill.

Save your work for use in Exercise 5-2.

PROBLEMS

Complete all assigned problems on the forms provided in your workbook.

PROBLEM 4-1

Recording transactions in T accounts; computing net income or net loss; preparing a balance sheet.
The T accounts for the accounting firm owned by Joseph Barbagallo, CPA, are provided in the workbook. The balances as of January 1 have been entered in the accounts.

Instructions:

1. Analyze the following transactions and record the effects in the T accounts. Identify each part of an entry by writing the letter of the transaction next to the amount.
2. Foot the accounts and enter the balances.
3. Compute the net income or net loss from operations.
4. Prepare a balance sheet as of January 31 of the current year.

Transactions:

a. Paid $2,000 for additional office equipment.
b. Paid $1,200 for office rent.
c. Received $400 for providing accounting services.
d. Paid $500 to creditors on account.
e. Paid $800 to employees for salaries.
f. Provided accounting services for $3,000 on credit.
g. Paid $40 for gas and oil for the automobile used in the business.
h. Barbagallo withdrew $600 from the business.
i. Paid $240 for repairs to the automobile used in the business.
j. Received $800 from clients on account.
k. Bought file cabinets for $400 and agreed to pay in 30 days.

Save your work for use in Problem 5-2.

PROBLEM 4-2

Recording transactions in T accounts; computing net income or net loss; preparing a balance sheet.
The Hooker Advertising Agency, owned by Kimberly Hooker, prepares magazine and newspaper ads and organizes fashion shows for clothing stores. The T accounts for the business are provided in the workbook. The balances as of April 1 have been entered in the accounts. Note that there are two revenue accounts—one for each type of service the business performs.

Instructions:

1. Analyze the following transactions and record the effects in the T accounts. Identify each part of an entry by writing the letter of the transaction next to the amount.
2. Foot the accounts and enter the balances.
3. Compute the net income or net loss from operations.
4. Prepare a balance sheet as of April 30 of the current year.

Transactions:

a. Organized a fashion show for Casual Stores for $2,000 on credit.
b. Paid $1,000 for rent.
c. Received $1,300 for preparing magazine advertisements.
d. Paid $50 for repairs to office equipment.
e. Received $400 from clients on account.
f. Bought supplies for $250 on credit.
g. Paid $600 to creditors on account.
h. Because the fashion show for Casual Stores (Transaction a) took an hour less than planned, Hooker reduced the bill by $100.
i. Returned damaged supplies and received credit for $50.
j. Hooker withdrew $400 for her personal use.
k. Prepared newspaper advertisements for $1,400 on credit.
l. Paid $750 for painting the office.
m. Bought computer software for $300 on credit.
n. Paid $1,800 to employees for salaries.

Save your work for use in Problem 5-3.

CASE STUDY

Write the answer to the case study on the form provided in your workbook.

Marilyn Wilco started a tutoring services for elementary school students who needed help with math or English. When preparing her owner's equity accounts, she used the following accounts:

Marilyn Wilco, Capital

Marilyn Wilco, Withdrawals

Revenue

Expenses

When using T accounts to analyze her transactions, she had difficulty understanding why revenue had a credit balance and expenses had a debit balance. It didn't make sense to her that the withdrawal account had a debit balance also.

Critical Thinking

- *What would you tell Wilco to help her understand how the account balances work?*

CHAPTER FIVE

The Trial Balance

OBJECTIVES

Upon completion of this chapter, you should be able to:

1. Prepare a trial balance.
2. Locate errors in the trial balance and ledger accounts.
3. Correct errors in the trial balance and ledger accounts.

Accounting Terminology

- Accounting errors
- Trial balance

INTRODUCTION

One of the major reasons for recording transactions in accounts is to provide the information needed for financial reports. However, before the information can be used to prepare these reports, it is necessary to check the accuracy of the entries that were recorded.

Remember that every entry consists of a debit and a credit. Therefore, the total of all the debits recorded in the accounts should equal the total of all the credits. This equality is verified by *taking a trial balance.* ■

Preparing a Trial Balance
Checking equality of total debits and total credits in ledger accounts.

■ PREPARING THE TRIAL BALANCE

The first step in preparing a trial balance is to find the balance of each account. This is done by pencil-footing the accounts, as described in Chapter 3.

Cash				Rebecca Van Lieu, Capital			
	10,000	(a)	800				12,000
(c)	2,000	(b)	500			(c)	2,000
(d)	1,000	(h)	300				14,000
(f)	1,000	(j)	100				
(i)	400	(k)	500				
12,200	14,400		2,200				

Accounts Receivable				Rebecca Van Lieu, Withdrawals			
(g)	800	(i)	400	(k)	500		
400							

Furniture and Equipment				Employment Fees			
	7,000					(f)	1,000
(a)	800					(g)	800
(e)	2,500						1,800
	10,300						

Loans Payable				Salaries Expense			
		(d)	1,000	(h)	300		

33

Accounts Payable				Repairs Expense	
(b)	500		5,000	(j) 100	
		(e)	2,500		
		7,000	7,500		

The accounts of Van Lieu Creative Solutions are shown on page 33 as they would appear after the balances have been determined.

The next step in preparing the trial balance is to list the accounts and their balances in pencil. Then the debits and credits are totaled. This work is often done on a ruled form, as shown below.

Trial Balance

VAN LIEU CREATIVE SOLUTIONS
TRIAL BALANCE
JULY 31, 20XX

Acct. No.	Account Name	Debit	Credit
	Cash	12 200 00	
	Accounts Receivable	400 00	
	Furniture and Equipment	10 300 00	
	Loans Payable		1 000 00
	Accounts Payable		7 000 00
	Rebecca Van Lieu, Capital		14 000 00
	Rebecca Van Lieu, Withdrawals	500 00	
	Employment Fees		1 800 00
	Salaries Expense	300 00	
	Repairs Expense	100 00	
	Totals	23 800 00	23 800 00

Steps in Preparing a Trial Balance:

- Find balances of accounts.
- List accounts and balances.
- Add balances to see if total debits and total credits are equal.

Note that the heading consists of three lines that answer these questions: Who? What? and When? The accounts are listed on the trial balance form in the order they appear in the ledger: assets, liabilities, capital, drawing, revenue, and expenses. The debit balances are recorded in the Debit money column, and the credit balances are recorded in the Credit money column. Note that the asset, withdrawals, and expense accounts are expected to have debit balances and that the liability, capital, and revenue accounts are expected to have credit balances. After all accounts and balances are listed, a single line is drawn across each money column with a ruler, and the balances are added. If the total of the two money columns agree, the trial balance is in balance. Then two lines are drawn under the totals. These lines indicate that the total debit balances equal the total credit balances, and the trial balance has been completed.

If the total debit balances do not equal the total credit balances, the trial balance is not in balance. This means that there is an error in the trial balance or in the accounts.

■ FINDING ERRORS IN THE TRIAL BALANCE AND THE ACCOUNTS

Time may be saved in finding errors by working back systematically from the trial balance to the accounts. It is usually possible to locate errors by completing one or more of the following steps.

1. Total the trial balance money columns again to make sure that the addition is correct.
2. Check to see whether any account balance has been omitted from the trial balance.

3. Compare the figures on the trial balance with the account balances to verify that the correct amounts have been listed on the trial balance and that they were placed in the proper money column.
4. Total the debits and credits in the accounts again, and compute the balances again.
5. Check the entries in the accounts to make sure that matching debit and credit were recorded for each transaction.

> **WWW Inquiry**
> Find the URL address for the Ruddick Corporation. Describe its two wholly owned subsidiaries.

■ ERRORS NOT REVEALED BY THE TRIAL BALANCE

Even if the trial balance is in balance, there is still a possibility that the accounts are not correct. Some errors that do not affect the equality of the trial balance totals are:

- Omitting a transaction completely.
- Debiting or crediting the wrong account.
- Entering the amount of the transaction incorrectly.
- Entering the same transaction twice.

■ CORRECTING ERRORS IN THE TRIAL BALANCE AND THE ACCOUNTS

Errors in the trial balance and in the account balances are easily corrected because these figures are written in pencil. If an error is located, erase it and write the correct amount in pencil. Errors in entries that have been written in ink are part of the permanent financial records. Therefore, they may never be erased or covered over with correction fluid or tape. Erasing or covering up errors will make the records suspect because it appears that someone may be falsifying the records. The type of correction required depends upon the type of error that was made. For example, assume that equipment was purchased for $850 on credit and the following entry was made.

> A transposition error occurs when two digits are swapped (e.g. $598 for $958). The difference will be divisible by 9.

Equipment	Accounts Payable
805	850

The error in Equipment is corrected by drawing a single line through the incorrect amount and then writing the correct amount above it, and initialing the correction.

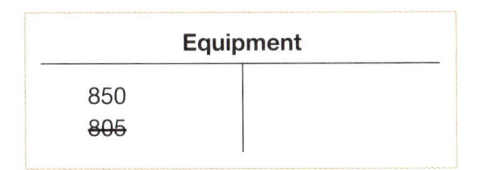

Equipment
850
~~805~~

If the wrong amount is debited or credited, then an entry should be recorded to correct the error. For example, the cost of gasoline and oil for a delivery truck was incorrectly debited to the asset account of Delivery Equipment, as shown below.

> **WWW Inquiry**
> Find the URL address for Barnes and Noble. What were net sales for the fourth quarter ending December 31 last year? (Hint: go to Quarterly financial reports)

Delivery Equipment	Cash
(a) 26	(a) 26

Because Delivery Expense rather than Delivery Equipment should have been debited, the following entry is required to correct the error. Note that this entry debits Delivery Expense and credits Delivery Equipment.

Delivery Equipment			Delivery Expense	
(a) 26	(b)	26	(b) 26	

CHAPTER 5 SUMMARY

- The accuracy of the accounts must be checked before financial reports are prepared.
- The procedure for checking the equality of the debits and credits in the accounts is called taking a trial balance.
- The first step in taking a trial balance is to find the balances of the accounts. The next step is to list the accounts and their balances. Then the debts and credits are totaled. The total of the debits should be equal to the total of the credits.
- The accounts are listed on the trial balance form in the order they appear in the ledger.
- If the trial balance is in balance, it is probable that the accounts in the ledger are correct. If the total debits and the total credits are not equal, the trial balance and the accounts must be checked to find and then correct the error.

CHAPTER APPLICATIONS

EXERCISES

Complete the following assignments on the forms provided in your workbook.

EXERCISE 5-1
Preparing a trial balance.
This is a continuation of Exercise 4-3.

Instructions:
1. Use the accounts from Exercise 4-3 to prepare a trial balance for Gerald White Management Consultant, as of June 30 of the current year.

EXERCISE 5-2
Preparing a trial balance. This is a continuation of Exercise 4-4.

Instructions:
1. Use the accounts from Exercise 4-4 to prepare a trial balance for Sandy Espe, Attorney at Law. Date the trial balance May 31 of the current year.

PROBLEMS

Complete all assigned problems on the forms provided in your workbook.

PROBLEM 5-1
Balancing accounts and preparing a trial balance.
The accounts of the Byelich Real Estate Agency, owned by Jim Byelich, are shown in the workbook.

Instructions:
1. Foot the accounts and enter the balances.
2. Prepare a trial balance as of March 31 of the current year.

PROBLEM 5-2
Preparing a trial balance. This is a continuation of Problem 4-1.

Instructions:
1. Use the accounts that were completed in Problem 4-1 to prepare a trial balance for the Barbagallo Accounting Service as of January 31 of the current year.

PROBLEM 5-3
Preparing a trial balance. This is a continuation of Problem 4-2.

Instructions:
1. Use the accounts that were completed in Problem 4-2 to prepare a trial balance for the Hooker Advertising Agency as of April 30 of the current year.

Save your work for use in Problem 6-2.

PROBLEM 5-4
Locating errors in a trial balance and accounts.
The typed version of the trial balance that follows was prepared from accounts that are shown in the workbook.

Instructions:

1. Follow the steps listed in Chapter 5 of the text to locate the errors in both the trial balance and the accounts.
2. Correct the errors and prepare a new trial balance.

ARCHIBALD BUILDERS
TRIAL BALANCE
JANUARY 31, 20XX

Cash	$22,638	
Equipment	31,920	
Accounts Payable		
Tim Archibald, Capital		$62,120
Tim Archibald, Withdrawals		800
Carpentry Fees		22
Rent Expense	150	
Salaries Expense	1,200	
Telephone Expense	48	
Totals	$57,856	$62,942

PROBLEM 5-5

Correcting errors in the accounts; preparing a trial balance. The accounts of Sound Systems, a firm owned by John Leidy, appear in the workbook. Transactions a through c have been recorded in the accounts. The following errors were found in the accounts.

- Leidy's $10,000 investment in the business was not recorded.
- The payment of $800 for rent in Transaction a was debited to John Leidy, Withdrawals.
- The $70 debit in Equipment in Transaction b should be $700.
- The capital account was debited for a $400 withdrawal in Transaction c.

Instructions:

1. Correct the errors in the accounts provided in the workbook. Use the identifying letters d through g for the correcting entries.
2. Foot the accounts and compute the balances.
3. Prepare a trial balance as of October 31 of the current year.

CASE STUDY

Write the answer to the case study on the form provided in your workbook.

Kathryn Kennedy's pet grooming business has been operating for one month. Kennedy prepared her financial records according to accepted accounting procedures. At month's end she had the following accounts and balances:

Cash	$2,202.
Accounts Receivable	$1,002.
Pet Grooming Equipment	$2,300.
Office Equipment	$2,800.
Accounts Payable	$2,300.
Kathryn Kennedy, Capital	$2,804.
Kathryn Kennedy, Withdrawals	$ 500.
Revenues	$1,800.
Expenses	$ 900.

Kennedy prepared her trial balance for the month and ended up with debit and credit balances of $8,304. She was pleased that her trial balance did, in fact, balance—proving that she had kept accurate records for the month.

When she explained her pride to her accountant, he indicated that even though the trial balance was equal, she may have made errors.

Critical Thinking

■ What errors might have been made that would still allow the balance to prove?

CHAPTER SIX

Financial Statements

Accounting Terminology

- Accounting period
- Balance sheet
- Financial statements
- Fiscal period
- Income statement
- Statement of owner's equity

OBJECTIVE

Upon completion of this chapter, you should be able to:

1. Prepare an income statement.
2. Prepare a statement of owner's equity.
3. Prepare a balance sheet.

INTRODUCTION

After the trial balance is in balance, formal reports summarizing the information in the accounts can be prepared. These reports are called *financial statements*. Financial statements show the financial position of a business and the results of its operations. ∎

■ THE ACCOUNTING PERIOD

Accounting Period: Period of time for which financial results of business operations are summarized.

Fiscal Year: Any accounting period of twelve consecutive months.

The period for which results are summarized is known as the *accounting period,* or *fiscal period.* The length of the accounting period is not the same for all businesses. Each owner chooses the period that seems best for his or her type of business. It may be one month, three months (quarterly period), six months (semiannual period), or twelve months (annual period). Whatever time period is chosen, it should be used consistently.

If a year is used for the accounting period, it need not be the calendar year (January 1 through December 31). It can be any twelve-month period covering the normal business year in an industry, such as July 1 through June 30. An accounting period of twelve consecutive months is called a *fiscal year.*

■ COMPLETION OF THE INCOME STATEMENT

Income Statement: Report of revenue, expenses, and net income or net loss, showing results of business operations for a period of time.

Look at the trial balance of Van Lieu Creative Solutions (see page 34). This trial balance will now be used to prepare the business's financial statements. The revenue and expense figures needed for the *income statement* are shown on the lower part of the trial balance.

The income statement is prepared on accounting paper with two money columns. The balance of the revenue account ($1,800) is entered in the second money column. This is followed by the balance of each of the expense accounts listed in the first money column. The expenses are added, and the total ($400) is written in the second money column. The total of the expenses is then subtracted from the revenue to find the net income ($1,800 − $400 = $1,400).

Of course, if the expenses had been greater than the revenue, the result would have been a net loss. This would have been shown on the income statement by using the words *Net Loss* instead of *Net Income.*

Observe that the heading of the income statement answers the three questions: Who? What? and When? The last line of the heading usually shows both the length of the business's accounting period and the ending date of the period. For example, a business with a

WWW Inquiry
Check out the Pepsi corporate website for a look at its financial reports.

monthly accounting period would use Month Ended January 31 of the current year on its income statement for January. Van Lieu Creative Solutions will have a monthly accounting period. However, since the business has been open for only a week, the heading of its current income statement says Week Ended July 31, 20XX.

Income Statement

Income Statement

VAN LIEU CREATIVE SOLUTIONS			
INCOME STATEMENT			
WEEK ENDED JULY 31, 20XX			
Revenue			
Employment Fees			1 800 00
Operating Expenses			
Salaries Expense	300 00		
Repairs Expense	100 00		
Total Operating Expenses			400 00
Net Income			1 400 00

■ COMPLETION OF THE STATEMENT OF OWNER'S EQUITY AND THE BALANCE SHEET

After the income statement is prepared, many businesses prepare a *statement of owner's equity,* or *capital statement.* This statement supplements the balance sheet by showing all the details of the changes in owner's equity during the accounting period. When a statement of owner's equity is used, the Owner's Equity section of the balance sheet can be kept very simple and easy to read. The illustration on page 28 and 29 shows how long and complex this section can be if there is no separate statement of owner's equity.

Statement of Owner's Equity: Report of changes in owner's equity during a period of time.

Preparing the Statement of Owner's Equity.
Like the income statement, the statement of owner's equity is prepared on two-column accounting paper. The heading again answers the questions: Who? What? and When?

VAN LIEU CREATIVE SOLUTIONS		
STATEMENT OF OWNER'S EQUITY		
WEEK ENDED JULY 31, 20XX		
Rebecca Van Lieu, Capital, July 24, 20XX		12 000 00
Additional Investment		2 000 00
Total Investment		14 000 00
Net Income	1 400 00	
Less Withdrawals	500 00	
Net Increase in Owner's Equity		900 00
Rebecca Van Lieu, Capital, July 31, 20XX		14 900 00

Statement of Owner's Equity

The information needed to prepare the statement of owner's equity comes from several sources. The amount of the owner's capital at the beginning of the period ($12,000) and the amount of the additional investment ($2,000) are taken from the Rebecca Van Lieu, Capital account on page 33. Notice that these two figures are written in the second money column and added to find Van Lieu's total investment ($12,000 + $2,000 = $14,000).

The net income for the period ($1,400) comes from the income statement and is listed in the first money column. The amount of the withdrawals ($500) comes from the balance of the drawing account shown on the trial balance on page 34. This figure is also listed in the first money column and is subtracted from the net income to find the net increase in owner's equity ($1,400 − $500 = $900).

WWW Inquiry
Find the URL address for JC Penney. What percentage of total assets did current assets represent on last year's balance sheet?

The net increase in owner's equity ($900) is written in the second money column. It is then added to the amount of the total investment ($14,000) to find the owner's capital at the end of the accounting period ($14,000 + $900 = $14,900).

Preparing the Balance Sheet.
Remember that a balance sheet shows the financial position of a business on any given day. Therefore, a balance sheet may be prepared at any time. However, one is always prepared at the end of the accounting period with the other statements.

If a statement of owner's equity is used, it is simple to prepare the balance sheet. The balances of the asset and liability accounts are taken from the trial balance (page 34). The Owner's Equity section of the balance sheet shows only one figure—the owner's capital at the end of the period. This figure comes from the statement of owner's equity.

Look at the following balance sheet. It shows that Rebecca Van Lieu's capital on July 31 of the current year is $14,900. This balance sheet was first prepared on accounting paper, as discussed in Chapter 1. Then, after it was proved to be correct, the balance sheet was typewritten. Notice that when financial statements are typewritten, dollar signs are used for the amounts.

VAN LIEU CREATIVE SOLUTIONS
BALANCE SHEET
JULY 31, 20XX

Assets			Liabilities and Owner's Equity		
Cash		$12,200	Liabilities		
Accounts Receivable		400	Loans Payable	$1,000	
Furniture and Equipment		10,300	Accounts Payable	7,000	
			Total Liabilities		$8,000
			Owner's Equity		
			Rebecca Van Lieu, Capital		14,900
			Total Liabilities and		
Total Assets		$22,900	Owner's Equity		$22,900

> **WWW Inquiry**
> Go to a website for a company of your choice and review the annual report. You will not find a trial balance. A trial balance is not a formal financial statement presented in a company's annual report. It is an internal statement prepared by the accountant to check the equality of debits and credits before the financial statements are prepared.

After the financial statements are completed, they are studied carefully by owners, managers, and accountants. These people interpret the information on the statements and use it to make decisions and plans.

CHAPTER 6 SUMMARY

- The accounting period is the period of time for which financial results are summarized. Another name for the accounting period is fiscal period.
- Most of the information used in preparing the financial statements comes from the trial balance, which is prepared on the last day of the accounting period.
- The income statement summarizes the revenue and expenses for an accounting period and shows how the net income or the net loss came about.
- The statement of owner's equity shows the details of the changes in owner's equity that occurred during an accounting period. This information may be reported on the balance sheet instead of being shown on a separate statement.
- The balance sheet shows the financial position of a business on one particular date.
- The financial statements permit owners, managers, and accountants to interpret business activities.

CHAPTER APPLICATIONS

EXERCISES

Complete the following assignments on the forms provided in your textbook.

EXERCISE 6–1

Classifying data for financial statements. The following items are reported on a firm's financial statements.

Instructions:
Indicate whether each of these items is shown on the income statement, the statement of owner's equity, or the balance sheet. Three items are reported on two statements.

1. Assets
2. Liabilities
3. Capital at the beginning of the period
4. Additional investments
5. Net income
6. Net loss
7. Revenue
8. Expenses
9. Capital at the end of the period

EXERCISE 6–2

Computing a net income and owner's equity.
Abigail Elyse operates a taxi service.

Instructions

1. Use the following data to compute the net income and owner's capital on June 30 of the current year.
2. Complete the following equation: Assets $70,678 = Liabilities $20,000 + Owner's Equity $_____.

Taxi Fares	$12,626	Abigail Elyse, Capital	
Salaries Expense	3,984	June 1, 20XX	$40,000
Repairs Expense	816	Additional Investment	4,000
Office Expense	148	Abigail Elyse, Withdrawals	1,000

EXERCISE 6–3

Computing a net loss and owner's equity. Lisa Savas operates an accounting consulting firm.

Instructions:

1. Use the following data to compute the net loss and the owner's capital on December 31 of the current year.
2. Complete the following equation: Assets $22,640 = Liabilities $6,070 + Owner's Equity $_____.

Consulting Fees	$5,670	Lisa Savas, Capital	
Salaries Expense	4,240	December 1, 20XX	$16,700
Rent Expense	1,250	Additional Investment	1,300
Telephone Expense	150	Lisa Savas,	
Advertising Expense	860	Withdrawals	600

PROBLEMS

Complete all assigned problems on the forms provided in your workbook.

PROBLEM 6–1

Preparing financial statements. The trial balance of the RMS Photo Studio, owned and operated by Kathleen Bonita, is given in the workbook.

Instructions:

1. Prepare an income statement for the month ended January 31 of the current year.
2. Prepare a statement of owner's equity for the month ended January 31 of the current year. The balance of the capital account on January 1 was $18,760. Bonita made an additional investment of $3,000 during the month.
3. Prepare a balance sheet dated January 31 of the current year.

PROBLEM 6–2

Preparing financial statements. This is a continuation of Problem 5–3. Use the trial balance that was completed for the Hooker Advertising Agency in Problem 5–3.

Instructions:

1. Prepare an income statement for the month ended April 30 of the current year.
2. Prepare a statement of owner's equity for the month ended April 30 of the current year
3. Prepare a balance sheet dated April 30 of the current year.

CASE STUDY

Write the answer to the case study on the form provided in your workbook.

Patty Hershey owns a car detailing service that provides on-your-work-site car care for customers who don't have time to take their cars to a specific location. Hershey's business has been very busy because satisfied customers tell others of her service.

After six months Hershey's accountant prepared her financial statements. She noticed that her income statement needed to be dated for the period of operation for which she was accounting. The balance sheet, she knew, captured a moment in time, and her owner's equity statement was for the same period of time as her income statement.

Hershey thought that all the statements should show a specific date, not a period of time. When she asked her accountant, Joe Barbagallo, about her confusion, he told her why the statements needed to be dated the way they were.

Critical Thinking

- *What were the reasons he gave? What are the accepted accounting procedures for dating financial reports?*

Chapters 1–6

PROJECT 1

Accounting for a Service Business

Contemporary Concepts, a home and office decorating business, is owned by Daniel Van Lieu. On December 1 the firm's accounts show the following balances. Complete the tasks listed below for this business. Use the forms in the workbook.

Cash	$30,400	Automobile	$18,000
Accounts Receivable	4,100	Accounts Payable	2,300
Office Equipment	10,400	Daniel Van Lieu, Capital	60,600

INSTRUCTIONS:

1. Enter the balances in the accounts.
2. Analyze the transactions and record their effects in the accounts. Identify each part of the entry by writing the letter of the transaction next to the amount.
3. Pencil-foot the accounts, and compute and enter the balances.
4. Prepare a trial balance as of December 31 of the current year.
5. Prepare an income statement for the month ended December 31 of the current year.
6. Prepare a statement of owner's equity for the month ended December 31 of the current year.
7. Prepare a balance sheet dated December 31 of the current year.

TRANSACTIONS:

a. Paid $1,050 for office rent.
b. Paid $325 for newspaper advertising.
c. Received $400 for preparing office space designs.
d. Paid $40 for gasoline and oil for the automobile.
e. Paid $750 to a creditor on account.
f. Received $600 from a client on account.
g. Paid $74 for postage stamps.
h. Paid $175 for the telephone bill.
i. Purchased a computer for $2,400 on credit; payment is due in 30 days.
j. Decorated a model apartment for $1,550 on credit.
k. Paid $32 for gasoline for the automobile.
l. Received $500 for interior decorating designs.
m. Received a $100 refund from the newspaper because one of the firm's advertisements did not appear in the Sunday supplement.
n. Van Lieu withdrew $500 from the business for personal use.

PART TWO

The Accounting Cycle

- **Chapter 7**
  The General Journal
- **Chapter 8**
  The General Ledger
- **Chapter 9**
  The Worksheet and the Financial Statements
- **Chapter 10**
  Closing the Ledger
- **Project 2**
  Accounting for a Merchandising Business

Once you have an understanding and working knowledge of the basic accounting equation, you will be introduced to the general journal, general ledger, financial worksheets, and financial statements. You will track transactions from the time they occurred to their effect upon individual accounts and how the information is presented from the General Journal to the ledger accounts. This information is then compiled using financial worksheets for the final presentation of the income statement, statement of owner's equity, and the balance sheet. There will be some similarities in part three as we begin studying the accounting of a merchandising business.

Accounting Careers

Landing the Job

■ WHAT IT WILL TAKE

- Command of the accounting cycle, ledgers, journals, and financial statements.
- Computer skills.
- Accuracy and efficiency.
- Ability to analyze problems and develop solutions.
- Salesmanship.
- Tactful and clear communication skills.
- Willingness to be a team player.

■ WHERE YOU FIT IN

- At a large public accounting firm like the "Big Four," or a small firm; providing accounting services to companies, the government, and individuals.
- Inside government.
- Within a corporation.

■ WHAT YOU CAN EARN

Payroll and timekeeping clerks $27,016
Bookkeeping, accounting, and auditing clerks $25,509
Billing clerks $24,437

■ JOB OUTLOOK

By 2010, the U.S. will need 36% more accountants than were employed in 2004. The areas requiring the most accountants will be firms that provide temps; tax firms; and the health care fields. Corporations employ two-thirds of all accountants.

ACTIVITY

- Check out your local newspaper for accounting employment opportunities.
- Find a company that you might want to work for in the future.
- Search the internet to see if the company is on the web.
- Locate the employment information on the site.
- Search the internet for sites that help you find a job.

CHAPTER SEVEN

The General Journal

OBJECTIVES

Upon completion of this chapter, you should be able to:

1. Record transactions in a general journal.
2. Use a chart of accounts.
3. Correct errors in the journal.

INTRODUCTION

Entering transactions into T accounts is a good way to learn the principles of debit and credit, but this arrangement is not adequate for keeping a record of business operations. The T account provides no information except the name of the account and the amount of each entry.

For example, the T accounts illustrating the $500 partial payment on account to a creditor—gave very little information.

Cash		Accounts Payable	
5,000	400	500	4,000
	500		

There is no way to tell from the Cash account or from the Accounts Payable account who was paid or when. This is why a business needs an easy-to-follow, day-by-day record of its transactions.

■ THE USE OF THE GENERAL JOURNAL

An accounting record known as a *journal* is used to list all the necessary information about a transaction in one place. The journal is the first accounting record of business transactions and is therefore referred to as a *record of original entry*. Entries are recorded in the journal in *chronological order*—in the order that the business transactions happen day by day. The process of recording these transactions in the journal is known as *journalizing,* or *recording journal entries.*

At least two accounts are affected by each transaction. The effect is recorded on the debit side of one account and the credit side of another account. This is known as the double-entry system of accounting.

There are a number of different types of journals. One common type is the *general journal,* which is illustrated below. Note that the information about Transaction (b) is much more complete when journalized as shown here.

Accounting Terminology

- Chart of accounts
- Chronological order
- Compound entry
- Double-entry accounting
- General journal
- Journal
- Journalizing
- Opening entry

The general journal is referred to as the book of original entry.

Journal: Chronological record of business operations.

Chronological Order: Order in which transactions happen day by day.

Journalizing: Recording transactions in the journal.

General Journal: A record in which all business transactions can be entered as they occur.

General Journal

GENERAL JOURNAL   Page 2

Date		Description	Post Ref.	Debit	Credit
20	XX				
July	28	Accounts Payable		500 00	
		Cash			500 00
		Paid Micro Systems on account			

Study the illustration carefully and observe the details listed below.

Double-Entry Accounting: The system of recording at least one debit and credit for each transaction.

Debits are always shown before credits.

- The year is entered at the top of the Date column. The month and day are written below the year. (The year and month need not be repeated after the first entry on a page, except when the year or month changes.)
- The name of the account being debited is written in the Description of Entry column, beginning at the left margin of that column. The debit amount is entered in the Debit money column. Debits are always recorded in the general journal before credits.
- The name of the account being credited is written on the next line of the Description of Entry column. It is indented about one-half inch from the left margin. The credit amount is entered in the Credit money column.
- A brief, clear explanation of the transaction follows on the next one or two lines of the Description of Entry column. This explanation gives additional information that is not shown by the account names.
- A blank line is left after the entry to separate it from the next entry. (This is one of several common methods used for separating entries from each other in the general journal.)
- The pages of the journal are numbered consecutively at the top right corner of each page.
- The narrow column to the left of the Debit money column is the Posting Reference column. Its use will be explained in the next chapter.

■ JOURNALIZING A BUSINESS'S TRANSACTIONS

Consider how the transactions for Guaranteed Delivery, a delivery service owned by Christopher Johns, would be recorded in a general journal. Johns bought this established business, and he begins his own operation on November 1. His balance sheet for that date is as follows:

Balance Sheet

GUARANTEED DELIVERY
BALANCE SHEET
NOVEMBER 1, 20XX

Assets		Liabilities and Owner's Equity	
Cash	32 000 00	Liabilities	
Accounts Receivable	2 000 00	Accounts Payable	20 000 00
Office Equipment	12 000 00	Owner's Equity	
Delivery Trucks	60 000 00	Christopher Johns, Capital	86 000 00
		Total Liabilities and	
Total Assets	106 000 00	Owner's Equity	106 000 00

Chart of Accounts: A list of all the accounts of a business arranged and numbered according to classification.

The firm's accountant has recommended John use the accounts shown below. Note that a number is assigned to each account for identification and reference purposes. Account numbers are usually assigned in the order in which the accounts appear on the financial statements. The arranged list of a business's accounts is known as a *chart of accounts.*

There are many numbering systems for accounts. The one shown here is a common type of numbering system.

GUARANTEED DELIVERY
CHART OF ACCOUNTS

Account Number	Name of Account
100–199	ASSETS
101	Cash
102	Accounts Receivable
111	Office Equipment
112	Delivery Trucks
200–299	LIABILITIES
201	Accounts Payable
300–399	OWNER'S EQUITY
301	Christopher Johns, Capital
303	Christopher Johns, Withdrawals
400–499	REVENUE
401	Delivery Service Fees
500–599	EXPENSES
501	Rent Expense
502	Truck Expense
503	Wages Expense

Johns asks the accountant to start a new set of financial records for the business on November 1. The accountant therefore makes an *opening entry* in the general journal to record the items listed on the balance sheet. This entry is shown on page 51. It is the first entry in the journal. Note that the accountant debits the asset and credits the liabilities and the owner's equity.

During the month of November, Johns records the business's transactions in the general journal, as shown on pages 51 and 52. Before making an entry, he analyzes each transaction and selects the correct account names from the chart of accounts. Johns' analysis of the November transactions is given below and on page 50. Refer to this analysis as you study the journal entries for Guaranteed Delivery.

Opening Entry: Journal entry that starts a new set of financial records.

Date	Description of Transactions	Analysis
Nov. 1	Paid $1,800 to Wilson Management for the November rent.	An increase in expenses decreases owner's equity (debit Rent Expense). An asset decreases (credit Cash).
5	Paid $1,000 to Compu Equipment for a new computer.	An asset increases (debit Office Equipment). An asset increases (credit Cash).
6	Received $650 from World Imports for providing delivery services.	An asset increases (debit Cash). An increase in revenue increases owner's equity (credit Delivery Service Fees).
10	Paid $400 to the Kenworth Truck Sales on account.	A liability decreases (debit Accounts Payable). An asset decreases (credit Cash).
13	Paid $150 for gasoline and oil for the trucks.	An increase in expenses decreases owner's equity (debit Truck Expense). An asset decreases (credit Cash).
15	Paid $2,500 for the truck driver's semimonthly wages.	An increase in expenses decreases owner's equity (debit Wages Expense). An asset decreases (credit Cash).

WWW Inquiry
Find the URL address for JC Penney. What amount of dividends were declared within the last three years? (Hint: go to the Consolidated Statements of Stockholders' Equity)

Nov. 18	Provided delivery services for $2,400 on credit to Riverview Medical Center.	An asset increases (debit Accounts Receivable). An increase in revenue increases owner's equity (credit Delivery Service Fees).
20	Received $3,500 for providing delivery services.	An asset increases (debit Cash). An increase in revenue increases owner's equity (credit Delivery Service Fees).
23	Christopher Johns invested an additional $5,000 in the business.	An asset increases (debit Cash). Owner's equity increases (credit Christopher Johns, Capital).
25	Received $1,500 from the Scientific Publishing Company on account.	An asset increases (debit Cash). An asset decreases (credit Accounts Receivable).
27	Bought an office safe for $1,500 on credit from the Kelly Safe Company.	An asset increases (debit Office Equipment). A liability increases (credit Accounts Payable).
29	Paid $2,500 for the truck drivers' semimonthly wages.	An increase in expenses decreases owner's equity (debit Wages Expense). An asset decreases (credit Cash).
30	Provide delivery services for $6,000 on credit to Bio-Tech, Inc.	An asset increases (debit Accounts Receivable). An increase in revenue increases owner's equity (credit Delivery Service Fees).
30	Christopher Johns withdrew $1,800 from the business for his personal use.	Owner's equity decreases (debit Christopher Johns, Withdrawals). An asset decreases (credit Cash).

Recording Transactions in the Journal

GENERAL JOURNAL Page 1

	Date		Description	Post Ref.	Debit	Credit
1	20 XX					
2	Nov	1	Cash		32 000 00	
3			Accounts Receivable		2 000 00	
4			Office Equipment		12 000 00	
5			Delivery Trucks		60 000 00	
6			Accounts Payable			20 000 00
7			Christopher Johns, Capital			86 000 00
8			Investment in the business			
9						
10		1	Rent Expense		1 800 00	
11			Cash			1 800 00
12			Paid November rent.			
13						
14		5	Office Equipment		1 000 00	
15			Cash			1 000 00
16			Purchased computer.			
17						
18		6	Cash		650 00	
19			Delivery Service Fees			650 00
20			Provided delivery services.			

GENERAL JOURNAL   Page 1

Date		Description	Post Ref.	Debit	Credit
20XX					
	10	Accounts Payable		400 00	
		Cash			400 00
		Paid Kenworth Truck Sales			
		on account.			
	13	Truck Expense		150 00	
		Cash			150 00
		Paid for gasoline and oil.			
	15	Wages Expense		2 500 00	
		Cash			2 500 00
		Paid semimonthly wages.			
	18	Accounts Receivable		2 400 00	
		Delivery Service Fees			2 400 00
		Provided services on credit to			
		Riverview Medical Center.			
				114 900 00	114 900 00

GENERAL JOURNAL   Page 2

Date		Description	Post Ref.	Debit	Credit
20XX					
Nov	20	Cash		3 500 00	
		Delivery Service Fees			3 500 00
		Provided delivery services.			
	23	Cash		5 000 00	
		Christopher Johns, Capital			5 000 00
		Additional investment.			
	25	Cash		1 500 00	
		Accounts Receivable			1 500 00
		Received cash from Scientific			
		Publishing Company on account.			
	27	Office Equipment		1 500 00	
		Accounts Payable			1 500 00
		Bought office safe from Kelly Safe			
		Company on credit.			
	29	Wages Expense		2 500 00	
		Cash			2 500 00
		Paid semimonthly wages.			
	30	Accounts Receivable		6 000 00	
		Delivery Service Fees			6 000 00
		Provided service on credit to			
		Bio-Tech, Inc.			
	30	Christopher Johns, Withdrawals		1 800 00	
		Cash			1 800 00
		Withdrawal by the owner.			
				21 800 00	21 800 00

> **WWW Inquiry**
> Find the URL address for America Online. What are the beginning and ending dates for America Online's fiscal year?

Note the pencil footings at the bottom of page 1 of the general journal and after the last entry on page 2. These footings are entered to prove that the total debits equal the total credits.

Journal entries are recorded in ink. No erasures are made. If a debit footing does not agree with a credit footing, an error has been made in recording an amount. To correct the error, a single line is drawn through the incorrect amount and the correct amount is written above it, and the correction is initialed as shown below. Then the pencil footing is erased and corrected.

General Journal

4	30	Christopher Johns, Withdrawals	1 800 00	1 800 00	4
5		Cash		800 00 *M.S*	5
6		Withdrawal by the owner.			6
7			21 800 00	21 800 00	7
8					8

An entry may require more than one debit or credit because more than two accounts may be affected. For example, an automobile repair shop may have separate accounts for its revenue from repairs and its revenue from towing. If a customer pays $100, of which $75 is for repairs and $25 is for towing, the entry would be journalized as shown below. Note that the debit is recorded before the credits and that the total of the debits and the total of the credits are equal. No matter how many accounts are involved in an entry, the debits and credits must always add up to equal dollar amounts.

General Journal

4	2	Cash	1 00 —		4
5		Repair Service Fees		75 —	5
6		Towing Service Fees		25 —	6
7		Provided repair and towing services.			7
8					8

Compound Entry: Journal entry with more than one debit or credit.

An entry that has more than one debit or credit is called a ***compound entry.*** The opening entry shown on page 50 is another example of a compound entry.

Instead of writing two zeros (00) in the cents column, many bookkeepers, accounting clerks, and accountants prefer to use a dash (-) to show that there are no cents. This is illustrated by the previous entry. Either method is acceptable as long as it is used consistently in the accounting records.

CHAPTER 7 SUMMARY

- Entering transactions in T accounts is not adequate for providing complete information about business activities. In addition to recording information in accounts, there is a need for a chronological (day-by-day) record of transactions. This record is called a journal.

- The journal is used to list essential information about each transaction as it occurs. The journal is known as the record of original entry because it is the first accounting record of a transaction.

- The general journal is a common type of journal.

- A systematically arranged list of a business's accounts is known as a chart of accounts. The chart shows account classifications (assets, liabilities, owner's equity, revenue, and expenses) as well as the name and number of each account. The number is used for identification and reference purposes.

- A journal entry may contain more than one debit or credit. This type of entry is called a compound entry. No matter how many accounts are involved, the total dollar amounts of the debits and credits in any one entry must be equal.

CHAPTER APPLICATIONS

EXERCISES

Complete the following assignments on the forms provided in your workbook.

EXERCISE 7–1

Establishing a chart of accounts. The accountant for the Florence Garage has recommended that the following accounts be used by the firm.

Instructions

1. Arrange the accounts according to the following classifications: assets, liabilities, owner's equity, revenue and expenses.
2. Assign an account number to each of the accounts, and prepare a chart of accounts.

Rent Expense	Accounts Receivable
Cash	Telephone Expense
Accounts Payable	Shannon Jobst, Withdrawals
Office Equipment	Towing Equipment
Salaries Expense	Repair Service Fees
Towing Service Fees	Shannon Jobst, Capital

EXERCISE 7–2

Journalizing transactions.

Instructions:

1. Journalize the following transactions that occurred at the Sikora Accounting Service during May of the current year.

Transactions:

May 5 Michael Sikora invested $15,000 cash and $5,000 of office equipment in his business.

10 Purchased two computers for $7,600 from Computer Systems. Paid $2,000 down and agreed to pay the balance in 30 days.

EXERCISE 7–3

Journalizing transactions.
Refer to Exercise 4–4 on page 30.

Instructions

1. Journalize the transactions. Use January 20 as the date for Transaction (a) and January 31 as the date for all other transactions.

PROBLEMS

Complete all assigned problems on the forms provided in your workbook.

PROBLEM 7–1

Journalizing transactions. Wilbur Clemens bought the Delta Cleaning Service on July 1 of the current year. His balance sheet was as follows:

DELTA CLEANING SERVICE
BALANCE SHEET
JULY 1, 20XX

Assets		Liabilities and Owner's Equity	
Cash	$7,000	Liabilities	
Accounts Receivable	2,250	Accounts Payable	$8,000
Supplies	200	Owner's Equity	
Cleaning Equipment	16,550	Wilbur Clemens, Capital	20,750
Office Equipment	2,750	Total Liabilities and	
Total Assets	$28,750	Owner's Equity	$28,750

Instructions:

1. Record the opening entry. Number the journal page 1, and enter the current year in the Date column.
2. Journalize the transactions for July, which are given below. Use the accounts listed in the chart of accounts that follows.
3. Pencil-foot at the bottom of each journal page and after the last transaction.

CHART OF ACCOUNTS

Assets		Revenue	
101	Cash	401	Cleaning Service Fees
103	Accounts Receivable		
104	Supplies	**Expenses**	
111	Cleaning Equipment	501	Rent Expense
112	Office Equipment	502	Telephone Expense
		503	Repairs and Maintenance Expense
Liabilities		504	Salaries Expense
202	Accounts Payable		

Owner's Equity
301 Wilbur Clemens, Capital
302 Wilbur Clemens, Withdrawals
399 Income Summary*

*This account is explained and used in Chapter 10.

Transactions:

July	1	Paid $850 for July rent.
	4	Purchased supplies for $570 on credit from Remco Cleaning Supplies.
	6	Received $350 for window cleaning services.
	8	Paid $35 for office equipment repairs.
	12	Provided floor waxing services for $450 on credit to the Manor Hotel.
	15	Paid $900 for salaries.
	18	Received $325 for cleaning and shampooing carpets.
	21	Received the $150 balance due from the Central Advertising Agency.
	25	Paid the Morsan Equipment Company $1,000 on account.
	25	Provided cleaning services for $275 on credit to the Central Advertising Agency.
	26	Purchased steam cleaning machines for $2,100 on credit from the Morsan Equipment Company.
	27	Received $300 on account from the Manor Hotel.
	28	Clemens withdrew $400 from the business for his personal use.
	31	Paid $900 for salaries.
	31	Paid $125 for the telephone bill.

Save your work for use in Problem 8–1.

PROBLEM 7–2

Journalizing transactions. Molly Gardzinski bought the Pacific Delivery Company on August 1 of the current year. The company offers two types of service—delivery by messenger and delivery by truck. Because Gardzinski wants to know her revenue from each type of service, she will use two revenue accounts. Her balance sheet is shown below.

Instructions:

1. Record the opening entry. Number the journal page 1, and enter the current year in the Date column.
2. Journalize the transactions for August. Use the accounts listed in the chart of accounts that follows.
3. Pencil-foot at the bottom of each journal page and after the last transaction.

PACIFIC DELIVERY COMPANY
BALANCE SHEET
AUGUST 1, 20XX

Assets		Liabilities and Owner's Equity	
Cash	$8,500	Liabilities	
Accounts Receivable	2,800	Accounts Payable	$4,600
Office Equipment	5,700	Owner's Equity	
Delivery Equipment	15,800	Molly Gardzinski, Capital	28,200
Total Assets	$32,800	Total Liabilities and Owner's Equity	$32,800

Transactions:

Aug.	1	Paid $960 for August rent.
	2	Received $1,580 for truck deliveries.
	3	Gardzinski invested an additional $1,000 in the business.
	4	Provided messenger service for $260 on credit to Martin Stockbrokers.
	7	Bought office equipment from Micro Center for $625. Paid $325 down and agreed to pay the balance in 30 days.
	10	Provided truck deliveries for $450 on credit and messenger service for $230 on credit to Larson's Department Store. The total amount billed to the store was $680.
	12	Paid $50 for gasoline and oil for the delivery truck.
	14	Received $70 from Klein Stores on account.
	15	Paid $1,200 in semimonthly wages for the truck driver and the messenger.
	16	Paid $86 for the telephone bill.
	18	Paid $500 to Ross Trucks on account.
	20	Bought a new tire for the delivery truck for $75 and agreed to pay the Central Garage in 30 days.
	24	Received $1,850 for truck deliveries and $450 for messenger service. The total cash received was $2,300.
	29	Paid $125 for truck repairs.
	31	Paid $1,200 in semimonthly wages to the truck driver and the messenger.
	31	Gardzinski withdrew $1,000 from the business for her personal use.
	31	Received $720 for truck deliveries and $340 for messenger service. The Total cash received was $1,060.

CHART OF ACCOUNTS

Assets
101 Cash
103 Accounts Receivable
111 Office Equipment
112 Delivery Equipment

Liabilities
202 Accounts Payable

Owner's Equity
301 Molly Gardzinski, Capital
302 Molly Gardzinski, Withdrawals
399 Income Summary*

Revenue
401 Truck Delivery Fees
402 Messenger Service Fees

Expenses
501 Rent Expense
502 Delivery Expense
503 Wages Expense
504 Office Expense

*This account is explained and used in Chapter 10.

Save your work for use in Problem 8–2.

CASE STUDY

Write the answer to the case study on the form provided in your workbook.

Using the General Journal

Craig Bowen owns a carburetor repair service. In the early stages of his business he used informal T accounts to keep track of his flow of business. He kept a running balance in each of the T accounts so he always knew the balance of each account.

However, when he tried to retrieve information about a particular transaction, he had difficulty tracking down the sequence of activity. A friend told him about the use of a general journal to analyze and record transactions.

Critical Thinking

- *Why should Bowen use a general journal? What advantage does the journal present to him?*
- *Considering accepted accounting practices, would there ever be a reason not to use a general journal?*

CHAPTER EIGHT

The General Ledger

Accounting Terminology

- Balance ledger form
- General ledger
- Ledger
- Posting
- Posting reference

OBJECTIVES

Upon completion of this chapter, you should be able to:

1. Post entries from a general journal to general ledger accounts.
2. Set up and arrange the general ledger accounts.
3. Complete the Balance columns of the general ledger accounts.
4. Correct errors in the general ledger.
5. Prepare a trial balance from the general ledger accounts.

INTRODUCTION

The journal gives a complete chronological record of a business's transactions. However, it is also necessary to sort this information so that related facts can be grouped and summarized. For example, all facts about cash must be grouped together. All facts about accounts payable transactions must also be grouped together. This is done in the ***ledger.*** The ledger is a book that contains a form for each account listed in the chart of accounts.

Sorting information about transactions involves transferring it from the journal to the ledger. Thus the ledger becomes the second record of transactions and is often called a record of final entry. The process of transferring information about transactions from the journal to the ledger is known as ***posting.***

Ledger account forms with columns are used instead of T accounts. An example of a four-column ***balance ledger form*** is shown below. ■

Ledger: Record that contains accounts.

Posting: Transferring information from the journal to the ledger.

Balance Ledger Form: Form of ledger account that always shows the account balance.

■ LEDGER ACCOUNT

- The account name and number are written at the top of each account.
- Four money columns follow the columns for the date, description, and posting reference.
- The first money column is used for entering debit amounts.
- The second is used for entering credit amounts.
- The third is used for debit balances.
- The fourth is used for credit balances.
- As each entry is posted from the journal, the account balance is recorded. Because the balance is recorded after each transaction, there is no need to pencil-foot accounts to compute their balances at the end of a period.

Balance Ledger Form

ACCOUNT Cash   ACCOUNT NO. 101

Date	Description	Post Ref.	Debit	Credit	Balance Debit	Balance Credit

■ POSTING TO THE LEDGER

The illustrations below show how the general journal entry for the payment of rent is posted to the ledger accounts. Note the following steps in posting the debit item from the general journal.

1. The year, month, and day are entered in the Date column. (After the first entry, the year and the month are not recorded except when continuing onto another page or when the year or the month changes.)
2. The Description column of the account is not used for most transactions. However, it is available for any special notations that might be helpful.
3. A J (for general journal) and the number of the journal page from which the entry came are written in the **Posting Reference** column of the account. Thus page 1 of the general journal would be recorded as J1. This makes it easy to trace the information in the ledger account back to the original journal entry.
4. The amount is entered in the Debit column of the ledger account being debited.
5. After the amount is recorded, the new balance of the account is entered in the appropriate balance column. In this case, the Debit Balance column is used.
6. The number of the ledger account is recorded in the Posting Reference column of the journal to show that the debit item was posted.

The credit item is then posted to the ledger account being credited by following similar steps. However, the amount is entered in the Credit column of the ledger account form. Study the posting of the rent payment to the Cash account shown below.

Posting Reference: The journal and page number of the entry.

GENERAL JOURNAL — Page 1

Date	Description	Post Ref.	Debit	Credit
20XX				
Nov. 1	Rent Expense		1 800 00	
	Cash			1 800 00
	Paid November rent.			

ACCOUNT Rent Expense — **ACCOUNT NO.** 501

Date	Description	Post Ref.	Debit	Credit	Balance Debit	Balance Credit
20XX Nov. 1	❷	❸ J1	❹ 1 800 00		❺ 1 800 00	

❶

GENERAL JOURNAL — Page 1

Date	Description	Post Ref.	Debit	Credit
20XX				
Nov. 1	Rent Expense	501	1 800 00	
	Cash	❻		1 800 00
	Paid November rent.			

ACCOUNT Cash — **ACCOUNT NO.** 101

Date	Description	Post Ref.	Debit	Credit	Balance Debit	Balance Credit
20XX Nov. 1		J1	32 000 00		32 000 00	
1		J1		1 800 00	30 200 00	

Posting to the Ledger

Posting Procedure:
- Enter date in account.
- Enter explanation in account if one is needed.
- Enter posting reference (journal page number) in account.
- Enter amount in account.
- Enter balance in account.
- Enter posting reference (account number) in the journal.

WWW Inquiry
Find the URL address for Outback Steak House. Search for information on quarterly reports, specifically the 3rd quarter of last year. What time period did this cover? What was the reported net income for the 3rd quarter of last year?

GENERAL JOURNAL   Page 1

Date	Description	Post Ref.	Debit	Credit
20 XX				
Nov. 1	Rent Expense	501	1 800 00	
	Cash	101		1 800 00
	Paid November rent.			

Note that the balance of $30,200 is computed and entered in the Debit Balance column. Then the number of the Cash account (101) is recorded in the Posting Reference column of the journal to show that the credit has been posted.

■ SETTING UP AND USING ACCOUNTS IN THE GENERAL LEDGER

Remember that an account must be provided for each financial item involved in the business—assets, liabilities, and owner's equity (including revenue and expenses). To make posting as simple as possible, a separate ledger sheet is used for each account. All accounts together make up the *general ledger.*

General Ledger: Entire group of accounts for a business's assets, liabilities, and owner's equity.

As discussed in Chapter 7, the accountant for Guaranteed Delivery prepared a chart of accounts (page 49) and recorded the opening entry in the general journal. Then the accountant set up a general ledger account for each item shown on the chart of accounts. The accountant did this by writing the account names and numbers at the top of the ledger sheets. Then the accountant posted the opening entry from the general journal to the general ledger.

When the general ledger accounts are set up, they are arranged in the order that they appear on the chart of accounts. This order will make it easy to prepare the financial statements. Note that the balance sheet accounts are placed first—assets accounts, liability accounts, owner's capital account, and owner's withdrawals account. Next come the income statement accounts—revenue accounts and expense accounts.

WWW Inquiry
Find the URL address for Coca-Cola. Who is the independent auditor that audited the financial statements prepared by Coca-Cola for its last fiscal year? (Hint: Go to the Report of Independent Auditors.)

After the transactions of Guaranteed Delivery have been entered in the general journal, they are posted to the general ledger. This is done on a daily basis in order to have up-to-date information in the accounts at all times.

Study the illustrations of the journal and the accounts below through page 61. Note the following about the illustrations.

- The account numbers in the journal are recorded as each item is posted. They show that the items were transferred from the journal to the ledger.

- In the ledger, the year and the month are written once. Only the day is used for later entries. (As already discussed, the month and year are not recorded again on the ledger sheet until there is a change.)

- The entries in the ledger accounts are recorded in ink. No erasures are made. If there is an error, it is corrected by following the procedures described on page 52.

- The posting reference in the ledger accounts changes from J1 to J2 when entries are posted from a new page of the journal.

Posting to the Ledger

GENERAL JOURNAL   Page 1

Date	Description	Post Ref.	Debit	Credit
20 XX				
Nov. 1	Cash	101	32 000 00	
	Accounts Receivable	102	2 000 00	
	Office Equipment	111	12 000 00	
	Delivery Trucks	112	60 000 00	
	Accounts Payable	201		20 000 00
	Christopher Johns, Capital	301		86 000 00
	Investment in the business.			

GENERAL JOURNAL   Page 1

	Date		Description	Post Ref.	Debit	Credit
1	20	XX				
2	Nov.	1	Rent Expense	501	1 800 00	
3			Cash	101		1 800 00
4			Paid November rent.			
5		5	Office Equipment	111	1 000 00	
6			Cash	101		1 000 00
7			Purchased computer.			
8		6	Cash	101	650 00	
9			Delivery Service Fees	401		650 00
10			Provided delivery services.			
11		10	Accounts Payable	201	400 00	
12			Cash	101		400 00
13			Paid Kenworth Truck Sales			
14			on account.			
15		13	Truck Expense	502	150 00	
16			Cash	101		150 00
17			Paid for gasoline and oil.			
18		15	Wages Expense	503	2 500 00	
19			Cash	101		2 500 00
20			Paid semimonthly wages.			
21		18	Accounts Receivable	102	2 400 00	
22			Delivery Service Fees	401		2 400 00
23			Provided services on credit to			
24			Riverview Medical Center			
25					114 900 00	114 900 00

GENERAL JOURNAL   Page 2

	Date		Description	Post Ref.	Debit	Credit
1	20	XX				
2	Nov.	20	Cash	101	3 500 00	
3			Delivery Service Fees	401		3 500 00
4			Provided delivery services.			
5		23	Cash	101	5 000 00	
6			Christopher Johns, Capital	301		5 000 00
7			Additional investment.			
8		25	Cash	101	1 500 00	
9			Accounts Receivable	102		1 500 00
10			Received cash from Scientific			
11			Publishing Company on account.			
12		27	Office Equipment	111	1 500 00	
13			Accounts Payable	201		1 500 00
14			Bought office safe from Kelly			
15			Safe Company on credit.			
16		29	Wages Expense	503	2 500 00	
17			Cash	101		2 500 00
18			Paid semimonthly wages.			
19		30	Accounts Receivables	102	6 000 00	
20			Delivery Service Fees	401		6 000 00
21			Provided Services Bio-Tec Inc.			
22		30	Christopher Johns, Withdrawals	302	1 800 00	
23			Cash	101		1 800 00
24			Withdrawal by the owner			
25					21 800 00	21 800 00

ACCOUNT: Cash — ACCOUNT NO. 101

Date	Description	Post Ref.	Debit	Credit	Balance Debit	Balance Credit
20XX Nov. 1		J1	32 000 00		32 000 00	
1		J1		1 800 00	30 200 00	
5		J1		1 000 00	29 200 00	
6		J1	650 00		29 850 00	
10		J1		400 00	29 450 00	
13		J1		150 00	29 300 00	
15		J1		2 500 00	26 800 00	
20		J2	3 500 00		30 300 00	
23		J2	5 000 00		35 300 00	
25		J2	1 500 00		36 800 00	
29		J2		2 500 00	34 300 00	
30		J2		1 800 00	32 500 00	

ACCOUNT: Accounts Receivable — ACCOUNT NO. 102

Date	Description	Post Ref.	Debit	Credit	Balance Debit	Balance Credit
20XX Nov. 1		J1	2 000 00		2 000 00	
18		J1	2 400 00		4 400 00	
25		J2		1 500 00	2 900 00	
30		J2	6 000 00		8 900 00	

ACCOUNT: Office Equipment — ACCOUNT NO. 111

Date	Description	Post Ref.	Debit	Credit	Balance Debit	Balance Credit
20XX Nov. 1		J1	12 000 00		12 000 00	
5		J1	1 000 00		13 000 00	
27		J2	1 500 00		14 500 00	

ACCOUNT: Delivery Trucks — ACCOUNT NO. 112

Date	Description	Post Ref.	Debit	Credit	Balance Debit	Balance Credit
20XX Nov. 1		J1	60 000 00		60 000 00	

ACCOUNT: Accounts Payable — ACCOUNT NO. 201

Date	Description	Post Ref.	Debit	Credit	Balance Debit	Balance Credit
20XX Nov. 1		J1		20 000 00		20 000 00
10		J1	400 00			19 600 00
27		J2		1 500 00		21 100 00

ACCOUNT	Christopher Johns, Capital						ACCOUNT NO.	301
			Post				Balance	
Date		Description	Ref.	Debit		Credit	Debit	Credit
20 XX								
Nov. 1			J1			86 000 00		86 000 00
23			J2			5 000 00		91 000 00

ACCOUNT	Christopher Johns, Withdrawals						ACCOUNT NO.	302
			Post				Balance	
Date		Description	Ref.	Debit		Credit	Debit	Credit
20 XX								
Nov. 30			J2	1 800 00			1 800 00	

ACCOUNT	Delivery Service Fees						ACCOUNT NO.	401
			Post				Balance	
Date		Description	Ref.	Debit		Credit	Debit	Credit
20 XX								
Nov. 6			J1			650 00		650 00
18			J1			2 400 00		3 050 00
20			J2			3 500 00		6 550 00
30			J2			6 000 00		12 550 00

ACCOUNT	Rent Expense						ACCOUNT NO.	501
			Post				Balance	
Date		Description	Ref.	Debit		Credit	Debit	Credit
20 XX								
Nov. 1			J1	1 800 00			1 800 00	

ACCOUNT	Truck Expense						ACCOUNT NO.	502
			Post				Balance	
Date		Description	Ref.	Debit		Credit	Debit	Credit
20 XX								
Nov. 13			J1	150 00			150 00	

ACCOUNT	Wages Expense						ACCOUNT NO.	503
			Post				Balance	
Date		Description	Ref.	Debit		Credit	Debit	Credit
20 XX								
Nov. 15			J1	2 500 00			2 500 00	
29			J2	2 500 00			5 000 00	

Posting to the Ledger (continued)

■ COMPLETING THE BALANCE COLUMNS OF THE ACCOUNTS

As each entry is posted from the journal, the ledger account balance is computed and recorded in either the Debit Balance or the Credit Balance column. The following procedure is used to complete the Balance columns.

- If an account has no balance and an amount is entered in the Debit column, the same amount is recorded in the Debit Balance column. Refer to the first entry in the Cash account on page 60.

- If an account has a debit balance and an amount is entered in the Debit column, the two amounts are added. The total is recorded in the Debit Balance column. This is shown in the entry in the Cash account on November 6. See page 60. The $650 debit is added to the debit balance of $29,200 from November 5.

- If an account has a debit balance and an amount is entered in the Credit column, the amount of the credit is subtracted from the debit balance. If the credit is smaller than the debit balance, the difference is entered in the Debit Balance column, as shown in the November 10 entry in the Cash account on page 60. Here the $400 credit is subtracted from the $29,850 debit balance, leaving $29,450 as the debit balance on November 10.

   If the credit amount is larger than the debit balance, the difference is recorded in the Credit Balance column.

- If an account has no balance and an amount is entered in the Credit column, the same amount is also entered in the Credit Balance column. Such is the case with the first entry in Accounts Payable on page 60.

- If an account has a credit balance and an amount is entered in the Credit column, the two amounts are added. The total is entered in the Credit Balance column. Refer to the entry on November 27 in Accounts Payable on page 60. The $1,500 credit is added to the $19,600 credit balance from the previous entry.

- If an account has a credit balance and an amount is entered in the Debit column, the amount of the debit is subtracted from the credit balance. If the debit is smaller than the credit balance, the difference is entered in the Credit Balance column. This is illustrated in the November 10 entry in Accounts Payable on page 60. In this case, the debit of $400 is subtracted from the $20,000 credit balance, resulting in a credit balance of $19,600 on November 10.

   If the debit is larger than the credit balance, the difference is recorded in the Debit Balance column.

■ CORRECTING ERRORS IN THE LEDGER

If an amount is incorrectly posted or posted to the wrong account, the error is corrected by drawing a single line through the incorrect data and writing the correct information above it. However, if the error involves a journal entry that was incorrectly recorded and posted to the wrong account, then another entry is required to correct the error. In the entry shown below, a purchase of office supplies was erroneously debited to Equipment and posted to the Equipment account.

Original Journal Entry

GENERAL JOURNAL — Page 1

Date	Description	Post Ref.	Debit	Credit
20 XX				
Dec. 1	Equipment	112	300 00	
	Accounts Payable	201		300 00
	Purchased supplies on credit from			
	Sterling Stationery.			

Because Supplies, rather than Equipment, should have been debited, the following entry is recorded to correct the error. Note the explanation in the entry.

Correcting Journal Entry

GENERAL JOURNAL — Page 1

Date	Description	Post Ref.	Debit	Credit
20 XX				
Dec. 31	Supplies	103	300 00	
	Equipment	112		300 00
	To correct December 1 entry in			
	which Equipment was debited in error.			

After the December 31 entry is posted, the ledger accounts are corrected and show the following balances. Notice that the Accounts Payable account was not affected by the error and, therefore, was not involved in the correcting entry.

Posting Correcting Entry

ACCOUNT Equipment   ACCOUNT NO. 112

Date	Description	Post Ref.	Debit	Credit	Balance Debit	Balance Credit
20XX Dec. 1	Balance	✓			5 000 00	
1		J12	300 00		5 300 00	
31		J12		300 00	5 000 00	

ACCOUNT Supplies   ACCOUNT NO. 103

Date	Description	Post Ref.	Debit	Credit	Balance Debit	Balance Credit
20XX Dec. 31		J12	300 00		300 00	

■ PROVING THE LEDGER

At the end of November, the account balances in the ledger for Guaranteed Delivery are used to prepare the trial balance shown below. The trial balance tests the accuracy of the entries in the ledger. Note that the account numbers are recorded in the first column of the trial balance for identification and reference purposes.

Although the journal, the ledger, and the trial balance are shown together in this chapter, keep in mind that each is a separate record and serves a different purpose. The journal provides a day-by-day listing of transactions. The ledger sorts this information and groups it by accounts. The trial balance proves the equality of the debits and credits in the ledger.

GUARANTEED DELIVERY
TRIAL BALANCE
NOVEMBER 30, 20XX

Acct. No.	Account Name	Debit	Credit
101	Cash	32 500 00	
102	Accounts Receivable	8 900 00	
111	Office Equipment	14 500 00	
112	Delivery Trucks	60 000 00	
201	Accounts Payable		21 100 00
301	Christopher Johns, Capital		91 000 00
302	Christopher Johns, Withdrawals	1 800 00	
401	Delivery Service Fees		12 550 00
501	Rent Expense	1 800 00	
502	Truck Expense	150 00	
503	Wages Expense	5 000 00	
	Totals	124 650 00	124 650 00

CHAPTER 8 SUMMARY

- The facts about a business's transactions are sorted and grouped by transferring the information from the journal to the *ledger.*

- An account must be provided in the *ledger* for each financial item in the business.

- The process of transferring information from the journal to the ledger is known as *posting*. Ledger account forms with columns are used to record detailed information about each entry.
- In the posting process, *posting references* are recorded to permit easy tracing of an entry from the journal to the ledger or from the ledger to the journal.
- Ledger accounts are arranged in an easy-to-follow order for preparing financial statements. Balance sheet accounts are first, and income statement accounts follow.
- After all postings for a month have been completed, a trial balance is taken to prove the accuracy of the ledger.

CHAPTER APPLICATIONS

EXERCISES

Complete the following assignments on the forms provided in your workbook.

EXERCISE 8–1

Recording data in four-column balance ledger accounts. T accounts for Cash and Accounts Payable are shown below.

Cash

20XX			20XX		
Jan.	1	16,000	Jan.	5	1,000
	10	2,000		15	500
	20	1,500		30	3,000
	15,000	19,500			4,500

Accounts Payable

20XX			20XX		
Jan.	7	500	Jan.	3	2,500
	14	500		28	1,000
	21	500		2,000	3,500
		1,500			

Instructions:

1. Your workbook contains four-column ledger accounts for Cash and Accounts Payable. The same entries that appear in the T accounts have been posted to the ledger. Calculate the balance after each posting.
2. Verify that your final balance for each account is the same as the balance shown in the T account.

EXERCISE 8–2

Correcting errors in the ledger. The following errors were found in the general ledger account.

Instructions

1. Determine how each of the following errors in the ledger accounts should be corrected.
2. If an entry is required to correct the error, give the entry.

Errors:

a. A $250 credit to Cash was posted as a credit of $25.
b. A $75 debit to Delivery Equipment should have been recorded as a debit to Repairs Expense in the journal and posted to Repairs Expense in the ledger.
c. A $400 debit balance in Telephone Expense was incorrectly recorded as $40.
d. A $1,200 debit balance in Accounts Receivable was entered in the Credit Balance column.
e. A $74 debit to Cash was posted as a debit of $47.

EXERCISE 8–3

Correcting the ledger and preparing a trial balance. The trial balance shown below does not balance. In examining the ledger accounts and journal entries, you discovered the errors listed below.

Instructions:

1. Determine the correct ledger account balances and prepare a new trial balance.

AMEND GRAPHICS
TRIAL BALANCE
JUNE 30, 20XX

Cash	$6,754	
Accounts Receivable	1,655	
Equipment	4,000	
Accounts Payable		$4,010
Zachary Amend, Capital		6,000
Zachary Amend, Withdrawals	1,000	
Fees		5,000
Rent Expense	1,600	
Telephone Expense	250	
Advertising Expense	10	
Totals	$15,269	$15,010

Errors:

a. A $250 received from a customer on account was not posted to Accounts Receivable.
b. A $500 withdrawal by the owner was journalized, but the entry was not posted to the ledger accounts.

c. A $54 credit to Accounts Receivable was posted as a $45 credit.

d. An entry for $800 debiting Rent Expense and crediting Cash was posted twice.

e. An entry for $100, debiting Advertising Expense and crediting Accounts Payable, was incorrectly posted to both ledger accounts as $10.

PROBLEMS

Complete all assigned problems on the forms provided in your workbook.

PROBLEM 8–1

Posting and preparing a trial balance. The chart of accounts for the Delta Cleaning Service is given on page 53 of the text.

Instructions:

1. Use the chart of accounts to open the ledger accounts. Transfer balances to General Ledger.
2. Post the journal entries that were recorded in Problem 7–1.
3. Prepare a trial balance as of July 31 of the current year.

Save your work for use in Problem 9–1.

PROBLEM 8–2

Posting and preparing a trial balance. The chart of accounts for the Pacific Delivery Company is given on page 54 of the text.

1. Use the chart of accounts to open the ledger accounts.
2. Post the journal entries that were recorded in Problem 7–2.
3. Prepare a trial balance as of August 31 of the current year.

Save your work for use in Problem 9–2.

Case Study

Write the answer to the case study on the form provided in your workbook.

Using Accounts in the General Ledger

Jay Stephens owns a photography service. Stephens initially recorded his accounts very informally. His accountant convinced him to use a general journal to analyze and record transactions and a general ledger to track the accounts. The process of analyzing and recording transactions in a general journal made sense to Stephens, but he was not sure about the use of accounts in the general ledger.

Critical Thinking

- What could you tell Stephens about accepted accounting procedures and the use of ledger accounts?

CHAPTER NINE

The Worksheet and the Financial Statements

Accounting Terminology

- Account-form balance sheet
- Report-form balance sheet
- Worksheet

OBJECTIVES

Upon completion of this chapter, you should be able to:

1. Record a trial balance on a worksheet.
2. Complete the worksheet.
3. Prepare the income statement, statement of owner's equity, and balance sheet from the worksheet.

INTRODUCTION

Journalizing transactions and posting them to the ledger are important activities. They provide the figures needed to determine the results of operations and the financial position of the business at the end of the accounting period.

Up to now, the financial statements have been prepared directly from the trial balance. However, a special form called a ***worksheet*** is often used to compute the net income or net loss and to plan the financial statements before they are prepared. This form serves the same purpose as a blueprint made by an architect in planning a house before it is built.

Note that the worksheet illustrated below has a series of columns that allow the trial balance items to be separated according to their use on the income statement or the balance sheet. ∎

Worksheet: Form used to compute the net income or net loss and to plan the preparation of financial statements.

GUARANTEED DELIVERY
WORKSHEET
MONTH ENDED NOVEMBER 30, 20XX

Acct. No.	Account Name	Trial Balance Debit	Trial Balance Credit	Income Statement Debit	Income Statement Credit	Balance Sheet Debit	Balance Sheet Credit
101	Cash	32 500 00				32 500 00	
102	Accounts Receivable	8 900 00				8 900 00	
111	Office Equipment	14 500 00				14 500 00	
112	Delivery Trucks	60 000 00				60 000 00	
201	Accounts Payable		21 100 00				21 100 00
301	Christopher Johns, Capital		91 000 00				91 000 00
302	Christopher Johns, Withdrawals	1 800 00				1 800 00	
401	Delivery Service Fees		12 550 00		12 550 00		
501	Rent Expense	1 800 00		1 800 00			
502	Truck Expense	150 00		150 00			
503	Wages Expense	5 000 00		5 000 00			
	Totals	124 650 00	124 650 00	6 950 00	12 550 00	117 700 00	112 100 00

■ PREPARING THE WORKSHEET

Since the worksheet is only a plan, it is usually prepared in pencil. The partially completed worksheet for Guaranteed Delivery for the month ended November 30 of the current year is shown on the previous page.

Note that the trial balance is recorded in the first two money columns of the worksheet. This is the same trial balance that was shown on page 63. Proceeding item by item, the accountant now transfers the trial balance amounts to the additional pairs of money columns. Each amount is recorded in the one money column where it belongs.

1. The debits for balance sheet items are listed in the Debit column of the Balance Sheet section. These amounts are the balances of the asset accounts and the owner's drawing account.
2. The credits for balance sheet items are listed in the Credit column of the Balance Sheet section. These amounts are the balances of the liability account and the owner's capital account.
3. The credits for income statement items are listed in the Credit column of the Income Statement section. On the worksheet shown here, there is only one income statement item with a credit amount. This is the balance of the revenue account.
4. The debits for income statement items are listed in the Debit column of the Income Statement section. These amounts are the balances of the expense accounts.

Note that a debit on the trial balance remains a debit when it is transferred to the other columns; a credit on the trial balance remains a credit when it is transferred.

The columns of the Income Statement section and the Balance Sheet section are totaled after all the amounts have been transferred. Note that double lines are not drawn under these columns yet. The result of operations—the net income or net loss—must be determined before the worksheet can be completed.

> **WWW Inquiry**
> Find the URL address for McDonalds Corporation. What were the total liabilities and shareholders' equity reported on its December 31 balance sheet of last year?

■ DETERMINING THE RESULT OF OPERATIONS

After the trial balance amounts have been classified on the worksheet, the result of operations can be determined quickly.

- The total of the Debit column in the Income Statement section shows the total expenses for the period.
- The total of the Credit column in the Income Statement section shows the total revenue for the period.
- The difference between the Debit and Credit columns in the Income Statement section is the net income (or net loss) from operations. (When revenue is greater than expenses, the result is a net income. When expenses are greater than revenue, the result is a net loss.)

Since the worksheet for Guaranteed Delivery lists total expenses of $6,950 and total revenue of $12,550, the net income for November is $5,600 ($12,550 − $6,950). The net income figure is now used in completing the worksheet. This two-step process is explained below.

1. The net income figure ($5,600) is entered in the Debit column of the Income Statement section under the expense total and added to that total. The two columns of the Income Statement section will then balance (unless a math error or some other type of error has been made).
2. The net income figure is also entered in the Credit column of the Balance Sheet section. After this amount is added to the previous total of the Credit column, the two columns of the Balance Sheet section will balance (unless an error has been made).

If the business had a net loss, the amount would be entered in the Credit column of the Income Statement section and the Debit column of the Balance Sheet section.

The following illustration shows how the worksheet for Guaranteed Delivery appears after the net income is recorded and the final totals are computed.

GUARANTEED DELIVERY
WORKSHEET
MONTH ENDED NOVEMBER 30, 20XX

Acct. No.	Account Name	Trial Balance Debit	Trial Balance Credit	Income Statement Debit	Income Statement Credit	Balance Sheet Debit	Balance Sheet Credit
101	Cash	32,500.00				32,500.00	
102	Accounts Receivable	8,900.00				8,900.00	
111	Office Equipment	14,500.00				14,500.00	
112	Delivery Trucks	60,000.00				60,000.00	
201	Accounts Payable		21,100.00				21,100.00
301	Christopher Johns, Capital		91,000.00				91,000.00
302	Christopher Johns, Withdrawals	1,800.00				1,800.00	
401	Delivery Service Fees		12,550.00		12,550.00		
501	Rent Expense	1,800.00		1,800.00			
502	Truck Expense	150.00		150.00			
503	Wages Expense	5,000.00		5,000.00			
	Totals	124,650.00	124,650.00	6,950.00	12,550.00	117,700.00	112,100.00
	Net Income			5,600.00			5,600.00
				12,550.00	12,550.00	117,700.00	117,700.00

Note that double lines are now drawn under the Income Statement and Balance Sheet columns to show that the worksheet is completed.

■ PREPARING FINANCIAL STATEMENTS

WWW Inquiry
Find the URL address for McDonalds Corporation. How much long-term debt does McDonalds report on its December 31 balance sheet of last year?

After the worksheet has been completed, the financial statements can be prepared easily because the planning has been done and the net income (or net loss) is known. (The value of the worksheet will become even more evident later when more complex financial statements are prepared.)

The Income Statement. The income statement for Guaranteed Delivery is illustrated below. It shows the result of operations (the net income) for November and how this result came about. The figures for the preparation of the income statement are taken from the Income Statement columns of the worksheet.

Income Statement

The amount of the net income on the Income Statement must be the same as that shown on the worksheet.

GUARANTEED DELIVERY
INCOME STATEMENT
MONTH ENDED NOVEMBER 30, 20XX

Revenue		
Delivery Service Fees		12,550.00
Operating Expenses		
Rent Expense	1,800.00	
Truck Expense	150.00	
Wages Expense	5,000.00	
Total Operating Expenses		6,950.00
Net Income		5,600.00

The Statement of Owner's Equity.
In addition to the balance sheet, Guaranteed Delivery uses a statement of owner's equity, which explains the details of the changes in owner's equity during the accounting period (see Chapter 6). When this statement is used, the Owner's Equity section of the balance sheet can be kept very simple.

Look at the statement of owner's equity below. The figures for the capital on November 1 and the additional investment are taken from the Christopher Johns, Capital account in the general ledger (see page 61). The figures for the net income and the withdrawals come from the Balance Sheet section of the worksheet. (The balance of the Christopher Johns, Withdrawals account shows the withdrawals.) The total investment, the net increase in the owner's equity, and the capital on November 30 are computed on the statement of owner's equity.

GUARANTEED DELIVERY
STATEMENT OF OWNERS EQUITY
MONTH ENDED NOVEMBER 30, 20XX

Christopher Johns, Capital, November 1		86 000 00
Additional Investment		5 000 00
Total Investment		91 000 00
Net Income	5 600 00	
Less Withdrawals	1 800 00	
Net Increase in Owner's Equity		3 800 00
Christopher Johns, Capital, November 30		94 800 00

Statement of Owner's Equity

The Balance Sheet.
After the statement of owner's equity is completed, the balance sheet is prepared to show the financial position of Guaranteed Delivery on November 30. The figures for the Assets section and the Liabilities section are taken from the Balance Sheet columns of the worksheet. Only one amount is listed in the Owner's Equity section of the balance sheet—the amount of capital on November 30. This comes from the statement of owner's equity.

GUARANTEED DELIVERY
BALANCE SHEET
NOVEMBER 30, 20XX

Assets		
Cash	32 500 00	
Accounts Receivable	8 900 00	
Office Equipment	14 500 00	
Delivery Trucks	60 000 00	
Total Assets		115 900 00
Liabilities and Owner's Equity		
Liabilities		
Accounts Payable		21 100 00
Owner's Equity		
Christopher Johns, Capital		94 800 00
Total Liabilities and Owner's Equity		115 900 00

Balance Sheet

Note: The amount of the owner's capital account is taken from the Statement of Owner's Equity.

Report-Form Balance Sheet: A balance sheet in which liabilities and owner's equity are placed under assets.

Account-Form Balance Sheet: A balance sheet in which assets are on the left side and liabilities and owner's equity are on the right side.

Note that the form of the balance sheet illustrated above is different from that shown previously. The liabilities and the owner's equity are listed below the assets instead of to the right of them. This is known as the *report-form balance sheet.* The change in arrangement does not affect the content or the equality of the statement. The totals show that the assets equal the liabilities plus the owner's equity, as they did in the *account-form balance sheet* used in earlier chapters.

CHAPTER 9 SUMMARY

- A special form known as a worksheet is often used to compute the net income or net loss and to plan the financial statements before they are prepared.

- The trial balance is completed in the first two money columns of the worksheet. Then the items on the trial balance are classified according to the financial statements on which they will appear. This is done by recording each amount in the proper statement section and column of the worksheet.

- The net income or net loss is the difference between the totals of the Debit and Credit columns in the Income Statement section of the worksheet.

- The net income is entered in two columns of the worksheet—the Debit column of the Income Statement section and the Credit column of the Balance Sheet section. A net loss would be recorded in the Credit column of the Income Statement section and the Debit column of the Balance Sheet section.

- The income statement is prepared from the figures in the Income Statement columns of the worksheet.

- The statement of owner's equity is prepared from figures in the owner's capital account in the general ledger and from figures in the Balance Sheet columns of the worksheet.

- The balance sheet is prepared from figures in the Balance Sheet columns of the worksheet and from the ending capital figures shown on the statement of owner's equity.

- In the report-form balance sheet, the liabilities and owner's equity are placed under the assets. The account-form balance sheet shows the assets on the left side and the liabilities and owner's equity on the right side.

CHAPTER APPLICATIONS

EXERCISES

Complete the following assignments using the forms provided in your workbook.

EXERCISE 9–1

Preparing a worksheet showing a net income.
The ledger account balances for InfoServices, a word processing service business, are given below.

Instructions:

1. Set up a six-column worksheet like the one shown on page 66. Use the accounts and balances to complete the worksheet for the month ended March 31 of the current year.

Save your work for use in Exercise 9–3.

Cash	$ 6,549	Janis Dofner,	
Accounts Receivable	2,050	Withdrawals	$ 950
Office Equipment	8,600	Word Processing	
Accounts Payable	1,860	Fees	3,740
Janis Dofner, Capital	14,699	Rent Expense	825
		Office Expense	1,200
		Advertising Expense	125

EXERCISE 9–2

Preparing a worksheet showing a net loss. The ledger account balances for the Ferry Studio are given below.

Instructions:

1. Set up a six-column worksheet like the one shown on page 66. Use the accounts and balances to complete the worksheet for the month ended June 30 of the current year.

Cash	$ 4,779	Thomas Ferry,	
Accounts Receivable	654	Withdrawals	$ 800
Photographic		Photography Fees	1,050
Equipment	8,927	Rent Expense	925
Accounts Payable	2,041	Advertising Expense	76
Thomas Ferry, Capital	13,197	Telephone Expense	127

Save your work for use in Exercise 9–4.

EXERCISE 9–3

Preparing financial statements. This is a continuation of Exercise 9–1. Refer to the worksheet for InfoServices completed in Exercise 9–1.

Instructions:

1. Prepare an income statement.
2. Prepare a statement of owner's equity.
3. Prepare a report-form balance sheet.

EXERCISE 9–4

Preparing financial statements. This is a continuation of Exercise 9–2. Refer to the worksheet for the Ferry Studio completed in Exercise 9–2.

Instructions:

1. Prepare an income statement.
2. Prepare a statement of owner's equity.
3. Prepare a report-form balance sheet.

PROBLEMS

Complete all assigned problems on the forms provided in your workbook.

PROBLEM 9–1

Preparing a worksheet and financial statements.
Refer to the trial balance for the Delta Cleaning Service that was completed in Problem 8–1.

Instructions:
Prepare the following.

a. A worksheet for the month ended July 31 of the current year.
b. An income statement.
c. A statement of owner's equity.
d. A report-form balance sheet.

Save your work for use in Problem 10–1.

PROBLEM 9–2

Preparing a worksheet and financial statements.
Refer to the trial balance for the Pacific Delivery Company that was completed in Problem 8–2.

Instructions:
Prepare the following.

a. A worksheet for the month ended August 31 of the current year.
b. An income statement.
c. A statement of owner's equity.
d. A report-form balance sheet.

Save your work for use in Problem 10–2.

Problem 9–3

Preparing a worksheet and financial statements.
The April 30 general ledger account balances for Midtown Cleaners are given below.

Instructions:
Complete the following.

a. A worksheet for the month ended April 30 of the current year.
b. An income statement.
c. A statement of owner's equity.
d. A report-form balance sheet.

Cash	$ 2,100	Betty Cox,	
Accounts Receivable	130	Withdrawals	$ 450
Cleaning Equipment	13,400	Cleaning Fees	1,420
Accounts Payable	520	Maintenance Expense	320
Betty Cox, Capital	15,010	Salaries Expense	500
		Utilities Expense	50

CASE STUDY

Write the answer to the Case Study on the form provided in your workbook.

Preparing Financial Statements

Sue Dintrone owns a child transportation business. Dintrone caters to parents needing desired safe and affordable transportation from school to day care where they would pick up their children after school. Dintrone understood the importance of using accepted accounting procedures in keeping accurate data when analyzing, recording, and posting daily transactions.

However, when she prepared her trial balance worksheet, she couldn't help wondering why it was necessary to prepare separate financial reports like the income statement, balance sheet, and owner's equity statement. All the information can be found on the trial balance of the worksheet. She wondered why she should go through the effort of preparing the additional statements.

Critical Thinking

- Why should Dintrone continue to follow accepted accounting practice and prepare the financial statements after preparing the worksheet?

CHAPTER TEN

Closing the Ledger

Accounting Terminology

- Accounting cycle
- Closing an account
- Closing entries
- Closing the ledger
- Income summary
- Permanent accounts
- Postclosing trial balance
- Temporary accounts

OBJECTIVES

Upon completion of this chapter, you should be able to:

1. Record closing entries.
2. Post the closing entries to the general ledger accounts.
3. Open new ledger accounts.
4. Prepare a postclosing trial balance.
5. Describe the accounting cycle.

INTRODUCTION

After the financial statements have been completed, the ledger must be made ready for the transactions of the next accounting period. ■

Consider the general ledger for Guaranteed Delivery (pages 60 through 61).

- One of the most important pieces of information about November operations is the fact that the business had a net income of $5,600. Although this fact is shown on the income statement (page 68), it does not yet appear in the business's permanent records—the journal and the ledger.

- The owner's capital account needs updating. The balance in the general ledger is now $91,000, but the statement of owner's equity (page 69) shows that it should be $94,800. This is the result of the net increase of $3,800 in owner's equity from November operations.

- The balances of the revenue and expense accounts represent transactions that took place during November. Remember that these accounts are used to determine the result of operations for each accounting period. The drawing account is another account that is used to gather information for each accounting period, and its balance must also be reduced to zero.

Closing the Ledger: Preparing the ledger at the end of a period so that it is ready to receive the next period's transactions.

Closing Entries: Journal entries that close revenue and expense accounts and transfer the net income or loss to the owner's equity account.

■ RECORDING THE CLOSING ENTRIES

The procedure used at the end of each accounting period to make the ledger ready for the next period's transactions is known as *closing the ledger.* This procedure begins with a series of *closing entries,* which are journalized and posted. The closing entries serve several purposes.

- They summarize the balances of the revenue and expense accounts so that the net income or net loss can be recorded.

- They transfer to the capital account the net increase or net decrease in owner's equity resulting from the current period's operations.

- They reduce the balances of the revenue, expense, and drawing accounts to zero so that these accounts can be used to record information for the next period.

The closing entries for Guaranteed Delivery are shown in the general journal below. Most of the information for these entries is taken from the Income Statement columns of the worksheet. Refer to the following partial worksheet for Guaranteed Delivery, which shows the accounts and balances used in recording the closing entries for November.

GUARANTEED DELIVERY
WORKSHEET
MONTH ENDED NOVEMBER 30, 20XX

Acct. No.	Account Name	Income Statement Debit	Income Statement Credit	Balance Sheet Debit	Balance Sheet Credit
302	Christopher Johns, Withdrawals			1 800 00	
401	Delivery Service Fees		12 550 00		
501	Rent Expense	1 800 00			
502	Truck Expense	150 00			
503	Wages Expense	5 000 00			
	Totals	6 950 00	12 550 00	117 700 00	112 100 00
		5 600 00			5 600 00
		12 550 00	12 550 00	117 700 00	117 700 00

Recording Closing Entries

GENERAL JOURNAL Page 3

	Date	Description	Post Ref.	Debit	Credit	
1	20XX	Closing Entries				1
2	Nov. 30	Delivery Service Fees	401	12 550 00		2
3		Income Summary	399		12 550 00	3
4		To close the revenue account				4
5		and transfer total revenue to				5
6		the summary account.				6
7						7
8	30	Income Summary	399	6 950 00		8
9		Rent Expense	501		1 800 00	9
10		Truck Expense	502		150 00	10
11		Wages Expense	503		5 000 00	11
12		To close the expense accounts				12
13		and transfer total expenses to				13
14		the summary account.				14
15						15
16	30	Income Summary	399	5 600 00		16
17		Christopher Johns, Capital	301		5 600 00	17
18		To close the summary account				18
19		and transfer net income to				19
20		the capital account.				20
21						21
22	30	Christopher Johns, Capital	301	1 800 00		22
23		Christopher Johns, Withdrawals	302		1 800 00	23
24		To close the withdrawals account				24
25		and transfer the balance to				25
26		the capital account.				26

Closing an Account: Reducing the balance of an account to zero by transferring the balance to another account.

Income Summary: An owner's equity account that is used to close accounts.

The steps needed to record the closing entries are as follows.

1. The first step is to close the revenue accounts. The revenue account balances are listed in the Income Statement Credit column. Because the Delivery Service Fees account has a credit balance of $12,550, it is closed by debiting it for this amount. Thus the balance is reduced to zero. A new account, Income Summary, is credited. This new owner's equity account is used only at the end of each period for the closing entries.

2. The second step is to close the expense accounts. The expense account balances are listed in the Income Statement Debit column. Because these accounts (Rent Expense, Truck Expense, and Wages Expense) have debit balances, each one is credited for the amount of its balance. This reduces each expense account balance to zero. The total of the Income Statement Debit column ($6,950) represents the total of all the expense account balances. This amount is debited to the Income Summary account.

3. The third step is to close the Income Summary account. This account now shows the same basic information as the income statement. The total of the revenue ($12,550) is recorded in the Credit column, and the total of the expenses ($6,950) is recorded in the Debit column. The balance of $5,600 ($12,550 − $6,950) represents the net income. The Income Summary account is closed by debiting it for $5,600 and crediting the amount to the owner's capital account.

Closing Entries
- Close revenue account to summary account.
- Close expense account to summary account.
- Close summary account to capital account.
- Close drawing account to capital account.

4. The fourth step is to close the withdrawals account. This account balance is shown in the Balance Sheet Debit column of the worksheet. The withdrawals account is closed by crediting it for $1,800 and debiting the same amount to the owner's capital account. This updates the capital account so that it shows the present capital of $94,800. Note that this amount agrees with the November 30 capital amount shown on both the statement of owner's equity and the balance sheet.

POSTING THE CLOSING ENTRIES

The posting of the closing entries to the actual ledger accounts is illustrated on pages 75 and 76. Note that an explanation is entered in each of the accounts.

Posting Closing Entries

ACCOUNT Cash   ACCOUNT NO. 101

Date	Description	Post Ref.	Debit	Credit	Balance Debit	Balance Credit
20 XX						
Nov. 1		J1	32 000 00		32 000 00	
1		J1		1 800 00	30 200 00	
5		J1		1 000 00	29 200 00	
6		J1	650 00		29 850 00	
10		J1		400 00	29 450 00	
13		J1		150 00	29 300 00	
15		J1		2 500 00	26 800 00	
20		J2	3 500 00		30 300 00	
23		J2	5 000 00		35 300 00	
25		J2	1 500 00		36 800 00	
29		J2		2 500 00	34 300 00	
30		J2		1 800 00	32 500 00	

Postclosing Entries (continued)

ACCOUNT __Accounts Receivable__ ACCOUNT NO. __102__

Date 20XX	Description	Post Ref.	Debit	Credit	Balance Debit	Balance Credit
Nov. 1		J1	2 000 00		2 000 00	
18		J1	2 400 00		4 400 00	
25		J2		1 500 00	2 900 00	
30		J2	6 000 00		8 900 00	

ACCOUNT __Office Equipment__ ACCOUNT NO. __111__

Date 20XX	Description	Post Ref.	Debit	Credit	Balance Debit	Balance Credit
Nov. 1		J1	12 000 00		12 000 00	
5		J1	1 000 00		13 000 00	
27		J2	1 500 00		14 500 00	

ACCOUNT __Delivery Trucks__ ACCOUNT NO. __112__

Date 20XX	Description	Post Ref.	Debit	Credit	Balance Debit	Balance Credit
Nov. 1		J1	60 000 00		60 000 00	

ACCOUNT __Accounts Payable__ ACCOUNT NO. __201__

Date 20XX	Description	Post Ref.	Debit	Credit	Balance Debit	Balance Credit
Nov. 1		J1		20 000 00		20 000 00
10		J1	400 00			19 600 00
27		J2		1 500 00		21 100 00

ACCOUNT __Christopher Johns, Capital__ ACCOUNT NO. __301__

Date 20XX	Description	Post Ref.	Debit	Credit	Balance Debit	Balance Credit
Nov. 1		J1		86 000 00		86 000 00
23		J2		5 000 00		91 000 00
30	Net income	J3		5 600 00		96 600 00
30	Withdrawals	J3	1 800 00			94 800 00

ACCOUNT __Christopher Johns, Withdrawals__ ACCOUNT NO. __302__

Date 20XX	Description	Post Ref.	Debit	Credit	Balance Debit	Balance Credit
Nov. 30		J2	1 800 00		1 800 00	
30	Closing	J3		1 800 00	—0—	

Postclosing Entries (continued)

ACCOUNT	Income Summary				ACCOUNT NO. 399	
Date	Description	Post Ref.	Debit	Credit	Balance Debit	Balance Credit
20XX Nov. 30	Revenue	J3		12 550 00		12 550 00
30	Expenses	J3	6 950 00			5 600 00
30	Net Income	J3	5 600 00			—0—

ACCOUNT	Delivery Service Fees				ACCOUNT NO. 401	
Date	Description	Post Ref.	Debit	Credit	Balance Debit	Balance Credit
20XX Nov. 6		J1		650 00		650 00
18		J1		2 400 00		3 050 00
20		J2		3 500 00		6 550 00
30		J2		6 000 00		12 550 00
30	Closing	J3	12 550 00			—0—

ACCOUNT	Rent Expense				ACCOUNT NO. 501	
Date	Description	Post Ref.	Debit	Credit	Balance Debit	Balance Credit
20XX Nov. 1		J1	1 800 00		1 800 00	
30	Closing	J3		1 800 00	—0—	

ACCOUNT	Truck Expense				ACCOUNT NO. 502	
Date	Description	Post Ref.	Debit	Credit	Balance Debit	Balance Credit
20XX Nov. 13		J1	150 00		150 00	
30	Closing	J3		150 00	—0—	

ACCOUNT	Wages Expense				ACCOUNT NO. 503	
Date	Description	Post Ref.	Debit	Credit	Balance Debit	Balance Credit
20XX Nov. 15		J1	2 500 00		2 500 00	
29		J2	2 500 00		5 000 00	
30	Closing	J3		5 000 00	—0—	

> **WWW Inquiry**
> Find the URL address for America Online. When was America Online founded and where is it based? (Hint: go to Management's Discussion and Analysis)

■ OPENING NEW LEDGER ACCOUNTS

After the closing entries are posted, the same ledger sheets can be used for the next accounting period. However, some accountants prefer to file the prior period's ledger and set up new ledger sheets for the current period.

When new ledger sheets are set up, the prior period's balances in the asset, liability, and capital accounts are entered in the appropriate Debit or Credit Balance column. The year, month, and day are entered in the Date column. The word *Balance* is entered in the Explanation column. Then a check mark (✓) is recorded in the Posting Reference column. The check mark indicates that the amount was not posted from a journal.

If the accountant for Guaranteed Delivery decided to set up new ledger sheets after the closing entries were posted, the Cash account would appear as shown below. This same procedure is used when more than one ledger sheet is needed during an accounting period.

Opening the New Ledger Account

ACCOUNT _Cash_   ACCOUNT NO. _101_

Date	Description	Post Ref.	Debit	Credit	Balance Debit	Balance Credit
20 XX Dec. 1	Balance	✓			32 500 00	

PREPARING THE POSTCLOSING TRIAL BALANCE

Before any transactions are recorded for the new period, another trial balance, called a *postclosing trial balance,* is prepared to check the equality of the debits and credits in the ledger. This is done whether new ledger sheets have been set up or the same ledger sheets are used. The postclosing trial balance for Guaranteed Delivery on November 30 is shown below.

Postclosing Trial Balance: Trial balance taken after closing entries are posted.

GUARANTEED DELIVERY
POSTCLOSING TRIAL BALANCE
NOVEMBER 30, 20XX

Acct. No.	Account Name	Debit	Credit
101	Cash	32 500 00	
102	Accounts Receivable	8 900 00	
111	Office Equipment	14 500 00	
112	Delivery Trucks	60 000 00	
201	Accounts Payable		21 100 00
301	Christopher Johns, Capital		94 800 00
	Totals	115 900 00	115 900 00

Note that the only open accounts listed on the postclosing trial balance are the ones that are still open (have balances)—the asset, liability, and owner's capital accounts. These accounts are often called *permanent accounts.* The revenue, expense, drawing, and summary accounts do not appear on the post-closing trial balance because they are closed. These accounts are often referred to as *temporary accounts.*

Permanent Accounts: Accounts that remain open from period to period.

Temporary Accounts: Accounts that are closed at the end of each period.

THE ACCOUNTING CYCLE

Accounting work follows a pattern. The same procedures are repeated in each accounting period. These procedures are referred to as the *accounting cycle.*

Accounting Cycle: Series of procedures repeated in each accounting period.

The methods used to complete accounting procedures vary from business to business. In some businesses, all accounting work is done by hand. In other businesses, computers play a major role in accounting work. However, no matter what method is used, the purpose of the accounting system remains the same—to provide information about the results of operations and financial position of the business. Management needs this information to control operations and make decisions.

The procedures that make up the accounting cycle are listed below. You are already familiar with most of these procedures.

1. Analyze transactions and record them in a journal.
2. Post the journal entries to the ledger accounts.
3. Prepare a trial balance to prove the ledger accounts.
4. Complete a worksheet to plan the financial statements.

WWW Inquiry
Find the URL address for America Online. What are the four product groups? (Hint: go to Management's Discussion and Analysis)

5. Prepare the financial statements.
6. Journalize and post adjusting entries and closing entries. (Adjusting entries are discussed in Chapter 23.)
7. Prepare a postclosing trial balance to prove the ledger accounts that remain open at the end of the period.

CHAPTER 10 SUMMARY

- The closing entries that are recorded at the end of each accounting period clear the revenue, expense, and drawing accounts so that they are ready for the next period's transactions.

- An account called Income Summary is used in the closing entries. The balances of the revenue and expense accounts are transferred to this account. Then the balance of Income Summary, which represents the net income (or net loss), is transferred to the owner's capital account.

- The balance of the owner's drawing account is transferred to the owner's capital account.

- After the closing entries have been posted, the revenue, expense, summary, and drawing accounts have zero balances.

- Before any transactions are recorded for the next accounting period, a postclosing trial balance is prepared to prove the equality of the debit and credit balances in the open accounts.

- The accounts that remain open from period to period are the permanent accounts—asset, liability, and owner's capital accounts. The accounts that are closed at the end of each period are the temporary accounts—revenue, expense, drawing, and summary accounts.

- The accounting cycle is a series of procedures that are repeated in each accounting period.

CHAPTER APPLICATIONS

EXERCISES

Complete the following assignments using the forms provided in your workbook.

EXERCISE 10–1

Recording closing entries. Refer to the partial worksheet shown below and record the closing entries. Date the entries May 31 of the current year.

	Income Statement Debit	Income Statement Credit	Balance Sheet Debit	Balance Sheet Credit
Fred Aiken, Capital				24,000
Fred Aiken, Withdrawals			1,000	
Rent Income		5,000		
Salaries Expense	3,200			
Insurance Expense	200			
Telephone Expense	100			
Totals	3,500	5,000	36,000	34,500
Net Income	1,500			1,500
	5,000	5,000	36,000	36,000

EXERCISE 10–2

Recording closing entries. Refer to the partial worksheet shown below and record the closing entries. Date the entries March 31 of the current year.

	Income Statement Debit	Income Statement Credit	Balance Sheet Debit	Balance Sheet Credit
Timothy Kristinsen, Capital				22,000
Timothy Kristinsen, Withdrawals			4,000	
Landscaping Fees		3,600		
Rent Expense	800			
Repairs Expense	600			
Salaries Expense	2,400			
Totals	3,800	3,600	21,800	22,000
Net Loss		200	200	
	3,800	3,800	22,000	22,000

PROBLEMS

Complete all assigned problems on the forms provided in your workbook.

PROBLEM 10–1

Preparing closing entries and a postclosing trial balance. This is a continuation of Problems 8–1 and 9–1. Refer to the worksheet prepared in Problem 9–1, and complete the closing procedure for the Delta Cleaning Service.

1. Record the closing entries in a general journal. Use 4 as the journal page number.
2. Post the closing entries to the general ledger accounts that were used for Problem 8–1.
3. Prepare a postclosing trial balance.

PROBLEM 10–2

Preparing closing entries and a postclosing trial balance. This is a continuation of Problems 8–2 and 9–2. Refer to the worksheet prepared in Problem 9–2, and complete the closing procedure for the Pacific Delivery Company.

1. Record the closing entries in a general journal.
2. Post the closing entries to the general ledger accounts that were used in Problem 8–2.
3. Prepare a postclosing trial balance.

CASE STUDY

Write the answer to the Case Study on the form provided in your workbook.

The Accounting Cycle

Wilson Sipe had operated his trading card business for nearly a year. As he prepared to close his financial records for the year, he journalized his closing entries, posted the closing entries to the appropriate ledger accounts, opened the new ledger accounts, and prepared his postclosing trial balance.

Although he followed accepted accounting procedures in keeping his financial records in order and the postclosing trial balance balanced, he wasn't sure why he needed to do everything he had done this year with his financial records.

> **Critical Thinking**
>
> - Explain the accounting cycle and why it was important that Sipe follow accepted accounting procedures.

PROJECT 2

Chapters 7–10

The Accounting Cycle

Scott Sutherland bought the Emily Floor Service on March 1. The firm's balance sheet for that date is as follows.

INSTRUCTIONS:

Complete the tasks listed below and on page 81 for this business. Use the forms in the workbook.

1. Record the opening entry in a general journal.
2. Open the following general ledger accounts.

    101 Cash
    102 Accounts Receivable
    103 Supplies
    111 Office Equipment
    112 Service Equipment
    113 Truck
    201 Accounts Payable
    301 Scott Sutherland, Capital
    302 Scott Sutherland, Withdrawals
    399 Income Summary
    401 Floor Service Fees
    501 Rent Expense
    502 Truck Expense
    503 Wages Expense
    504 Telephone Expense
    505 Advertising Expense
    506 Office Cleaning Expense

3. Post the opening entry to the ledger accounts.
4. Journalize the transactions.
5. Post the journal entries to the ledger accounts.
6. Prepare a worksheet.

Emily Floor Service
Balance Sheet
March 1, 20XX

Assets

Cash	$ 3,500
Accounts Receivable	1,300
Supplies	1,150
Office Equipment	3,250
Service Equipment	8,800
Truck	12,000
Total Assets	**$30,000**

Liabilities and Owner's Equity

Liabilities
  Accounts Payable $4,400

Owner's Equity
  Scott Sutherland, Capital 25,600

Total Liabilities and Owner's Equity $30,000

7. Prepare an income statement for the month ended March 31 of the current year.
8. Prepare a statement of owner's equity for the month ended March 31 of the current year.
9. Prepare a report-form balance sheet, dated March 31 of the current year.
10. Record the closing entries in the general journal. Record these entries immediately after the last transaction journalized on March 31.
11. Post the closing entries.
12. Prepare a postclosing trial balance.

TRANSACTIONS

Mar.	1	Paid $800 for the March rent.
Mar.	2	Received $700 from Suburban Real Estate, a customer, on account. (This money is for work done in February when the previous owner was operating the business.)
Mar.	6	Bought a sander for $375 on credit from the Gray Equipment Company.
Mar.	7	Received $550 for installing linoleum.
Mar.	8	Received $600 from Baldwin Securities in payment of the balance due for work done in February.
Mar.	10	Paid $1,850 in wages to employees.
	10	Paid $25 for gasoline for the truck.
Mar.	12	Paid $150 for supplies.
Mar.	13	Received $1,750 for installing floor tiles.
Mar.	15	Paid $1,000 to Crown Floor Machines, a creditor, on account. (This payment is for a purchase made by the previous owner in February.)
	15	Scott Sutherland invested an additional $2,000 in the business.
Mar.	17	Paid $175 for an office file cabinet.
	17	Refinished floors at Ty's Restaurant for $2,350 on credit.
Mar.	19	Received $685 for repairing a floor.
Mar.	20	Paid $190 to the Office Maintenance Company for cleaning the office.
Mar.	22	Paid $125 for a newspaper ad.
Mar.	23	Received $1,940 for installing floor tiles.
	23	Paid $87 for the telephone bill.
Mar.	24	Paid $2,400 to United Floor Tiles, a creditor, on account for a purchase made in February.
	24	Paid $1,850 in wages to employees.
Mar.	26	Received $1,250 for refinishing a floor.
Mar.	28	Paid $275 for supplies.
Mar.	30	Installed floor tiles at the Fashion Boutique for $1,725 on credit.
Mar.	31	Paid $42 for gasoline for the truck.
	31	Scott Sutherland withdrew $700 for his personal use.

PART THREE

Recording Financial Data

- **Chapter 11**
  Introduction to Merchandising Businesses: Sales
- **Chapter 12**
  Introduction to Merchandising Businesses: Purchases
- **Chapter 13**
  Accounting for Purchases
- **Chapter 14**
  Accounting for Sales
- **Chapter 15**
  The Sales Journal
- **Chapter 16**
  The Purchases Journal
- **Chapter 17**
  The Cash Receipts Journal
- **Chapter 18**
  The Cash Payments Journal
- **Chapter 19**
  The Accounts Receivable Ledger
- **Chapter 20**
  The Accounts Payable Ledger
- **Project 3**

Part Three will introduce you to the operations of a merchandising business. You will be able to see the differences in the accounting processes between service businesses (parts one and two) and a merchandising enterprise. The recording of transactions that affect sales and purchases are integral to a merchandising business. You will track the purchase of inventory for resale, the sale of that inventory, and the use of special journals. Working with the sales, purchases, cash receipts, and cash payments journals will prepare you for adjustments and adjusting entries to be presented in Part Four.

Accounting Careers

You Mean Accountants Have to Write?

Writing is an essential function of an accountant's job. Contrary to stereotype, accountants do not sit in a cluttered office and crunch numbers all day with little or no interaction with others. Not only do accountants deal with financial information; they must interpret, analyze, and explain that information to others. Part of the CPA exam involves writing essays that are graded for clarity and expression of ideas as well as for technical content.

■ BECOMING AN EFFECTIVE WRITER

- Know your audience. Are you writing to a group already knowledgeable about your subject, or do you need to start from the beginning?
- Think about content. What idea or ideas are you trying to convey to the reader? Be concise and deal with a limited number of ideas.
- Organize your thoughts in a logical pattern so the reader can understand how to perform the task or interpret the information.

ACTIVITY

- Look for examples of effective and ineffective writing. Bring examples of both to class.
- Talk to a CPA. Ask how much of his/her workday is spent in writing and other communication tasks. Ask to see a representative writing sample.

CHAPTER ELEVEN

Introduction to Merchandising Businesses

Sales

OBJECTIVES

On completion of this chapter, you should be able to:

1. Describe the differences between cash, charge account, and credit card sales.
2. Compute sales tax.
3. Use credit terms.
4. Compute the discount and amount of payment due on an invoice.
5. Apply the procedure for handling sales returns and allowances.

Accounting Terminology

- Allowance
- Cash discount
- Charge accounts
- Credit cards
- Credit memorandum
- Inventory
- Invoice
- Merchandise
- Merchandising business
- Retailers
- Sales returns and allowances
- Sales slip
- Sales tax
- Source documents
- Statement of account
- Wholesalers

INTRODUCTION

Up to this point, we have been concerned with the accounting procedures and financial records of service businesses. These businesses provide a service, such as repairing computers or delivering packages. We now turn our attention to the ***merchandising business.*** This type of business earns its revenue by selling ***merchandise,*** or goods, that it has purchased. Merchandise the business has in stock or storage is called ***inventory.***

Merchandising businesses are usually either wholesalers or retailers. ***Wholesalers*** normally buy merchandise from the manufacturers or producers and sell it at a higher price to retailers. Some wholesalers also sell to large consumers, such as hotels and hospitals. Wholesalers are often called ***distributors.***

Retailers normally buy merchandise from wholesalers and sell it at a higher price to individual consumers. However, some manufacturers and producers allow retailers (especially large retailers) to buy directly. Department stores, supermarkets, and drugstores are all examples of retailers. ■

■ SELLING AT RETAIL

A few retailers sell only for cash. Most retailers provide the option for customers to pay cash or to purchase on credit. By providing credit, businesses allow customers to obtain merchandise immediately and pay for it at a later time. Many retailers provide their own store credit card as well as allowing customers to charge purchases to a commercial credit card such as MasterCard, Visa, Discover, or American Express.

Cash Sales. When merchandise is sold for cash, the retailer usually uses a cash register to record the sale and the receipt of cash from their customers. Some cash registers require that the cashier enter the sale manually. On such registers, the cashier enters the price, and then selects a preprogrammed key to account for the category of the item being sold.

Merchandising Business: A business that earns its revenue by selling merchandise that it has purchased.

Merchandise: Goods purchased for resale.

Inventory Merchandise the business has in stock or storage is called inventory.

Wholesalers: Merchandising businesses that sell to retailers and large consumers.

Retailers: Merchandising businesses that sell to individual consumers.

In larger stores cashiers scan the products by the bar code printed on the product or package. Scanning is usually done by sliding the product across a laser reader or by pointing a handheld scanner at the bar code and depressing the trigger. In addition, by touching certain keys on the cash register, the product and the cost is automatically tallied. The information concerning the sale is stored on the business's database and in the cash register. The customer is given a receipt listing the items purchased and the costs. The use of a scanner usually provides greater detail about the items purchased than a cash register that requires the cashier to enter the price, etc.

The cash register is widely used in retail businesses to record both cash and credit sales. This machine has several advantages for retailers:

- It transmits details of all sales transactions to inventory and other accounting records.
- It prints a receipt for each customer.
- It provides a cash drawer for sorting the currency and coins received from customers and for storing this money until a bank deposit can be made.

At the end of each cashier's work day, the register provides a printout that lists the total of the cash and credit sales and other information. This tape is usually called the *detailed audit tape.*

Computerization of the point-of-sale process has greatly facilitated inventory maintenance. Point of sale (POS) systems provide increased speed and accuracy for cashiers and are easy to use—even by new cashiers. The result for retailers is greater productivity for employees and shorter checkout lines for customers.

Charge Accounts: A type of credit offered by retailers to their customers.

Sales Slips: Form listing information about a retail sale, usually a credit sale.

Store Charge Accounts. A retailer may offer a store charge account. A few small stores still enter charge sales manually. However, most retailers issue a credit card to their charge customers. When a sale on account is made, the cashier enters the customer's charge account number or simply swipes the card through a machine that reads the account number from the magnetic strip on the back of the card. The cash register generates a detailed receipt for the customer as well as a copy for the customer to sign. The cashier gives the detailed receipt to the customer and keeps the signed copy in a secure section of the cash register.

> **WWW Inquiry**
> Find the URL address for the May Department Stores Company. How much did current assets increase last year?

Sales on account are summarized monthly and a statement is sent to the customer. The statement is a reminder to the customer that payment is due. Before paying the statement, it should be checked for accuracy. It is not uncommon for errors to appear on computerized statements. The customer should compare amounts on the monthly statement with the detailed receipt from each sale. Discrepancies should be reported to the store's credit department immediately.

Many retailers add a finance charge if the customer does not pay by a specified time. Payment may be required as soon as the statement of account is received, or the customer may be allowed an additional payment period, such as 30 days.

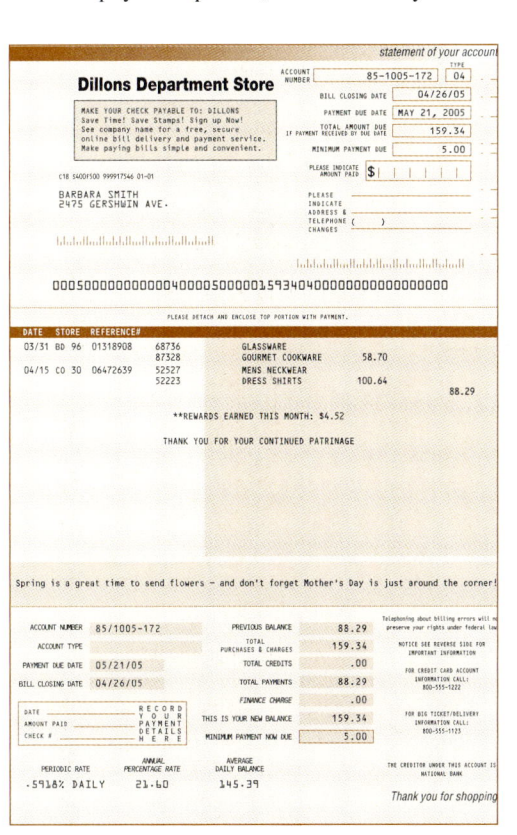

Statement of Account: Form that is sent to a customer who buys on credit to show transactions for a specified period and the total owed.

Credit Cards: A type of credit provided by credit card companies for use in retail businesses.

Credit Card Sales. Some retailers do not provide charge accounts, but they allow customers to use *credit cards* to buy on credit. Customers can obtain credit from credit card companies, such as MasterCard, Visa, Discover, and American Express. These credit cards can be used in a large number of retail establishments.

There are several differences between retail charge accounts and credit cards. Retailers who accept credit cards collect their money from the credit card companies rather than from the customers. The credit card companies send bills to the customers and receive payment from them.

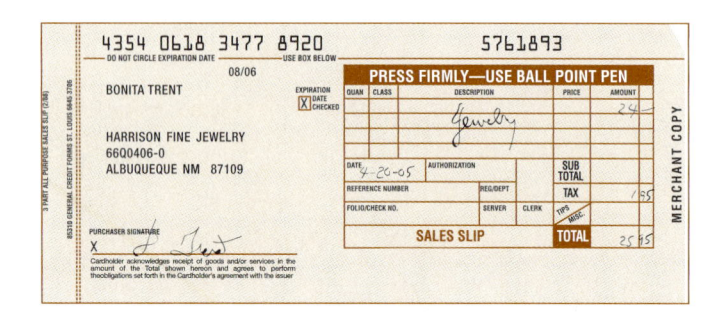

This arrangement is helpful to the retailers because it simplifies their accounting work. They do not have to prepare monthly bills and maintain charge account records. However, the retailers must pay a fee to the credit card companies. This fee is a small percentage of each credit card sale.

When retailers make credit card sales, the procedure is essentially the same as for charges to the customer's store charge account. The customer presents the credit card, the card number is entered or the card is read by the register, a receipt and a store copy are generated.

In some instances, however, credit card sales are recorded on special sales slips that the credit card company gives to the retailer. After listing information about the sale on one of these sales slips, the retailer places the form and the customer's credit card in an imprinting device. This device transfers the customer's name and credit card number from the card to the sales slip.

Sales Tax: A tax levied on retail sales.

Sales Tax. Retailers are also responsible for charging sales taxes imposed by states, cities, and counties. The tax is computed and listed separately on cash register tapes and sales slips. At regular intervals, monthly or quarterly, the retailer sends the total amount of the tax from all sales to the appropriate governmental agency. Note how the sales tax is computed and entered on the sales slip shown on page 87. The total amount of the sale $26, is multiplied by 5.75 percent (0.575) to determine the sales tax of $1.50.

■ SELLING AT WHOLESALE

Most selling at the wholesale level is done on credit. When merchandise is shipped, the wholesaler sends a form called an *invoice* to the customer. The invoice is a bill for the merchandise sold.

Invoice: Form used to record details of a sale and to bill the customer.

A typical invoice is shown below. It was prepared in duplicate so that the wholesaler could keep a copy. The invoice lists the same kind of information as the sales slips used by retailers to record their credit sales. Note that no sales tax is charged by wholesalers. Only retail sales require sales tax.

Some wholesalers send a monthly statement of account to their customers in addition to their invoices for the individual sales.

Source Documents: Business papers that contain important facts about transactions.

Cash register tapes, sales slips, and invoices are often referred to as *source documents* because they contain the important facts about transactions. They are the source of the information that is used to make accounting entries for the transactions.

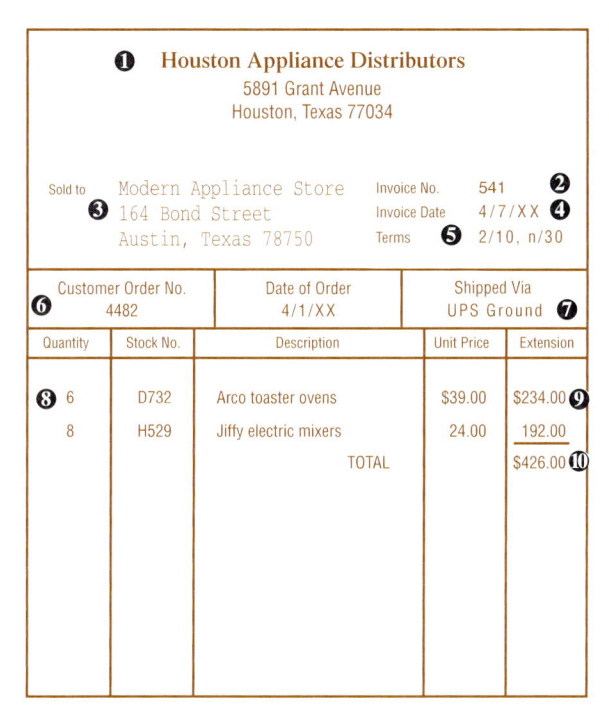

❶	**Houston Appliance Distributors**				
	5891 Grant Avenue				
	Houston, Texas 77034				

Sold to	Modern Appliance Store ❸ 164 Bond Street Austin, Texas 78750	Invoice No. Invoice Date Terms	541 ❷ 4/7/XX ❹ ❺ 2/10, n/30
❻ Customer Order No. 4482	Date of Order 4/1/XX	Shipped Via UPS Ground ❼	
Quantity	Stock No.	Description	Unit Price	Extension
❽ 6	D732	Arco toaster ovens	$39.00	$234.00 ❾
8	H529	Jiffy electric mixers	24.00	192.00
		TOTAL		$426.00 ❿

Recording Sales in Wholesale Businesses

The invoice is the form that is used to record detailed information about a sale and to bill the customer. This form usually includes the following items:

1. The seller's name and address, which are preprinted.
2. The invoice number, which is often preprinted also. (This practice makes it easier for the seller to keep track of all invoices.)
3. The customer's name and address.
4. The invoice date.
5. The credit terms, which show when the customer must pay for the merchandise.
6. The number and date of the customer's order.
7. The transportation company used to ship the merchandise.
8. The quantity, stock number, description, and unit price of each type of merchandise shipped.
9. The extension is the total amount owed for each type of merchandise. This amount is found by multiplying the unit price by the quantity.
10. The invoice total. This amount is found by adding all the extensions. (Note that wholesalers do not charge sales tax.)

■ CREDIT TERMS

The credit terms on an invoice show when the customer must pay for the merchandise. To encourage early payment, wholesalers often include a *cash discount* in their credit terms. The cash discount is a deduction from the invoice total. The customer can obtain this deduction by paying within a short discount period.

Cash Discount: Deduction from invoice total given for early payment.

Some common credit terms are explained below.

- n/30—The letter *n* stands for "net" and the figure 30 stands for "30 days." Thus the net (full) amount of the invoice must be paid within 30 days of the invoice date. To determine the end of the credit period, the exact number of days must be counted, starting with the day after the invoice date. For example, an invoice dated July 19 with terms of n/30 would be due on August 18.

July 20–31	12 days
August 1–18	18 days
	30 days

Note that the credit terms *n/30* do not include a cash discount.

- 2/10, n/30—The first part of these terms (*2/10*) means that a cash discount of 2 percent will be allowed if the invoice is paid within 10 days of its date (the discount period). Otherwise, the customer must pay the full amount of the invoice within 30 days. This is shown in the second part of the terms (*n/30*). Consider an invoice for $500, dated July 19, with terms of 2/10, n/30. If the invoice is paid by July 29 (10 days after July 19), the customer can take a discount of $10 ($500 × 0.02 = $10). Thus the amount due is $490.

2/10, n/30: A cash discount of 2% is allowed if paid within 10 days. If not, the balance is due in 30 days.

Amount of invoice	$500
Less 2 percent discount	10
Amount due	$490

If payment is not made by July 29, no discount is permitted. In this case, the customer must pay $500 by August 18 (the end of the 30-day credit period).

- **3/10, n/30 EOM**—The letters *EOM* are an abbreviation for "end of month." When credit terms include EOM, the days of the discount period are counted after the last day of the month in which the invoice is dated. For example, suppose that an invoice is dated July 19 and has terms of 3/10, n/30 EOM. To obtain the 3 percent cash discount, the customer must pay by August 10 (10 days after July 31). Otherwise the customer must pay the full amount of the invoice by August 30 (30 days after July 31).

There are many variations on the basic credit terms described here.

Note that discounts apply to the selling price of the merchandise only. Discounts cannot be taken on sales tax or on returns and allowances. For example, Judith Walsh received an invoice and a credit memorandum from the same supplier. The credit terms shown on the invoice were 2/10, n/30.

Invoice 415	$800 × 5% sales tax = $40 =	$840
Less Credit Memorandum 82	100 × 5% sales tax = 5 =	105
	$700	$735
	Less discount (2% × $700)	−14
	Net amount due	$721

In the preceding example, the discount is allowed on the selling price of the merchandise less the amount of the return or allowance. Note that the computation of the discount does not include the sales tax.

■ SALES RETURNS AND ALLOWANCES

Allowance: A reduction in the price of merchandise that may be damaged or not completely satisfactory.

Credit Memorandum: Form showing the deduction from a customer's account for a return or allowance.

Businesses try to sell merchandise that will please their customers. However, sometimes a customer will return the merchandise or request an allowance. An *allowance* is a reduction in the price of merchandise that may be damaged or not completely satisfactory.

When merchandise is sold for cash, many businesses provide a cash refund if the customer returns the goods in salable condition or asks for an allowance. The procedure for handling returns and allowances on credit sales involves the use of a form called a *credit memorandum,* or *credit slip.* This form shows that the seller will deduct the amount of the return or allowance from the customer's account balance. The credit memorandum shown below consists of an original and at least one copy. The seller sends the original to the customer and keeps the copy for reference.

If sales tax was charged at the time of the sale, then the sales tax on the return or allowance must be included in the refund or added to the credit memorandum.

WWW Inquiry
Find the URL address for the May Department Stores Company. What were net earnings as a percentage of revenues for last year?

Houston Appliance Distributors
5891 Grant Avenue
Houston, Texas 77034

Sold to: Economy Appliance Center
24 Hilton Shopping Mall
San Antonio, TX 78201

Credit Memorandum No. 1
Date: 5/6/XX

Quantity	Stock No.	Description	Unit Price	Extension
2	C128	Arco broilers sold on Invoice 543	$40.00	$80.00

Explanation: Arrived in damaged condition.

CHAPTER 11 SUMMARY

- A merchandising business earns revenue by selling merchandise (goods) that it has purchased. Merchandising businesses are usually either wholesalers or retailers.
- Some retailers sell only for cash, and others sell both for cash and on credit. Charge accounts and credit cards are two common types of credit used in retail stores. Wholesalers make most of their sales on credit.
- When sales are made, merchandising businesses must record information about them on source documents. Retailers prepare cash register tapes and sales slips. Wholesalers prepare invoices. An invoice is a bill for the merchandise.
- States, cities, and counties may impose a sales tax. The retailer collects this tax from customers and periodically remits it to the appropriate governmental agency.
- Wholesalers often include a cash discount in their credit terms to encourage early payment. This discount is deducted from the invoice total if payment is made within a specified number of days.
- When a customer returns merchandise that was sold on credit or receives an allowance on such merchandise, a credit memorandum, or credit slip, is issued.

CHAPTER APPLICATIONS

EXERCISES

Complete the following assignments on the forms provided in your workbook.

EXERCISE 11-1

Computing sales tax.

Instructions:
Compute the sales tax and total sales slip amount for each of the following.

	Sale	Sales Tax
a.	$30.00	6%
b.	$60.00	8%
c.	$87.43	6%

EXERCISE 11-2

Determining the last day of the discount period. To obtain a discount, the following invoices must be paid by the last day of the discount period.

Instructions:
Use the invoice date and the terms to determine the end of the discount period.

	Invoice Date	Terms
a.	May 10	2/10, n/30
b.	Oct. 25	3/10, n/30
c.	June 30	3/10, n/30 EOM
d.	Dec. 4	3/10, n/30 EOM

PROBLEMS

Complete all assigned problems on the forms provided in your workbook.

PROBLEM 11-1

Computing sales tax. Syvertsen Office Supply collects a 6 percent sales tax on all sales of stationery and office supplies.

Instructions:
Compute the following for each sale.

Sales Slip Amount Excluding Sales Tax

a. $59.27
b. $34.26
c. $87.98
d. $2.59

1. The amount of sales tax.
2. The total sales slip amount.

PROBLEM 11-2

Computing discounts. Jurist Electronics allows its customers credit terms of 2/10, n/30. During July, the invoices listed below were issued.

Invoices

a. July 5, $197.46
b. July 11, $339.50
c. July 22, $80.32
d. July 31, $46.53

Instructions:

Determine the following.

1. The last day of the discount period.
2. The amount of discount that would be allowed if the customer pays within the discount period.
3. The amount of the payment if the discount is deducted.

PROBLEM 11-3

Computing an invoice amount, a credit memorandum amount, and a discount. On August 2, General Office Furniture sold the following items to Byelich Real Estate.

a. 2 office desks, each $1,075
b. 3 office chairs, each $216
c. 2 desk lamps, each $49.25

On August 5, General Office Furniture shipped the items to Byelich Real Estate and issued Invoice 329. The invoice listed a 5 percent sales tax and showed credit terms of 2/10, n/30 EOM.

On August 6, Byelich Real Estate reported that one of the desks was scratched. General Office Furniture offered a $100 allowance on the damaged desk if the customer would keep it. Byelich Real Estate agreed; therefore, General Office Furniture issued Credit Memorandum 72 on August 8. Byelich Real Estate paid the balance due on August 10.

Instructions:
Compute the following:

1. The total amount of Invoice 329, including sales tax.
2. The total amount of Credit Memorandum 72, including sales tax.
3. The last day of the discount period.
4. The amount of the discount.
5. The amount of the payment.

PROBLEM 11-4

Computing the discount period, the amount of discount, and the amount of payment. Information about seven invoices issued by various wholesalers is given in the tables in the workbook.

Instructions:

1. For each invoice listed in the first table, enter the last day of the discount period (if any) and the last day of the credit period.
2. The dates when the invoices were actually paid are shown in the second table. For each invoice, enter the amount of the payment. Then indicate whether the payment was late—made after the end of the credit period. (Look at the due dates in the first table as you work on the second table. Remember that a cash discount should only be taken if payment is made on or before the last day of the discount period.)

CASE STUDY

Write the answer to the case study on the form provided in your workbook.

Accuracy

In reviewing the books for a local business where you work, you notice that sales of merchandise on account was actually recorded as cash sales. You know that the entry is incorrect and would like to point it out to the owner.

> **Critical Thinking**
>
> ■ *How would you describe the effect an incorrect entry has on the accounts?*
>
> *Hint: Think about the account balances and what they mean to the operation of the business.*

CHAPTER TWELVE

Introduction to Merchandising Businesses: Purchases

OBJECTIVES

Upon completion of this chapter, you should be able to:

1. Apply the procedure for checking the accuracy of invoices.
2. Use an unpaid invoice file.
3. Explain the difference between FOB shipping point and FOB destination.
4. Demonstrate the procedure for handling purchases returns and allowances.
5. Compute purchases discounts.

INTRODUCTION

Merchandising businesses earn revenue by purchasing merchandise and then selling it at a higher price. As discussed in Chapter 11, wholesalers normally purchase merchandise from manufacturers or distributors, and retailers normally purchase merchandise from wholesalers. ■

■ PURCHASING MERCHANDISE

Businesses that purchase merchandise must have orderly procedures for checking the accuracy of invoices and for making prompt payments. As we have discussed, the buyer receives an invoice from the seller for each purchase. To the seller, this form is a *sales invoice.* To the buyer, it is a *purchase invoice.*

Sometimes the invoice is included with the shipment, and sometimes it is sent separately. When the invoice arrives, the buyer must check to see that the merchandise has actually been received and that the quantities, unit prices, extensions, total amount, and credit terms are correct. The *extensions* are the mathematical result of multiplying the quantity by the unit price. If there are errors, the buyer reports them to the seller. If the invoice is accurate, it is accepted for payment.

As soon as the invoice is checked and accepted, the due date for payment must be computed. This should be done quickly in order to take advantage of any discount.

A business must also have an efficient method for keeping track of the due dates of all invoices so that payments can be made on time. Every effort should be made to pay promptly for the following reasons.

- The buyer will obtain a cash discount by paying within the discount period. During a year, this practice will save a great deal of money.
- If it is not possible to pay within the discount period, the buyer should be sure to pay by the end of the credit period. Otherwise, the seller may charge a late payment penalty. Also, constant late payments will give a business a poor credit rating. Some sellers may refuse to provide any more credit.

Accounting Terminology

- Extensions
- FOB destination
- FOB shipping point
- Free on board
- Purchase invoice
- Purchases discounts
- Purchases returns and allowances
- Sales discounts
- Sales invoice
- Tickler file
- Unpaid invoice file

Invoices: The buyer receives an invoice from the seller for each purchase. To the seller, this form is a sales invoice. To the buyer it is a purchase invoice.

Extensions: The sum arrived at by multiplying the quantity by the unit price.

93

Unpaid Invoice File: File in which unpaid invoices are arranged by due dates.

One simple way of keeping track of due dates is to use an *unpaid invoice file.* All approved invoices are placed in this file according to the dates on which they are to be paid. Each morning, the accounting clerk looks at the file and takes out any invoices that are due for payment. An unpaid invoice file is shown below.

CONTROLLING PURCHASE INVOICES
Many businesses use a processing stamp to help control purchase invoices. When the buyer receives the invoice, it is stamped with a rubber stamp. As the invoice is checked, recorded, and paid, the necessary information is written in the stamped area. Note that the due date is also entered.

An unpaid invoice file is another aid in handling purchase invoices efficiently. This type of file is often called a *tickler file.*

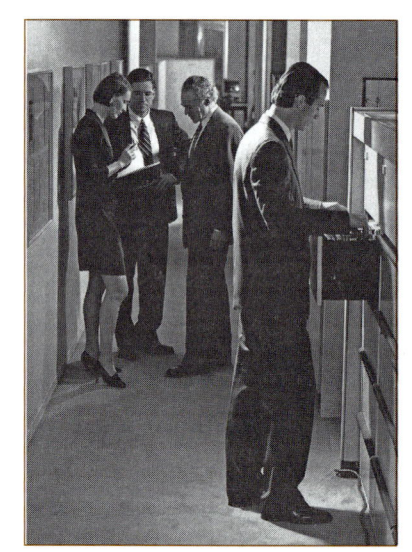

■ TRANSPORTATION CHARGES

When a business purchases merchandise, it may be required to pay transportation charges from the supplier's warehouse. These charges are an added cost of the merchandise.

Transportation charges may cover parcel post, motor freight, railway freight, or air freight. The invoice issued by the supplier usually shows who will pay the transportation charges. The term *FOB shipping point* on the invoice means that the purchaser must pay. The term *FOB destination* means that the supplier must pay. (The abbreviation *FOB* stands for *free on board.*)

FOB: Free on board.

FOB Shipping Point: The purchaser pays transportation charges.

FOB Destination: The supplier pays transportation charges.

Payment of the transportation charges can be handled in two ways. In some cases, the supplier lists the transportation charges on the invoice. The purchasers pays the supplier for both the merchandise and the transportation charges when the invoice becomes due. The second way is that the shipping or transportation company bills the purchaser separately.

■ PURCHASES RETURNS AND ALLOWANCES

In a well-run business, all merchandise purchases are carefully inspected soon after they arrive. If any goods are unsatisfactory, they are returned to the supplier or an allowance is requested. When a business returns goods or receives an allowance, there is a decrease in the cost of its merchandise purchases.

Most businesses expect a cash refund if they return goods purchased for cash or request an allowance on such goods. If merchandise is purchased on credit, the supplier usually issues a credit memorandum for a return or allowance. The credit memorandum shows that the supplier will reduce the purchaser's account balance by the amount of the return or allowance. The credit memorandum shows that the supplier will reduce the purchaser's account balance by the amount of the return allowance.

WWW Inquiry
Find the URL address for Yum Brands. What revenue accounts are shown on its most recent income statement?

PURCHASE DISCOUNTS

Cash discounts are called **sales discounts** by the seller and **purchase discounts** by the buyer. These discounts apply to the cost of merchandise only. They are not calculated on transportation charges, sales tax, or returns and allowances. For example, an invoice with terms of 2/10, n/30 lists merchandise of $800 and transportation charges of $65. The discount may be taken on the price of the goods only ($800 × 0.02 = $16). Then the amount to be paid ($849) is calculated by deducting the discount from the total of the invoice ($865 − $16 = $849).

When merchandise purchased on credit is returned or an allowance is given, the discount is calculated on the net purchase amount. For example, merchandise was purchased for $1,100 on terms of 2/10, n/30, and items costing $100 arrived in damaged condition. The damaged items were returned, and a credit memorandum for $100 was issued by the supplier. When the invoice is paid, the return is deducted from the cost of the merchandise before the discount and the amount of the payment are computed.

Sales Discount: Cash discount offered by the seller.

Purchase Discount: Cash discount offered by the buyer.

Invoice total	$1,100	Net purchase	$1,000
Less return	100	Less discount	20
Net purchase	$1,000	Amount of payment	$980
Rate of discount	0.02		
Amount of discount	$20		

WWW Inquiry
Find the URL address for TRICON Global Restaurants, Inc. What restaurants are owned by this company?

CHAPTER 12 SUMMARY

- A purchase invoice is a bill that a buyer receives for a purchase of merchandise.
- Invoices must be paid within the discount period to obtain the cash discount.
- An unpaid invoice file is used to keep track of due dates.
- FOB shipping point means that the purchaser must pay the transportation charges. FOB destination means that the seller must pay the transportation charges.
- Purchases returns and allowances decrease the cost of merchandise purchased.
- A credit memorandum shows that the supplier will reduce the purchaser's account balance by the amount of the return or allowance.
- Purchases discounts apply only to the cost of merchandise. They are not allowed on transportation charges, sales tax, or returns and allowances.

CHAPTER APPLICATIONS

EXERCISES

Complete the following assignments using the forms provided in your workbook.

EXERCISE 12-1

Computing due dates.

Instructions:
Use the invoice dates and credit terms listed below to determine the due date required to obtain the discount for each of the following invoices if a discount is offered.

	Date of Invoice	Credit Terms
a.	January 6	n/30
b.	March 8	2/10, n/30
c.	July 17	2/15, n/30
d.	August 7	3/10, n/30 EOM
e.	August 20	2/10, n/30 EOM

EXERCISE 12-2

Paying transportation charges.

Instructions:
For each of the following invoices, determine whether the buyer or the seller will pay the transportation charges.

a. Invoice 726, FOB Destination
b. Invoice 409, FOB Shipping Point

EXERCISE 12-3
Computing cash discounts and amounts of payment.

Instructions:
For each of the following invoices, compute the discount (if one is offered) and the amount of the payment that would be made to the creditor.

	Merch. Pur.	Trans. Charges	Pur. Ret. and Allow.	Terms
a.	$1,000			2/10, n/30
b.	$1,000	$60		2/10, n/30
c.	$1,000		$100	2/10, n/30
d.	$1,000	$60	$100	2/10, n/30
e.	$1,000	$60	$100	n/30

PROBLEMS

Complete all assigned problems on the forms provided in your workbook.

PROBLEM 12-1
Checking the accuracy of the invoices. During the first week of September, the Leonetti Furniture Store received the two invoices shown in the workbook.

Instructions:
1. Check the accuracy of the extensions and totals on these invoices.
2. If there is an error, cross out the incorrect amount and write the correct one above it. When you complete work on an invoice, enter your initials in the Extensions/Total section of the processing stamp.

Remember that an extension is found by multiplying the unit price of an item by its quantity.

PROBLEM 12-2
Determining due dates, discounts, and amounts of payment. Refer to the corrected invoices used for Problem 12-1 in the workbook.

Instructions:
Compute the following.

1. The due date required to obtain the discount.
2. The amount of the discount.
3. The amount of the payment.

CASE STUDY

Write the answer to the case study on the form provided in your workbook.

Discounts
Sharon Harrison owns a business that sells golfing equipment both at the retail and wholesale levels. Ms. Harrison rarely takes advantage of buying discounts saying that she wouldn't save that much money.

Ms. Harrison hires you as a part-time clerical worker and you notice that if she paid the bills in a more timely fashion, she could take advantage of the discounts offered her. You think there are good reasons why she should take advantage of the discounts offered.

> **Critical Thinking**
>
> ■ *What will you tell her the major advantages are to paying invoices within the period of time that allows her to take the discounts?*

CHAPTER THIRTEEN

Accounting for Purchases

OBJECTIVES

Upon completion of this chapter, you should be able to:

1. Record the entries for the purchase of merchandise for cash and on credit.
2. Record the entries for the purchase of supplies and other assets.
3. Record purchases discounts.
4. Record the entries for freight in.
5. Record the entries for purchases returns and allowances.

Accounting Terminology

- Freight in
- Merchandise purchases
- Purchases discount
- Purchases returns and allowances

INTRODUCTION

In the previous chapter, we discussed the procedures for handling purchases and source documents such as invoices and credit memorandums. These source documents provide the information needed to record purchases, transportation charges, and purchases returns and allowances. ■

■ RECORDING PURCHASES OF MERCHANDISE

The purchase of merchandise for resale is recorded in an account called Merchandise Purchases. This account is usually referred to as a *cost account* and is a temporary account. Like the expense accounts, it decreases owner's equity.

The Merchandise Purchases account is debited for the amount of each purchase. The account to be credited depends on the terms of the purchase. The Cash account is used for a cash purchase, and the Accounts Payable account is used for a credit purchase. These two kinds of merchandise purchases are journalized and posted in the following illustrations.

Purchases of merchandise for resale are debited to the cost account Merchandise Purchases.

GENERAL JOURNAL   Page **3**

Recording Merchandise Purchases

	Date		Description	Post Ref.	Debit	Credit	
1	20	XX					1
2	Mar.	2	Merchandise Purchases	501	880 00		2
3			Cash	101		880 00	3
4			Purchased merchandise.				4
5							5
6		4	Merchandise Purchases	501	1150 00		6
7			Accounts Payable	202		1150 00	7
8			Purchased merchandise on credit				8
9			from American Electric, Invoice				9
10			J7632, dated 3/1/XX, terms				10
11			2/10, n/30.				11

Recording Merchandise Purchases (continued)

ACCOUNT Merchandise Purchases						ACCOUNT NO. 501	
Date	Description	Post Ref.	Debit	Credit	Balance Debit	Balance Credit	
20XX							
Mar. 2		J3	880 00		880 00		
4		J3	1 150 00		2 030 00		

ACCOUNT Cash						ACCOUNT NO. 101	
Date	Description	Post Ref.	Debit	Credit	Balance Debit	Balance Credit	
20XX							
Feb. 26		J1	12 000 00		12 000 00		
Mar. 2		J3		880 00	11 120 00		

ACCOUNT Accounts Payable						ACCOUNT NO. 202	
Date	Description	Post Ref.	Debit	Credit	Balance Debit	Balance Credit	
20XX							
Mar. 4		J3		1 150 00		1 150 00	

■ RECORDING OTHER PURCHASES

Purchases of permanent assets are debited to an appropriate asset account, such as Office Equipment.

Be careful to record only **purchases of merchandise for resale** in the Merchandise Purchases account. Purchases of permanent assets, such as computers, copiers, and delivery equipment, should be debited to an appropriate asset account and credited to Cash or Accounts Payable. The procedure for recording these purchases is the same in both service and merchandising businesses.

Purchases of supplies are debited to the asset account Supplies.

Purchases of supplies that will be used over a period of several months are usually debited to an asset account called Supplies. For example, a wholesaler records a purchase of cartons, bubble wrap, sealing tape, and shipping labels, which it needs to send merchandise to customers, as follows:

Recording Other Purchases

		GENERAL JOURNAL			Page 3	
	Date	Description	Post Ref.	Debit	Credit	
1	20XX					1
2	Mar.					2
6	5	Supplies	115	430 00		6
7		Cash	101		430 00	7
8		Purchased shipping cartons,				8
9		bubble wrap, sealing tape, and				9
10		shipping labels.				10

■ RECORDING AMOUNTS PAID FOR PURCHASES OF MERCHANDISE ON CREDIT

The amount to be paid for merchandise bought on credit depends on whether a cash discount is involved. (Remember that cash discounts are not allowed on transportation charges or on returns and allowances.) If there is no cash discount, the buyer must pay the total amount of the invoice. This transaction is recorded in the same way as the payments on account discussed in earlier chapters. Accounts Payable is debited, and Cash is credited.

If the credit terms of the purchase include a cash discount and the buyer pays within the discount period, the amount of the payment is less than the total of the invoice. For example, consider an invoice for $1,150 on which a discount of 2 percent is taken. The amount to be paid is $1,127.

> **WWW Inquiry**
> Find the URL address for Kraft Foods. List the business divisions for Kraft Foods.

Total of invoice	$1,150
Less 2 percent discount	23
Amount of payment	$1,127

Three accounts are used to record this transaction. The total of the invoice is debited to Accounts Payable. The amount of cash actually paid is credited to Cash. The amount of the discount is credited to a cost account called Purchases Discount. The following illustrations show how this payment is journalized and posted. Notice that the entire debt has been discharged by a smaller payment because of the cash discounts. Accounts payable is therefore debited for the full amount.

A cash discount for a purchase of merchandise is credited to the cost account Purchases Discount when the invoice is paid.

GENERAL JOURNAL Page 3

Date	Description	Post Ref.	Debit	Credit
20XX Mar. 10	Accounts Payable	202	1,150.00	
	Cash	101		1,127.00
	Purchases Discount	504		23.00
	Paid American Electric for			
	Invoice J7632 less discount.			

Recording Purchases Discounts

ACCOUNT **Accounts Payable** ACCOUNT NO. **202**

Date	Description	Post Ref.	Debit	Credit	Balance Debit	Balance Credit
20XX Mar. 4		J3		1,150.00		1,150.00
10		J3	1,150.00			-0-

Posting the Journal Entry

ACCOUNT **Cash** ACCOUNT NO. **101**

Date	Description	Post Ref.	Debit	Credit	Balance Debit	Balance Credit
20XX Mar. 10		J3		1,127.00	8,389.00	

ACCOUNT **Purchases Discount** ACCOUNT NO. **504**

Date	Description	Post Ref.	Debit	Credit	Balance Debit	Balance Credit
20XX Mar. 10		J3		23.00		23.00

Notice that the Purchases Discount account has a credit balance unlike the other cost and expense accounts, which have debit balances. This is because purchase discounts reduce the cost of the purchases recorded in the Merchandise Purchases account.

■ RECORDING TRANSPORTATION CHARGES ON MERCHANDISE PURCHASES

Freight In, another cost account, is debited for the transportation charges on all incoming merchandise purchases. Payment for transportation charges can be handled in two ways. If the purchaser pays the transportation company directly, Freight In is debited, and Cash is credited. If the seller lists the transportation charges on the invoice, then the purchaser owes the seller for both the merchandise and the transportation charges. In this case, a compound entry is recorded.

Transportation charges on incoming merchandise are debited to the cost account Freight In.

Recording Transportation Charges

GENERAL JOURNAL — Page 4

Date	Description	Post Ref.	Debit	Credit
20XX				
Mar. 20	Merchandise Purchases		600 00	
	Freight In		45 00	
	Accounts Payable			645 00
	Purchased merchandise on credit			
	from United Manufacturing Co.;			
	Invoice 1223, dated 3/18/XX,			
	terms 2/10, n/30.			

■ RECORDING PURCHASES RETURNS AND ALLOWANCES

Purchases returns and allowances are credited to the cost account Purchases Returns and Allowances.

When a business returns goods or receives an allowance, there is a decrease in the cost of its merchandise purchases. This decrease is recorded in a cost account called Purchases Returns and Allowances.

Returns and Allowances on Cash Purchases. Businesses expect a cash refund if they return goods or request an allowance on goods that were purchased for cash. Suppose that an item costing $30 is found to be defective. The defective merchandise is returned to the seller, and a check for $30 is issued to the purchaser. The purchaser records the receipt of the check by a debit to Cash and a credit to Purchases Returns and Allowances.

Recording Purchase Returns and Allowances

GENERAL JOURNAL — Page 4

Date	Description	Post Ref.	Debit	Credit
20XX				
Mar. 21	Cash		30 00	
	Purchases Returns and Allowances			30 00
	Refund for the return of defective			
	merchandise.			

Returns and Allowances on Credit Purchases. If the return or allowance applies to merchandise that was purchased on credit, the seller issues a credit memorandum. As a result, the buyer owes less money to the seller. Thus Accounts Payable is debited and Purchases Returns and Allowances is credited. This account is really the credit side of the merchandise purchases account. However, because management needs to know how much merchandise is being returned, a separate account is used.

		GENERAL JOURNAL			Page __4__	
	Date	Description	Post Ref.	Debit	Credit	
1	20 XX					1
2	Mar.					2
6	25	Accounts Payable		50 00		6
7		Purchases Returns and Allowances			50 00	7
8		Received Credit Memorandum 19				8
9		from Alfieri Distributing for the				9
10		return of merchandise purchased				10
11		on Invoice 327.				11

WWW Inquiry
Find the URL address for General Mills. List some cereals and snacks produced by General Mills.

CHAPTER 13 SUMMARY

- Purchases of merchandise for resale are debited to a cost account called Merchandise Purchases.
- Purchases of assets, such as equipment, are debited to an appropriate asset account. Supplies purchased in large amounts for use during several months are considered assets and are debited to the asset account Supplies.
- When a cash discount is offered and payment is made in time to take advantage of it, the buyer credits the amount of the discount to a cost account called Purchases Discount.
- The purchaser may be required to pay transportation charges on merchandise. These charges are debited to the Freight In account.
- The Purchases Returns and Allowances account is used to record the decrease in the cost of merchandise purchases that results when a business returns goods or receives allowances.
- Purchases Returns and Allowances is credited for all returns and allowances. If the business is given a cash refund, the Cash account is debited. However, if the amount is deducted from a balance that the business owes, Accounts Payable is debited.

CHAPTER APPLICATIONS

EXERCISES

Complete the following assignments using the forms provided in your workbook.

EXERCISE 13-1

Analyzing purchases transactions for a merchandising business.

Instructions:
For each of the following transactions, give the titles of the accounts that would be debited and credited.

Transactions:

a. Purchased merchandise for cash.
b. Purchased merchandise on credit.
c. Purchased office supplies for cash.
d. Purchased office supplies on credit.
e. Paid transportation charges on a shipment of merchandise purchased.
f. Received credit from the seller for a return of damaged merchandise.
g. Received credit from the seller for a return of damaged office supplies.
h. Paid a creditor's invoice less a cash discount.

EXERCISE 13-2

Accounting for purchases of merchandise and assets.
Listed below are some of the accounts used by Oliver Industries.

Cash	$6,000	Merchandise	
Supplies	200	Purchases	–0–
Office Equipment	2,800	Purchases Returns	
Accounts Payable	–0–	and Allowances	–0–
David Oliver, Capital	9,000	Purchases Discounts	–0–

Instructions:

1. Set up T accounts, and enter the balances.
2. Analyze each of the following transactions, and record the effects in the T accounts.
3. Compute the balance of each account.

4. Prepare a trial balance as of August 31 of the current year.

Transactions:

a. Purchased merchandise for $3,400 on credit from Whitcur Manufacturing; the terms are 2/10, n/30.

b. Purchased shipping cartons on credit for $320; the terms are n/30.

c. Purchased file cabinets on credit for $500; the terms are n/30.

d. Returned damaged merchandise to Whitcur Manufacturing and received a credit of $400.

e. Returned damaged shipping cartons and received a credit of $120 from the seller.

f. Issued Check 92 for $2,940 to Whitcur Manufacturing for the balance due less a 2 percent discount of $60.

EXERCISE 13-3

Accounting for purchases, transportation charges, returns and allowances, and discounts.

Instructions:

1. Set up the following T accounts for Stereo Systems, and enter the balances.

Cash	$9,000	Freight In	–0–
Accounts Payable	–0–	Purchases Returns	
Matthew Dempsey,		and Allowances	–0–
Capital	9,000		
Merchandise Purchases	–0–	Purchases Discount	–0–

2. Analyze each of the following transactions, and record the effects in the T accounts.

3. Compute the balance of each account.

4. Prepare a trial balance as of May 31 of the current year.

Transactions:

a. Purchased merchandise for $5,000 on credit from Newtown Products; the terms are 2/10, n/30.

b. Purchased merchandise for $4,000 plus transportation charges of $300 from Crystal Electronics. The invoice total is $4,300, and the terms are 2/10, n/30.

c. Paid $125 for transportation charges on the shipment of merchandise from Newtown Products.

d. Returned damaged merchandise and received a credit of $1,000 from Crystal Electronics.

e. Issued Check 207 for $4,900 to pay Newtown Products for its $5,000 invoice less a 2 percent discount of $100.

EXERCISE 13-4

Accounting for purchases, transportation charges, and returns and allowances.

Instructions:

1. Set up T accounts for Cash; Supplies; Accounts Payable; Shawn Kendig, Capital; Merchandise Purchases; Freight In; and Purchases Returns and Allowances.

2. Analyze each of the following transactions, and record the effects in the T accounts.

3. Compute the balance of each account.

4. Prepare a trial balance for Saxon Stores as of May 31 of the current year.

Transactions:

a. Kendig invested $10,000 in the business.

b. Purchased merchandise for $3,000 on credit.

c. Purchased office supplies for $400 on credit.

d. Paid $200 for a cash purchase of merchandise.

e. Paid $30 for transportation charges on merchandise purchased.

f. Purchased merchandise for $1,000 plus transportation charges of $70. The invoice total is $1,070, and the terms are n/30.

g. Returned damaged merchandise and received a credit of $100 from the seller.

h. Issued a check for $3,000 to pay a creditor's invoice.

i. Returned damaged office supplies and received a credit of $25 from the seller.

j. Received a freight bill for $50 on a shipment of merchandise purchased. Payment is due in 30 days.

PROBLEMS

Complete all assigned problems on the forms provided in your workbook.

PROBLEM 13-1

Accounting for purchases, transportation charges, discounts, and returns.

Ocean City Wholesale purchases merchandise from various manufacturers and then sells it to retailers. The ledger account balances as of April 1 of the current year and transactions for April are shown below.

Instructions:

1. Open the ledger accounts and enter the balances.

2. Record the transactions in the general journal. Use 4 as the journal page number.

3. Foot the journal.

4. Post the journal entries to the ledger accounts.
5. Prepare a trial balance as of April 30 of the current year.

101	Cash	$40,000	502	Freight In	–0–
202	Accounts Payable	–0–	503	Purchases Returns and Allowances	–0–
301	Niccole Hank, Capital	40,000	504	Purchases Discounts	–0–
501	Merchandise Purchases	–0–			

Transactions:

Apr. 1 Purchased merchandise for $2,800 from West Manufacturing; Invoice A62, dated 3/31, terms 2/10, n/30.

3 Paid $59 for transportation charges on the shipment of merchandise from West Manufacturing.

5 Purchased merchandise for $2,500 plus transportation charges of $125 from Elias Productions; Invoice 251, dated 4/4, terms 1/10, n/30.

10 Paid $2,744 to West Manufacturing for Invoice A62 ($2,800) less discount ($56).

12 Returned merchandise to Elias Productions and received Credit Memorandum C57 for $500.

14 Paid $2,105 to Elias Productions for the balance due on Invoice 251 less the $20 discount.

Apr. 24 Purchased merchandise for $3,000 from Software Systems; Invoice 601, dated 4/23, terms 2/10, n/30.

30 Paid $65 for transportation charges on the shipment of merchandise from Software Systems.

CASE STUDY

Write the answer to the case study on the form provided in your workbook.

Purchases and the Cost of Merchandise

In your accounting class you are studying purchases and the cost of merchandise. You are learning about transportation costs, and one of your fellow students thinks that merchandise should be valued at the original cost plus other costs associated with the purchase of the merchandise, like transportation.

You think that the cost of transportation for buying and receiving the merchandise is an expense of the business, and shouldn't be included in the value of the inventory.

Critical Thinking

- *Give reasons to support both cases—adding the cost of freight to the cost of merchandise and for considering it as a separate cost item.*

CHAPTER FOURTEEN

Accounting for Sales

Accounting Terminology

- Merchandise inventory
- Credit sales
- Sales discount
- Sales returns and allowances
- Sales tax

OBJECTIVES

Upon completion of this chapter, you should be able to:

1. Record the entries for the sale of merchandise for cash or on credit.
2. Record sales discount.
3. Record the entries for sales returns and allowances.
4. Record sales tax.

INTRODUCTION

In Chapter 11, the procedures for handling sales and source documents such as sales slips, invoices, and credit memorandums were discussed. These source documents provide the information for recording sales, sales returns and allowances, and sales tax.

RECORDING SALES OF MERCHANDISE

Sales is the revenue account that is credited for cash or credit sales of merchandise. This account is similar to Employment Fees and Delivery Service Fees, which were used in earlier chapters for recording sales of services. Look at the entries below. The amount of each sale of merchandise is credited to Sales. The offsetting debit is to Cash or Accounts Receivable, depending on the terms of the sale.

Sales of merchandise are credited to the revenue account Sales.

When sales are made, either the asset account cash or accounts receivable is debited.

Recording Sales of Merchandise

GENERAL JOURNAL Page 3

Date	Description	Post Ref.	Debit	Credit
20XX Mar. 7	Cash	101	76000	
	Sales	401		76000
	Cash sales for first week			
	of March.			
8	Accounts Receivable	112	30000	
	Sales	401		30000
	Sold merchandise on credit			
	to Shane Appliance store;			
	Invoice 536; terms 3/15, n/60.			

104

Recording Sales of Merchandise (continued)

ACCOUNT Cash **ACCOUNT NO.** 101

Date	Description	Post Ref.	Debit	Credit	Balance Debit	Balance Credit
20XX Mar. 7		J3	760 00		15 760 00	

ACCOUNT Accounts Receivable **ACCOUNT NO.** 112

Date	Description	Post Ref.	Debit	Credit	Balance Debit	Balance Credit
20XX Mar. 8		J3	300 00		300 00	

ACCOUNT Sales **ACCOUNT NO.** 401

Date	Description	Post Ref.	Debit	Credit	Balance Debit	Balance Credit
20XX Mar. 7		J3		760 00		760 00
Mar. 8		J3		300 00		1 060 00

■ RECORDING AMOUNTS RECEIVED FROM SALES OF MERCHANDISE ON CREDIT

If a credit sale does not involve a cash discount, the amount received from the customer is recorded by debiting Cash and crediting Accounts Receivable. However, if the seller offers a cash discount and the customer pays in time to obtain it, three accounts must be used in recording the amount received. For example, suppose that a seller allows a 3 percent discount on an invoice of $300. The customer deducts $9 for the discount, and the seller receives $291.

Total of invoice	$300
Less 3 percent discount	9
Amount received	$291

The amount of cash actually received from the customer is debited to Cash. The amount of the discount is debited to a revenue account called Sales Discount. The total of the invoice is credited to Accounts Receivable. Study the entry shown below.

WWW Inquiry
Find the URL address for Walgreens. Compute net earnings as a percentage of net sales for the most recent annual report.

A cash discount for a sale of merchandise is debited to the revenue account Sales Discount when the money is received for the invoice.

Recording a Cash Discount

GENERAL JOURNAL Page 4

	Date	Description	Post Ref.	Debit	Credit	
1	20XX					1
2	Mar. 23	Cash	101	291 00		2
3		Sales Discount	403	9 00		3
4		Accounts Receivable	112		300 00	4
5		Received from Shane Appliance				5
6		Store for Invoice 536 less discount.				6
7						7

To the buyer, a cash discount is a ***purchase discount.*** To the seller, it is a ***sales discount.*** Notice that the Sales Discount account is debited, whereas the Sales account is credited. This is because sales discounts represent a reduction in revenue. Notice also that Accounts Receivable is credited for the full amount because the entire debt has been discharged by a smaller payment.

■ RECORDING SALES RETURNS AND ALLOWANCES

Sales returns and allowances are debited to the revenue account Sales Returns and Allowances.

When a customer returns merchandise or receives an allowance, there is a decrease in revenue for the business. This decrease is recorded by debiting the revenue account Sales Returns and Allowances and crediting either Cash or Accounts Receivable.

Returns and Allowances on Cash Sales.
Many businesses provide a cash refund if customers return merchandise or ask for an allowance on goods that were sold for cash. For example, suppose that merchandise sold for $25 cash was found to be defective. The customer returned the item and was given a $25 refund check.

Recording Sales Returns and Allowances for Cash Sales

GENERAL JOURNAL Page 3

Date	Description	Post Ref.	Debit	Credit
20XX Mar. 17	Sales Returns and Allowances	402	25 00	
	Cash	101		25 00
	Issued Check 35 as a refund			
	for the return of defective			
	merchandise.			

Returns and Allowances on Credit Sales.
As discussed on page 90, the procedure for handling returns and allowances on credit sales involves the use of a credit memorandum. When the seller issues a credit memorandum, the customer is given credit in the form of a reduction in the amount owed.

Recording Sales Returns and Allowances for Credit Sales

GENERAL JOURNAL Page 3

Date	Description	Post Ref.	Debit	Credit
20XX Mar. 13	Sales Returns and Allowances	402	80 00	
	Accounts Receivable	112		80 00
	Issued Credit Memorandum 11			
	to Virginia Appliances for the			
	return of merchandise sold on			
	Invoice 543.			

■ RECORDING SALES TAX

Sales tax is credited to the liability account Sales Tax Payable.

When a sales slip or invoice includes sales tax, the tax is collected from the customer, and either Cash or Accounts Receivable is debited. Because the sales tax is owed to the state or city taxing authority, it is credited to a liability account called Sales Tax Payable. The entries shown below illustrate the procedure used to record the tax.

Recording Sales Tax

GENERAL JOURNAL Page 1

	Date	Description	Post Ref.	Debit	Credit	
1	20 XX					1
2	Jan.					2
5	2	Cash	101	10 60		5
6		Sales Tax Payable	203		60	6
7		Sales	401		10 00	7
8		Cash sale plus 6% sales tax.				8
9						9
10	3	Accounts Receivable	112	36 04		10
11		Sales Tax Payable	203		2 04	11
12		Sales	401		34 00	12
13		Sold merchandise on credit to				13
14		Steven Sanchez, Sales Slip 2007.				14
15						15

■ SALES RETURNS AND ALLOWANCES AND SALES TAX

Customers often return merchandise or receive an allowance from retail firms that charge sales tax. In such instances, the customer must be given a refund or a credit for the sales tax as well as for the price of the merchandise.

As a result of a return or allowance, the retailer no longer owes the original amount of tax to the sales tax agency. This means that the Sales Tax Payable account must be debited to record the decrease in the liability. For example, assume that a cash customer returns a $10 item with 6 percent sales tax that was purchased on January 2. She would receive a refund of $10.60. Note that Sales Tax Payable and Sales Returns and Allowances are debited. When a credit memorandum is issued to a charge customer, Accounts Receivable rather than Cash would be credited. If Steven Sanchez returned the merchandise purchased on Sales Slip 2007, the entry would be recorded as shown in the following illustration.

When a return or allowance involves sales tax, debit the sales tax to Sales Tax Payable and debit the amount of the return or allowance to Sales Returns and Allowances.

Recording Sales Tax Transactions

GENERAL JOURNAL Page 1

	Date	Description	Post Ref.	Debit	Credit	
1	20 XX					1
2	Jan.					2
5	5	Sales Tax Payable	203	60		5
6		Sales Returns and Allowances	402	10 00		6
7		Cash	101		10 60	7
8		Refund for the return of				8
9		merchandise plus sales tax.				9
10						10
11	7	Sales Tax Payable	203	2 04		11
12		Sales Returns and Allowances	402	34 00		12
13		Accounts Receivable	112		36 04	13
14		Issued Credit Memorandum 29				14
15		to Steven Sanchez for the return				15
16		of merchandise sold on Sales				16
17		Slip 2007.				17
18						18

RECORDING TYPICAL TRANSACTIONS FOR A MERCHANDISING BUSINESS

Ross Maddalon was the manager of an office supply business for a number of years. When the owner retired, he bought the business and named it Maddalon Office Supply. His firm sells office supplies, microcomputers, and computer products for cash and on credit. Charge customers are allowed credit terms of 1/10, n/30. A sales tax of 6 percent is imposed on all sales.

The chart of accounts for the business is shown below. Notice that certain account numbers have been skipped so that new accounts can be added later as needed. This is a common practice that allows new accounts to be added in their correct numeric order. Also notice that the assets include an account called Merchandise Inventory. The stock of merchandise that a business has on hand for resale is referred to as *merchandise inventory*. This is one of the assets that Ross Maddalon obtained when he bought the business.

Merchandise Inventory: Stock of merchandise that a business has on hand for resale to its customers.

ROSS MADDALON OFFICE SUPPLY
CHART OF ACCOUNTS

Number	Account	Number	Account
100–199	ASSETS	400–499	REVENUE
101	Cash	401	Sales
112	Account Receivable	402	Sales Returns and Allowances
114	Merchandise Inventory	403	Sales Discounts
115	Supplies		
116	Prepaid Insurance	500–599	COSTS AND EXPENSES
126	Store Equipment	501	Merchandise Purchases
128	Office Equipment	502	Freight In
132	Building	503	Purchases Returns and Allowances
134	Land	504	Purchases Discounts
200–299	LIABILITIES	511	Salaries Expense
202	Accounts Payable	512	Telephone Expense
203	Sales Tax Payable	513	Electricity Expense
300–399	OWNER'S EQUITY		
301	Ross Maddalon, Capital		
302	Ross Maddalon, Withdrawals		
399	Income Summary		

On April 1 of the current year, Maddalon began operations as the new owner. During the month of April, the transactions described below and on page 109 were completed. The general journal entries to record the beginning investment and the transactions for April are shown on pages 110 through 113. After you read the description of each transaction, study the related journal entry.

WWW Inquiry
Find the URL address for Walgreens. What is the percentage of change in inventories for the last two years?

Date	Description of Transactions
Apr. 1	Ross Maddalon began operations with the following assets and liabilities: Cash, $11,000; Accounts Receivable, $2,400; Merchandise Inventory, $8,000; Supplies, $600; Store Equipment, $6,000; Office Equipment, $12,000; Building, $30,000; Land, $10,000; and Accounts Payable, $5,000. His owner's equity is $75,000 (assets of $80,000 minus liabilities of $5,000).
2	Paid $2,400 to the National Insurance Company for a two-year insurance policy.

Apr. 2 Purchased a computer for $4,200 on credit from Display Systems, terms n/30.
3 Purchased merchandise for $800 from Allied Office Products; Invoice 1167, dated 4/1, terms 3/10, n/60.
3 Paid $320 to Cohen Packaging for supplies.
5 Paid $2,800 to Office Forms for Invoice B2895. This payment is for a purchase made on credit by the previous owner in March.
6 Returned damaged supplies that were purchased from Cohen Packaging and received a $60 refund.
7 Received $1,696 for cash sales during the first week of April; total sales of $1,600 plus sales tax of $96.
7 Sold merchandise for $800 plus $48 in sales tax (a total of $848) to Data Processors; Invoice 541, terms 1/10, n/30.
9 Received $900 from Sensor Publishing (a customer) for Invoice 538, dated March 10.
9 Refunded $53 to a cash customer for the return of damaged merchandise; $50 for the goods plus $3 sales tax.
9 Paid $776 to Allied Office Products for Invoice 1167 ($800) less discount ($24).
11 Paid $450 for a cash purchase of merchandise.
14 Paid $1,275 for semimonthly salaries.
14 Paid $350 for the electric bill.
14 Paid $135 for the telephone bill.
14 Received $2,385 for cash sales during the second week of April; total sales of $2,250 plus sales tax of $135.
16 Ross Maddalon invested an additional $2,000 in the business.
16 Sold merchandise for $1,300 plus sales tax of $78 (a total of $1,378) to Rosenberg Securities; Invoice 542, terms 1/10, n/30.
16 Returned defective merchandise purchased on April 11 and received a $30 refund from the supplier.
17 Received $840 from Data Processors for Invoice 541 ($848) less discount ($8).
17 Paid $600 for a showcase for the store.
18 Purchased merchandise for $3,600 plus transportation charges of $75 (a total of $3,675) from Arco Calculators; Invoice 6281, dated 4/16, terms 1/10, n/30.
21 Received $2,279 for cash sales during the third week in April: total sales of $2,150 plus sales tax of $129.
24 Received $1,365 from Rosenberg Securities for Invoice 542 ($1,378) less discount ($13).
24 Sold merchandise for $1,250 plus sales tax of $75 (a total of $1,325) to Barbagallo & Co., CPAs; Invoice 543, terms 1/10, n/30.
24 Purchased merchandise for $3,750 from E-Tron Computer Products; Invoice 327, dated 4/21, terms 3/10 EOM.
24 Paid $3,639 to Arco Calculators for Invoice 6281 ($3,675) less discount ($36).
25 Paid $85 to Universal Trucking for transportation charges on the shipment of merchandise from E-Tron Computer Products.
28 Received $4,929 for cash sales during the fourth week in April: total sales of $4,650 plus sales tax of $279.
28 Issued Credit Memorandum 101 for $106 to Barbagallo & Co., CPAs for the return of damaged merchandise; $100 for the goods plus sales tax of $6.
30 Sold merchandise for $950 plus sales tax of $57 (a total of $1,007) to Data Processors; Invoice 544, terms 1/10, n/30.
30 Paid $1,275 for semimonthly salaries.
30 Returned damaged merchandise to E-Tron Computer Products and received Credit Memorandum 481 for $150.
30 Purchased merchandise for $4,200 plus transportation charges of $125 (a total of $4,325) from Allied Office Products; Invoice 1191, dated 4/28, terms 3/10, n/60.
30 Ross Maddalon withdrew $1,000 from the business for his personal use.

Journalizing Transactions

GENERAL JOURNAL
Page 1

Date	Description	Post Ref.	Debit	Credit
20XX				
Apr. 1	Cash		11,000.00	
	Accounts Receivable		2,400.00	
	Merchandise Inventory		8,000.00	
	Supplies		600.00	
	Store Equipment		6,000.00	
	Office Equipment		12,000.00	
	Building		30,000.00	
	Land		10,000.00	
	Accounts Payable			5,000.00
	Ross Maddalon, Capital			75,000.00
	Investment in the business.			
2	Prepaid Insurance		240.00	
	Cash			240.00
	Paid insurance premium in advance			
	for a two-year period.			
2	Office Equipment		420.00	
	Accounts Payable			420.00
	Purchased a computer on credit			
	from Display Systems; terms n/30.			
3	Merchandise Purchases		800.00	
	Accounts Payable			800.00
	Purchased merchandise on credit			
	from Allied Office Products; Invoice			
	1167, dated April 1, terms 3/10, n/60.			
3	Supplies		320.00	
	Cash			320.00
	Purchased store supplies.			
5	Accounts Payable		2,800.00	
	Cash			2,800.00
	Paid Office Forms for Invoice B2895.			
6	Cash		60.00	
	Supplies			60.00
	Returned damaged supplies.			
7	Cash		1,696.00	
	Sales Tax Payable			96.00
	Sales			1,600.00
	Cash sales for first week of April.			
7	Accounts Receivable		848.00	
	Sales Tax Payable			48.00
	Sales			800.00
	Sold merchandise on credit to Data			
	Processors; Invoice 541; terms			
	1/10, n/30.			
			93,124.00	93,124.00

Journalizing Transactions (continued)

GENERAL JOURNAL   Page 2

	Date	Description	Post Ref.	Debit	Credit
1	20XX				
2	Apr. 9	Cash		900 00	
3		Accounts Receivable			900 00
4		Received payment from Sensor			
5		Publishing for Invoice 538.			
6					
7	9	Sales Returns and Allowances		50 00	
8		Sales Tax Payable		3 00	
9		Cash			53 00
10		Refund for the return of damaged			
11		merchandise.			
12					
13	9	Accounts Payable		800 00	
14		Cash			776 00
15		Purchases Discount			24 00
16		Paid Allied Office Products for			
17		Invoice 1167 less discount.			
18					
19	11	Merchandise Purchases		450 00	
20		Cash			450 00
21		Purchased merchandise.			
22					
23	14	Salaries Expense		1 275 00	
24		Cash			1 275 00
25		Paid semimonthly salaries.			
26					
27	14	Electricity Expense		350 00	
28		Cash			350 00
29		Paid electric bill.			
30					
31	14	Telephone Expense		135 00	
32		Cash			135 00
33		Paid telephone bill.			
34					
35	14	Cash		2 385 00	
36		Sales Tax Payable			135 00
37		Sales			2 250 00
38		Cash sales for second week			
39		of April.			
40					
41	16	Cash		2 000 00	
43		Ross Maddalon, Capital			2 000 00
44		Additional investment.			
45					
46	16	Accounts Receivable		1 378 00	
47		Sales Tax Payable			78 00
48		Sales			1 300 00
49		Sold merchandise on credit to			
50		Rosenberg Securities; Invoice 542,			
51		terms 1/10, n/30.			
52				9 726 00	9 726 00

Journalizing Transactions (continued)

GENERAL JOURNAL Page 3

	Date		Description	Post Ref.	Debit	Credit	
1	20	XX					1
2	Apr.	16	Cash		30 00		2
3			Purchases Returns and Allowances			30 00	3
4			Returned defective merchandise.				4
5							5
6		17	Cash		840 00		6
7			Sales Discount		8 00		7
8			Accounts Receivable			848 00	8
9			Received payment from Data				9
10			Processors for Invoice 541				10
11			less discount.				11
12							12
13		17	Store Equipment		600 00		13
14			Cash			600 00	14
15			Purchased a showcase.				15
16							16
17		18	Merchandise Purchases		3 600 00		17
18			Freight In		75 00		18
19			Accounts Payable			3 675 00	19
20			Purchased merchandise on credit				20
21			from Arco Calculators; Invoice 6281;				21
22			dated April 16, terms 1/10, n/30.				22
23							23
24		21	Cash		2 279 00		24
25			Sales Tax Payable			129 00	25
26			Sales			2 150 00	26
27			Cash sales for third week of April.				27
28							28
29		24	Cash		1 365 00		29
30			Sales Discount		13 00		30
31			Accounts Receivable			1 378 00	31
32			Received payment from Rosenberg				32
33			Securities for Invoice 542				33
34			less discount.				34
35							35
36		24	Accounts Receivable		1 325 00		36
37			Sales Tax Payable			75 00	37
38			Sales			1 250 00	38
39			Sold merchandise on credit to				39
40			Barbagallo & Co., CPAs; Invoice				40
41			543, terms 1/10, n/30.				42
43							43
44		24	Merchandise Purchases		3 750 00		44
45			Accounts Payable			3 750 00	45
46			Purchased merchandise on credit				46
47			from E-Tron Computer Products,				47
48			Invoice 327, dated April 21, terms				48
49			5/10 EOM.				49
50					13 885 00	13 885 00	50
51							51
52							52

GENERAL JOURNAL

Page 4

Journalizing Transactions (continued)

Date		Description	Post Ref.	Debit	Credit
20XX					
Apr.	24	Accounts Payable		3675 00	
		Cash			3639 00
		Purchases Discount			36 00
		Paid Arco Calculators for Invoice			
		6281 less discount.			
	25	Freight In		85 00	
		Cash			85 00
		Paid freight charges on shipment			
		from E-Tron Computer Products.			
	28	Cash		4929 00	
		Sales Tax Payable			279 00
		Sales			4650 00
		Cash sales for fourth week of April.			
	28	Sales Returns and Allowances		100 00	
		Sales Tax Payable		6 00	
		Accounts Receivable			106 00
		Issued Credit Memorandum 101 to			
		Barbagallo & Co., CPAs.			
	30	Accounts Receivable		1007 00	
		Sales Tax Payable			57 00
		Sales			950 00
		Sold merchandise on credit to			
		Data Processors; Invoice 544,			
		terms 1/10, n/30.			
	30	Salaries Expense		1275 00	
		Cash			1275 00
		Paid semimonthly salaries.			
	30	Accounts Payable		150 00	
		Purchases Returns and Allowances			150 00
		Received Credit Memorandum 481			
		from E-Tron Computer Products.			
	30	Merchandise Purchases		4200 00	
		Freight In		125 00	
		Accounts Payable			4325 00
		Purchased merchandise on credit			
		from Allied Office Products;			
		Invoice 1191, dated April 28,			
		terms 3/10, n/60.			
	30	Ross Maddalon, Withdrawals		1000 00	
		Cash			1000 00
		Withdrawal for personal use.			
				16552 00	16552 00

CHAPTER 14 SUMMARY

- Sales of merchandise are credited to a revenue account called Sales.
- When a customer deducts a cash discount, the amount is debited to the Sales Discount account.
- The Sales Returns and Allowances account is used to record the decrease in sales revenue that results when a customer returns merchandise or receives an allowance. This account is debited for all returns and allowances. If the customer is given a cash refund, the Cash account is credited. If the amount is deducted from a balance that the customer owes, the Accounts Receivable account is credited.
- States, cities, and counties may impose a sales tax. The retailer collects this tax from customers. When sales are made, the amount of sales tax is credited to the liability account Sales Tax Payable.
- If a refund or a credit for a sales return or allowance involves sales tax, Sales Tax Payable is debited for the amount of the tax and Sales Returns and Allowances is debited for the amount of the return or allowance.

CHAPTER APPLICATIONS

EXERCISES

Complete the following assignments on the forms provided in your workbook.

EXERCISE 14-1

Analyzing sales transactions for a wholesale merchandising business.

Instructions:
For each of the following transactions, record the titles of the accounts involved and indicate whether they would be debited or credited.

Transactions:

a. Sold merchandise on credit.
b. Sold merchandise for cash.
c. Issued a credit memorandum to a customer for a return of defective merchandise previously sold on credit.
d. Refunded cash to a customer for a return of damaged merchandise previously sold for cash.
e. Received cash from a credit customer in payment of an invoice.
f. Received cash from a credit customer in payment of an invoice less a discount.

EXERCISE 14-2

Analyzing sales transactions for a retail merchandising business.

Instructions:
For each of the following transactions, record the titles of the accounts involved and indicate whether each account would be debited or credited. Sales tax is charged on each sale.

Transactions:

a. Sold merchandise for cash.
b. Sold merchandise on credit.
c. Refunded the price of damaged merchandise plus sales tax to a cash customer.
d. Issued a credit memorandum to a charge customer for the price of defective merchandise plus related sales tax.
e. Received cash on account from a charge customer.

EXERCISE 14-3

Accounting for sales, returns and allowances, and discounts.

Instructions:

1. Set up the following T accounts, and enter the balances.
2. Analyze each of the following transactions, and record the effects in the T accounts.
3. Compute the balance of each account.
4. Prepare a trial balance for Garden Products as of September 30 of the current year.

Cash	$10,000	Sales Returns	
Accounts Receivable	–0–	and Allowances	–0–
Gabriel Michaels,		Sales Discount	–0–
Capital	10,000		
Sales	–0–		

Transactions:

a. Sold merchandise for $1,000 to Pennwood Stores; terms 2/10, n/30.
b. Sold merchandise for $500 to Colleen Distributing; terms 2/10, n/30.
c. Allowed a $100 credit to Pennwood Stores for the return of damaged merchandise.
d. Received $392 from Pennwood Stores to settle its account within the discount period.
e. Received $980 from Colleen Distributing as the balance due on its account within the discount period.

EXERCISE 14-4

Accounting for sales, sales tax, and returns and allowances.

Instructions:

1. Set up T accounts for Cash, Accounts Receivable, Sales, Sales Tax Payable, and Sales Returns and Allowances.
2. Analyze each of the following transactions, and record the effects in the T accounts.
3. Compute the balance of each account.
4. Then add the debit balances and the credit balances to prove that the totals are equal.

Transactions:

a. Sold merchandise for $200 plus sales tax of $12 to Jessica James on credit.
b. Sold merchandise for $300 plus sales tax of $18 to Ty Jordan on credit.
c. Allowed a $53 credit to Jessica James for the return of damaged merchandise; $50 for the goods plus sales tax of $3.
d. Received $159 from Jessica James as the balance due on her account.
e. Gave an allowance of $106 to Ty Jordan to reduce the price of damaged merchandise; $100 for the goods plus sales tax of $6.
f. Received the balance due from Ty Jordan.

PROBLEMS

Complete all assigned problems on the forms provided in your workbook.

PROBLEM 14-1

Accounting for sales, sales tax, and sales returns and allowances. The Oreland Furniture Store charges a 5 percent sales tax on all sales. On June 1 of the current year, the general ledger shows the following accounts and balances.

101 Cash	$30,000	301 Sharon Griffiths, Capital	$30,000
112 Accounts Receivable	–0–	401 Sales	–0–
203 Sales Tax Payable	–0–	402 Sales Returns and Allowances	–0–

Instructions:

1. Open the general ledger accounts, and enter the balances.
2. Record the June transactions in the general journal. Use *1* as the page number of the journal.
3. Foot the journal.
4. Post the journal entries to the ledger accounts.
5. Prepare a trial balance as of June 30 of the current year.

Transactions:

June 3 Sold merchandise for $420 on credit to Grace Maynard; Sales Slip 1201, $400 for the goods plus sales tax of $20.

7 Sold merchandise for $1,161.30 in cash during the first week of June; $1,106 for the goods plus sales tax of $55.30.

9 Sold merchandise for $630 on credit to Rachel Spinrad; Sales Slip 1202, $600 for the goods plus sales tax of $30.

13 Issued Credit Memorandum 28 for $105 to Rachel Spinrad for damaged merchandise that she returned; $100 for the goods plus sales tax of $5.

14 Sold merchandise for $1,279.95 in cash during the second week of June; $1,219 for the goods plus sales tax of $60.95.

16 Sold merchandise for $598.50 on credit to Rita Ponzio, Sales Slip 1203, $570 for the goods plus sales tax of $28.50.

21 Sold merchandise for $1,554 in cash during the third week of June; $1,480 for the goods plus sales tax of $74.

24 Received $420 in cash from Grace Maynard in payment of Sales Slip 1201.

28 Sold merchandise for $1,077.30 in cash during the fourth week of June; $1,026 for the goods plus sales tax of $51.30.

CASE STUDY

Write the answer to the case study on the form provided in your workbook.

Sales Transactions

In studying the use of T accounts in analyzing sales transactions, you understand that when sales are made on account, the T accounts affected are accounts receivable and sales.

You have learned that the account, Accounts Receivable, is debited because it is an asset account; and that Sales is credited because it is a revenue account. One of your friends thinks, therefore, that Sales should be debited when a customer returns merchandise.

Critical Thinking

■ *What can you tell her to help her understand how a sales returns and allowances account would be used?*

CHAPTER FIFTEEN

The Sales Journal

Accounting Terminology

- Cross-footing
- Posting reference *S*
- Sales journal
- Special journal

OBJECTIVES

Upon completion of this chapter, you should be able to:

1. Record sales of merchandise on credit in a sales journal.
2. Total, prove, and rule the sales journal.
3. Post from the sales journal.

INTRODUCTION

Every business has certain types of transactions that take place often and require similar journal entries. For example, the general journal prepared by Maddalon Office Supply during April shows four entries for sales of merchandise on credit. From these entries, 12 separate postings had to be made to the general ledger.

As Maddalon Office Supply expands its business activities, it will have many more credit sales each month. This will lead to even greater repetition in its journal entries and postings. ■

Sales Transactions in the General Journal

GENERAL JOURNAL   Page 1

Date		Description	Post Ref.	Debit	Credit
20XX					
Apr.					
	7	Accounts Receivable	112	848 00	
		Sales Tax Payable	203		48 00
		Sales	401		800 00
		Sold merchandise on credit to			
		Data Processors; Invoice 541,			
		terms 1/10, n/30.			
	16	Accounts Receivable	112	1 378 00	
		Sales Tax Payable	203		78 00
		Sales	401		1 300 00
		Sold merchandise on credit to			
		Rosenberg Securities; Invoice 542,			
		terms 1/10, n/30.			
	24	Accounts Receivable	112	1 325 00	
		Sales Tax Payable	203		75 00
		Sales	401		1 250 00
		Sold merchandise on credit to			
		Barbagallo & Co., CPAs; Invoice 543,			
		terms 1/10, n/30.			

GENERAL JOURNAL
Page 1

	Date	Description	Post Ref.	Debit	Credit	
1	20 XX					1
2	Apr.					2
5	30	Accounts Receivable	112	1 007 00		5
6		Sales Tax Payable	203		57 00	6
7		Sales	401		950 00	7
8		Sold merchandise on credit to				8
9		Data Processors; Invoice 544,				9
10		terms 1/10, n/30.				10

Sales Transactions in the General Journal (Continued)

■ RECORDING TRANSACTIONS IN THE SALES JOURNAL

One way to reduce repetition in journalizing and posting is to have a *special journal* for all sales of merchandise on credit. Since this special journal is used to record *only sales of merchandise on credit,* it is called *a sales journal.*

Maddalon Office Supply will be using a sales journal from now on. The business's credit sales for April are shown below as they would be recorded in the sales journal.

Special Journal: Journal in which only one kind of transaction is entered. The Sales Journal is an example of a special journal.

Sales Journal: Chronological record of credit sales of merchandise.

SALES JOURNAL
FOR MONTH OF APRIL, 20XX
Page 1

	Date	Inv. No.	Customer's Account Name	✔	Accounts Receivable Debit	Sales Tax Payable Credit	Sales Credit	
1	20 XX							1
2	Apr. 7	541	Data Processors		848 00	48 00	800 00	2
3	16	542	Rosenberg Securities		1 378 00	78 00	1 300 00	3
4	24	543	Barbagallo & Co., CPAs		1 325 00	75 00	1 250 00	4
5	30	544	Data Processors		1 007 00	57 00	950 00	5

Sales Transactions in the Sales Journal

Notice the advantages of the sales journal.

- All entries for sales of merchandise on credit are grouped together in one place in chronological order rather than being scattered throughout the general journal. Thus information about credit sales can be located quickly and easily.
- The important facts about each transaction are written on a single line. These facts include the date, the invoice number, the name of the customer, the amount of the receivable, the sales tax, and the amount of the sale.
- There is no need to enter account names or to write a long explanation for each transaction.
- It allows for greater division of labor—one person can be put in charge of entering sales.

The source of information for each entry in the sales journal is the sales invoice or sales slip. Maddalon Office Supply uses a duplicate copy of the sales invoice that is sent to each customer who buys on credit.

Because the source documents are numbered in order and the numbers are recorded in the sales journal, it is easy to check that all credit sales have been entered. Also, the correct source document is always available as a quick reference. The copies of the sales invoices or sales slips are filed for this purpose after the journalizing is completed.

WWW Inquiry
Find the URL address for General Electric. What was the change in revenues for the last two years?

■ POSTING FROM THE SALES JOURNAL

Another major advantage of the special sales journal is that it simplifies the posting of credit sales to the general ledger. At the end of each month, the money columns of the sales

Cross-Footing: Adding the totals of all Debit columns and the totals of all Credit columns to prove that they are equal.

Posting of Monthly Totals from Sales Journal with Three Money Columns: Accounts Receivable Debit Sales Tax Payable Credit Sales Credit

Posting Reference for Sales Journal: The letter *S* and the journal page number.

Posting from the Sales Journal

journal are pencil-footed. The footings are then checked for accuracy by *cross-footing*. Cross-footing proves that the total of the Debit columns equal the total of the Credit column ($4,558 = $258 + $4,300). This procedure verifies that equal debits and credits were recorded during the month. After the equality of the debits and credits is proved, the column totals are written in regular-size ink figures and the journal is ruled. Then each column total is posted separately: a single debit to the Accounts Receivable accounts; a single credit to the Sales Tax Payable account; and a single credit to the Sales account.

As each column total is posted to an account in the general ledger, the ledger account number is written in parentheses below the total in the journal.

Observe how the sales journal is totaled and how the postings are recorded. In the ledger accounts, the abbreviation *S* and the journal page number are written in the Posting Reference column to identify the postings from the sales journal.

SALES JOURNAL
FOR MONTH OF APRIL, 20XX   Page 1

Date	Inv. No.	Customer's Account Name	✓	Accounts Receivable Debit	Sales Tax Payable Credit	Sales Credit
20XX						
Apr. 7	541	Data Processors		848 00	48 00	800 00
16	542	Rosenberg Securities		1378 00	78 00	1300 00
24	543	Barbagallo & Co., CPAs		1325 00	75 00	1250 00
30	544	Data Processors		1007 00	57 00	950 00
30		Totals		4558 00	258 00	4300 00
				(112)	(203)	(401)

ACCOUNT Accounts Receivable   **ACCOUNT NO.** 112

Date	Description	Post Ref.	Debit	Credit	Balance Debit	Balance Credit
20XX Apr.						
30		S1	4558 00		6852 00	

ACCOUNT Sales Tax Payable   **ACCOUNT NO.** 203

Date	Description	Post Ref.	Debit	Credit	Balance Debit	Balance Credit
20XX Apr.						
30		S1		258 00		258 00

ACCOUNT Sales   **ACCOUNT NO.** 401

Date	Description	Post Ref.	Debit	Credit	Balance Debit	Balance Credit
20XX Apr.						
30		S1		4300 00		4300 00

WWW Inquiry
Find the URL address for General Electric. What does General Electric report for net earnings per share for the last three years?

The single posting to each account saves time and reduces the possibility of error. Remember that when the general journal was used, 12 separate postings were needed to transfer the same information to the general ledger.

The sales journal can be easily adapted to meet the special needs of a business. For instance, if it is the custom of a business to add delivery charges to a bill, there can be a separate column for this. A wholesaler who does not charge sales tax would have no need for the Sales Tax Payable Credit column in the Sales Journal above.

CHAPTER 15 SUMMARY

- The sales journal is a special journal that is used for recording sales of merchandise on credit. It allows a business to save time and avoid repetition in the journalizing and posting of its credit sales.
- The sales journal organizes in one place all the information about credit sales. The columns further organize all the information for one transaction on a single line.
- The information needed for entries in the sales journal is taken from copies of the sales invoices or from copies of the sales slips.
- At the end of each month, the figures in the sales journal are added and cross-footed. The column totals are posted to the general ledger as a debit to the Accounts Receivable account, a credit to the Sales Tax Payable account, and a credit to the Sales account.
- The form of the journal can be tailored to meet the specific needs of each business.

CHAPTER APPLICATIONS

EXERCISES

Complete the following assignments on the forms provided in your workbook.

EXERCISE 15-1

Identifying transactions to be recorded in a sales journal.

Instructions:
Analyze the following transactions and decide which ones should be recorded in a sales journal.

Transactions:
a. Sold merchandise on credit.
b. Sold a used computer from the office for cash.
c. Sold merchandise for cash.
d. Sold used computer printer on credit.
e. Sold merchandise to a customer on terms of 2/10, n/30.

EXERCISE 15-2

Posting from a sales journal. Page 6 of a sales journal shows the following totals as of June 30 of the current year: Accounts Receivable, $5,300; Sales Tax Payable, $300; and Sales, $5,000.

Instructions:
Write the answers to the following questions in your workbook.

1. What information would be recorded in the Posting Reference column of each of the ledger accounts to show that the amounts have been posted from the sales journal?
2. What information would be entered in the sales journal to show that the amounts have been posted to the ledger accounts?

EXERCISE 15-3

Identifying transactions to be recorded in a sales journal. Refer to Exercise 14-2.

Instructions:
Identify, by letter, which transaction should be recorded in a sales journal that provides columns for Accounts Receivable, Sales Tax Payable, and Sales.

EXERCISE 15-4

Designing and posting from a sales journal. The Asbury Market uses four revenue accounts to record sales of meat and poultry, produce, dairy products, and nonfood items. Sales tax is charged on all nonfood items. During January, the market issued 1,040 sales slips to credit customers.

Instructions:
a. List the columns that you would include in the sales journal for the Asbury Market.
b. If the market recorded the January credit sales in a general journal, how many times would the title of the Accounts Receivable account be written? How many debit postings would be made to the Accounts Receivable account?
c. If the market used a sales journal during January, how many debit postings would be made to the Accounts Receivable account? How many debit postings would be made to the Accounts Receivable account during the year?

PROBLEMS

Complete all assigned problems on the forms provided in your workbook.

PROBLEM 15-1

Using a sales journal and a general journal. The Shippensburg Appliance Store sells merchandise that is subject to a 5 percent sales tax. The store uses a general journal and a sales journal that provides columns for Accounts Receivable, Sales Tax Payable, and Sales.

Instructions:

1. Record the February transactions in the proper journal. Use 2 as the page number of each journal.
2. Foot and cross-foot the sales journal. Enter the totals and rule the journal.

Transactions:

Feb. 3   Sold merchandise on credit for $360 plus sales tax of $18 to Dan Vann; Invoice 201.

5   Sold merchandise on credit for $240 plus sales tax of $12 to Grace Maynard; Invoice 202.

8   Issued Invoice 203 for $86 plus sales tax of $4.30 to Meghan Kennedy, a charge customer.

11   Allowed a credit of $25 plus sales tax of $1.25 to Dan Vann for the return of defective merchandise; Credit Memorandum 22.

13   Sold merchandise on credit for $180 plus sales tax of $9 to Rita Ponzio; Invoice 204.

15   Received $1,472.39 from accounts receivable.

17   Issued Invoice 205 for $274 plus sales tax of $13.70 to Melissa Tressalt, a charge customer.

21   Accepted the return of merchandise bought by Rita Ponzio on February 13; Invoice 204. Full credit was allowed on Credit Memorandum 23.

24   Sold merchandise on credit for $200 plus sales tax of $10 to Katie Urffer; Invoice 206.

28   Sold merchandise on credit for $90 plus sales tax of $4.50 to George Wells; Invoice 207.

Save your work for use in Problem 15-2.

PROBLEM 15-2

Posting from a sales journal and a general journal. This problem is a continuation of Problem 15-1. The ledger account balances for the Shippensburg Appliance Store on February 1 of the current year are as follows.

101	Cash	$10,947.62
112	Accounts Receivable	1,472.39
203	Sales Tax Payable	–0–
301	Joan Brennan, Capital	12,420.01
401	Sales	–0–
402	Sales Returns and Allowances	–0–

Instructions:

1. Open the ledger accounts and enter the balances.
2. Post from the sales journal and the general journal completed in Problem 15-1 to the ledger accounts.
3. Prepare a trial balance.

CASE STUDY

Write the answer to the case study on the form provided in your workbook.

Journalizing and Posting Transactions

As you prepare the sales journal, you wonder if it would be easier to just use the ledger accounts and enter the information directly in them instead of the two-step process of journalizing and then posting to the ledger accounts.

> **Critical Thinking**
>
> ■ *Explain why it is important to journalize and then post to the ledger accounts.*

CHAPTER SIXTEEN

The Purchases Journal

OBJECTIVES

Upon completion of this chapter, you should be able to:

1. Record purchases of merchandise on credit in a purchases journal.
2. Total, prove, and rule the purchases journal.
3. Post from the purchases journal.

Accounting Terminology

- Posting reference *P*
- Purchases journal

INTRODUCTION

The use of a sales journal simplifies accounting work and saves time. To achieve even more efficiency, many businesses also have a special journal for purchases of merchandise on credit.

The recording of credit purchases in the general journal involves the same kind of repetition as the recording of credit sales in the general journal. Look at the following general journal entries. They show four purchases of merchandise on credit made by Maddalon Office Supply during April. From these entries, ten separate postings were needed to transfer the information to the general ledger. ■

Purchases Transactions

GENERAL JOURNAL — Page 1

	Date	Description	Post Ref.	Debit	Credit
1	20XX				
2	Apr.				
5	3	Merchandise Purchases	501	800 00	
6		Accounts Payable	202		800 00
7		Purchased merchandise on credit			
8		from Allied Office Products; Invoice			
9		1167, dated April 1, terms 3/10, n/60.			
10					
15	18	Merchandise Purchases	501	3 600 00	
16		Freight In	502	75 00	
17		Accounts Payable	202		3 675 00
18		Purchased merchandise on credit			
19		from Arco Calculators; Invoice 6281,			
20		dated April 16, terms 1/10, n/30.			
21					
25	24	Merchandise Purchases	501	3 750 00	
26		Accounts Payable	202		3 750 00
27		Purchased merchandise on credit			
28		from E-Tron Computer Products;			
29		Invoice 327, dated April 21,			
30		terms 3/10 EOM.			

121

Purchases Transactions (Continued)

GENERAL JOURNAL Page 1

	Date	Description	Post Ref.	Debit	Credit	
1	20 XX					1
2	Apr.					2
5	30	Merchandise Purchases	501	4 200 00		5
6		Freight In	502	125 00		6
7		Accounts Payable	202		4 325 00	7
8		Purchased merchandise on credit				8
9		from Allied Office Products; Invoice				9
10		1191, dated April 28, terms 3/10, n/60.				10

Purchases Journal:
Chronological record of credit purchases of merchandise.

By using a *purchases journal* as well as a sales journal, Maddalon Office Supply will further reduce repetition in the journalizing and posting of its transactions. Purchases of merchandise on credit can be recorded easily and quickly in the special purchases journal.

Note that purchases of merchandise for cash, purchases of supplies, and purchases of permanent assets cannot be entered in the purchases journal. This special journal is used to record *only purchases of merchandise on credit.* At this point, purchases other than merchandise for credit will be recorded in the general journal.

■ RECORDING TRANSACTIONS IN THE PURCHASES JOURNAL

The purchases journal offers the same type of advantage as the sales journal. All journal entries for purchases of merchandise on credit are grouped together in one place. The column headings permit the important facts about each transaction to be recorded in a minimum amount of space and with a minimum amount of work. A single line is needed to enter a purchase. No account titles are used. Only the name of the creditor is entered. The use of the purchases journal also permits further division of labor.

The purchases of merchandise on credit made by Maddalon Office Supply during April are shown below as they would be recorded in a purchases journal.

PURCHASES JOURNAL
FOR MONTH OF APRIL, 20XX Page 1

	Date	Creditor's Account Credited	Post. Ref.	Invoice No.	Invoice Date	Terms	Accounts Payable Credit	Merch Purchases Debit	Freight in Debit	
1	20 XX									1
2	Apr. 3	Allied Office Products		1167	4/1/XX	3/10, n/60	800 00	800 00		2
3	18	Arco Calculators		6281	4/16/XX	1/10, n/30	3 675 00	3 600 00	75 00	3
4	24	E-Tron Computer Products		327	4/21/XX	3/10 EOM	3 750 00	3 750 00		4
5	30	Allied Office Products		1191	4/28/XX	3/10, n/60	4 325 00	4 200 00	125 00	5
6										6

The source documents for entries in the purchases journal are the purchase invoices received from suppliers. The procedures for handling the purchase invoice were discussed in Chapter 12.

The invoice on page 123 is recorded on the first line of the purchases journal shown above. Notice that the date used for the journal entry (April 3) is the date on which the invoice was received. (This date appears in the processing stamp.) The date that the supplier prepared the invoice (April 1) is recorded in the Invoice Date column of the journal. The other important facts taken from the invoice are the name of the supplier, the invoice number, the credit terms, and the total of the purchase.

WWW Inquiry
Find the URL address for Disney. What is Disney's overriding objective?

Observe that Maddalon Office Supply uses a processing stamp on its purchase invoices. After an invoice is entered in the purchases journal, the number of the journal page is written in the stamped area. Then the invoice is placed in an unpaid invoices file until the due date for payment. When payment is made, information about the payment is recorded in the stamped area of the invoice. Finally, the invoice is placed in a paid invoices file in case it is needed for future reference.

ALLIED OFFICE PRODUCTS
162 Oxford Street
Newark, NJ 07102

INVOICE NO. **1167**

SOLD TO: MADDALON OFFICE SUPPLY
5755 Magnolia Trail
Mercerville, NJ 08619

INVOICE DATE: 4/1/XX
TERMS: 3/10, n/60

DATE OF ORDER: 3/2/XX
CUSTOMER ORDER NO.: 081
SHIPPED VIA: Ward Motor Freight
SALES REPRESENTATIVE: Sadowski

QUAN.	STOCK NO.	DESCRIPTION	UNIT PRICE	EXTENSION
50	A113X20	Reams of bond paper	$9.82	$491.00
100	A164X68	Reams of duplicator paper	3.09	309.00
		TOTAL		$800.00

Date Received: 4/3/XX
Quantities & Prices: JGB
Extensions & Total: AML
Due Date: 4/11/XX
Journal Page No.: P1
Payment Date:
Check No.:

WWW Inquiry
Find the URL address for Walgreens. Was any increase in selling, occupancy, and administrative expenses for the last two years offset by the increase in net sales for the same period?

The form used for the purchases journal may vary. Some businesses arrange the columns of this journal in a different order. Other businesses add more columns so that they can record additional information.

■ POSTING FROM THE PURCHASES JOURNAL

At the end of each month, the figures in the money columns of the purchases journal are pencil-footed and then checked for accuracy by cross-footing. If the total of the Debit columns equals the total of the Credit column, the totals are then written in ink. The total of the Merchandise Purchases column represents the cost of all the purchases of merchandise on credit made during the month. This amount is posted as a single debit to the Merchandise Purchases account. The total of the Freight In column is posted as a single debit to Freight In, and the total of the Accounts Payable column is posted as a single credit to Accounts Payable.

Notice that the account numbers are placed in parentheses beneath the totals in the journal. The abbreviation *P* and the journal page number are used in the Posting Reference column of the general ledger accounts to identify postings from the purchases journal.

Posting of Monthly Totals from Purchases Journal with Three Money Columns:
Accounts Payable Credit
Merchandise Purchases Debit
Freight In Debit

Posting Reference for Purchases Journal: The letter *P* and the journal page number.

PURCHASES JOURNAL
FOR MONTH OF APRIL, 20XX
Page 1

	Date		Creditor's Account Credited	Post. Ref.	Invoice No.	Invoice Date	Terms	Accounts Payable Credit	Merch Purchases Debit	Freight in Debit	
1	20	XX									1
2	Apr.	3	Allied Office Products		1167	4/1/XX	3/10, n/60	800 00	800 00		2
3		18	Arco Calculators		6281	4/16/XX	1/10, n/30	3675 00	3600 00	75 00	3
4		24	E-Tron Computer Products		327	4/21/XX	3/10 EOM	3750 00	3750 00		4
5		30	Allied Office Products		1191	4/28/XX	3/10, n/60	4325 00	4200 00	125 00	5
6		30	Totals					12550 00	12350 00	200 00	6
7								(202)	(501)	(502)	7
8											8

Posting from the Purchases Journal

ACCOUNT **Accounts Payable** ACCOUNT NO. **202**

Date		Description	Post Ref.	Debit	Credit	Balance Debit	Balance Credit
20	XX						
Apr.							
	30		P1		12550 00		21600 00

ACCOUNT **Merchandise Purchases** ACCOUNT NO. **501**

Date		Description	Post Ref.	Debit	Credit	Balance Debit	Balance Credit
20	XX						
Apr.							
	30		P1	12350 00		12350 00	

ACCOUNT **Freight In** ACCOUNT NO. **502**

Date		Description	Post Ref.	Debit	Credit	Balance Debit	Balance Credit
20	XX						
Apr.							
	30		P1	200 00		285 00	

CHAPTER 16 SUMMARY

- The purchases journal is a special journal for recording purchases of merchandise on credit.
- The information about each transaction is taken from a purchase invoice and is entered on a single line of the purchases journal.
- The journal entry for each purchase shows the date the invoice was received, the supplier's name, the invoice number, the invoice date, the credit terms, and the amount of the purchase.
- At the end of the month, the figures in the purchases journal are added and cross-footed. The column totals are posted as a debit to the Merchandise Purchases account, a debit to the Freight In account, and a credit to the Accounts Payable account.

CHAPTER APPLICATIONS

EXERCISES

Complete the following assignments on the forms provided in your workbook.

EXERCISE 16-1

Identifying transactions to be recorded in a purchases journal.

Instructions:
Analyze the following transactions and decide which transactions would be recorded in a purchases journal.

a. Purchased merchandise for cash.
b. Purchased merchandise on credit.
c. Purchased office equipment for cash.
d. Purchased office equipment on credit.
e. Purchased merchandise on terms of 2/10, n/30.

EXERCISE 16-2

Posting from a purchases journal. On May 31 of the current year, Page 5 of a purchases journal shows the following totals: Accounts Payable, $14,477; Merchandise Purchases, $14,021; and Freight In, $456.

Instructions:
Answer the following questions on the forms provided.

1. What information would be recorded in the Posting Reference column of each of the ledger accounts to show that the amounts have been posted from the purchases journal?
2. What information would be entered in the purchases journal to show that the amounts have been posted to the ledger accounts?

EXERCISE 16-3

Identifying transactions to be recorded in a purchases journal. Refer to Exercise 13-4.

Instructions:
Identify, by letter, which transactions should be recorded in a purchases journal that provides columns for Accounts Payable, Merchandise Purchases, and Freight In.

EXERCISE 16-4

Designing and posting from a purchases journal.
The Lamp Lighter uses three cost accounts for merchandise purchases: Lamp Purchases, Fixture Purchases, and Shade Purchases. All the purchase invoices that the store receives include freight charges to cover the manufacturer's cost of shipping the merchandise. During the year, the store received 170 invoices for lamps, 150 invoices for fixtures, and 130 invoices for shades.

Instructions:

1. List the columns that you would include in the purchases journal for the Lamp Lighter.
2. Answer the questions on the forms provided.

   a. If the Lamp Lighter recorded each purchase of merchandise in a general journal, what would have been the total number of debits posted to the purchases accounts during the year? How many debits would have been posted to Freight In during the year?

   b. If the Lamp Lighter recorded the invoices in a purchases journal, how many debit and credit postings would have been made during the year?

PROBLEMS

Complete all assigned problems on the forms provided in your workbook.

PROBLEM 16-1

Using a purchases journal and a general ledger.
Lakehurst Lumber purchases lumber and building materials from various suppliers. Its accounting records include a general journal and a purchases journal that provides columns for Accounts Payable, Merchandise Purchases, and Freight In.

Instructions:

1. Record the September transactions in the proper journal. Use *1* as the page number of each journal.
2. Foot and cross-foot the purchases journal. Enter the totals and rule the journal.

Transactions:

Sept. 4 Purchased merchandise for $897.60 plus freight of $64.57 from U.S. Timber; Invoice 413, dated September 1; terms are 2/10, n/30.

7 Purchased merchandise for $1,347.91 plus freight of $98.63 from North East Lumber; Invoice A97, dated September 5; terms are net 30.

11 Issued a check for $944.22 to U.S. Timber in payment of Invoice 413 for $962.17 less a $17.95 discount.

16 Purchased merchandise for $1,126.75 from Canadian Forest Products; Invoice C82, dated September 14; terms are 3/10, n/30.

18 Issued a check for $126 to pay freight charges on the shipment of merchandise from Canadian Forest Products.

Sept. 19 Returned damaged merchandise to North East Lumber and received Credit Memorandum 418 for $145.

24 Issued a check for $1,092.95 to Canadian Forest Products in payment of Invoice C82 for $1,126.75 less a $33.80 discount.

26 Purchase office equipment for $475 from Halifax Furniture; Invoice 1046, dated September 22; terms are n/60.

30 Purchased merchandise for $1,027.54 plus freight of $75.60 from Atlantic Saw Mill; Invoice W930, dated September 24; terms are 2/10, n/30.

Save your work for use in Problem 16-2.

PROBLEM 16-2

Posting from a purchases journal and a general journal. This problem is a continuation of Problem 16-1. The ledger account balances for Lakehurst Lumber on September 1 of the current year are as follows.

101	Cash	$ 8,194.20
120	Office Equipment	5,726.00
202	Accounts Payable	2,072.44
301	Young Oh, Capital	11,847.76
501	Merchandise Purchases	–0–
502	Freight In	–0–
503	Purchases Returns and Allowances	–0–
504	Purchases Discounts	–0–

Instructions:

1. Open the ledger accounts and enter the balances.
2. Post from the purchases journal and the general journal completed in Problem 16-1 to the ledger accounts.
3. Prepare a trial balance.

CASE STUDY

Write the answer to the case study on the form provided in your workbook.

Purchases Journal

Michaels' Landscaping uses a general journal along with special journals to record transactions. Mr. Michaels allows you to record the transactions from the source documents. When attempting to record purchases for cash, Mr. Michaels made you wonder whether you should use the purchases journal. When you ask Mr. Michaels, he tells you that only purchases on account should be journalized in the purchases journal.

Critical Thinking

■ *What are the reasons he might give you for using the purchases journal only for purchases on account?*

CHAPTER SEVENTEEN

The Cash Receipts Journal

OBJECTIVES

Upon completion of this chapter, you should be able to:

1. Record transactions in a cash receipts journal.
2. Total, prove, and rule the cash receipts journal.
3. Post from the cash receipts journal.
4. Record bank credit card sales.

Accounting Terminology

- Cash receipts journal
- Discount on credit card sales
- Memorandum entry
- Posting reference *CR*

INTRODUCTION

Cash transactions are very common in most businesses. Cash is constantly received and constantly paid out. For example, during April, Maddalon Office Supply had ten transactions involving the receipt of cash. ■

GENERAL JOURNAL Page 1

Cash Transactions

	Date		Description	Post Ref.	Debit	Credit	
1	20	XX					1
2	Apr.						2
5		6	Cash	101	60 00		5
6			Supplies	115		60 00	6
7			Returned damaged supplies.				7
8							8
15		7	Cash	101	1 696 00		15
16			Sales Tax Payable	203		96 00	16
17			Sales	401		1 600 00	17
18			Cash sales for first week of April.				18
19							19
25		9	Cash	101	900 00		25
26			Accounts Receivable	112		900 00	26
27			Received payment from Sensor				27
28			Publishing for Invoice 538.				28
29							29
35		14	Cash	101	2 385 00		35
36			Sales Tax Payable	203		135 00	36
37			Sales	401		2 250 00	37
38			Cash sales for second week of April.				38
39							39
45		16	Cash	101	2 000 00		45
46			Ross Maddalon, Capital	301		2 000 00	46
47			Additional investment.				47
48							48

127

Cash Transactions (continued)

GENERAL JOURNAL
Page 2

Date	Description	Post Ref.	Debit	Credit
20XX				
Apr.				
16	Cash	101	30 00	
	Purchases Returns and Allowances	503		30 00
	Returned defective merchandise.			
17	Cash	101	840 00	
	Sales Discount	403	8 00	
	Accounts Receivable	112		848 00
	Received payment from			
	Data Processors for			
	Invoice 541 less discount.			
21	Cash	101	2279 00	
	Sales Tax Payable	203		129 00
	Sales	401		2150 00
	Cash sales for third week of April.			
24	Cash	101	1365 00	
	Sales Discount	403	13 00	
	Accounts Receivable	112		1378 00
	Received payment from Rosenberg			
	Securities for Invoice 542 less			
	discount.			
28	Cash	101	4929 00	
	Sales Tax Payable	203		279 00
	Sales	401		4650 00
	Cash sales for fourth week of April.			

Notice that the Cash account was debited ten times during the month (not including the opening entry). The journal entries for cash receipts required ten separate postings to the Cash account in the general ledger.

Cash Receipts Journal: Chronological record of cash receipts.

Obviously the use of a special *cash receipts journal* will make the accounting system of Maddalon Office Supply more efficient. Like the sales journal and the purchases journal, the cash receipts journal offers important advantages. All the cash receipts transactions will be grouped together in one place. The journalizing of these transactions will be easier and quicker, and their posting will be greatly simplified.

■ SETTING UP A CASH RECEIPTS JOURNAL

The cash receipts journal that Maddalon Office Supply will use is shown on page 129. The transactions for April have been recorded in this journal.

Notice that this journal has six money columns. All debits are entered in the last two money columns. The Sales Discount Debit column is used to record any sales discounts taken by credit customers who are paying invoices within the discount period. The Cash Debit column is used to record the amount of cash received in each transaction.

The credits section of the cash receipts journal contains four money columns. The Accounts Receivable Credit column is used to record the amounts that credit customers are paying on account. The Sales Tax Payable Credit column is used to record the sales tax received from cash sales. The Sales Credit column is used to record the amounts received from cash sales.

The last credit money column—Other Accounts—is used to record the credit entries for cash received from sources other than cash sales, sales tax, and amounts collected from credit customers. For example, the credit entry for an additional investment by the owner is recorded in this column.

CASH RECEIPTS JOURNAL
FOR MONTH OF APRIL, 20XX

Page 1

	Date	Explanation	Accounts Receivable Credit	Sales Tax Payable Credit	Sales Credit	Other Accounts Credit Account Name	Post Ref.	Amount	Sales Discount Debit	Cash Debit	
1	20XX										1
2	Apr. 1	Balance on									2
3		hand, $11,000									3
4	6	Cash refund				Supplies		60 00		60 00	4
5	7	Cash sales		96 00	1 600 00					1 696 00	5
6	9	Sensor									6
7		Publishing	900 00							900 00	7
8	14	Cash sales		135 00	2 250 00					2 385 00	8
9	16	Investment				Ross Maddalon,		2 000 00		2 000 00	9
10						Capital					10
11	16	Ret. merch.				Pur. Ret. & Allow.		30 00		30 00	11
12	17	Data									12
13		Processors	848 00						8 00	840 00	13
14	21	Cash sales		129 00	2 150 00					2 279 00	14
15	24	Rosenberg									15
16		Securities	1 378 00						13 00	1 365 00	16
17	28	Cash sales		279 00	4 650 00					4 929 00	17

■ RECORDING TRANSACTIONS IN THE CASH RECEIPTS JOURNAL

Since the cash receipts journal has special money columns for the accounts commonly used by the business in recording cash receipts transactions, it is easy to record entries in this journal. Observe the following about the entries for April.

- The notation **Balance on hand, $11,000** is written on the first line of the journal. This figure comes from the Cash account. It is customary to record the amount of cash on hand at the beginning of each month in the cash receipts journal. Because this notation simply provides information and is not a regular entry to be posted, the amount is listed in the Explanation column. A line is drawn through the Cash Debit column. The notation of the cash balance is called a *memorandum entry.*

- The entry on April 6 records a cash refund for the return of damaged supplies. The debit part of the entry is recorded in the Cash Debit column. Because there is no special column for the Supplies account, the credit part of the entry must be recorded in the amount column for Other Accounts. Notice that it is necessary to write the name of the account to be credited when this money column is used.

- The entries for April 7, 14, 21, and 28 involve cash received from weekly cash sales. Each entry records the amount of cash received in the Cash Debit column, the sales tax in the Sales Tax Payable Credit column, and the amount of the sales in the Sales Credit column.

Memorandum Entry: Journal entry that is not to be posted.

> **WWW Inquiry**
> Find the URL address for Texas Instruments. What is the change in accounts payable and accrued expenses for the last two years?

- The entry for April 9 involves cash received from a credit customer who is paying an invoice after the discount period. Thus there is no sales discount, and the customer has sent a check for the full amount of the invoice. The amount received is recorded in the Cash Debit column and the Accounts Receivable Credit column.

- The first entry for April 16 involves cash received from an additional investment by the owner. The debit part of the entry is recorded in the Cash Debit column. Since there is no special column for the Ross Maddalon, Capital account, the credit part of the entry must be recorded in the column for Other Accounts, and the account title is written in Account Name column.

- The second entry for April 16 records a cash refund for the return of defective merchandise. The debit is entered in the Cash Debit column, and the credit to Purchases Returns and Allowances is recorded in the Other Accounts Amount column.

- The entries for April 17 and 24 involve cash received from credit customers who are paying invoices within the discount period. Thus each of these customers has deducted a sales discount from the total of the invoice. The amount actually received is recorded in the Cash Debit column. The amount of the sales discount is recorded in the Sales Discount Debit column. The total of the invoice is recorded in the Accounts Receivable Credit column.

Notice that the essential facts about each transaction can be recorded on a single line in the cash receipts journal. Also notice that the debits and credits for the transactions in the cash receipts journal are exactly the same as they were in the general journal.

Cash receipts may be currency, coins, checks, and money orders.

Cash received by a business may be in several forms: currency (paper money), coins, checks, and money orders. When cash is received, it is usually recorded on a source document, such as cash register tapes or remittance slips for checks received from customers, and then deposited in the bank. Most businesses deposit their cash often in order to safeguard it. Many businesses provide a separate memorandum column for deposits just to check that all cash received has been deposited in the bank.

■ POSTING FROM THE CASH RECEIPTS JOURNAL

Posting from Cash Receipts Journal:
- During month, post individual credits from Other Accounts column.
- At end of month, post totals of rest of columns.

During the month, each amount appearing in the Other Accounts Credit column of the cash receipts journal is posted individually to the account named in the entry. Thus the refund for the return of supplies was posted individually to the Supplies account in the general ledger on April 6. The number of this account (115) was then written in the Post. Ref. column next to the amount.

At the end of each month, all the money columns of the cash receipts journal are added and pencil footings are written in these columns. The totals are checked by cross-footing before being entered in ink. First the totals of the debit columns are added together. Then the totals of the credit columns are added together.

Debit totals:	$21 + $16,484 = $16,505
Credit totals:	$3,126 + $639 + $10,650 + $2,090 = $16,505

If the sum of each group of column totals is the same, equal debits and credits were recorded during the month. After the equality of the debits and credits is proven, the column totals are written in regular-size ink figures, and the cash receipts journal is ruled.

Posting Reference for Cash Receipts Journal:
The letters *CR* and the journal page number.

As each column total is posted to an account in the general ledger, the account number is written in parentheses below the total in the journal. The total of the Other Accounts Amount column is not posted. An *X* is therefore written in parentheses below this total. (Remember that these credits were posted as individual items.) The abbreviation *CR* and the journal page number are entered in the general ledger accounts to identify that the postings were from the cash receipts journal.

CASH RECEIPTS JOURNAL
FOR MONTH OF APRIL, 20XX

Page 1

	Date	Explanation	Accounts Receivable Credit	Sales Tax Payable Credit	Sales Credit	Other Accounts Credit — Account Name	Post Ref.	Amount	Sales Discount Debit	Cash Debit	
1	20 XX										1
2	Apr. 1	Balance on									2
3		hand, $11,000									3
4	6	Cash refund				Supplies	115	60 00		60 00	4
5	7	Cash sales		96 00	1600 00					1696 00	5
6	9	Sensor									6
7		Publishing	900 00							900 00	7
8	14	Cash sales		135 00	2250 00					2385 00	8
9	16	Investment				Ross Maddalon,	301	2000 00		2000 00	9
10						Capital					10
11	16	Ret. merch.				Pur. Ret. & Allow.	503	30 00		30 00	11
12	17	Data									12
13		Processors	848 00						8 00	840 00	13
14	21	Cash sales		129 00	2150 00					2279 00	14
15	24	Rosenberg									15
16		Securities	1378 00						13 00	1365 00	16
17	28	Cash sales		279 00	4650 00					4929 00	17
18	30	Totals	3126 00	639 00	10650 00			2090 00	21 00	16484 00	18
19			(112)	(203)	(401)			(X)	(403)	(101)	19

ACCOUNT Cash   ACCOUNT NO. 101

Date	Description	Post Ref.	Debit	Credit	Balance Debit	Balance Credit
20 XX						
Apr. 1		J1	11000 00		11000 00	
30		CR1	16484 00		27484 00	

ACCOUNT Accounts Receivable   ACCOUNT NO. 112

Date	Description	Post Ref.	Debit	Credit	Balance Debit	Balance Credit
20 XX						
Apr. 1		J1	2400 00		2400 00	
28		J1		106 00	2294 00	
30		S1	4558 00		6852 00	
30		CR1		3126 00	3726 00	

ACCOUNT Supplies   ACCOUNT NO. 115

Date	Description	Post Ref.	Debit	Credit	Balance Debit	Balance Credit
20 XX						
Apr. 1		J1	60 00		60 00	
3		J1	320 00		920 00	
6		CR1		60 00	860 00	

ACCOUNT	Sales Tax Payable				ACCOUNT NO. 203	
Date	Description	Post Ref.	Debit	Credit	Balance Debit	Balance Credit
20XX Apr.						
30		S1		258 00		249 00
30		CR1		639 00		888 00

ACCOUNT	Ross Maddalon, Capital				ACCOUNT NO. 301	
Date	Description	Post Ref.	Debit	Credit	Balance Debit	Balance Credit
20XX Apr. 1		J1		75 000 00		75 000 00
16		CR1		2 000 00		77 000 00

ACCOUNT	Sales				ACCOUNT NO. 401	
Date	Description	Post Ref.	Debit	Credit	Balance Debit	Balance Credit
20XX Apr. 30		S1		4 300 00		4 300 00
30		CR1		10 650 00		14 950 00

ACCOUNT	Sales Discount				ACCOUNT NO. 403	
Date	Description	Post Ref.	Debit	Credit	Balance Debit	Balance Credit
20XX Apr. 30		CR1	21 00		21 00	

ACCOUNT	Purchases/Returns and Allowances				ACCOUNT NO. 503	
Date	Description	Post Ref.	Debit	Credit	Balance Debit	Balance Credit
20XX Apr. 16		CR1		30 00		30 00

Remember that the general journal entries for these transactions required 26 separate postings. When a cash receipts journal is used, the same information can be transferred to the general ledger with three individual postings and five postings of column totals.

■ BANK CREDIT CARD SALES

Many retail businesses allow customers to use bank credit cards, such as MasterCard, Visa, Discover, and American Express. This arrangement is convenient because the retailer can offer charge account services but does not have to wait for payment, keep charge account records or send monthly statements to its customers.

Chapter 17 The Cash Receipts Journal   133

When a retailer makes a sale involving a bank credit card the transaction is recorded when the credit card is swiped through a unit attached to the computer. The transaction information is stored on the computer's database and transmitted to the credit card company. The data will be used for inventory control by the business.

The sales slip that is generated is signed by the purchaser as proof of purchase. The buyer keeps a copy and the seller keeps a copy. In businesses without computer technology a special multicopy sales slip form supplied by the bank is processed through a small mechanical imprinting device. A copy of the sale goes to the seller, buyer and the credit card company.

As the sale is being recorded the retailer will know instantly if the credit card is valid and can be used for the transaction. If, after being swiped through the computer, the card is found to be invalid or stolen, the seller must keep the card. If the buyer has reached the credit limit, the sale will not be processed.

At the end of the day or selling period, the seller adds the amounts of all the sales slips for bank credit card sales. The total is entered on a summary form, such as the one shown below. Notice that the retailer has also entered a discount. This is a fee that the bank charges for handling credit card sales. The discount is a percentage of the total sales. In this case, the rate is three percent. After the discount is computed, it is subtracted from the total sales, to find the net amount that the retailer will receive ($179.80 − $5.39 = $174.41).

Discount on Credit Card Sales: A fee charged for handling credit card sales.

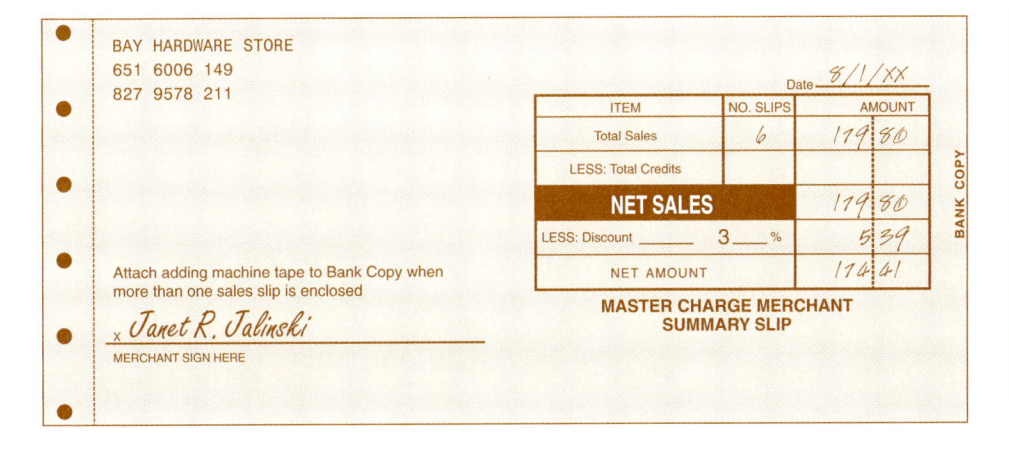

BAY HARDWARE STORE
651 6006 149
827 9578 211

Date 8/1/XX

ITEM	NO. SLIPS	AMOUNT
Total Sales	6	119 80
LESS: Total Credits		
NET SALES		119 80
LESS: Discount ___3___%		5 39
NET AMOUNT		174 41

MASTER CHARGE MERCHANT SUMMARY SLIP

Attach adding machine tape to Bank Copy when more than one sales slip is enclosed

x *Janet R. Jalinski*
MERCHANT SIGN HERE

BANK COPY

Bay Hardware Store
Credit Card Sales
August 1, 20XX

    00 T
  24.00
  32.70
  27.90
  41.50
  34.80
  18.90
 179.80 T

Bank credit card sales are treated as cash sales by the retailer. After the deposit is made, these sales are entered in the cash receipts journal. The Cash account is debited for the net amount of the sales. An account called Credit Card Fee Expense is debited for the discount. The Sales account is credited for the total sales. A journal entry for credit card sales is shown below.

WWW Inquiry
Find the URL address for Texas Instruments. What is the change in the provision for income taxes as reported on the income statements for the last two years?

CASH RECEIPTS JOURNAL
FOR MONTH OF APRIL, 20XX   Page __1__

	Date	Explanation	Sales Credit	Other Accounts Credit — Account Name	Post Ref.	Amount	Credit Card Fee Expense	Cash Debit	
1	20 XX								1
2	Aug. 1	Balance on hand, $2,640							2
3	1	Daily cash sales	426 50					426 50	3
4	1	Daily credit card sales	179 80				5 39	174 41	4
5									5

Some banks do not deduct the discount when the credit card sales slips are deposited. Instead, they add the total amount of these sales to the retailer's account. At the end of the month, the bank computes the total discount for the period and deducts it from the account balance. When the bank statement arrives, the retailer makes an entry in the general journal or in the cash payments journal (discussed in Chapter 18). The Credit Card Fee Expense account is debited, and the Cash account is credited. With this procedure, no entries are made for the discount during the month. (Each entry in the cash receipts journal consists of a debit to Cash and a credit to Sales for the total of the credit card sales.)

CHAPTER 17 SUMMARY

- The cash receipts journal is a special journal in which all of a business's cash receipt transactions are recorded in chronological order. It groups together the entries for cash receipts.

- The use of a cash receipts journal makes an accounting system more efficient. It eliminates repetition in the journalizing and posting of cash receipts. The cash receipts journal usually has several special money columns that simplify the recording of routine entries. These columns are for the accounts (such as Accounts Receivable, Sales Tax Payable, Sales, Sales Discount, and Cash) that a business uses most often in recording cash receipts. The Other Accounts section is used for credits to accounts for which there are no special columns.

- A memorandum entry is made in the cash receipts journal to record the cash balance at the beginning of each month.

- The totals of the debits and credits must be equal for each transaction recorded in the cash receipts journal.

- The amounts in the Other Accounts column are posted individually during the month to the general ledger accounts indicated in the journal entries. The totals of the other amounts columns are posted at the end of the month to the general ledger accounts named in the column headings.

- Before posting any column totals, it is necessary to check their accuracy. A process called cross-footing is used for this purpose.

- The form of the cash receipts journal may vary according to the needs of a business.

- Many retail businesses make bank credit card sales. The bank charges a discount (fee) for handling such sales. The discount is subtracted from the total of the sales. The bank adds the net amount of the credit card sales to the retailer's checking account after the retailer deposits the necessary forms.

- Bank credit card sales are treated as cash sales by the retailer. They are recorded in the cash receipts journal.

- The Credit Card Fee Expense account is debited for the amount of the discount that the bank deducts.

CHAPTER APPLICATIONS

EXERCISES

Complete the following assignments on the forms provided in your workbook.

EXERCISE 17-1

Interpreting entries in a cash receipts journal.

Instructions:
Give an explanation for each entry listed in the following cash receipts journal.

Cash Receipts Journal

	Acct. Rec. Credit	Sales Credit	Other Accounts	Amount	Sales Disc. Debit	Cash Debit
a.			Cameron Matthews, Capital	1,000		1,000
b.	500					500
c.		600				600
d.	400				8	392
e.			Office Equip.	100		100

EXERCISE 17-2

Identifying special journals and entries. The Current Wire and Cable Company records transactions in a cash receipts journal (CR), a sales journal (S), a purchases journal (P), and a general journal (J).

Instructions:

1. Analyze each of the following transactions and write the abbreviation of the journal that would be used to record the transaction.
2. List the titles of the accounts that would be debited and credited.

Transaction

Example: *Purchased equipment on credit.*

Journal	Account(s) Debited	Account(s) Credited
J	Equipment	Accounts Payable

Transactions:

1. Sold merchandise for cash.
2. Purchased office supplies on credit.
3. Sold used equipment for cash.
4. Sold merchandise on credit.
5. Gave an allowance to a charge customer for damaged merchandise.
6. Received cash from a charge customer on account.
7. Purchased merchandise on credit.
8. Received an additional cash investment from Linda Welch, the owner.
9. Received credit from a supplier for damaged merchandise.
10. Received credit from a supplier for damaged office supplies.

EXERCISE 17-3

Posting from special journals.

Instructions:

1. Set up T accounts for Ream Art Supplies for the following items, and enter the balance on the appropriate side of each account.

Cash	$5,000	Sales Discount	$200
Accounts Receivable	2,500	Merchandise	
Accounts Payable	1,000	Purchases	15,000
Sales Tax Payable	700	Freight In	500
Blair Ream, Capital	11,000	Purchases Returns	
Sales	10,000	and Allowances	600
Sales Returns and		Purchases Discount	300
Allowances	400		

2. Enter the following column totals from the special journals and the following amounts from the general journal entries in the T accounts.
3. Foot the accounts.
4. Prepare a trial balance dated April 30.

Sales Journal	
Accounts Receivable	$5,350
Sales Tax Payable	350
Sales	5,000
Purchases Journal	
Accounts Payable	$4,150
Merchandise Purchases	4,000
Freight In	150
Cash Receipts Journal	
Accounts Receivable	$5,000
Sales Tax Payable	420
Sales	6,000
Sales Discount	100
Cash	11,320
General Journal	
Sales Returns and Allowances	100
Sales Tax Payable	7
Accounts Receivable	107
Accounts Payable	200
Purchases Returns and Allowances	200

PROBLEMS

Complete all assigned problems on the forms provided in your workbook.

PROBLEM 17-1

Using a cash receipts journal and preparing a trial balance. Cape May Food Products, a wholesaler of groceries, uses a cash receipts journal. The firm's ledger account balances on April 1 of the current year are as follows.

101	Cash	$5,492.81
112	Accounts Receivable	3,175.63
120	Office Equipment	7,800.00
301	Steve Wagoner, Capital	$16,468.44
401	Sales	–0–
403	Sales Discount	–0–

Instructions:

1. Open the ledger accounts, and enter the April 1 balances.
2. Record the April transactions in the cash receipts journal. Number the journal page 4 and make a memorandum entry of the beginning cash balance in the journal.

3. Post the items in the Other Accounts Amount column of the journal to the ledger accounts.
4. Pencil-foot the columns of the journal, and cross-foot to prove their accuracy.
5. Enter the column totals and rule the journal.
6. Post the column totals to the ledger accounts.
7. Prepare a trial balance.

Transactions:

Apr. 2 Received $130.50 from Sanchez's Market for Invoice 845.
  4 Received $320.10 from Clemens Groceries for Invoice 848; $330 less discount of $9.90.
  7 Sold merchandise for $792.75 in cash during the first week of April.
  9 Sold a used office file for $30 in cash.
  10 Received $236.45 from Briggs' Diner for Invoice 844.
  12 Received $281.30 from Kissimmee Foods for Invoice 849; $290 less discount of $8.70.
  14 Sold merchandise for $845.75 in cash during the second week of April.
  16 Received $192.35 from Briggs' Diner for Invoice 846.
Apr. 18 Received $240.85 from Tom's Inn for Invoice 847.
  20 Steve Wagoner made an additional cash investment of $5,000 in the business.
  21 Sold merchandise for $690.25 in cash during the third week of April.
  24 Received $223.10 from Kissimmee Foods for Invoice 851; $230 less discount of $6.90.
  27 Received $388 from the Food Mart for Invoice 852; $400 less discount of $12.
  28 Sold merchandise for $820.95 in cash during the fourth week of April.
  30 Received $315.90 from Briggs' Diner for Invoice 850.

PROBLEM 17-2

Using a cash receipts journal, a sales journal, and a general journal and preparing a trial balance.
Dintrone Aluminum Products uses a cash receipts journal, a sales journal, and a general journal. On May 1 of the current year, the firm's ledger accounts showed the following balances.

101	Cash	$8,912.42	401	Sales	–0–
112	Accounts Receivable	4,329.15	402	Sales Returns and Allowances	–0–
301	Sue Dintrone, Capital	13,241.57	403	Sales Discount	–0–

1. Open the ledger accounts, and enter the May 1 balances.
2. Record the May transactions in the appropriate journal. Number each journal page 1 and make a memorandum entry of the beginning cash balance in the cash receipts journal.
3. Post the entries from the Other Accounts section of the cash receipts journal and from the general journal on a daily basis.
4. Pencil-foot the columns of the cash receipts journal, and cross-foot to prove their accuracy. Then enter the column totals.
5. Rule the cash receipts journal and the sales journal.
6. Post the column totals to the ledger accounts.
7. Prepare a trial balance.

Transactions:

May 3 Received $2,057.35 from Texas Hardware in payment of the balance due on its account.
  5 Received $837.52 for a cash sale.
  8 Sold merchandise for $3,600 to Allegretto Plumbing; Invoice C97, terms 2/10, n/30.
  10 Sold merchandise for $2,700 to Mesquite Roofing: Invoice C98, terms 2/10, n/30.
  12 Received $627.86 for a cash sale.
  14 Accepted a return of damaged merchandise from Mesquite Roofing, and issued Credit Memorandum 29 for $186.
  18 Received $3,528 from Allegretto Plumbing in payment of Invoice C97 less a $72 discount.
  20 Received $2,463.72 from Mesquite Roofing in payment of its account less a $50.28 discount.
  24 Dintrone invested an additional $4,000 in the business.
  26 Sold merchandise for $3,150 to Demshick Construction; Invoice C99, terms 2/10, n/30.
  27 Received $2,271.80 from Tremont Lumber in payment of the balance due on its account.
  31 Received $421.53 for a cash sale.

CASE STUDY

Write the answer to the case study on the form provided in your workbook.

Cash Receipts Journal

You begin working for James Castagnera, a local businessperson who sells new and used books. When looking at Castagnera's books, you notice that for cash transactions he uses the general journal. Having studied the cash receipts journal, you know that it is more efficient to use a special journal for the receipt of cash.

> **Critical Thinking**
>
> ■ When you approach Castagnera with your suggestion to begin using a separate cash receipts journal, he asks you "why?" What will you tell him?

CHAPTER EIGHTEEN

The Cash Payments Journal

OBJECTIVES

Upon completion of this chapter, you should be able to:

1. Record transactions in a cash payments journal.
2. Total, prove, and rule the cash payments journal.
3. Post from the cash payments journal.

Accounting Terminology

- Cash payments journal
- Check stubs
- Posting reference *CP*

INTRODUCTION

Businesses must pay out cash for a number of reasons: to make cash purchases of equipment and supplies, to make cash purchases of merchandise, to settle invoices for credit purchases, and to take care of operating expenses such as wages, electricity, and telephone service. In addition, there may be regular cash withdrawals by the owner. Observe the following 14 entries for cash payments that were recorded in the general journal of Maddalon Office Supply during April.

The general journal entries for cash payments during the month required 31 separate postings to general ledger accounts.

Cash Payment Entries

GENERAL JOURNAL Page 1

Date	Description	Post. Ref.	Debit	Credit
20XX				
Apr.				
2	Prepaid Insurance	116	240 00	
	Cash	101		240 00
	Paid insurance premium in advance			
	for a two-year period.			
3	Supplies	115	32 00	
	Cash	101		32 00
	Purchased store supplies.			
5	Accounts Payable	202	280 00	
	Cash	101		280 00
	Paid Office Forms for Invoice B2895.			
9	Sales Returns and Allowances	402	50 00	
	Sales Tax Payable	203	3 00	
	Cash	101		53 00
	Refund for the return of damaged			
	merchandise.			

137

138 Part Three Recording Financial Data

Cash Payment Entries (continued)

GENERAL JOURNAL

Page 2

Date	Description	Post. Ref.	Debit	Credit
20XX Apr.				
9	Accounts Payable	202	800 00	
	Cash	101		776 00
	Purchases Discount	504		24 00
	Paid Allied Office Products for			
	Invoice 1167 less discount.			
11	Merchandise Purchases	501	450 00	
	Cash	101		450 00
	Purchased merchandise.			
14	Salaries Expense	511	1275 00	
	Cash	101		1275 00
	Paid semimonthly salaries.			
14	Electricity Expense	513	350 00	
	Cash	101		350 00
	Paid electric bill.			
14	Telephone Expense	512	135 00	
	Cash	101		135 00
	Paid telephone bill.			
17	Store Equipment	126	600 00	
	Cash	101		600 00
	Purchased a showcase.			
24	Accounts Payable	202	3675 00	
	Cash	101		3639 00
	Purchases Discount	504		36 00
	Paid Arco Calculators for			
	Invoice 6281 less discount.			
25	Freight In	502	85 00	
	Cash	101		85 00
	Paid freight charges on shipment			
	from E-Tron Computer Products.			
30	Salaries Expense	511	1275 00	
	Cash			1275 00
	Paid semimonthly salaries.			
30	Ross Maddalon, Withdrawals	302	100 00	
	Cash	101		100 00
	Withdrawal for personal use.			

Notice that the journal entries for cash payments required 14 separate postings to the credit side of the Cash account in the general ledger.

Maddalon Office Supply will further increase the efficiency of its accounting system by adding a special *cash payments journal.* This journal will provide the same kind of advantages as the other special journals. It will group together information about all of the

Cash Payments Journal: Chronological record of cash payments.

business's cash payments, and it will eliminate repetition in the journalizing and posting of these transactions.

■ SETTING UP A CASH PAYMENTS JOURNAL

The cash payments journal that Maddalon Office Supply will use is shown below. This journal was set up in a similar manner to the business's cash receipts journal. A special money column is provided for accounts that will be used often in recording cash payments. The special money columns make it easier to enter transactions and permit the summary posting of totals at the end of each month.

CASH PAYMENTS JOURNAL
FOR MONTH OF APRIL, 20XX
Page 1

Date	Ck. No.	Explanation	✓	Accounts Payable Debit	Merch. Purchase Debit	Other Accounts Debit Account Name	Post. Ref.	Amount	Purchase Discount Credit	Cash Credit
20XX										
Apr. 2	101	Insurance premium				Prepaid Insurance	116	240 00		240 00
3	102	Store supplies				Supplies	115	32 00		32 00
5	103	Office Forms		280 00						280 00
9	104	Cash refund				Sales Ret. & Allow.	402	50 00		
						Sales Tax Payable	203	3 00		53 00
9	105	Allied Office Products		800 00					24 00	776 00
11	106	Merchandise purchase			450 00					450 00
14	107	Semimonthly salaries				Salaries Expense	511	1275 00		1275 00
14	108	Electric bill				Electricity Expense	513	350 00		350 00
14	109	Telephone bill				Telephone Expense	512	135 00		135 00
17	110	Showcase				Store Equipment	126	600 00		600 00
24	111	Arco Calculators		3675 00					36 00	3639 00
25	112	Freight charges				Freight In	502	85 00		85 00
30	113	Semimonthly salaries				Salaries Expense	511	1275 00		1275 00
30	114	Withdrawal				R. Maddalon, Withdrawals	302	1000 00		1000 00
30		Totals		7275 00	450 00			7493 00	60 00	15158 00
				(202)	(501)			(X)	(504)	(101)

The Accounts Payable Debit section is used to record the amounts being paid to creditors on account. The Merchandise Purchases Debit column is used to record the amounts of cash purchases of merchandise. The amounts column in the Other Accounts section is used to record the debit entries for all other types of payments, such as payments for cash purchases of equipment or supplies and payments for expenses.

The Purchases Discount Credit column is used to record the discounts taken on purchase invoices that are paid within the discount period. The Cash Credit column is used to record the amount of each cash payment.

Notice that the cash payments journal also includes a Check No. column. In a well-run business, payments are made by check. The checks have consecutive numbers, and these numbers are listed in the cash payments journal when the transactions are recorded. (The preparation of checks and the use of a checking account will be discussed in Chapter 24.)

> **WWW Inquiry**
> Find the URL address for Hewlett Packard. On the balance sheet under stockholders' equity, what was the number of common shares of stock issued and outstanding last year?

■ RECORDING TRANSACTIONS IN THE CASH PAYMENTS JOURNAL

Observe the following about the entries in the cash payments journal of Maddalon Office Supply.

- The entries for April 2, 3, and 17 involve payments for cash purchases of assets. The amount of each payment is recorded in the Other Accounts Debit column and the Cash Credit column. The Other Accounts Debit column must be used because there are no special columns for the Prepaid Insurance, Supplies, and Store Equipment accounts.

- The entry for April 5, the second entry on April 9, and the entry on April 24 involve payments that were made to settle invoices for credit purchases. The payment on April 5 was made after the discount period. Since there was no discount, the amount is recorded in the Accounts Payable Debit column and the Cash Credit column. The payments on April 9 and 24 were made in time to take advantage of the discounts. The total of each of these invoices is recorded in the Accounts Payable Debit column. The amount of the discount is recorded in the Purchases Discount Credit column. The amount of cash actually paid is recorded in the Cash Credit column.

- The first entry on April 9 records a refund to a cash customer. Notice that two lines are used to debit the Sales Returns and Allowances account and the Sales Tax Payable accoun . Then the total amount of the refund is recorded in the Cash Credit column.

- The entry for April 11 involves a payment for the cash purchase of merchandise. The amounts are recorded in the Merchandise Purchases Debit column and the Cash Credit column.

- The entries for April 14 and the first entry for April 30 involve payments for expenses; the entry on April 25 involves a payment for freight charges. The amounts are recorded in the Other Accounts Debit section (because there are no special columns for the expense and Freight In accounts) and the Cash Credit column.

- The second entry for April 30 involves a payment for a cash withdrawal by the owner. The amount is recorded in the Other Accounts Amount column and the Cash Credit column.

Unlike the general journal, the cash payments journal makes it possible to enter most payments on a single line. However, the same accounts are used, and equal debits and credits are still recorded for each payment.

The information needed to journalize cash payments usually comes from the checkbook of a business. A checkbook contains a check stub that contains the critical payment information and the check. In most checkbooks, the checks and check stubs are pre-numbered so there is less chance of a clerical error when recording the information in the cash payments journal. For example, the following three check stubs provided the information for the entries of April 2, 3, and 5 in the cash payments journal of Maddalon Office Supply.

> **WWW Inquiry**
> Find the URL address for Hewlett Packard. On the balance sheet under stockholders' equity, how many shares of preferred stock are authorized?

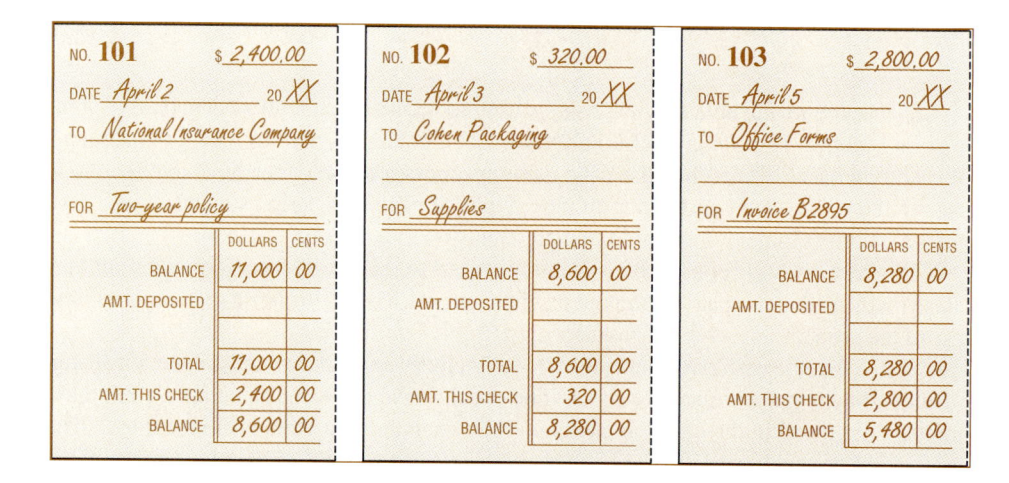

NO. 101	$2,400.00
DATE April 2	20 XX
TO National Insurance Company	
FOR Two-year policy	
	DOLLARS / CENTS
BALANCE	11,000 00
AMT. DEPOSITED	
TOTAL	11,000 00
AMT. THIS CHECK	2,400 00
BALANCE	8,600 00

NO. 102	$320.00
DATE April 3	20 XX
TO Cohen Packaging	
FOR Supplies	
	DOLLARS / CENTS
BALANCE	8,600 00
AMT. DEPOSITED	
TOTAL	8,600 00
AMT. THIS CHECK	320 00
BALANCE	8,280 00

NO. 103	$2,800.00
DATE April 5	20 XX
TO Office Forms	
FOR Invoice B2895	
	DOLLARS / CENTS
BALANCE	8,280 00
AMT. DEPOSITED	
TOTAL	8,280 00
AMT. THIS CHECK	2,800 00
BALANCE	5,480 00

The form of the cash payments journal varies from business to business. For example, some firms add columns for expense accounts that they use often in recording cash payments. The number of columns used and the headings must suit the needs of each business.

■ POSTING FROM THE CASH PAYMENTS JOURNAL

During the month, the amounts in the Other Accounts section are posted to the general ledger accounts named in the entries. The posting of the April 2 entry to the Prepaid Insurance account is shown below. The rest of the entries in the Other Accounts section are posted in the same way.

ACCOUNT **Prepaid Insurance** ACCOUNT NO. **116**

Date	Description	Post. Ref.	Debit	Credit	Balance Debit	Balance Credit
20XX Apr. 2		CP1	240 00		240 00	

At the end of each month, all the money columns of the cash payments journal are added and checked for accuracy.

> Debit totals: $7,275 + $450 + $7,493 = $15,218
>
> Credit totals: $60 + $15,158 = $15,218

After the equality of the debits and credits is proved, the column totals are entered and the cash payments journal is ruled. Then the totals are posted to the general ledger accounts named in the column headings. As these postings are made, the account numbers are written in parentheses below the totals in the journal. The total of the Other Accounts Amount column is, of course, not posted because the amounts were posted individually during the month. Thus an *X* is placed in parentheses below this total. The abbreviation *CP* and the journal page number are entered in the general ledger accounts to identify the postings from the cash payments journal.

ACCOUNT **Cash** ACCOUNT NO. **101**

Date	Description	Post. Ref.	Debit	Credit	Balance Debit	Balance Credit
20XX Apr. 1		J1	1 100 00		1 100 00	
30		CR1	16 484 00		27 484 00	
30		CP1		15 158 00	12 326 00	

ACCOUNT **Accounts Payable** ACCOUNT NO. **202**

Date	Description	Post. Ref.	Debit	Credit	Balance Debit	Balance Credit
20XX Apr. 1		J1		500 00		500 00
2		J1		420 00		920 00
30		J1	15 00			905 00
30		P1		1 255 00		2 160 00
30		CP1	727 500			1 432 500

Posting from Cash Payments Journal:
- During month, post individual debits from Other Accounts Amount column.
- At end of month, post totals of rest of columns.

Posting Reference for Cash Payments Journal:
The letters *CP* and the journal page number.

ACCOUNT	Merchandise Purchases						ACCOUNT NO. 501	
			Post.				Balance	
Date		Description	Ref.	Debit		Credit	Debit	Credit
20 XX								
Apr. 30			P1	1235000			1235000	
30			CP1	45000			1280000	

ACCOUNT	Purchases Discount						ACCOUNT NO. 504	
			Post.				Balance	
Date		Description	Ref.	Debit		Credit	Debit	Credit
20 XX								
Apr. 30			CP1			6000		6000

Notice that 4 postings of column totals and 11 individual postings were made to transfer the information from the cash payments journal to the general ledger. However, when the general journal was used for recording cash payments, 31 separate postings were needed. Additional special columns would mean an even greater savings in postings.

■ PAYMENT OF SALES TAX

Sales tax is paid to appropriate government entity on a monthly or quarterly basis.

As discussed previously, retail businesses that collect sales tax from their customers are required to pay the tax to the state and possibly to a city or county tax agency. The tax is paid on a monthly or quarterly basis.

The following entry is made in the cash payments journal when the tax is sent to the sales tax agency. The Sales Tax Payable account is debited, and the Cash account is credited.

CASH PAYMENTS JOURNAL
FOR MONTH OF MAY 20XX Page 2

	Date	Ck. No.	Explanation	✓	Accounts Payable Debit	Merch. Purchase Debit	Other Accounts Account Name	Post. Ref.	Amount	Purchase Discount Credit	Cash Credit	
1	20 XX											1
2	May 3	118	April sales tax sent									2
3			to state				Sales Tax Payable	203	88800		88800	3
4												4

The debit to the Sales Tax Payable account is posted individually from the cash payments journal. After the posting, the balance of the account is zero. The taxes collected from customers and held during the month have now been paid to the sales tax agency.

■ THE GENERAL JOURNAL

The general journal is used for entries that cannot be made in the special journals.

Although Maddalon Office Supply has set up special journals for sales, purchases, cash receipts, and cash payments, it will still keep the general journal. This journal will now be used for any entries that cannot be made in the special journals. For example, the opening entry and closing entries must be recorded in the general journal. Credit purchases and sales of permanent assets such as equipment must also be recorded in the general journal.

CHAPTER 18 SUMMARY

- The cash payments journal is a special journal that is used for recording a business's cash payments. It groups together all entries for these transactions.
- A cash payments journal increases the efficiency of an accounting system by eliminating repetitious journalizing and posting.
- The cash payments journal usually has several special money columns that simplify the recording of routine entries. These columns are for the accounts that a business uses most often to record its cash payments, such as Accounts Payable, Merchandise Purchases, Purchases Discount, and Cash. A section called Other Accounts is also set up for debits to accounts for which there are no special columns.
- The source of information for entries in the cash payments journal is usually the checkbook of a business.
- The totals of the debits and credits must be equal for each transaction recorded in the cash payments journal.
- The debits in the Other Accounts section are posted individually during the month to the general ledger accounts indicated in the journal entries. The totals of the rest of the columns are posted at the end of the month to the general ledger accounts named in the column headings.
- The accuracy of the column totals must be checked before they are posted.
- A retailer who is responsible for collecting sales tax must send the sales tax to a government agency at regular intervals, such as every month. At this time, the Sales Tax Payable account is debited, and the Cash account is credited.
- After special journals are added to an accounting system, there is still a need for the general journal. This journal will be used for any entries that cannot be made in the special journals.

CHAPTER APPLICATIONS

EXERCISES

Complete the following assignments on the forms provided in your workbook.

EXERCISE 18-1

Interpreting entries in a cash payments journal.

Instructions:
Give an explanation for each entry listed in the following cash payments journal.

Cash Payments Journal

	Acct. Pay. Debit	Merch. Purch. Debit	Other Accounts	Amount	Purch. Disc. Credit	Cash Credit
a.	500					500
b.		300				300
c.			Supplies	100		100
d.	800				16	784
e.			Wang Lu, Withdrawals	400		400

EXERCISE 18-2

Matching entries to special columns in a cash payments journal. Sapora Electronics uses a cash payments journal that provides special columns for the following.

Debits	Credits
a. Accounts Payable	d. Purchases Discount
b. Merchandise Purchases	e. Cash
c. Other Accounts	

Instructions:
For each of the following transactions write the letters of the columns in which the amounts would be entered.

Transactions:
1. Issued Check 52 for the purchase of merchandise.
2. Issued Check 53 to pay a creditor's invoice less a 2 percent discount.
3. Issued Check 54 to purchase supplies.
4. Issued Check 55 for a withdrawal by the owner.
5. Issued Check 56 to a customer as a refund for returned merchandise. (The merchandise was originally sold for cash.)

EXERCISE 18-3

Matching transactions to special journals. Richboro Products, owned by Wags Carlisle, records transactions in the following journals.

CR   A cash receipts journal with columns for Accounts Receivable, Sales Tax Payable, Sales, Other Accounts, Sales Discount, and Cash.

CP   A cash payments journal with columns for Accounts Payable, Merchandise Purchases, Other Accounts, Purchases Discount, and Cash.

P   A purchases journal with columns for Accounts Payable, Merchandise Purchases, and Freight In.

S   A sales journal with columns for Accounts Receivable, Sales Tax Payable, and Sales.

J   A general journal.

Instructions:
For each of the following transactions write:

a. The abbreviation of the journal that would be used in recording the transaction.
b. The account(s) that would be debited.
c. The account(s) that would be credited.

Transaction

Example: *Issued a check to pay the rent.*

Journal	Account(s) Debited	Account(s) Credited
CP	Rent Expense	Cash

Transactions:

1. Received cash and sales tax from cash sales.
2. Received an allowance from a creditor for damaged merchandise.
3. Purchased office equipment on credit; terms are net 30.
4. Issued a check to a creditor in payment of the balance due.
5. Accepted a return of merchandise from a charge customer and allowed full credit on her account. The credit memorandum covered both the price of the goods and sales tax.
6. Received a check from a charge customer in payment of the balance due on his account.
7. Received an invoice for merchandise purchased on credit plus freight charges; terms are 2/10, n/30.
8. Refunded cash to a customer for the return of damaged merchandise. The merchandise was originally sold for cash. Sales tax was charged.
9. Sold merchandise on credit to a charge customer. The total of the invoice included a 5 percent sales tax.
10. Purchased store equipment for cash.
11. The owner invested cash in the business.
12. Received a check from a customer in payment of her account less a 2 percent discount.
13. Paid a creditor's invoice within the discount period and deducted a 2 percent discount.
14. The owner withdrew cash from the business.

PROBLEMS

Complete all assigned problems on the forms provided in your workbook.

PROBLEM 18-1

Using a cash payments journal. The Flower Shop, owned and operated by Ellen Shank, sells plants, seeds, and gardening tools. The firm uses a cash payments journal. Selected accounts from the firm's general ledger are listed below.

101 Cash	504 Purchases Discount
114 Supplies	511 Salaries Expense
302 Ellen Shank, Withdrawals	513 Telephone Expense
501 Merchandise Purchases	517 Utilities Expense

Instructions:

1. Record each of the following transactions in the cash payments journal. Number the journal page *1*.
2. Pencil-foot the column totals of the cash payments journal, and cross-foot to prove their accuracy.
3. Enter the column totals and rule the journal.

Transactions:

July 2   Issued Check 464 for $235.85 to Plants, Inc., to pay Invoice 1026.
5   Issued Check 465 for $125.50 to make a cash purchase of wrapping paper and other store supplies.
6   Issued Check 466 for $400 to make a cash purchase of merchandise.
10   Issued Check 467 for $120 to pay the telephone, cell phone, and beeper bill.
12   Issued Check 468 for $97 to Drew & Hall to pay Invoice 721; $100 less discount of $3.
15   Issued Check 469 for $800 for a cash withdrawal by Ellen Shank, the owner.
20   Issued Check 470 for $990.25 to make a cash purchase of merchandise.
24   Issued Check 471 for $294 to Yamamoto's Nursery to pay Invoice 589; $300 less discount of $6.
25   Issued Check 472 for $137.50 to pay the electric bill.
28   Issued Check 473 for $7.35 to make a cash purchase of office supplies.
30   Issued Check 474 for $300 to make a cash purchase of merchandise.
31   Issued Check 475 for $500 to pay the monthly wages of the salesclerk.

PROBLEM 18-2

Using a cash payments journal and preparing a trial balance. Hess Tool Supply sells hand tools and consumer hardware. The firm uses a cash payments journal. Its general ledger accounts and their balances on May 1 of the current year are as follows.

101	Cash	$28,620.48
114	Supplies	160.00
124	Equipment	16,500.00
202	Accounts Payable	8,080.48
301	Amber Hess, Capital	42,200.00
302	Amber Hess, Withdrawals	5,000.00
501	Merchandise Purchases	–0–
502	Freight In	–0–
504	Purchases Discount	–0–
511	Rent Expense	–0–
513	Salaries Expense	–0–
515	Telephone Expense	–0–
517	Advertising Expense	–0–

Instructions:

1. Open the ledger accounts and enter the balances.
2. Record each of the following transactions in the cash payments journal. Number the journal page 5.
3. Post the items in the Other Accounts Debit column of the journal on a daily basis.
4. Pencil-foot the columns of the journal, and cross-foot to prove their accuracy. Then enter the column totals and rule the journal.
5. Post the column totals to the ledger accounts.
6. Prepare a trial balance.

Transactions:

May 1 Issued Check 502 for $1,200 to Prudential Realtors for the May rent.
 3 Issued check 503 for $588 to Metric Die to pay Invoice 624; $600 less a $12 discount.
 5 Issued Check 504 for $250 to E-Media for radio advertising.
 8 Issued Check 505 for $230 to Tremont Supplies for shipping boxes, bubble wrap, and strapping tape.
 10 Issued Check 506 for $360 for the cash purchase of merchandise from Stanley Tools.
 12 Issued Check 507 for $56 to Fast Freight to cover transportation charges on incoming merchandise.
 13 Issued Check 508 for $156.75 to pay the telephone bill.
 15 Issued Check 509 for $1,950 to pay salaries for the first half of the month.
 22 Issued Check 510 for $980 to Felton Tools to cover Invoice 981; $1,000 less a $20 discount.
 24 Issued Check 511 for $700 to Amber Hess as a withdrawal for personal use.
 26 Issued Check 512 for $240 to Office Systems for the purchase of file cabinets.
 28 Issued Check 513 for $460 for the cash purchase of merchandise from Ace Tool Works.
 30 Issued Check 514 for $686 to Gilmour Supplies, to pay Invoice 297; $700 less a $14 discount.
 31 Issued Check 515 for $1,950 to pay salaries for the second half of the month.

CASE STUDY

Write the answer to the case study on the form provided in your workbook.

Accounting Procedures

You are employed part-time as a clerk at Bowen Painting. The owner, Mr. Bowen has limited knowledge of accounting. You notice that he uses special journals for Sales, Purchases, Cash Receipts, and Cash Payments. One of your duties is to journalize the transactions from source documents. While Mr. Bowen is an excellent painter, he does not follow appropriate accounting procedures. You find that he has written checks without completing the check stubs most of the time.

Critical Thinking

- *What effect will this habit have on the keeping of the books? How will your duties be affected? What is the resulting impact on the business?*

CHAPTER NINETEEN

The Accounts Receivable Ledger

Accounting Terminology

- Accounts receivable ledger
- Balance ledger form
- Control account
- Notes receivable
- Promissory note
- Schedule of accounts receivable
- Schedule of accounts receivable by age
- Statement of account
- Subsidiary ledger

OBJECTIVES

Upon completion of this chapter, you should be able to:

1. Post to the accounts receivable ledger.
2. Prepare a schedule of accounts receivable.
3. Prepare a statement of account.
4. Prepare and use a schedule of accounts receivable by age.
5. Record transactions involving notes receivable.

INTRODUCTION

All the accounting systems discussed in the previous chapters contained a single ledger—the general ledger. However, many businesses also use other types of ledgers. These ledgers do not replace the general ledger. They are intended to increase the efficiency of the accounting system and provide additional information to management. ■

During April, Maddalon Office Supply sold merchandise on credit to several customers. At the end of April, the Accounts Receivable account in the general ledger showed the following information.

- The total amount owed by credit customers at the beginning of the month ($2,400).
- The decrease in accounts receivable as a result of a return of merchandise by a credit customer ($106). This amount was posted from the general journal.
- The increase in accounts receivable as a result of sales to credit customers during the month ($4,558). This amount was posted from the sales journal.
- The decrease in amounts receivable as a result of cash collected from credit customers during the month ($3,126). This amount was posted from the cash receipts journal.
- The balance still owed by credit customers at the end of the month ($3,726).

ACCOUNT	Accounts Receivable				ACCOUNT NO. 112	
Date	Description	Post. Ref.	Debit	Credit	Balance Debit	Balance Credit
20XX Apr. 1		J1	2400 00		2400 00	
28		J1		106 00	2294 00	
30		S1	4558 00		6852 00	
30		CR1		3126 00	3726 00	

Although the owner, Ross Maddalon, knows that the $3,726 is the total amount still owed by credit customers, he does not know who owes this money. He also does not know how much each customer owes. To find this information, Ross Maddalon would have to look at all the entries in the sales journal and compute the total amount sold to each customer during the month. He would have to check through the cash receipts journal and compute the total amount collected from each customer. Then he would have to search through the general journal to locate any sales returns and allowances. The amount still owed by each customer would be computed by subtracting the cash collections and returns and allowances from sales. This method is inefficient and time-consuming, and it can easily lead to errors.

A better way to know how much money is owed by each credit customer is to use a separate account for each customer. Most businesses do not keep these accounts in the general ledger. Instead, they place all accounts for credit customers in another ledger called the *accounts receivable ledger.* Since the general ledger is the business's main ledger, the accounts receivable ledger is referred to as a *subsidiary ledger.*

Accounts Receivable Ledger: Ledger that contains accounts for credit customers.

The accountant for Maddalon Office Supply has set up an accounts receivable ledger for the business. One of the accounts from this subsidiary ledger is shown below.

Subsidiary Ledger: Ledger that is used for a single type of account and is subordinate to the general ledger.

NAME Data Processors
ADDRESS 164 Clinton Avenue
Totowa, NJ 07511   **TERMS** 1/10, n/30

Date	Description	Post. Ref.	Debit	Credit	Balance
20 XX					
Apr. 7	Invoice 541	S1	848 00		848 00
17		CR1		848 00	–0–
30	Invoice 544	S1	1007 00		1007 00

Notice that a *balance ledger form* with three money columns is used. This form provides a continuous record of the account balance. Whenever a transaction is posted, the current balance is entered in the Balance column. (Because each account in the accounts receivable ledger normally has a debit balance, a form with only one balance column is used.)

Balance Ledger Form: Form of ledger account that always shows the account balance.

■ POSTING TO THE ACCOUNTS RECEIVABLE LEDGER

Entries should be posted to the accounts receivable ledger on a daily basis. It is important to have available the up-to-date balance of each customer's account. The entries may come from any journal, but usually arise in the sales, cash receipts, and general journals.

During April, the journal entries shown on page 148 were posted to the accounts receivable ledger of Maddalon Office Supply. The accounts from this ledger appear on pages 148 and 149.

SALES JOURNAL
FOR MONTH OF APRIL 20XX   Page 1

Date	Inv. No.	Customer's Account	✔	Accounts Receivable Debit	Sales Tax Payable Credit	Sales Credit
20 XX						
Apr. 7	541	Data Processors	✔	848 00	48 00	800 00
16	542	Rosenberg Securities	✔	1378 00	78 00	1300 00
24	543	Barbagallo & Co., CPAs	✔	1325 00	75 00	1250 00
30	544	Data Processors	✔	1007 00	57 00	950 00
30		Totals		4558 00	258 00	4300 00
				(112)	(203)	(401)

CASH RECEIPTS JOURNAL
FOR MONTH OF APRIL, 20XX

Page 1

Date	Explanation	Accounts Receivable ✓ Credit	Sales Tax Payable Credit	Sales Credit	Other Accounts Credit - Account Name	Post. Ref.	Amount	Sales Discounts Debit	Cash Debit
20XX Apr. 1	Balance on hand, $11,000 ✓								
9	Sensor Publishing ✓	900 00							900 00
17	Data Processors ✓	848 00						8 00	840 00
24	Rosenberg Securities ✓	1378 00						13 00	1365 00
30	Totals	3126 00 (112)	639 00 (203)	10650 00 (401)			2090 00 (X)	21 00 (403)	16484 00 (101)

GENERAL JOURNAL

Page 1

Date	Description	Post. Ref.	Debit	Credit
20XX Apr. 28	Sales Returns and Allowances	402	100 00	
	Sales Tax Payable	203	6 00	
	Accounts Receivable/Barbagallo & Co., CPAs	112 ✓		106 00
	Issued Credit Memorandum 101 for the return of damaged merchandise sold on Invoice 543.			

The accounts receivable ledger now contains four accounts, which are arranged in alphabetical order. As the business gains more credit customers, additional accounts will be placed in the accounts receivable ledger.

Posting to the Subsidiary Ledger

NAME Barbagallo & Co.
ADDRESS 36 Main Street
Paterson, New Jersey 07512   **TERMS** 1/10, n/30

Date	Description	Post. Ref.	Debit	Credit	Balance
20XX Apr. 24	Invoice 543	S1	1325 00		1325 00
28	Credit Memorandum #101	J1		106 00	1219 00

NAME Data Processors
ADDRESS 164 Clinton Avenue
Totowa, New Jersey 07511 **TERMS** 1/10, n/30

	Date		Description	Post. Ref.	Debit	Credit	Balance	
1	20	XX						1
2	Apr.	7	Invoice 541	S1	848 00		848 00	2
3		17		CR1		848 00	—0—	3
4		30	Invoice 544	S1	1007 00		1007 00	4
5								5

NAME Rosenberg Securities
ADDRESS 315 Union Avenue
Clifton, New Jersey 07011 **TERMS** 1/10, n/30

	Date		Description	Post. Ref.	Debit	Credit	Balance	
1	20	XX						1
2	Apr.	16	Invoice 542	S1	1378 00		1378 00	2
3		24		CR1		1378 00	—0—	3
4								4
5								5

NAME Sensor Publishing
ADDRESS 47 Lincoln Avenue
Montclair, New Jersey 07043 **TERMS** 1/10, n/30

	Date		Description	Post. Ref.	Debit	Credit	Balance	
1	20	XX						1
2	Apr.	1	Balance	✓			2400 00	2
3		9		CR1		900 00	1500 00	3
4								4
5								5

Observe the following about the accounts receivable ledger.

- When the ledger is set up, the name, address, and terms for each credit customer are recorded on a separate ledger sheet or card. If any of the customers owe money, an entry is made to record the amount owed. This is the opening balance for the customer's account. On April 1, Sensor Publishing owed $2,400 to Maddalon Office Supply. Look at the account for this customer to see how the balance was recorded. The same type of entry must be made when a ledger sheet is filled, and the customer's balance must be transferred to another sheet.

- Each transaction listed in the sales journal is posted individually to a customer's account in the accounts receivable ledger. For example, notice how the entry of April 7 was posted to the account for Data Processors. The date of the transaction (April 7) is written in the Date column of the account. The invoice number (541) is written in the Description column to identify the sale. The amount ($848) is entered in the Debit column. (Remember that sales on credit increase the asset Accounts Receivable. Increases in assets are recorded as debits.) Because Data Processors had no previous balance, the amount of the sale is also written in the Balance column.

WWW Inquiry
Find the URL address for Wal-Mart. On what date did Wal-Mart Stores incorporate, and on what date was Wal-Mart stock first made available for sale to the public?

WWW Inquiry
Find the URL address for Heidelberg. What is the change in receivables for Heidelberg between the last two annual reports?

Thus the balance of this customer's account on April 7 is $848. The abbreviation *S* and the journal page number *1* are written in the Posting Reference column of the account to identify the source of the entry. A check mark is placed in the sales journal to show that the transaction was posted to the subsidiary ledger.

- Each transaction listed in the Accounts Receivable Credit column of the cash receipts journal is posted individually to a customer's account in the accounts receivable ledger. For example, notice how the entry of April 9 was posted to the account for Sensor Publishing. The date of the transaction (April 9) is written in the Date column. The amount ($900) is entered in the Credit column. (Remember that cash received from credit customers decreases the asset Accounts Receivable. Decreases in assets are recorded as credits.) The amount of cash received is subtracted from the previous balance to find the current balance ($2,400 − $900 = $1,500). The current balance is entered in the Balance column. The abbreviation *CR* and the journal page number *1* are written in the Posting Reference column of the account. A check mark is placed in the cash receipts journal to indicate that the transaction was posted to the subsidiary ledger.

- Each return or allowance is entered in the general journal and posted to both the general ledger and the subsidiary ledger accounts involved. Look at the general journal entry on page 148. Notice that the accountant uses a diagonal line in both the Description of Entry column and the Posting Reference column. The 112 means that $106 was posted to the Accounts Receivable account in the general ledger. The check mark means that $106 was also posted to the account for Barbagallo & Co., CPAs in the accounts receivable ledger. In the account for Barbagallo & Co., CPAs, the credit memorandum number (101) is written in the Description column and *J1* is written in the Posting Reference column.

■ PROVING THE ACCOUNTS RECEIVABLE LEDGER

At the end of the month, the accounts receivable ledger must be proved. To do this, a *schedule of accounts receivable* is prepared.

Schedule of Accounts Receivable: List of customer's accounts with unpaid balances.

1. The name and account balance for each customer with an unpaid balance are listed on the schedule form. This information is taken from the accounts receivable ledger.
2. The balances are added to find the total amount owed by all credit customers.
3. The total of the schedule of accounts receivable is compared with the balance of the Accounts Receivable account in the general ledger. The two amounts must be the same.
4. Even though the totals agree, there may still be an error, such as posting the correct amount to the wrong customer's account.

Proving the Accounts Receivable Ledger

MADDALON OFFICE SUPPLY
SCHEDULE OF ACCOUNTS RECEIVABLE
APRIL 30, 20XX

	Customer	Balance
1	Barbagallo & Co., CPAs	1 219 00
2	Data Processors	1 007 00
3	Sensor Publishing	1 500 00
4	Total	3 726 00

ACCOUNT Accounts Receivable   ACCOUNT NO. 112

Date	Description	Post. Ref.	Debit	Credit	Balance Debit	Balance Credit
20 XX Apr. 1		J1	2 400 00		2 400 00	
28		J1		106 00	2 294 00	
30		S1	4 558 00		6 852 00	
30		CR1		3 126 00	3 726 00	

The Accounts Receivable account in the general ledger is known as a ***control account*** because its balance summarizes the balances of all the accounts in a subsidiary ledger. In this case, the balance of Accounts Receivable should be the total amount owed by all credit customers. A control account provides a link between a subsidiary ledger and the general ledger. Notice that the total of the schedule of accounts receivable prepared at Maddalon Office Supply on April 30 agrees with the balance of the Accounts Receivable account on that date.

Control Account: General ledger account that summarizes the balances of accounts in a subsidiary ledger.

■ PREPARING THE STATEMENTS OF ACCOUNT

Most businesses send a ***statement of account*** to each credit customer at regular intervals. Usually, this statement is prepared monthly. Some statements of account show all transactions with the customer during the period and the balance at the end of the period. Other statements of account show only the customer's final balance. The information for preparing a statement of account is taken from the accounts receivable ledger. Some businesses simply make a photocopy of the customer's ledger account sheet and mail it to the customer.

The statement of account below was prepared at Maddalon Office Supply on April 30. Compare this statement with the ledger account for Data Processors on page 149.

Statement of Account: A periodic statement sent to a customer to report the balance that the customer owes.

STATEMENT OF ACCOUNT
MADDALON OFFICE SUPPLY
5755 Magnolia Trail
Mercerville, NJ 08619

Data Processors
164 Clinton Avenue
Totowa, NJ 07511

DATE: 4 / 30 / XX

DATE	DESCRIPTION	CHARGES	CREDITS	BALANCE
Apr. 1	Previous Balance			00
7	Invoice 541	848 00		848 00
17	Payment		848 00	
30	Invoice 544	1,007 00		1,007 00

■ AGING THE ACCOUNTS RECEIVABLE

The management of a business needs to know whether credit customers are paying their invoices on time. To obtain this information, some firms prepare a *schedule of accounts receivable by age* at the end of each month. The following procedure is used.

1. The name and account balance of each customer is listed on the schedule.
2. The entries in the accounts receivable ledger are examined to see which invoices are current and which are past due. The amounts of the current invoices are recorded in the Current column of the schedule.
3. The past-due invoices are classified according to how many days have gone by since the credit period ended. The amounts of these invoices are recorded in the Past Due columns of the schedule.
4. The columns of the schedule are added to find the total of the current invoices and the total of the past-due invoices in each age group.

Schedule of Accounts Receivable by Age: List of customer's account balances classified according to the age of unpaid invoices.

STANDARD AUTO PRODUCTS
SCHEDULE OF ACCOUNTS RECEIVABLE BY AGE
NOVEMBER 30, 20XX

Customer	Balance	Current	Past Due 1–30 Days	Past Due 31–60 Days	Past Due Over 60 Days
Berger's Service Station	$1,335	$910	$425		
Dale's Garage	770	770			
Elmwood Auto Service	250			$150	$100
Paragon Auto Repairs	1,100	800	100	200	
Totals	$3,455	$2,480	$525	$350	$100

The schedule of accounts receivable by age shown above was prepared at Standard Auto Products, a distributor of auto parts and supplies. The information on this schedule helps management to control credit.

■ NOTES RECEIVABLE

A credit customer will sometimes request an extension of time to pay the balance due on an account. In order to set a definite date for payment, the seller may want the customer to issue a *promissory note.* Such notes usually bear interest.

When a business obtains a promissory note from a credit customer, the amount owed is no longer a part of the asset Accounts Receivable. Instead, the amount owed becomes part of the asset *Notes Receivable.* This change must be entered in the seller's financial records.

On May 23, Data Processors asked Maddalon Office Supply for an extension of 60 days in which to pay an invoice. Data Processors issued a promissory note for $1,007, the amount owed. The note is for 60 days and bears interest at 12 percent. When Maddalon Office Supply receives the note, the transaction is entered in the general journal and posted to the general ledger and the accounts receivable ledger.

Promissory Note: A written promise to pay a stated amount of money on a specified date.

Notes Receivable: Promissory notes that a business has received.

GENERAL JOURNAL   Page 4

Date	Description	Post Ref.	Debit	Credit
20XX May 23	Notes Receivable	111	1007 00	
	Accounts Receivable/Data Processors	112 ✓		1007 00
	Received a 60-day, 12% note.			

ACCOUNT Notes Receivable   ACCOUNT NO. 111

Date	Description	Post. Ref.	Debit	Credit	Balance Debit	Balance Credit
20XX May 23		J4	1,007.00		1,007.00	

ACCOUNT Accounts Receivable   ACCOUNT NO. 112

Date	Description	Post. Ref.	Debit	Credit	Balance Debit	Balance Credit
20XX Apr. 30		CR1		3,126.00	3,726.00	
May 23		J4		1,007.00	2,719.00	

NAME Data Processors
ADDRESS 164 Clinton Avenue
Totowa, New Jersey 07511   **TERMS** 1/10, n/30

	Date	Description	Post. Ref.	Debit	Credit	Balance	
1	20XX						1
2	Apr. 7	Invoice 541	S1	848.00		848.00	2
3	17		CR1		848.00	–0–	3
4	30	Invoice 544	S1	1,007.00		1,007.00	4
5	May 23	60-day, 12% note	J4		1,007.00	–0–	5

The Notes Receivable account is debited to record the new asset that the business gained. Two accounts are credited—the Accounts Receivable account in the general ledger and the customer's account in the accounts receivable ledger.

The note issued by Data Processors will become due on July 22. When Maddalon Office Supply receives the money, an entry is made in the cash receipts journal. The Cash account is debited for the total received ($1,027.14). The Notes Receivable account is credited for the amount of the note ($1,007), and the Interest Income account is credited for the amount of the interest on the note ($20.14).

Another advantage of receiving notes from customers is that if the business is in need of ready cash, it may be able to sell the note to its bank. The bank will advance the cash for a small fee.

CASH RECEIPTS JOURNAL
FOR MONTH OF JULY 20XX   Page 4

	Date	Explanation	Accounts Receivable Credit ✓	Sales Tax Payable Credit	Sales Credit	Other Accounts Account Name	Post. Ref.	Amount	Sales Discounts Debit	Cash Debit	
1	20XX										1
2	July										2
3	22	Note—				Notes Receivable	111	1,007.00			3
4		Data									4
5		Processors				Interest Income	491	20.14		1,027.14	5

CHAPTER 19 SUMMARY

- The accounts receivable ledger is a subsidiary ledger that contains an account for each credit customer.
- Transactions involving credit customers are posted to the accounts receivable ledger from the sales journal, the cash receipts journal, and the general journal. This posting work should be done on a daily basis so that the balances can always be kept up to date.
- At the end of each month, the accounts receivable ledger is proved. First, a schedule of accounts receivable is prepared. Then the total of the schedule is compared with the balance of the Accounts Receivable account in the general ledger. The two amounts should be the same.
- The Accounts Receivable account in the general ledger is a control account. It shows the total amount owed by all credit customers.
- A statement of account is sent to each credit customer. In most businesses, this is done monthly. The statement of account reports the balance due from the customer.
- Some businesses prepare a schedule of accounts receivable by age. This schedule shows whether customers are paying their invoices on time.
- Promissory notes received by a business are an asset and are known as notes receivable. The interest on these notes is revenue. The Notes Receivable account is debited when a note is obtained and credited when the money is received for the note. The Interest Income account is credited for the amount of interest received.

CHAPTER APPLICATIONS

EXERCISES

Complete the following assignments on the forms provided in your workbook.

EXERCISE 19-1

Posting to the accounts receivable ledger and proving the ledger. Ledger account balances and partial journals are shown below.

Instructions:
1. Set up T accounts for Accounts Receivable and for the subsidiary ledger accounts.
2. Enter the balances in these accounts.
3. Post from the partial journals to these accounts.
4. Compute the account balances.
5. Total the subsidiary ledger account balances, and prove the total to the balance in the control account.

General Ledger

Accounts Receivable	$2,900

Subsidiary Ledger

Data Resources	–0–
Info Systems	$1,200
Microtech	700
Solutions Inc.	1,000

Sales Journal

Data Resources	$1,500
Info Systems	2,000
Microtech	2,500
Solutions Inc.	3,000
	$9,000

Cash Receipts Journal

Microtech	$ 700
Info Systems	1,200
Data Resources	1,500
Solutions Inc.	1,000
	$4,400

EXERCISE 19-2

Posting to a customer's account.

Instructions:
Set up a balance ledger for Del Rocco Systems. The address is 100 Fourth Avenue, Brooklyn, NY 11200, and the terms are n/10. Assume that you are posting each of the following transactions from page 5 of the sales journal, the cash receipts journal, or the general journal. Enter the date, posting reference, debit or credit amount, and the balance in the customer's account.

Transactions:

May	1	Sold merchandise for $3,000 on credit, Invoice 196.
	9	Received $2,000 on account.
	11	Sold merchandise for $4,000 on credit, Invoice 217.
	15	Issued Credit Memorandum 72 for $1,000 for the return of defective merchandise sold on Invoice 217.
	20	Received $1,500 on account.
	28	Received a 30-day, 10 percent promissory note for $2,500 to settle the balance of the overdue account.

EXERCISE 19-3

Aging the accounts receivable. Forest Grove Distributing prepares a schedule of accounts receivable by age at the end of each month. This schedule is similar to the one given on page 152. On April 30, the accounts receivable ledger shows the following customer, credit terms, dates, and amounts of their unpaid invoices.

Customer	Terms	Invoice Date	Amount
Furniture Mart	2/10, n/30	Apr. 20	$1,602.74
Maples and Oaks	n/30	Jan. 3	1,459.60
Spruce Stores	2/10, n/30	Feb. 18	2,064.22
Seasoned Wood	n/30	Mar. 15	1,576.83

Instructions:
Using the data from the accounts receivable ledger, prepare a schedule of accounts receivable by age. Date the schedule April 30 of the current year.

EXERCISE 19-4

Accounting for notes receivable and interest income.

Instructions:

1. Set up T accounts for Cash, Notes Receivable, Accounts Receivable, Sales, and Interest Income.
2. Analyze each of the following transactions, and record the effects in the T accounts.
3. Compute the balance of each account, and prove that the total of debit balances equals the total of the credit balances.

Transactions:

a. Sold merchandise for $3,600 to Data Systems on credit.
b. Received a 60-day, 10 percent promissory note for $3,600 from Data Systems as an extension of credit on its account.
c. Received $3,660 from Data Systems in payment of its note plus interest of $60.
d. Sold merchandise for $5,000 to Dynamic Software on credit.
e. Received a 30-day, 12 percent promissory note for $5,000 from Dynamic Software.
f. Received $5,050 from Dynamic Software in payment of its note plus interest of $50.

PROBLEMS

Complete all assigned problems on the forms provided in your workbook.

PROBLEM 19-1

Posting to a customer's account. Carr Hardware Distributors is setting up an accounts receivable ledger for its credit customers.

Instructions:

1. Open an account for Reynolds Hardware Store, 2112 Racing Drive, Charleston, WV 25301. The terms of sale are n/30. The balance on July 1 is $320.

2. Assume that the sales journal, the cash receipts journal, and the general journal show the following transactions with Reynolds Hardware Store during July and August. Enter these transactions in the customer's account. The posting references are *S7* for the sales journal, *CR10* for the cash receipts journal, and *J3* for the general journal.

Transactions:

July 6 Sold merchandise for $250 on credit, Invoice 121.
  10 Received $320 on account.
  15 Sold merchandise for $120 on credit, Invoice 205.
Aug. 1 Received $250 for Invoice 121.
  7 Sold merchandise for $475 on credit, Invoice 309.
  12 Received $120 for Invoice 205.
  28 Sold merchandise for $200 on credit, Invoice 454.
  30 Issued Credit Memorandum 31 for $50 for the return of damaged merchandise sold on Invoice 454.

PROBLEM 19-2

Using the sales journal, the cash receipts journal, the general journal, the general ledger, and the accounts receivable ledger. Wing Lu Packaging is a distributor of wrapping and packaging products. During February, the firm sold merchandise with a 5 percent sales tax on credit to the following customers.

Tozzi Markets	Herman's Grocery
944 Wayne Drive	1339 Broad Street
West Trenton, NJ 08601	Bridgewater, NJ 08807
Bogert's Bonanza	Aiello Market
1776 Freedom Road	92 Black Horse Pike
Washington Crossing, PA 18976	Williamstown, NJ 08028

Instructions:
Complete the following accounting work for the business. Use the current year.

1. Open general ledger accounts for Cash 101, Accounts Receivable 112, Equipment 141, Sales Tax Payable 203, Sales 401, Sales Returns and Allowances 402, and Sales Discount 403.

2. Enter the February 1 balances in the following general ledger accounts: Cash, $5,000; Accounts Receivable, $755; and Equipment, $8,280.

3. Open accounts for the credit customers in the accounts receivable ledger. The terms of sale are 2/20, n/60.

4. Enter the February 1 balances in the customer's accounts: Tozzi Market, $250; Bogert's Bonanza,

$125; Herman's Grocery, $300; and Aiello Market, $80.

5. Make a memorandum entry of the beginning cash balance in the cash receipts journal.
6. Record each of the transactions given on the next page in the sales journal, the cash receipts journal, or the general journal. Use *1* as the page number for each journal.
7. Post the entries from the sales journal, from the Accounts Receivable Credit column of the cash receipts journal, and from the general journal to the accounts receivable ledger on a daily basis.
8. Post the entries from the general journal and from the Other Accounts Credit column of the cash receipts journal to the general ledger on a daily basis.
9. Pencil-foot the sales journal and the cash receipts journal, and prove their accuracy by cross-footing.
10. Total and rule the sales journal and the cash receipts journal.
11. Post the totals of the sales journal and the cash receipts journal.
12. Prepare a schedule of accounts receivable, dated February 28. Compare the total of the schedule with the balance of the Accounts Receivable account in the general ledger. The two amounts should be the same.
13. Prepare a detailed statement of account for Aiello Market as of February 28.

Transactions:

Feb. 3 Sold merchandise for $200 plus $10 sales tax on credit to the Herman's Grocery, Invoice 76.
  4 Received $245.24 from the Tozzi Market for Invoice 72; $250 less a discount of $4.76.
  6 Sold merchandise for $100 plus $5 sales tax on credit to Aiello Market, Invoice 77.
  7 Received $1,640.42 for cash sales of $1,562.30 plus $78.12 sales tax during the first week of February.
  10 Sold merchandise for $90 plus $4.50 sales tax on credit to Bogert's Bonanza, Invoice 78.
  11 Sold merchandise for $180 plus $9 sales tax on credit to the Tozzi Market, Invoice 79.
  12 Received $122.62 from Bogert's Bonanza for Invoice 73; $125 less a discount of $2.38.
  13 Issued Credit Memorandum 56 for $42 to Aiello Market for the return of damaged merchandise that was sold for $40 plus $2 sales tax.
  13 Sold merchandise for $210 plus $10.50 sales tax on credit to Aiello Market, Invoice 80.

Feb. 14 Received $1,302.65 for cash sales of $1,240.62 plus $62.03 sales tax during the second week of February.
  17 Received $294.29 from the Herman's Grocery for Invoice 74; $300 less a discount of $5.71.
  18 Sold merchandise for $285 plus $14.25 sales tax on credit to Bogert's Bonanza, Invoice 81.
  18 Received $78.48 from Aiello Market for Invoice 75; $80 less a discount of $1.52.
  21 Received $1,030.26 for cash sales of $981.20 plus $49.06 sales tax during the third week of February.
  22 Received $206 from the Herman's Grocery for Invoice 76; $210 less a discount of $4.
  24 Received $65 from the sale of used office equipment.
  24 Sold merchandise for $200 plus $10 sales tax on credit to the Tozzi Market, Invoice 82.
  24 Received $61.80 from Aiello Market for Invoice 77 less Credit Memorandum 56; $63 less a discount of $1.20.
  25 Sold merchandise for $150 plus $7.50 sales tax on credit to Aiello Market, Invoice 83.
  27 Sold merchandise for $170 plus $8.50 sales tax on credit to the Herman's Grocery, Invoice 84.
  27 Received $185.40 from the Tozzi Market for Invoice 79; $189 less a discount of $3.60.
  27 Issued Credit Memorandum 57 for $31.50 to Bogert's Bonanza for the return of damaged merchandise that was sold for $30 plus $1.50 sales tax.
  28 Received $216.30 from Aiello Market for Invoice 80; $220.50 less a discount of $4.20.
  28 Received $1,199.26 for cash sales of $1,142.15 plus $57.11 sales tax during the fourth week of February.

CASE STUDY

Write the answer to the case study on the form provided in your workbook.

Proving Your Work

You have been taught in accounting class that the debit postings must equal the credit postings, but you have been posting the same amounts to the Accounts Receivable account in the general ledger and also to the customer's account in the subsidiary ledger.

Critical Thinking

■ *Why does this not put your accounts out of balance?*

CHAPTER TWENTY

The Accounts Payable Ledger

OBJECTIVES

Upon completion of this chapter, you should be able to:

1. Post to the accounts payable ledger.
2. Prepare a schedule of accounts payable.
3. Record transactions involving notes payable.

Accounting Terminology

- Accounts payable ledger
- Notes payable
- Schedule of accounts payable

INTRODUCTION

The use of an account receivable ledger improves the efficiency of an accounting system. A record of all transactions with credit customers is available in one place. Also, the amount owed by each credit customer is always known. Similar benefits can be achieved for accounts payable by setting up an accounts payable ledger.

During April, Maddalon Office Supply made several purchases of merchandise on credit. At the end of April, the Accounts Payable account in the general ledger showed the following information.

- The total amount owed to creditors at the beginning of the month ($5,000).
- The increase in accounts payable as a result of a purchase of office equipment on credit ($4,200). This amount was posted from the general journal.
- The decrease in accounts payable as a result of a return of merchandise to a creditor ($150). This amount was posted from the general journal.
- The increase in accounts payable as a result of purchases of merchandise from creditors during the month ($12,550). This amount was posted from the purchases journal.
- The decrease in accounts payable as a result of payments to creditors during the month ($7,275). This amount was posted from the cash payments journal.
- The balance owed to creditors at the end of the month ($14,325).

WWW Inquiry

Find the URL address for Dell Computer Corporation. In what state did Dell Computer Corporation incorporate and where is its current headquarters?

ACCOUNT: Accounts Payable   ACCOUNT NO. 202

Date	Description	Post. Ref.	Debit	Credit	Balance Debit	Balance Credit
20XX Apr. 1	Balance	✓				5,000.00
2		J1		4,200.00		9,200.00
30		J1	150.00			9,050.00
30		P1		12,550.00		21,600.00
30		CP1	7,275.00			14,325.00

157

It is important for Ross Maddalon, the owner, to know the total amount that the business owes to creditors. However, to manage operations effectively, he needs more information about the accounts payable. He must know which creditors the money is owed to and how much must be paid to each one. A good way to obtain such information is to keep separate accounts for the individual creditors. These accounts are usually placed in a subsidiary ledger called the *accounts payable ledger.*

Accounts Payable Ledger: Ledger that contains accounts for creditors.

The accountant for Maddalon Office Supply has set up an accounts payable ledger for the business. The form used for these accounts is a balance ledger form with three money columns. (Because each account in the accounts payable ledger normally has a credit balance, a form with only one balance column is appropriate.)

■ POSTING TO THE ACCOUNTS PAYABLE LEDGER

Entries should be posted to the accounts payable ledger on a daily basis so that the balances can be kept up to date. The entries usually come from the purchases journal, the cash payments journal, and the general journal.

During April, the journal entries shown below and on page 159 were posted to the accounts payable ledger of Maddalon Office Supply.

The accounts payable ledger now contains five accounts, which are arranged alphabetically. These accounts appear on pages 159 and 160. As the business expands operations and deals with more creditors, additional accounts will be placed in the accounts payable ledger.

PURCHASES JOURNAL
FOR MONTH OF APRIL, 20XX Page 1

	Date	Creditor's Account Credited	Post. Ref.	Invoice No.	Invoice Date	Terms	Accounts Payable Credit	Merch. Purchases Debit	Freight in Debit	
1	20 XX									1
2	Apr. 3	Del Rocco Office Products	✓	1167	4/1/XX	3/10, n/60	800 00	800 00		2
3	18	Arco Calculators	✓	6281	4/16/XX	1/10, n/30	3675 00	3600 00	75 00	3
4	24	E-Tron Computer Products	✓	327	4/21/XX	3/10 EOM	3750 00	3750 00		4
5	30	Del Rocco Office Products	✓	1191	4/28/XX	3/10, n/60	4325 00	4200 00	125 00	5
6	30	Totals					12550 00	12350 00	200 00	6
7							(202)	(501)	(502)	7
8										8

CASH PAYMENTS JOURNAL
FOR MONTH OF APRIL, 20XX Page 1

	Date	Ck. No.	Explanation	✓	Accounts Payable Debit	Merch. Purch. Debit	Other Accounts Debit Account Name	Post. Ref.	Amount	Purch. Disc. Credit	Cash Credit	
1	20 XX											1
2	Apr.											2
3												3
5	5	103	Office Forms	✓	2800 00						2800 00	5
6												6
10	9	105	Del Rocco Office									10
11			Products	✓	800 00					24 00	776 00	11
12												12
15	24	111	Arco Calculators	✓	3675 00					36 00	3639 00	15
20	30		Totals		7275 00	450 00			7493 00	60 00	15158 00	20
21					(202)	(501)			(X)	(504)	(101)	21
22												22

Posting to the Accounts Payable Ledger

GENERAL JOURNAL   Page 1

	Date	Description	Post. Ref.	Debit	Credit	
1	20 XX					1
2	Apr.					2
5	2	Office Equipment	128	4 2 0 0 00		5
6		Accounts Payable/Display Systems	202 ✓		4 2 0 0 00	6
7		Purchased a word processor on				7
8		credit; Invoice 796, terms n/30.				8
9						9
15	30	Accounts Payable/E-Tron Computer				15
16		Products	202 ✓	1 5 0 00		16
17		Purchases Returns and Allowances	503		1 5 0 00	17
18		Received Credit Memorandum 481.				18
19						19

NAME Del Rocco Office Products
ADDRESS 162 Oxford Street
Newark, New Jersey 07102   TERMS 3/10, n/60

	Date	Description	Post. Ref.	Debit	Credit	Balance	
1	20 XX						1
2	Apr. 3	Invoice 1167, 4/1/XX	P1		8 0 0 00	8 0 0 00	2
3	9		CP1	8 0 0 00		—0—	3
4	30	Invoice 1191, 4/28/XX	P1		4 3 2 5 00	4 3 2 5 00	4
5							5

NAME Arco Calculators
ADDRESS 122 Madison Avenue
New York, New York 10020   TERMS 1/10, n/30

	Date	Description	Post. Ref.	Debit	Credit	Balance	
1	20 XX						1
2	Apr. 18	Invoice 6281, 4/16/XX	P1		3 6 7 5 00	3 6 7 5 00	2
3	24		CP1	3 6 7 5 00		—0—	3
4							4
5							5

NAME Display Systems
ADDRESS 97 Grand Avenue
Englewood, New Jersey 07631   TERMS n/30

	Date	Description	Post. Ref.	Debit	Credit	Balance	
1	20 XX						1
2	Apr. 2	Invoice 796, 4/2/XX	J1		4 2 0 0 00	4 2 0 0 00	2
3							3
4							4
5							5

NAME	E-Tron Computer Products
ADDRESS	39 Vista Boulevard
	San Diego, California 92115

TERMS 3/10 EOM

	Date	Description	Post. Ref.	Debit	Credit	Balance
1	20 XX					
2	Apr. 24	Invoice 327, 4/21/XX	P1		3 750 00	3 750 00
3	30	Credit Memorandum 481	J1	150 00		3 600 00

NAME	Office Forms
ADDRESS	548 Main Street
	Newark, New Jersey 07102

TERMS n/60

	Date	Description	Post. Ref.	Debit	Credit	Balance
1	20 XX					
2	Apr. 1	Balance	✓			5 000 00
3	5		CP1	2 800 00		2 200 00

> **WWW Inquiry**
> Find the URL address for Wal-Mart. What is the Supplier Proposal Packet used by Wal-Mart?

Observe the following about the accounts payable ledger.

- When the ledger is set up, each creditor's name, address, and terms are recorded on a separate ledger sheet or card. If the business owes money to any of the creditors, an entry is made to record the amount owed. This is the opening balance of the creditor's account. On April 1, Maddalon Office Supply owed $5,000 to a creditor—Office Forms. Look at the account for this creditor to see how the balance was recorded. The same type of entry must be made when a ledger sheet is filled, and the creditor's balance must be transferred to another sheet.

- Each transaction listed in the purchases journal is posted individually to a creditor's account in the accounts payable ledger. For example, notice how the entry of April 3 was posted to the account for Del Rocco Office Products. The date of the transaction (April 3) is written in the Date column of the account. The invoice number (1167) and the invoice date (4/1/XX) are written in the Description column. This information identifies the purchase. The amount ($800) is entered in the Credit column of the account. (Remember that purchases on credit increase the liability Accounts Payable. Increases in liabilities are recorded as credits.) Because there was no previous balance for Del Rocco Office Products, the amount of the purchase is also written in the Balance column. Thus the balance of this creditor's account on April 3, is $800. The abbreviation *P* and the journal page number *1* are written in the Posting Reference column of the account to identify the source of the entry. A check mark is placed in the purchases journal to show that the transaction was posted.

- If a creditor's account already has a balance when a purchase is posted, the amount of the purchase must be added to the previous balance. For example, suppose that a purchase of $1,000 is posted to the account of E-Tron Computer Products on May 1. The amount of the purchase would be recorded in the Credit column. Then this amount would be added to the previous balance to find the new balance ($3,600 + $1,000 = $4,600). The new balance would be entered in the Balance column.

- Each transaction listed in the Accounts Payable Debit column of the cash payments journal is posted to a creditor's account in the accounts payable ledger. For example, notice how the entry of April 5 was posted to the account for Office Forms. The date of the transaction (April 5) is written in the Date column. The amount ($2,800) is entered in the Debit column. (Remember that payments to creditors decrease the liability Accounts Payable. Decreases in liabilities are recorded as debits.) The amount of the payment is subtracted from the previous balance to find the new balance ($5,000 − $2,800 = $2,200). The new balance is entered in the Balance column. The abbreviation *CP* and the journal page number *1* are written in the Posting Reference column of the account. A check mark is placed in the cash payments journal to show that the transaction was posted.

- Each time Accounts Payable is debited or credited in the general journal, the entry is posted individually to a creditor's account in the accounts payable ledger. Look at the general journal entries on page 159. Notice that the accountant uses a diagonal line in both the Description of Entry column and the Posting Reference column. The *202* means that the amount was posted to the Accounts Payable account in the general ledger. The check mark means that the amount was also posted to the creditor's account in the account's payable ledger.

Observe the postings made from the general journal to the accounts for Display Systems and E-Tron Computer Products in the accounts payable ledger on pages 159 and 160. In the Display Systems account, the invoice number (796) is written in the Description column and *J1* is written in the Posting Reference column. In the E-Tron Computer Products account, the credit memorandum number (481) is written in the Description column and *J1* is written in the Posting Reference column.

■ PROVING THE ACCOUNTS PAYABLE LEDGER

At the end of the month, the accounts payable ledger must be proved. A *schedule of accounts payable* is used to do this.

1. The name and account balance for each creditor with an unpaid balance are listed on the schedule form. This information is taken from the accounts payable ledger.
2. The balances are added to find the total amount owed to all creditors.
3. The total of the schedule of accounts payable is compared with the balance of the Accounts Payable account in the general ledger. The two amounts must be the same.

Schedule Of Accounts Payable: List of creditor's accounts with unpaid balances.

The Accounts Payable account in the general ledger is a control account because its balance is the total amount owed to all creditors. This account provides a link between the subsidiary ledger and the general ledger. Notice that the total of the schedule of accounts payable prepared at Maddalon Office Supply on April 30 agrees with the balance of the Accounts Payable account on that date.

MADDALON OFFICE SUPPLY
SCHEDULE OF ACCOUNTS PAYABLE
APRIL 30, 20XX

	Customer	Balance
1	Del Rocco Office Products	4 3 2 5 00
2	Display Systems	4 2 0 0 00
3	E-Tron Computer Products	3 6 0 0 00
4	Office Forms	2 2 0 0 00
5	Total	14 3 2 5 00

Proving the Accounts Payable Ledger

ACCOUNT	Accounts Payable				ACCOUNT NO. 202	
Date	Description	Post. Ref.	Debit	Credit	Balance Debit	Balance Credit
20XX						
Apr. 1		J1		500 00		500 00
2		J1		420 00		920 00
30		J1	150 00			905 00
30		P1		1255 00		2160 00
30		CP1	727 50			1432 50

■ NOTES PAYABLE

If a business does not have enough cash to pay the balance owed to a creditor, it will usually request some extra time. The creditor may grant the extra time but ask for a promissory note. This arrangement gives the creditor more assurance of receiving its money. The note provides a written promise to pay and sets a definite date for the payment. In some businesses, notes are used routinely.

Assume that Maddalon Office Supply issues a note for $2,200 to Office Forms on May 29. The note will run for 60 days and bear interest at 12 percent. This note does not pay the debt. It merely changes the form of the liability from an account payable to a note payable. (Promissory notes given to creditors are called *notes payable*.) Because the form of the liability has changed, the following entry is made in the general journal of Maddalon Office Supply. This entry is posted to the general ledger and the accounts payable ledger.

Notes Payable: Promissory notes that a business has issued.

GENERAL JOURNAL Page 4

	Date	Description	Post. Ref.	Debit	Credit	
1	20XX					1
2	May					2
5	29	Accounts Payable/Office Forms	202 ✓	220 00		5
6		Notes Payable	201		220 00	6
7		Issued a 60-day, 12% note.				7
8						8

ACCOUNT	Accounts Payable				ACCOUNT NO. 202	
Date	Description	Post. Ref.	Debit	Credit	Balance Debit	Balance Credit
20XX						
Apr. 1		J1		500 00		500 00
2		J1		420 00		920 00
30		J1	150 00			905 00
30		P1		1255 00		2160 00
30		CP1	727 50			1432 50
May 29		J4	220 00			1212 50

ACCOUNT	Notes Payable				ACCOUNT NO. 201	
Date	Description	Post. Ref.	Debit	Credit	Balance Debit	Balance Credit
20XX						
May 29		J4		220 00		220 00

NAME	Office Forms					
ADDRESS	548 Main Street					
	Newark, New Jersey 07102			TERMS	n/60	

	Date		Description	Post. Ref.	Debit	Credit	Balance	
1	20	XX						1
2	Apr.	1	Balance	✓			5 000 00	2
3		5		CP1	2 800 00		2 200 00	3
4	May	29	60-day, 12% note	J4	2 200 00		–0–	4
5								5

The Accounts Payable account in the general ledger and the creditor's account in the accounts payable ledger are debited to record the decrease in their balances. The Notes Payable account is credited to record the new liability.

The note given to Office Forms will become due on July 28. When Maddalon Office Supply issues the check, an entry is made in the cash payments journal. The Notes Payable account is debited for the amount of the note ($2,200), and the Interest Expense account is debited for the amount of interest ($44). The Cash account is credited for the total amount paid ($2,244).

**CASH PAYMENTS JOURNAL
FOR MONTH OF JULY, 20XX**

Page 7

	Date	Ck. No.	Explanation	✓	Accounts Payable Debit	Merch. Purch. Debit	Other Accounts Debit Account Name	Post. Ref.	Amount	Purch. Disc. Credit	Cash Credit	
1	20 XX											1
2	July											2
3		28	164	Note—Office Forms				Notes Payable	201	2 200 00			3
4								Interest Expense	591	44 00		2 244 00	4

CHAPTER 20 SUMMARY

- The accounts payable ledger is a subsidiary ledger that contains an individual account for each creditor.

- Transactions with the creditors are posted to the accounts payable ledger from the purchases journal, the cash payments journal, and the general journal. This posting should be done on a daily basis so that the balances can be kept up to date.

- At the end of each month, the accounts payable ledger is proved. First, a schedule of accounts payable is prepared. Then the total of the schedule is compared with the balance of the Accounts Payable account in the general ledger. The two amounts should be the same.

- The Accounts Payable account in the general ledger is a control account. It shows the total amount owed to all creditors.

- Promissory notes given by a business are a liability and are known as notes payable. The interest on these notes is an expense. The Notes Payable account is credited when a note is issued and debited when the note is paid. The Interest Expense account is debited for the amount of interest paid.

CHAPTER APPLICATIONS

EXERCISES

Complete the following assignments on the forms provided in your workbook.

EXERCISE 20-1

Posting to the accounts payable ledger and proving the ledger. Ledger account balances and partial journals are shown below.

General Ledger		Subsidiary Ledger	
Accounts Payable	$7,000	Apollo Sounds	$1,500
		Arista Plastics	900
		Lincoln Resources	1,100
		Madre Leasing	3,500

Purchases Journal		Cash Payments Journal	
Apollo Sounds	$1,000	Madre Leasing	$3,500
Arista Plastics	2,000	Apollo Sounds	1,000
Lincoln Resources	3,000	Lincoln Resources	1,100
Madre Leasing	2,200	Arista Plastics	2,900
	$8,200		$8,500

Instructions:

1. Set up T accounts for Accounts Payable and for the subsidiary ledger accounts.
2. Enter the balances in these accounts.
3. Post from the partial journals to these accounts.
4. Compute the account balances.
5. Total the subsidiary ledger account balances, and prove the total to the balance in the control account.

EXERCISE 20-2

Posting to a creditor's account.

Instructions:

1. Set up a balance ledger form for Menz Electronics. The address is 1280 Benson Drive, Dayton, OH 45402, and the terms are n/10. Assume that you are posting each of the following transactions from page 6 of the purchases journal, the cash payments journal, or the general journal.
2. Enter the date, posting reference, debit or credit amount, and the balance in the creditor's account.

Transactions:

June 2   Purchased merchandise for $2,000 on credit, Invoice 501.
     10   Purchased merchandise for $3,000 on credit, Invoice 547.
     12   Issued Check 492 for $2,000 to pay Invoice 501.
     15   Received Credit Memorandum 87 for $500 to cover the return of defective merchandise purchased on Invoice 547.
     22   Issued a 60-day, 10 percent promissory note to settle the balance of the account.

EXERCISE 20-3

Using special journals and subsidiary ledgers. Display Systems records transactions in a sales journal (*S*), a purchases journal (*P*), a cash receipts journal (*CR*), a cash payments journal (*CP*), and a general journal (*J*). Entries are posted from the five journals to the accounts receivable ledger and the accounts payable ledger.

Instructions:

1. For each transaction listed below, identify the journal that is used to record the transaction.
2. Determine which of the transactions will be posted to the accounts receivable ledger and which will be posted to the accounts payable ledger.
3. Decide whether the subsidiary ledger account will be debited or credited. If a transaction will not be posted to a subsidiary ledger, leave the columns blank.

Transaction

Example: *Purchased equipment on credit.*

Journal	Accounts Receivable	Accounts Payable
J		Cr.

1. Sold merchandise on credit.
2. Purchased office supplies on credit.
3. Sold merchandise for cash.
4. Purchased merchandise for cash.
5. Issued a check to a creditor.
6. Received a check from a customer in payment of the balance of her account.
7. Purchased office equipment for cash.
8. Received a credit memorandum from a creditor for the return of merchandise.
9. Purchased office supplies for cash.
10. Issued a credit memorandum to a customer for the return of merchandise.

EXERCISE 20-4

Accounting for notes payable and interest.

Instructions:

1. Set up T accounts and enter the balances shown below.

Cash	$7,000	Merchandise Purchases	$2,000
Notes Payable	–0–	Freight In	–0–
Accounts Payable	9,000	Interest Expense	–0–

2. Analyze each of the following transactions and record the effects in the T accounts.
3. Compute the balance of each account and prove that the total of the debit balances equals the total of the credit balances.

Transactions:

a. Purchased merchandise for $3,000 from Rosequist Manufacturing on credit, Invoice 522.
b. Issued a 60-day, 12 percent promissory note for $3,000 to Rosequist Manufacturing in settlement of Invoice 522.

c. Issued Check 347 for $3,060 to Rosequist Manufacturing in payment of the promissory note plus interest of $60.

d. Purchased merchandise for $2,600 plus freight charges of $100 from McGarth Industries, Invoice 633 due in 30 days.

e. Issued a 90-day, 12 percent promissory note for $2,700 to McGarth Industries in settlement of Invoice 633.

f. Issued Check 362 for $2,781 to McGarth Industries in payment of the promissory note plus interest of $81.

PROBLEMS

Complete all assigned problems on the forms provided in your workbook.

PROBLEM 20-1

Posting to a creditors account. Cutler's Furniture Store is setting up an accounts payable ledger for its creditors.

Instructions:

1. Open an account for Lesher Manufacturing Company, 121 Clark Street, Mankato, MN 56001. The terms are n/30. The balance on September 1 of the current year is $562.85.

2. Assume that the purchases journal and the cash payments journal show the following transactions with the Lesher Manufacturing Company during September and October of the current year. Enter these transactions in the creditor's account. The posting references are *P9* for the purchases journal and *CP12* for the cash payments journal.

Transactions:

Sept.	10	Purchased merchandise for $387 on credit; Invoice 4321, dated 9/8.
	14	Paid $562.85 on account.
	26	Purchased merchandise for $720 on credit; Invoice 4537, dated 9/24.
Oct.	3	Purchased merchandise for $693.45 on credit; Invoice 4762, dated 10/1.
	5	Paid $387 for Invoice 4321.
	19	Purchased merchandise for $1,288.30 on credit; Invoice 5023, dated 10/17.
	21	Paid $720 for Invoice 4537.
	28	Paid $693.45 for Invoice 4762.

PROBLEM 20-2

Using the purchases journal, the cash payments journal, the general journal, the general ledger, and the accounts payable ledger. Majestic Photo Products is a retail store that sells cameras and film. Most of the merchandise is purchased on credit from four suppliers.

Instructions:

1. Open the general ledger accounts for Cash 101; Equipment 113; Accounts Payable 202; Jim Hyslop, Withdrawals 302; Merchandise Purchases 501; Freight In 502; Purchases Returns and Allowances 503; and Purchases Discounts 504.

2. Enter the September 1 balances in the following general ledger accounts: Cash, $8,760; Equipment, $2,550; and Accounts Payable, $1,875. Use the current year.

3. Open the accounts for the following creditors in the accounts payable ledger.

Clarity Photo
Marsh Road
Hilton Head, SC 29925

Rodriguez Camera
214 Alamo Trail
San Antonio, TX 78201

Saporo Corporation
1010 Electronics Drive
Frederick, MD 21701

New Hope Distributors
811 Main Street
New Hope, PA 18969

4. Enter the September 1 balances in the creditor's accounts: Clarity Photo, $350; Saporo Corporation, $475; Rodriguez Camera, $650; and New Hope Distributors, $400.

5. Record each of the following transactions in the purchases journal, the cash payments journal, or the general journal. Use *1* as the page number for each journal.

6. Post the entries from the purchases journal, from the Accounts payable Debit column of the cash payments journal, and from the general journal to the accounts payable ledger on a daily basis.

7. Post the entries from the Other Accounts Debit column of the cash payments journal and from the general journal to the general ledger on a daily basis.

8. Pencil-foot the purchases journal and the cash payments journal. Prove their accuracy by cross-footing.

9. Total and rule the purchases journal and the cash payments journal.

10. Post the totals of the purchases journal and the cash payments journal.

11. Prepare a schedule of accounts payable, dated September 30. Compare the total of the schedule with the balance of the Accounts Payable account in the general ledger. The two amounts should be the same.

Transactions:

Sept. 4 Purchased merchandise for $280 plus a freight charge of $20 on credit from Clarity Photo; Invoice 1361, dated 9/1, terms 2/20, n/60.

4 Issued Check 221 for $630.50 to Rodriguez Camera to pay Invoice 716; $650 less a discount of $19.50.
5 Issued Check 222 for $343 to Clarity Photo to pay Invoice 1282; $350 less a discount of $7.
6 Purchased merchandise for $295 plus a freight charge of $16 on credit from the Saporo Corporation; Invoice 382, dated 9/4, terms n/30.
8 Issued Check 223 for $392 to New Hope Distributors to pay Invoice 4512; $400 less a discount of $8.
10 Purchased merchandise for $600 on credit from New Hope Distributors; Invoice 4623; dated 9/8, terms 2/10 EOM.
12 Issued Check 224 for $300 to make a cash purchase of merchandise.
12 Received Credit Memorandum C381 for $65 from the Saporo Corporation for the return of damaged merchandise.
13 Purchased merchandise for $175 on credit from Rodriguez Camera; Invoice 797, dated 9/11, terms 3/10, n/30.
15 Issued Check 225 for $285 to purchase equipment for the office.
17 Purchased merchandise for $340 plus a freight charge of $18 on credit from the Saporo Corporation; Invoice 441, dated 9/15, terms n/30.
18 Issued Check 226 for $475 to the Saporo Corporation to pay Invoice 291.
19 Issued Check 227 for $294.40 to Clarity Photo to pay Invoice 1361; $300 less a discount of $5.60.
20 Purchased merchandise for $330 plus a freight charge of $20 on credit from Clarity Photo; Invoice 1558, dated 9/18, terms 2/20, n/60.
20 Issued Check 228 for $169.75 to Rodriguez Camera to pay Invoice 797; $175 less a discount of $5.25.
22 Purchased merchandise for $718 on credit from New Hope Distributors; Invoice 4830, dated 9/20, terms 2/10 EOM.
25 Purchased merchandise for $467 plus a freight charge of $21 on credit from the Saporo Corporation; Invoice 506, dated 9/23, terms n/30.
25 Received Credit Memorandum 109 for $110 from New Hope Distributors for the return of damaged merchandise.
26 Purchased merchandise for $222 on credit from Rodriguez Camera; Invoice 882, dated 9/24, terms 3/10, n/30.
27 Issued Check 229 for $200 to make a cash purchase of merchandise.
29 Issued Check 230 for $950 for a cash withdrawal by Jim Hyslop, the owner.
30 Issued Check 231 for $311 to the Saporo Corporation to pay Invoice 382.

CASE STUDY

Write the answer to the case study on the form provided in your workbook.

Posting Errors

You learned in accounting class that even though a subsidiary ledger has been proven, there can be errors in posting to the incorrect accounts. Sometimes amounts are posted to the wrong accounts so that the totals still prove, but the incorrect accounts are not correct.

Critical Thinking

- *How will such posting errors be discovered and corrected?*

Chapters 11–20

PROJECT 3

Accounting for a Merchandising Business

On February 1 of the current year, Jennifer Jenkins opened the Jenkins Lumber Company. The chart of accounts for this business follows.

Ms. Jenkins sells merchandise on credit to local builders. She also makes cash sales to individuals who need lumber for home repairs and improvements. Most of the merchandise is purchased on credit from four suppliers. Use the forms in your workbook to complete the project.

INSTRUCTIONS:

1. Record the opening entry in the general journal. Use 1 as the journal page number. Ms. Jenkins' investment consisted of the following items: Cash, $15,000; Merchandise Inventory, $18,000; Office Equipment, $4,000; and Warehouse Equipment, $7,000. Post the opening entry to the general ledger accounts.

2. Record a memorandum entry of the cash balance in the cash receipts journal.

3. Record each of the transactions for February in the proper journal. The business has a general journal and special journals for sales, purchases, cash receipts, and cash payments. Use *1* as the page number for each journal.

4. Post individual entries daily to the subsidiary ledgers in the following order. Post to the accounts receivable ledger from the sales journal, from the Accounts Receivable Credit column of the cash receipts journal, and from the general journal. Post to the accounts payable ledger from the purchases journal, from the Accounts Payable Debit column of the cash payments journal, and from the general journal.

5. Post individual entries daily to the general ledger from the Other Accounts Credit column of the cash receipts journal, from the Other Accounts Debit column of the cash payments journal, and from the general journal.

6. At the end of the month, pencil-foot the journals. Prove the accuracy of the journals by cross-footing.

7. Total and rule the special journals.

8. Post the totals from the special journals.

9. Prepare a schedule of accounts receivable and a schedule of accounts payable. Compare the totals of the schedules with the balances of the control accounts in the general ledger. The amounts should be the same.

10. Prepare a trial balance.

Jenkins Lumber Company
Chart of Accounts

Assets
101 Cash
112 Accounts Receivable
113 Allowance for Uncollectible Accounts*
114 Merchandise Inventory
115 Supplies
116 Prepaid Insurance
126 Office Equipment
127 Accumulated Depreciation—Office Equipment*
128 Warehouse Equipment
129 Accumulated Depreciation—Warehouse Equipment*

Liabilities
202 Accounts Payable
231 Sales Tax Payable

Owner's Equity
301 Jennifer Jenkins, Capital
302 Jennifer Jenkins, Withdrawals
399 Income Summary

Revenue
401 Sales
402 Sales Returns and Allowances
403 Sales Discount

Costs and Expenses
501 Merchandise Purchases
502 Freight In
503 Purchases Returns and Allowances
504 Purchases Discount
511 Advertising Expense
512 Telephone Expense
513 Depreciation Expense—Office Equipment*
514 Depreciation Expense—Warehouse Equipment*
516 Rent Expense
517 Supplies Expense*
518 Utilities Expense
519 Wages Expense
521 Uncollectible Accounts Expense*
522 Insurance Expense*

*These accounts will be used in Project 4.

TRANSACTIONS:

Feb. 1 Issued Check 101 for $800 to pay the monthly rent for the building in which the business is located.

Feb. 2 Sold merchandise for $950 plus $47.50 sales tax (a total of $997.50) on credit to Archibald Builders; Invoice A1, terms 2/10, n/30.

2 Issued Check 102 for $1,320 to Farmers Insurance for fire and liability insurance. (Debit Prepaid Insurance.)

2 Issued Check 103 for $337.50 to pay for supplies that will be used in the business.

Feb. 3 Purchased merchandise for $1,300 plus a $40 freight charge (a total of $1,340) on credit from Mountain Lumber Company; Invoice 1364, dated 2/1, terms 1/30, n/60.

3 Sold merchandise for $1,680 plus $84 sales tax (a total of $1,764) on credit to McKnight Developers; Invoice A2, terms 1/10, n/60.

Feb. 5 Purchased merchandise for $870 plus a $35 freight charge (a total of $905) on credit from Pine Forest Products; Invoice 3176, dated 2/3, terms 2/10, n/30.

Feb. 6 Issued Check 104 for $150 to pay for a newspaper advertisement.

6 Received $2,071.13 for cash sales of $1,972.50 plus $98.63 sales tax during the first week of February. *Be sure to post the individual entries as directed in Instructions 4 and 5.*

Feb. 8 Sold merchandise for $1,654.80 plus $82.74 sales tax (a total of $1,737.54) on credit to Betterbuilt Homes; Invoice A3, terms 2/10, n/30.

Feb. 10 Received $978.50 from Archibald Builders for Invoice A1, $997.50 less a $19 discount.

Feb. 11 Sold merchandise for $652 plus $32.60 sales tax (a total of $684.60) on credit to Cross Country Construction; Invoice A4, terms 2/10, n/30.

11 Issued Check 105 for $887.60 to Pine Forest Products for Invoice 3176; $905 less a $17.40 discount.

Feb. 13 Received $1,747.20 from McKnight Developers for Invoice A2, $1,764 less a $16.80 discount.

13 Received $2,092.97 for cash sales of $1,993.30 plus $99.67 sales tax during the second week of February. *Be sure to post the individual entries.*

Feb. 15 Purchased merchandise for $725 plus a $26 freight charge (a total of $751) on credit from Bay Building Materials; Invoice 1738, dated 2/13, terms n/30.

15 Issued Check 106 for $1,980 to pay the wages of employees for the first half of the month.

Feb. 17 Sold merchandise for $1,520 plus $76 sales tax (a total of $1,596) on credit to Jorga Construction Company; Invoice A5, terms 1/10, n/60.

Feb. 18 Purchased merchandise for $2,464 plus a $54 freight charge (a total of $2,518) on credit from Mountain Lumber Company; Invoice 1426, dated 2/15, terms 1/30, n/60.

Feb. 19 Issued Check 107 for $152.70 to pay the telephone bill.

19 Issued Check 108 for $1,500 to purchase steel shelves for the warehouse.

Feb. 20 Received $671.56 from Cross Country Construction for Invoice A4, $684.60 less a $13.04 discount.

20 Received $2,588.04 for cash sales of $2,464.80 plus $123.24 sales tax during the third week of February. *Be sure to post the individual entries.*

Feb. 22 Received $120 from the sale of used office file cabinets.

22 Issued Check 109 for $450 for the cash purchase of merchandise.

Feb. 22 Accepted a return of damaged merchandise sold to Jorga Construction Company on Invoice A5. Issued Credit Memorandum C1 for $105. Of this amount, $100 is for the merchandise and $5 is for the sales tax.

Feb. 23 Purchased merchandise for $456 plus a freight charge of $24 (a total of $480) on credit from Sierra Wood Products; Invoice 786, dated 2/20, terms 2/10, n/30.

Feb. 24 Purchased merchandise for $760 plus a $28 freight charge (a total of $788) on credit from Pine Forest Products; Invoice 3285, dated 2/22, terms 2/10, n/30.

Feb. 25 Sold merchandise for $1,330 plus $66.50 sales tax (a total of $1,396.50) on credit to Betterbuilt Homes; Invoice A6, terms 2/10, n/30.

Feb. 26 Returned damaged merchandise that was purchased from Sierra Wood Products on Invoice 786. Received Credit Memorandum 375 for $150.

Feb. 27 Issued Check 110 for $175 to pay the electric bill.

27 Issued Check 111 for $1,980 to pay the wages of employees for the second half of the month.

27 Issued Check 112 for $1,000 for a withdrawal by Jennifer Jenkins, the owner.

27 Issued Check 113 for $1,327 to Mountain Lumber Company for Invoice 1364; $1,340 less a $13 discount.

27 Received $2,530.50 for cash sales of $2,410 plus $120.50 sales tax during the fourth week of February. *Be sure to post the individual entries.*

Save your work for use in Project 4.

PART FOUR

Summarizing and Reporting Financial Information

- **Chapter 21**
  Worksheet Adjustments
- **Chapter 22**
  Cost of Goods Sold and Statements
- **Chapter 23**
  Adjusting and Closing the General Ledger
- **Project 4**

After working with special journals, you will sense that in order for the accounting for a merchandising business to be precise, you must consider things like depreciation, inventory changes, and the collection of debts. In Part Four you will learn to compute the cost of goods sold, which is a critical concept in understanding how inventory changes affect the bottom line for a merchandising business. In addition you will prepare the necessary end-of-period statements for the business and prepare the accounts for the next accounting period. Parts One through Four helped you understand the accounting necessary in service and merchandising businesses. Part Five will help you understand the importance of cash management in these businesses. ■

Accounting Careers

What's Ethics Got to Do with It?

■ CONFLICT HAPPENS

Accounting isn't cut and dried. If you pursue a career in accounting, you will quickly learn that in some situations there is not a clear line between the *Required,* the *Permissible,* and the *Forbidden.* The American Institute of Certified Public Accountants has a Professional Code of Ethics. However, there will be times when you won't be able to look up the answers. Establishing a clear-cut strategy for resolving conflicts will ensure that you make ethical and moral decisions and do not respond in an inappropriate manner when a dilemma occurs.

■ TACKLING ETHICAL DILEMMAS

- Gather resources and advice
- List the facts
- List personal advantages
- List the ethical issues
- State your objectives
- Know what other parties have at stake—their objectives and their pressures on you.
- Review the relevant rules
- Write down the undesirable choices
- Brainstorm alternatives
- Apply the rules to the alternatives
- Know the consequences for yourself and others
- Plan a course of action.

ACTIVITY

- Obtain and read a copy of the AICPA's Professional Code of Ethics for Certified Public Accountants.
- Divide the class into groups with each group responsible for writing up a skit dealing with ethical decisions. Exchange skits and role play several different outcomes for the same skit.

CHAPTER TWENTY-ONE

Worksheet Adjustments

OBJECTIVES

Upon completion of this chapter, you should be able to:

1. Explain the need for worksheet adjustments.
2. Describe how the adjustments are calculated and recorded on the worksheet.
3. Explain the procedure for writing off an uncollectible account receivable.
4. Complete the Adjusted Trial Balance section of the worksheet.

INTRODUCTION

At the end of each accounting period, a trial balance is prepared to verify the equality of the debits and credits in the general ledger. The trial balance is usually entered on a worksheet. Remember that the *worksheet* is a form used to compute the net income or net loss and to plan and speed up the preparation of the financial statements.

Certain information about a business's operations such as changes in the merchandise inventory, supplies used, expired insurance, estimated uncollectible accounts, and depreciation have not yet been recorded in the accounting records. *Adjustments* are entered on the worksheet to provide such information for the financial statements. ■

■ THE NEED FOR ADJUSTMENTS

It is important that the financial statements present a complete picture of the results of operations and the condition of the business. For example, the income statement should report all revenues earned and all expenses incurred during the accounting period. In order to accurately determine the net income or net loss, the revenues and expenses charged to a period must be those that pertain to that period. This is the *matching principle* of accounting.

The trial balance prepared for Maddalon Office Supply on April 30 does not include the amounts of several of the expenses the actual amount incurred during April—the expenses for supplies; for insurance; for depreciation of the store equipment, the office equipment, and the building; and for estimated uncollectible accounts receivable. Worksheet adjustments must be recorded so that these expenses can be shown on the income statement and subtracted from the revenue for the month.

The adjustments ensure that the asset account balances are updated and that they show the correct amount at the end of the accounting period.

■ THE ADJUSTMENT FOR MERCHANDISE INVENTORY

When the trial balance is prepared, the general ledger shows the amount of merchandise inventory that was on hand at the start of the accounting period. However, changes occurred in this inventory during the period because goods were purchased and sold.

Accounting Terminology

- Adjustments
- Beginning inventory
- Book value
- Contra account
- Depreciation
- Disposal value
- Ending inventory
- Inventory sheet
- Long-term assets
- Matching principle
- Physical inventory
- Prepaid insurance
- Property, plant, and equipment
- Straight-line method
- Uncollectible accounts
- Useful life
- Worksheet
- Worksheet adjustments
- Writing off a customer's account

Worksheet: Form used to compute the net income or net loss and to plan the preparation of financial statements.

Worksheet Adjustments: Amounts that are recorded on the worksheet to update the account balances with information not yet recorded in the accounting records.

Matching Principle: All revenues earned and all expenses incurred during an accounting period must be used to determine the net income or net loss.

Beginning Inventory: Merchandise on hand at the start of an accounting period.

Ending Inventory: Merchandise on hand at the end of an accounting period.

Physical Inventory: An actual count of merchandise on hand.

Inventory Sheet: Form listing information about a physical inventory.

On April 1, Maddalon Office Supply had a *beginning inventory* totaling $8,000. Because no entries are recorded in the Merchandise Inventory account, the balance of the account is still $8,000 on April 30, when the trial balance is prepared.

The following steps must be taken to determine the amount of the *ending inventory*.

1. An actual count is made of all merchandise on hand. This count is called a *physical inventory*.
2. Information about each item is listed on an *inventory sheet*. This information includes the stock number, description, quantity, and unit cost.
3. The total cost for each item is computed. The unit cost is multiplied by the quantity. The resulting amount is entered on the inventory sheet.
4. The total cost for the merchandise on hand is computed. This is done by adding the costs of all the items. The overall total is recorded at the bottom of the last inventory sheet.

The inventory sheet below shows that Maddalon Office Supply had an ending inventory of $12,000 on April 30. The Merchandise Inventory account must now be updated on the worksheet. The balance of the account must be changed so that it will show the ending inventory for the period. This is done in two adjusting entries.

INVENTORY SHEET	April 30, 20XX			No. 6
COUNTED BY J.S.		COMPUTED BY JR		
LISTED BY RV		CHECKED BY AL		
STOCK NO.	DESCRIPTION	QUANTITY	UNIT COST	TOTAL
3624L	Printing calculator	8	130 00	1,040 00
2376X	10 Digit calculator	24	23 50	564 00
			TOTAL	12,000 00

1. The amount of the beginning inventory ($8,000) is taken off the books by closing the account balance into the Income Summary account. Look at the worksheet on pages 178 and 179. Notice that it has a special section for adjustments. The debit of $8,000 is entered on the line for the Income Summary account, and the credit of $8,000 on the line for the Merchandise Inventory account. The letter (a) is placed next to both of the $8,000 figures to identify the two parts of the first adjustment.
2. The second adjusting entry (b) debits the amount of the ending inventory ($12,000) to the Merchandise Inventory account and credits the Income Summary account for the same amount. This entry updates and records the correct inventory balance on April 30.

WWW Inquiry
Find the URL address for Kellogg's, the cereal and convenience food company. What percentage of total current liabilities does accounts payable represent on the most recent balance sheet?

■ THE ADJUSTMENT FOR SUPPLIES USED

When Maddalon Office Supply began operations on April 1, it had store supplies totaling $600. Because these supplies were expected to last for several months, their cost was debited to the asset account Supplies. During April, the firm bought additional supplies; and on April 30 the Supplies account had a balance of $860. However, some of the supplies were used during the month. On April 30, a count was made of the remaining supplies. The quantity on hand was multiplied by the unit cost of the items to find the total amount of supplies on hand at the end of the month. The amount of supplies used was then determined as shown below.

Cost of supplies available during month	$860
Less inventory of supplies on hand at end of month	620
Cost of supplies used during month	$240

The cost of supplies used is an expense for the business. An adjustment must be made to transfer this amount from the Supplies account to the Supplies Expense account. The adjustment for supplies used is recorded by entering a debit of $240 on the line for the Supplies Expense account and a credit of $240 on the line for the Supplies account. The letter (c) is placed next to both the $240 figures to identify the two parts of the adjustment.

■ THE ADJUSTMENT FOR EXPIRED INSURANCE

Many businesses buy insurance to protect their property. The amount paid for insurance usually covers a year or several years. For this reason, the amount is debited to an asset account—the Prepaid Insurance account. At the end of each accounting period, part of the insurance protection is used up. An adjustment must be made to charge the cost of the expired insurance to the operations of the period. This adjustment consists of a debit to the Insurance Expense account and a credit to the Prepaid Insurance account.

On April 2, Maddalon Office Supply purchased a two-year insurance policy for $2,400. At the end of each month during the two-year period, an adjustment of $100 will be made for expired insurance: $2,400 ÷ 24 months = $100. The letter (d) in the Adjustments section of the worksheet identifies the debit to Insurance Expense and the credit to Prepaid Insurance.

Prepaid Insurance: An asset that will last for the term of the policy.

■ THE ADJUSTMENT FOR DEPRECIATION

Businesses usually own certain types of property that will be used for a number of years. Land, buildings, machinery, and equipment are examples of such property. These items are called *property, plant, and equipment, long-term assets,* or *fixed assets.*

All long-term assets except land eventually wear out, become obsolete, or become inadequate. They have a limited *useful life.* When a long-term asset is purchased, an estimate is made of its useful life. This estimate is usually based on the previous experience of the business, common practices in its industry, and guidelines published by the Internal Revenue Service.

Long-term assets are used in operating a business. They provide services that the business needs to function effectively and earn revenue. The cost of each long-term asset must therefore be charged to operations. During the useful life of the long-term asset, every accounting period bears part of the cost. The amount that is charged to operations is called *depreciation.* The only long-term asset that is not subject to depreciation is land.

Adjustments are entered on the worksheet to record depreciation. Aside from land, Maddalon Office Supply has three types of long-term assets. To determine the depreciation for a long-term asset, it is necessary to consider its cost, its disposal value, and its estimated useful life. The *disposal value,* also called *scrap value* or *salvage value,* is the amount that a business expects to receive when the long-term asset is traded in or scrapped. The computation of monthly depreciation for the building owned by Maddalon Office Supply is shown on page 176.

Property, Plant, and Equipment, or Long-Term Assets: Property that will be used for a number of years.

Useful Life: Estimated number of years that a long-term asset will be used in a business.

Depreciation: Part of the cost of a long-term asset that is charged to operations.

Disposal, Scrap, or Salvage Value: Amount that a business expects to receive when a long-term asset is traded in or scrapped.

Purchase Date	Description	Original Cost	− Disposal Value	= Total Depreciation	÷ Estimated Useful Life	= Yearly Depreciation	÷ 12	= Monthly Depreciation
20XX								
April 1	Store Equipment	$6,000	$708	$5,292	7 years	$756	12	$63
17	Store Equipment	600	120	480	5 years	96	12	8*
		$6,600						$71†
1	Office Equipment	$12,000	$1,200	$10,800	5 years	$2,160	12	$180
2	Office Equipment	4,200	504	3,696	4 years	924	12	77
		$16,200						$257
1	Building	$30,000	$6,000	$24,000	25 years	$960	12	$80

*During April, no depreciation can be taken on this item because it was purchased after April 15.
†The monthly depreciation recorded for store equipment in April is $63.

Depreciation of Building

$30,000 (original cost) − $6,000 (disposal value) = $24,000 (total depreciation)

$24,000 (total depreciation) ÷ 25 (estimated years of useful life) = $960 (yearly depreciation)

$960 (yearly depreciation) ÷ 12 (months) = $80 (monthly depreciation)

Straight-Line Method: Method of computing depreciation in which an equal amount is assigned to each period.

There are several methods of computing depreciation. The one used by Maddalon Office Supply is called the *straight-line method.* With this method, an equal amount of depreciation is assigned to each accounting period.

Depreciation is an expense. When the adjustments for depreciation are recorded, the amount for each type of long-term asset is debited to a separate expense account. Look at the worksheet on pages 178 and 179. The adjustments for depreciation are identified by the letters (e) through (g). Notice that there is a separate accumulated depreciation account for each type of long-term asset. This account is credited for the amount of depreciation.

Book Value: Portion of the original cost of a long-term asset that has not yet been depreciated.

The accumulated depreciation account will provide a record of the total depreciation taken on each type of long-term asset. The *book value* of the long-term asset can be computed at any time by subtracting the total depreciation from the original cost. For example, the book value of the building owned by Maddalon Office Supply is $29,920 after the depreciation for April is recorded. The Building account shows an original cost of $30,000. The Accumulated Depreciation—Building account shows total depreciation of $80.

Contra Account: Account used to record deductions from the balance of a related account.

The accumulated depreciation account is called a *contra account* because it has a credit balance, which is contrary to the normal balance for an asset account. As you have seen, the credit balance of the accumulated depreciation account is subtracted from the debit balance of the related long-term asset account to determine book value.

■ THE ADJUSTMENTS FOR DOUBTFUL ACCOUNTS

From experience, business managers know that some credit customers will not be able to pay their bills when the amounts become due. Estimated uncollectible amounts owed by credit customers are referred to as *uncollectible accounts,* or *bad debts.* They represent an expense for the business.

Uncollectible Accounts: Estimated uncollectible amounts owed by credit customers.

There is no way to tell in advance which customers will fail to pay. However, uncollectible accounts expense should be recorded in each accounting period so that it can be matched against revenue earned during the period. This is done by estimating the doubtful accounts for the period.

A number of methods can be used to estimate the amount of uncollectible accounts receivable. One common method is to take a percentage of the accounts receivable at the end of the period. For example, Maddalon Office Supply expects the rate of loss on accounts receivable to be 2 percent. The amount of the doubtful accounts expense for the period is $75 ($3,726 accounts receivable × 0.02 = $74.52, rounded off to the nearest whole dollar = $75).

An adjustment for the estimated loss from doubtful accounts is entered on the worksheet and identified by the letter (h). Notice that the Uncollectible Accounts Expense account is debited and a contra asset account called Allowance for Uncollectible Accounts is credited.

■ WRITING OFF A CUSTOMER'S ACCOUNT

When a bill becomes overdue, various steps are taken to obtain payment from the customer. The business sends collection letters and may hire a collection agency. If such efforts are not successful, the customer's account is *written off.* This is done by recording the following entry in the general journal.

Writing Off a Customer's Account: Reducing the balance of the account to zero because it is uncollectible.

GENERAL JOURNAL   Page 10

Date	Description	Post Ref.	Debit	Credit
20 XX				
Aug. 30	Allowance for Uncollectible Accounts	113	65 00	
	Accounts Receivable/Central Realty	112 ✓		65 00
	Write-off of uncollectible account.			

Allowance for Uncollectible Accounts is debited for the amount being written off. Two accounts are credited for this amount. The Accounts Receivable account in the general ledger must be credited to decrease its balance by the uncollectible amount. The customer's account in the accounts receivable ledger must be credited to reduce its balance to zero.

The Uncollectible Accounts Expense account is not involved in this transaction. It is only used when the estimated loss from uncollectible accounts for a period is recorded.

■ COMPLETING THE ADJUSTMENTS SECTION OF THE WORKSHEET

After the adjustments are entered on the worksheet of Maddalon Office Supply, the Adjustments section can be completed. The amounts in the two columns of the Adjustments section are added. The total of the Debit column should equal the total of the Credit column.

■ THE ADJUSTED TRIAL BALANCE SECTION OF THE WORKSHEET

Notice that Maddalon Office Supply uses a worksheet with ten money columns. This worksheet provides a special section for preparing an adjusted trial balance. The amounts in the Adjustments section must be combined with the amounts in the Trial Balance section to determine the new account balances. The following procedure is used to complete the Adjusted Trial Balance section.

WWW Inquiry
Find the URL address for Kellogg's. What is the percentage change in inventories between the last two years?

- If an account has a debit balance in the Trial Balance section and no adjustment, the same debit balance is entered in the Adjusted Trial Balance section. Refer to the following accounts on the worksheet of Maddalon Office Supply: Cash; Accounts Receivable; Store Equipment; Office Equipment; Building; Land; Ross Maddalon, Drawing; Sales Returns and Allowances; Sales Discount; Merchandise Purchases; Freight In; Salaries Expense; Telephone Expense; and Electricity Expense.

- If an account has a debit balance in the Trial Balance section and a debit amount in the Adjustments section, the two amounts are added. The total is entered in the Debit column of the Adjusted Trial Balance section. This does not occur on the worksheet of Maddalon Office Supply.

- If an account has a debit balance in the Trial Balance section and both a debit and credit amount in the Adjustments section, the debits are added and the credit is subtracted. Refer to the Merchandise Inventory account. The account had a debit balance of $8,000 and was adjusted by a debit of $12,000 and a credit of $8,000, which results in a debit balance of $12,000.

- If an account has a debit balance in the Trial Balance section and a credit amount in the Adjustments section, the credit amount is subtracted from the debit balance. The difference is entered in the Debit column of the Adjusted Trial Balance section. Refer to the worksheet of Maddalon Office Supply. The Supplies account had a debit balance of $860 when the trial balance was prepared. This account was credited for $240 to record the adjustment for supplies used. There is now a debit balance of $620 ($860 − $240 = $620). The same type of computation was used to determine the debit balance for Prepaid Insurance that appears in the Adjusted Trial Balance section.

MADDALON OFFICE SUPPLY
WORKSHEET
MONTH ENDED APRIL 30, 20XX

	Acct. No.	Account Name	Trial Balance Debit	Trial Balance Credit	Adjustments Debit	Adjustments Credit	
1	101	Cash	12 326 00				1
2	112	Accounts Receivable	3 726 00				2
3	113	Allowance for Uncollectible Accounts				(h) 75 00	3
4	114	Merchandise Inventory	8 000 00		(b) 12 000 00	(a) 8 000 00	4
5	115	Supplies	860 00			(c) 240 00	5
6	116	Prepaid Insurance	2 400 00			(d) 100 00	6
7	126	Store Equipment	6 600 00				7
8	127	Accumulated Depreciation—Store Equipment				(e) 63 00	8
9	128	Office Equipment	16 200 00				9
10	129	Accumulated Depreciation—Office Equipment				(f) 257 00	10
11	132	Building	30 000 00				11
12	133	Accumulated Depreciation—Building				(g) 80 00	12
13	134	Land	10 000 00				13
14	202	Accounts Payable		14 325 00			14
15	203	Sales Tax Payable		888 00			15
16	301	Ross Maddalon, Capital		77 000 00			16
17	302	Ross Maddalon, Drawing	1 000 00				17
18	399	Income Summary			(a) 8 000 00	(b) 12 000 00	18
19	401	Sales		14 950 00			19
20	402	Sales Returns and Allowances	150 00				20
21	403	Sales Discount	21 00				21
22	501	Merchandise Purchases	12 800 00				22
23	502	Freight In	285 00				23
24	503	Purchases Returns and Allowances		180 00			24
25	504	Purchases Discount		60 00			25
26	511	Salaries Expense	2 550 00				26
27	512	Telephone Expense	135 00				27
28	513	Electricity Expense	350 00				28
29	515	Supplies Expense			(c) 240 00		29
30	517	Insurance Expense			(d) 100 00		30
31	527	Depreciation Expense—Store Equipment			(e) 63 00		31
32	528	Depreciation Expense—Office Equipment			(f) 257 00		32
33	529	Depreciation Expense—Building			(g) 80 00		33
34	531	Uncollectible Accounts Expense			(h) 75 00		34
35		Totals	107 403 00	107 403 00	20 815 00	20 815 00	35
36							36

Chapter 21 Worksheet Adjustments 179

- If an account has no balance in the Trial Balance section and a debit amount in the Adjustments section, the same debit amount is entered in the Adjusted Trial Balance section. Refer to Supplies Expense, Insurance Expense, the Depreciation Expense Accounts, and Uncollectible Accounts Expense on the worksheet of Maddalon Office Supply.
- If an account has a credit balance in the Trial Balance section and no adjustment, the same credit balance is entered in the Adjusted Trial Balance section. Refer to the following accounts on the worksheet of Maddalon Office Supply: Accounts Payable; Sales Tax Payable; Ross Maddalon, Capital; Sales; Purchases Returns and Allowances; and Purchases Discounts.
- If an account has a credit balance in the Trial Balance section and a credit amount in the Adjustments section, the two amounts are added. The total is entered in the Credit column of the Adjusted Trial Balance section. This does not occur on the worksheet of Maddalon Office Supply.

| | Adjusted Trial Balance || Income Statement || Balance Sheet ||
	Debit	Credit	Debit	Credit	Debit	Credit
1	12 3 2 6 00					
2	3 7 2 6 00					
3		7 5 00				
4	12 0 0 0 00					
5	6 2 0 00					
6	2 3 0 0 00					
7	6 6 0 0 00					
8		6 3 00				
9	16 2 0 0 00					
10		2 5 7 00				
11	30 0 0 0 00					
12		8 0 00				
13	10 0 0 0 00					
14		14 3 2 5 00				
15		8 8 8 00				
16		77 0 0 0 00				
17	1 0 0 0 00					
18	8 0 0 0 00	12 0 0 0 00				
19		14 9 5 0 00				
20	1 5 0 00					
21	2 1 00					
22	12 8 0 0 00					
23	2 8 5 00					
24		1 8 0 00				
25		6 0 00				
26	2 5 5 0 00					
27	1 3 5 00					
28	3 5 0 00					
29	2 4 0 00					
30	1 0 0 00					
31	6 3 00					
32	2 5 7 00					
33	8 0 00					
34	7 5 00					
35	119 8 7 8 00	119 8 7 8 00				
36						

- If an account has no balance in the Trial Balance section and a credit amount in the Adjustments section, the same credit amount is entered in the Adjusted Trial Balance section. Refer to Allowance for Uncollectible Accounts and the accumulated depreciation accounts on the worksheet of Maddalon Office Supply.
- The Income Summary account is an exception to the above procedures. On this line of the worksheet, both the beginning and the ending inventory amounts are transferred to the Adjusted Trial Balance columns because both figures will be used later on the income statement.

After all account balances are recorded in the Adjusted Trial Balance section, the columns are added to prove the equality of the debits and credits.

CHAPTER 21 SUMMARY

- At the end of the accounting period, certain information about operations does not appear in the general ledger. Adjustments must be entered on the worksheet to provide this information for the financial statements.
- The financial statements should present a complete picture of the results of operations and the condition of the business. The revenues and expenses for the accounting period must be matched in order to determine the net income or net loss accurately.
- The Merchandise Inventory account must be updated to show the value of the ending inventory.
- Determining the ending inventory involves counting all merchandise on hand, listing information about the merchandise on inventory sheets, computing the cost of each item, and computing the total cost of all merchandise.
- The Merchandise Inventory account is adjusted by two entries: (a) debit Income Summary and credit Merchandise Inventory for the cost of the beginning inventory and (b) debit Merchandise Inventory and credit Income Summary for the cost of the ending inventory.
- An adjustment must be made for the amount of supplies used during the accounting period. The Supplies Expense is debited, and the Supplies account is credited.
- When insurance is purchased, the amount paid is debited to an asset account—the Prepaid Insurance account. At the end of each accounting period, an adjustment must be made for expired insurance. The Insurance Expense account is debited, and the Prepaid Insurance account is credited.
- The cost of a long-term asset must be charged to operations during its estimated useful life. Each accounting period must bear part of the cost. The amount charged to operations is called depreciation.

- An adjustment must be made to record depreciation for each long-term asset at the end of the accounting period. A depreciation expense account is debited, and an accumulated depreciation account is credited.
- An accumulated depreciation account provides a record of the total depreciation taken on a long-term asset. The balance of this account is subtracted from the balance of the related long-term asset account to find the book value.
- Uncollectible accounts, or bad debts, are estimated uncollectible amounts owed by credit customers. At the end of each accounting period, the losses from uncollectible accounts receivable are estimated. An adjusting entry for this amount is recorded on the worksheet. Uncollectible Accounts Expense is debited, and Allowance for Uncollectible Accounts is credited.
- These offsetting accounts, such as accumulated depreciation and allowance for uncollectible accounts are contra accounts.
- It is necessary to estimate the amount of doubtful accounts because most losses from the current period's sales will probably not occur until the next period. However, the uncollectible accounts expense for the current period must be matched against the revenue earned in that period.
- When a customer's account is found to be uncollectible, it is written off. Allowance for Uncollectible Accounts is debited. Two accounts are credited—the Accounts Receivable account in the general ledger and the customer's account in the accounts receivable ledger.
- The 10-column worksheet has special sections for recording adjustments and preparing an adjusted trial balance. The amounts in the Trial Balance section and the Adjustments section are combined. The resulting account balances are entered in the Adjusted Trial Balance section. The exception is the Income Summary accounts where both adjustments are transferred to the Adjusted Trial Balance section.

CHAPTER APPLICATIONS

EXERCISES

Complete the following assignments on the forms provided in your workbook.

EXERCISE 21-1

Calculating adjustments for supplies used and expired insurance.

Instructions:
Give the adjustment required in each of the following cases.

a. The Supplies account has a balance of $1,200. An inventory of supplies at the end of the month shows that $700 of the supplies are on hand.

b. The Prepaid Insurance account has a balance of $2,400. The expired insurance for the month is $200.

EXERCISE 21-2

Computing and recording depreciation. Bubba Juke Electronics owns five types of long-term assets.

Instructions:

1. Use the following information to compute the monthly depreciation of these assets.
2. Record the required adjustments for the month.

Description	Original Cost	Disposal Value	Estimated Useful Life
Delivery Equipment	$32,000	$3,200	6 years
Warehouse Equipment	16,400	1,640	10 years
Office Equipment	7,200	720	5 years
Store Equipment	10,800	1,140	7 years
Building	66,760	13,000	28 years

EXERCISE 21-3

Calculating estimated uncollectible accounts.

Instructions:
Give the adjustment for uncollectible accounts required in each of the following cases.

a. Accounts receivable is $10,000, and the rate of loss is expected to be 2 percent.

b. Accounts receivable is $50,000, and the rate of loss is expected to be 3 percent.

EXERCISE 21-4

Preparing the Adjusted Trial Balance section of a worksheet.

Instructions:

1. Using the data from the following partial worksheet, combine the amounts in the Adjustments section with the amounts in the Trial Balance section, and enter the figures in the Adjusted Trial Balance columns. Add the columns to prove the equality of the debits and credits.

Save your work for use in Exercise 22-4 and Exercise 23-5.

MIDTOWN SPORTSWEAR
WORKSHEET (PARTIAL)
MONTH ENDED APRIL 30, 20XX

	Trial Balance		Adjustments	
	Debit	Credit	Debit	Credit
Cash	5,000			
Accounts Receivable	3,500			
Allowance for Uncollectible Accounts				(f) 70
Merchandise Inventory	6,000		(b) 9,000	(a) 6,000
Supplies	500			(c) 200
Prepaid Insurance	1,200			(d) 100
Equipment	8,000			
Accumulated Depreciation Equipment				(e) 50
Accounts Payable		4,000		
Jeffrey Burke, Capital		17,700		
Jeffrey Burke, Withdrawals	800			
Income Summary			(a) 6,000	(b) 9,000
Sales		19,000		
Merchandise Purchases	10,000			
Rent Expense	2,000			
Salaries Expense	3,600			
Supplies Expense			(c) 200	
Insurance Expense			(d) 100	
Depreciation Expense			(e) 50	
Uncollectible Accounts Expense			(f) 70	
Miscellaneous Expense	100			
	40,700	40,700	15,420	15,420

PROBLEMS

Complete all assigned problems on the forms provided in your workbook.

PROBLEM 21-1

Recording worksheet adjustments and preparing an adjusted trial balance. Dawn Eisenhardt started Bucks Furniture Wholesalers on March 1 of the current year. At the end of the first month of operations, the general ledger account showed these balances.

Account No.	Account	Balance
101	Cash	$4,500
112	Accounts Receivable	1,750
113	Allowance for Uncollectible Accounts	
114	Merchandise Inventory	20,000
115	Supplies	350
116	Prepaid Insurance	1,020
124	Delivery Equipment	18,500
125	Accumulated Depreciation—Delivery Equipment	
126	Warehouse Equipment	13,000
127	Accumulated Depreciation—Warehouse Equipment	
202	Accounts Payable	2,700
301	Dawn Eisenhardt, Capital	47,620
302	Dawn Eisenhardt, Withdrawals	1,000
399	Income Summary	
401	Sales	28,600
402	Sales Returns and Allowances	260
403	Sales Discount	310
501	Merchandise Purchases	15,500
502	Freight In	500
503	Purchases Returns and Allowances	2,000
504	Purchases Discount	290
511	Depreciation Expense—Delivery Equipment	
512	Depreciation Expense—Warehouse Equipment	
513	Rent Expense	800
514	Supplies Expense	
515	Wages Expense	3,500
516	Utilities Expense	220
517	Insurance Expense	
518	Uncollectible Accounts Expense	

Instructions:

1. Set up the worksheet for the month ended March 31 of the current year. Enter the heading, the account numbers, and the account names.
2. Complete the Trial Balance section of the worksheet.
3. Complete the Adjustments section of the worksheet. The merchandise inventory on March 31 is $21,325. During the month, supplies costing $90 were used. Expired insurance is $85. The depreciation of the delivery equipment is $270, and the depreciation of the warehouse equipment is $125. Uncollectible accounts are estimated to be $75.
4. Complete the Adjusted Trial Balance section of the worksheet. Make sure that the debits and credits are equal.

Save your work for use in Problem 22-1.

PROBLEM 21-2

Recording worksheet adjustments and preparing an adjusted trial balance. Jeff Finsen owns Rancocas Toy Distributors. The business uses a quarterly accounting period. On December 31 of the current year, the general ledger accounts contained the balances shown below.

Instructions:

1. Set up the worksheet for the quarter ended December 31 of the current year. Enter the heading, the account numbers, and the account names.
2. Complete the Trial Balance section of the worksheet.
3. Complete the Adjustments section of the worksheet. The merchandise inventory on December 31 is $17,390. The supplies on hand total $280. Expired insurance is $120. The depreciation of the office equipment is $250, and the depreciation of the warehouse equipment is $400. Doubtful accounts are estimated to be $125.
4. Complete the Adjusted Trial Balance section of the worksheet. Prove that the total of the Debit column equals the total of the Credit column.

Save your work for use in Problem 22-2.

Account No.	Account	Balance
101	Cash	$3,575
112	Accounts Receivable	2,140
113	Allowance for Uncollectible Accounts	
114	Merchandise Inventory	18,600
115	Supplies	420
116	Prepaid Insurance	1,440
132	Office Equipment	6,960
133	Accumulated Depreciation—Office Equipment	360
134	Warehouse Equipment	16,000
135	Accumulated Depreciation—Warehouse Equipment	630
202	Accounts Payable	1,760
301	Jeff Finsen, Capital	45,325
302	Jeff Finsen, Withdrawals	3,200
399	Income Summary	
401	Sales	34,000
402	Sales Returns and Allowances	560
403	Sales Discount	620
501	Merchandise Purchases	22,500
502	Freight In	430
503	Purchases Returns and Allowances	485
504	Purchases Discount	225
511	Depreciation Expense—Office Equipment	
512	Depreciation Expense—Warehouse Equipment	
513	Rent Expense	1,950
514	Supplies Expense	
515	Wages Expense	3,840
516	Utilities Expense	550
517	Insurance Expense	
518	Uncollectible Accounts Expense	

CASE STUDY

Write the answer to the case study on the form provided in your workbook.

The Matching Principle

In accounting class you learned how to compute and record adjusting entries for merchandise inventory, supplies, insurance, depreciation, and uncollectible accounts. You learned that adjustments reflected the accounting procedure called the *matching principle*.

Critical Thinking

- Why is it necessary to adjust some accounts at the end of an accounting period?

CHAPTER TWENTY-TWO

Cost of Goods Sold and Statements

Accounting Terminology

- Classified balance sheet
- Current assets
- Current liabilities
- Long-term liabilities
- Plant and equipment
- Solvency

OBJECTIVES

Upon completion of this chapter, you should be able to:

1. Complete a 10-column worksheet.
2. Prepare the income statement, statement of owner's equity, and balance sheet from the worksheet.

INTRODUCTION

After the Adjusted Trial Balance columns of the worksheet are added and the total of the Debit column equals the total of the Credit column, the worksheet can be completed and the financial statements can be prepared. ■

■ COMPLETING THE 10-COLUMN WORKSHEET

The following procedures are used to prepare the last two sections of the worksheet—the Income Statement section and the Balance Sheet section.

1. The balances of the asset, liability, and owner's equity accounts shown in the Adjusted Trial Balance section are recorded in the proper columns of the Balance Sheet section.

2. Both the debit and credit amounts shown on the Income Summary line are extended to the Debit and Credit columns in the Income Statement section.

3. The balances of the revenue, cost, and expense accounts shown in the Adjusted Trial Balance section are recorded in the proper columns of the Income Statement section.

4. The columns of the Income Statement section and the Balance Sheet section are totaled.

5. The total of the Debit column in the Income Statement section is subtracted from the total of the Credit column ($27,190 − $25,106 = $2,084). The difference is the net income for the period. This amount is entered below the total of the Debit column. (There is a net income because the revenue exceeds the costs

and expenses. However, if the total of the Debit column is greater than the total of the Credit column, the business has a net loss. The costs and expenses exceed the revenue.)

6. The total of the Credit column in the Balance Sheet section is subtracted from the total of the Debit column ($94,772 − $92,688 = $2,084). The difference is the same as the net income. This amount is entered below the total of the Credit column.

7. The columns of the Income Statement section and the Balance Sheet section are totaled again. In each section, the debits and credits should be equal.

PREPARING THE FINANCIAL STATEMENTS

The completed worksheet provides the information needed for the financial statements.

The Income Statement.

The income statement shown on page 188 was prepared at Maddalon Office Supply. It reports the results of operations for the month ended April 30.

The income statement for Maddalon Office Supply consists of five sections.

- The Operating Revenue section shows information about the revenue that the business earned from selling merchandise during the accounting period. The total of Sales Returns and Allowances and Sales Discount is subtracted from Sales to find the net sales ($14,950 − $171 = $14,779).

- The Cost of Goods Sold section shows information about the cost that the business incurred for the merchandise it sold during the accounting period. Notice that Merchandise Purchases and Freight In are added to compute the delivered cost of purchases ($12,800 + $285 = $13,085). Then the total of the Purchases Returns and Allowances and Purchases Discount is subtracted from the delivered cost of purchases to find the net delivered cost of purchases ($13,085 − $240 = $12,845). The beginning inventory and the net delivered cost of purchases are added to find the total merchandise available for sale ($8,000 + $12,845 = $20,845). Then the ending inventory is subtracted from the total merchandise available for sale to find the cost of goods sold ($20,845 − $12,000 = $8,845).

- The Gross Profit on Sales section contains a single figure. This figure is the difference between the revenue earned from selling merchandise and the cost of that merchandise. The amount of gross profit on sales for the accounting period is computed by subtracting the cost of goods sold from the net sales ($14,779 − $8,845 = $5,934).

- The Operating Expenses section shows information about the expenses the business incurred to conduct its operations during the accounting period. The amounts of the individual expenses are added to find the total operating expenses ($3,850).

- The Net Income section contains a single figure. This figure is the profit of the business for the accounting period. The total of the operating expenses is subtracted from the gross profit on sales to find the net income ($5,934 − $3,850 = $2,084).

> **WWW Inquiry**
> Return to the URL address for Kellogg's. What was the change in cost of goods sold in the two most recent years?

MADDALON OFFICE SUPPLY
WORKSHEET
MONTH ENDED APRIL 30, 20XX

Acct. No.	Account Name	Trial Balance Debit	Trial Balance Credit	Adjustments Debit	Adjustments Credit
101	Cash	12,326.00			
112	Accounts Receivable	3,726.00			
113	Allowance for Uncollectible Accounts				(h) 75.00
114	Merchandise Inventory	8,000.00		(b) 12,000.00	(a) 8,000.00
115	Supplies	860.00			(c) 240.00
116	Prepaid Insurance	2,400.00			(d) 100.00
126	Store Equipment	6,600.00			
127	Accumulated Depreciation—Store Equipment				(e) 63.00
128	Office Equipment	16,200.00			
129	Accumulated Depreciation—Office Equipment				(f) 257.00
132	Building	30,000.00			
133	Accumulated Depreciation—Building				(g) 80.00
134	Land	10,000.00			
202	Accounts Payable		14,325.00		
203	Sales Tax Payable		888.00		
301	Ross Maddalon, Capital		77,000.00		
302	Ross Maddalon, Drawing	1,000.00			
399	Income Summary			(a) 8,000.00	(b) 12,000.00
401	Sales		14,950.00		
402	Sales Returns and Allowances	150.00			
403	Sales Discount	21.00			
501	Merchandise Purchases	12,800.00			
502	Freight In	285.00			
503	Purchases Returns and Allowances		180.00		
504	Purchases Discount		60.00		
511	Salaries Expense	2,550.00			
512	Telephone Expense	135.00			
513	Electricity Expense	350.00			
515	Supplies Expense			(c) 240.00	
517	Insurance Expense			(d) 100.00	
527	Depreciation Expense—Store Equipment			(e) 63.00	
528	Depreciation Expense—Office Equipment			(f) 257.00	
529	Depreciation Expense—Building			(g) 80.00	
531	Uncollectible Accounts Expense			(h) 75.00	
	Totals	107,403.00	107,403.00	20,815.00	20,815.00
	Net Income				

	Adjusted Trial Balance Debit	Adjusted Trial Balance Credit	Income Statement Debit	Income Statement Credit	Balance Sheet Debit	Balance Sheet Credit	
1	1232600				1232600		1
2	37260				37260		2
3		7500				7500	3
4	120000				120000		4
5	6200				6200		5
6	23000				23000		6
7	66000				66000		7
8		6300				6300	8
9	162000				162000		9
10		2570				2570	10
11	300000				300000		11
12		800				800	12
13	100000				100000		13
14		143250				143250	14
15		8880				8880	15
16		770000				770000	16
17	10000				10000		17
18	80000	120000	80000	120000			18
19		149500		149500			19
20	1500		1500				20
21	210		210				21
22	128000		128000				22
23	2850		2850				23
24		1800		1800			24
25		600		600			25
26	25500		25500				26
27	1350		1350				27
28	3500		3500				28
29	2400		2400				29
30	1000		1000				30
31	630		630				31
32	2570		2570				32
33	800		800				33
34	7500		7500				34
35	1198780	1198780	251060	271900	947720	926880	35
36			20840			20840	36
37			271900	271900	947720	947720	37
38							38

MADDALON OFFICE SUPPLY
INCOME STATEMENT
MONTH ENDED APRIL 30, 20XX

Operating Revenue			
Sales			$14,950
Less: Sales Returns and Allowances		$ 150	
Sales Discount		21	171
Net Sales			$14,779
Cost of Goods Sold			
Merchandise Inventory, April 1		$ 8,000	
Merchandise Purchases	$12,800		
Freight In	285		
Delivered Cost of Purchases	$13,085		
Less: Purchases Returns and Allowances	$180		
Purchases Discount	60	240	
Net Delivered Cost of Purchases		12,845	
Total Merchandise Available for Sale		$20,845	
Less: Merchandise Inventory, April 30		12,000	
Cost of Goods Sold			8,845
Gross Profit on Sales			$ 5,934
Operating Expenses			
Salaries Expense		$ 2,550	
Telephone Expense		135	
Electricity Expense		350	
Supplies Expense		240	
Insurance Expense		100	
Depreciation Expense—Store Equipment		63	
Depreciation Expense—Office Equipment		257	
Depreciation Expense—Building		80	
Uncollectible Accounts Expense		75	
Total Operating Expenses			3,850
Net Income from Operations			$ 2,084

Notice that the income statement for a merchandising business is more complex than the income statement for a service business. A merchandising business must report cost of goods sold and gross profit on sales as well as revenue, expenses, and net income or net loss.

At the end of the next period, Maddalon Office Supply will have promissory notes received from customers and issued to creditors. Therefore, Interest Income and Interest Expense accounts will appear on the income statement. Interest Income will be reported in the Other Income section of the income statement. Interest Expense will be reported in the Other Expenses section. These sections are listed at the bottom of the income statement as shown at the top of page 189.

WWW Inquiry
Return to the URL address for Kellogg's. What was the depreciation and amortization expense for the most recent year? (Hint: go to the consolidated statement of cash flows for this information.)

        Net Income from Operations
            Other Income
                Interest Income
                    Total Income From All Sources
            Other Expenses
                Interest Expense
            Net Income

The Statement of Owner's Equity.

After the income statement is completed, the statement of owner's equity is prepared. Remember that this financial report shows the changes in owner's equity that occur during an accounting period. The statement of owner's equity shown below was prepared at Maddalon Office Supply. It covers the month ended April 30.

The amount of capital at the start of the month ($75,000) and the additional investment made during the month ($2,000) are taken from the capital account in the general ledger. The net income for the month ($2,084) and the owner's withdrawals ($1,000) come from the worksheet. The rest of the amounts are computed on the statement of owner's equity.

MADDALON OFFICE SUPPLY
STATEMENT OF OWNER'S EQUITY
MONTH ENDED APRIL 30, 20XX

Ross Maddalon, Capital, April 1		$75,000
Additional Investment		2,000
Total Investment		$77,000
Net Income	$2,084	
Less Withdrawals	1,000	
Net Increase in Owner's Equity		1,084
Ross Maddalon, Capital, April 30		$78,084

The Classified Balance Sheet.

The balance sheet given on page 190 was prepared at Maddalon Office Supply on April 30. It shows the financial position of the business at the end of the accounting period.

The amounts of the assets and liabilities are taken from the worksheet. The amount of capital comes from the statement of owner's equity. This amount ($78,084) is the capital on April 30 after the net income has been added and the withdrawals have been subtracted.

In accounting, assets are usually classified into two groups: current assets and plant and equipment (or long-term assets). Liabilities are also classified into two groups: current liabilities and long-term liabilities. Maddalon Office Supply uses a *classified balance sheet.* This type of balance sheet shows related assets and liabilities in groups.

Current assets consist of cash, items that will be turned into cash within a year, and items that will be used up within a year. Maddalon Office Supply has the following current assets on April 30: cash, accounts receivable, merchandise inventory, supplies, and prepaid insurance. The accounts receivable will be turned into cash as customers pay their bills. The merchandise inventory will be turned into cash as goods are sold. The supplies and prepaid insurance will be used up in operations as the year goes on.

Allowance for Uncollectible Accounts is a contra asset. It is subtracted from Accounts Receivable to show the amount that the business expects to collect from its credit customers.

Plant and equipment consists of property that a business uses for a number of years. Maddalon Office Supply lists the following assets as plant and equipment on April 30: store equipment, office equipment, building, and land. Notice that the balance sheet shows three amounts for store equipment, office equipment, and building: the original cost, the

Classified Balance Sheet: Type of balance sheet that shows related assets and liabilities in groups.

Current Assets: Cash, items that will be turned into cash within a year, and items that will be used up within a year.

Plant and Equipment: Property that will be used for a number of years.

accumulated depreciation, and the book value. The accumulated depreciation accounts are contra assets. The book value of each long-term asset is determined by subtracting the balance of the accumulated depreciation account from the original cost.

MADDALON OFFICE SUPPLY
BALANCE SHEET
APRIL 30, 20XX

Assets

Current Assets			
Cash		$12,326	
Accounts Receivable	$ 3,726		
Less Allowance for Uncollectible Accounts	75	3,651	
Merchandise Inventory		12,000	
Supplies		620	
Prepaid Insurance		2,300	
Total Current Assets			$30,897
Plant and Equipment			
Store Equipment	$ 6,600		
Less Accumulated Depreciation	63	$ 6,537	
Office Equipment	16,200		
Less Accumulated Depreciation	257	15,943	
Building	30,000		
Less Accumulated Depreciation	80	29,920	
Land		10,000	
Total Plant and Equipment			62,400
Total Assets			**$93,297**

Liabilities and Owner's Equity

Current Liabilities		
Accounts Payable	$14,325	
Sales Tax Payable	888	
Total Current Liabilities		$15,213
Owner's Equity		
Ross Maddalon, Capital		78,084
Total Liabilities and Owner's Equity		**$93,297**

Current liabilities are debts that must be paid within a year. Maddalon Office Supply has two current liabilities on April 30: accounts payable and sales tax payable.

Long-term liabilities are debts that extend for more than a year. Maddalon Office Supply does not have any long-term liabilities on April 30. However, if the business had a 20-year mortgage on its building, this debt would be listed on the balance sheet as a long-term liability.

The classified balance sheet helps management to judge the ***solvency*** of the business—the ability of the business to pay its debts when they become due. A company may own expensive land and equipment; however, when it has to pay its debts, it cannot count on these assets to provide the necessary funds. For example, management compares the amounts of the current assets and the current liabilities. The current assets will provide the money needed to pay the current liabilities. On April 30, Maddalon Office Supply has current liabilities of $15,213. However, the current assets total $30,897. Thus the business should be able to pay its debts without difficulty.

Current Liabilities: Debts that must be paid within a year.

Long-Term Liabilities: Debts that extend for more than a year.

Solvency: Ability of a business to pay its debts.

CHAPTER 22 SUMMARY

- After the Adjusted Trial Balance section of the worksheet is completed, the balances for all accounts except the Income Summary account are transferred from the Adjusted Trial Balance section to the Income Statement and Balance Sheet sections of the worksheet.
- The Income Summary debit and credit amounts are recorded in the Income Statement section of the worksheet. The net income is entered below the totals of the Debit column in the Income Statement section and the Credit column in the Balance Sheet section. Then these sections are totaled again.
- The completed worksheet provides the information needed to prepare the financial statements.
- The income statement for a merchandising business shows cost of goods sold and gross profit on sales as well as revenue, expenses, and net income or net loss.
- The cost of goods sold is computed in the following way. The beginning inventory and the net delivered cost of purchases are added to find the total merchandise available for sale. Then the ending inventory is subtracted from the total merchandise available for sale.
- The gross profit on sales is computed by subtracting the cost of goods sold from the net sales.
- Assets are classified into two groups. Current assets consist of cash, items that will be turned into cash within a year, and items that will be used up within a year. Plant and equipment consists of property that a business will use for a number of years.
- Liabilities are also classified into two groups. Current liabilities are debts that must be paid within a year. Long-term liabilities are debts that extend for more than a year.
- The classified balance sheet shows assets and liabilities in groups.

CHAPTER APPLICATIONS

EXERCISES

Complete the following assignments on the forms provided in your workbook.

EXERCISE 22-1

Completing a worksheet. A partially completed worksheet is shown below.

Instructions:

1. Complete the Income Statement and Balance Sheet sections.

Save your work for use in Exercise 22-2 and Exercise 23-5.

ALL BRANDS DISTRIBUTING
WORKSHEET (PARTIAL)
MONTH ENDED MAY 31, 20XX

	Adjusted Trial Balance	
	Debit	Credit
Cash	8,000	
Merchandise Inventory	8,000	
Accounts Payable		5,000
Dave Fletcher, Capital		11,000
Dave Fletcher, Withdrawals	1,000	
Income Summary	7,000	8,000
Sales		15,000
Merchandise Purchases	9,000	
Selling Expenses	4,000	
Office Expenses	2,000	
	39,000	39,000

EXERCISE 22-2

Preparing financial statements. Refer to the worksheet that you completed in Exercise 22-1.

Instructions:
Prepare an income statement, a statement of owner's equity, and a balance sheet for All Brands Distributing.

EXERCISE 22-3

Computing net sales and cost of goods sold.

Instructions:
Use the partial worksheet shown below to complete the Operating Revenue, Cost of Goods Sold, and Gross Profit on Sales sections of an income statement.

FISHMAN FURNITURE
WORKSHEET (PARTIAL)
MONTH ENDED MAY 31, 20XX

	Income Statement		Balance Sheet	
	Debit	Credit	Debit	Credit
Merchandise Inventory	8,000	10,000	10,000	
Sales		18,000		
Sales Returns and Allowances	1,200			
Sales Discount	400			
Merchandise Purchases	11,000			
Freight In	2,000			
Purchases Returns and Allowances		1,000		
Purchases Discount		200		

191

EXERCISE 22-4

Preparing a worksheet and financial statements. Refer to Exercise 21-4.

Instructions:

1. Complete the Income Statement section and Balance Sheet section for the worksheet of Midtown Sportswear.
2. Prepare an income statement, a statement of owner's equity, and a classified balance sheet.

PROBLEMS

Complete all assigned problems on the forms provided in your workbook.

PROBLEM 22-1

Preparing a worksheet and financial statements. Complete the following activities for Bucks Furniture Wholesalers.

Instructions:

1. Complete the worksheet that you started in Problem 21-1.
2. Prepare an income statement for the month ended March 31.
3. Prepare a statement of owner's equity for the month ended March 31. The balance of the capital account on March 1 was $44,620. The owner made an additional investment of $3,000 during the month.
4. Prepare a classified balance sheet dated March 31.

Save your work for use in Problem 23-1.

PROBLEM 22-2

Preparing a worksheet and financial statements. Complete the following activities for Rancocas Toy Distributors.

Instructions:

1. Complete the worksheet that you started in Problem 21-2.
2. Prepare an income statement for the quarter ended December 31.
3. Prepare a statement of owner's equity for the quarter ended December 31. The balance of the capital account on October 1 was $40,325. The owner made an additional investment of $5,000 during the quarter.
4. Prepare a classified balance sheet dated December 31.

Save your work for use in Problem 23-2.

PROBLEM 22-3

Preparing a worksheet. A worksheet for the Delmuth Wholesale Grocery Company is shown in the workbook. This worksheet contains the trial balance prepared on March 31. Complete the following activities for the business.

Instructions:

1. Prepare the Adjustments section of the worksheet. The merchandise inventory on March 31 is $9,800. During March, supplies costing $130 were used, and insurance costing $60 expired. The depreciation for the delivery equipment is $150, and the depreciation for the warehouse equipment is $30. Uncollectible accounts are estimated to be $50.
2. Prepare the Adjusted Trial Balance, Income Statement, and Balance Sheet sections of the worksheet.

CASE STUDY

Write the answer to the case study on the form provided in your workbook.

Cost of Goods Sold

You are the owner of a store that sells the latest electronic toys. After the holiday selling season, one of your clerks who was hired to count inventory was responsible for counting and calculating the cost of the merchandise still available to sell. Following the count, she reported that the inventory was valued at $18,000. The next day she recalculated and came up with an inventory of $22,000.

> **Critical Thinking**
>
> ■ What effect does the change have on the cost of goods sold? What effect does the change have upon net income?

CHAPTER TWENTY-THREE

Adjusting and Closing the General Ledger

OBJECTIVES

Upon completion of this chapter, you should be able to:

1. Journalize adjusting and closing entries.
2. Post the adjusting and closing entries.
3. Prepare a postclosing trial balance.

Accounting Terminology

- Adjusting entries
- Closing entries

INTRODUCTION

After the financial statements are prepared, adjusting entries must be journalized and posted. The purpose of these entries is to make the amounts in the general ledger agree with the amounts reported on the financial statements and to reduce the balances of the temporary accounts to zero. ■

■ RECORDING THE ADJUSTING ENTRIES

A business must have a permanent record of the adjustments that appear on the worksheet. The following general journal shows the adjusting entries recorded at Maddalon Office Supply on April 30. The amounts were obtained from the Adjustments section of the worksheet. (Refer to the identifying letters on the worksheet on pages 186 and 187.)

Adjusting the General Ledger: Making the amounts in the general ledger agree with the amounts on the financial statements.

GENERAL JOURNAL   Page 2

	Date		Description	Post. Ref.	Debit	Credit	
1	20	XX	Adjusting Entries				1
2	Apr.	30	Income Summary	399	800 00		2
3			Merchandise Inventory	114		800 00	3
4			To close the beginning inventory.				4
5							5
6		30	Merchandise Inventory	114	1200 00		6
7			Income Summary	399		1200 00	7
8			To record the ending inventory.				8
9							9
10		30	Supplies Expense	515	240 00		10
11			Supplies	115		240 00	11
12			To record cost of supplies used				12
13			during April.				13

General Journal (continued)

	Date		Description	Post. Ref.	Debit	Credit	
15	Apr.	30	Insurance Expense	517	100 00		15
16			Prepaid Insurance	116		100 00	16
17			To record cost of expired				17
18			insurance for April.				18
19							19
20		30	Depreciation Expense—Store Equipment	527	63 00		20
21			Accumulated Depreciation—				21
22			Store Equipment	127		63 00	22
23			To record depreciation for April.				23
24		30	Depreciation Expense—Office Equipment	528	257 00		24
25			Accumulated Depreciation—				25
26			Office Equipment	129		257 00	26
27			To record depreciation for April.				27
28							28
29		30	Depreciation Expense—Building	529	80 00		29
30			Accumulated Depreciation—Building	133		80 00	30
31			To record depreciation for April.				31
32							32
33		30	Uncollectible Accounts Expense	531	75 00		33
34			Allowance for Uncollectible Accounts	113		75 00	34
35			To record estimated uncollectible				35
36			accounts for April.				36
37					20 815 00	20 815 00	37
38							38

Study the general ledger accounts on pages 195 through 201 to see how the adjusting entries are posted.

■ RECORDING THE CLOSING ENTRIES

Closing the General Ledger: Making the general ledger ready to receive the next period's transactions.

After the adjusting entries are posted, closing entries must be recorded. These entries reduce the balances of the temporary accounts to zero and transfer the results of operations to the capital account.

The closing entries recorded at Maddalon Office Supply are explained below and on page 195.

GENERAL JOURNAL Page 3

	Date		Description	Post. Ref.	Debit	Credit	
1	20	XX	Closing Entries				1
2	Apr.	30	Sales	401	14 950 00		2
3			Purchases Returns and Allowances	503	180 00		3
4			Purchases Discount	504	60 00		4
5			Income Summary	399		15 190 00	5
6			To close temporary accounts with				6
7			credit balances.				7
8							8
9		30	Income Summary	399	17 106 00		9
10			Sales Returns and Allowances	402		150 00	10
11			Sales Discount	403		21 00	11
12			Merchandise Purchases	501		12 800 00	12
13			Freight In	502		285 00	13
14			Salaries Expense	511		2 550 00	14
15			Telephone Expense	512		135 00	15
16			Electricity Expense	513		350 00	16

General Journal (continued)

17		Supplies Expense	515	240 00	
18		Insurance Expense	517	100 00	
19		Depreciation Expense—			
20		Store Equipment	527	63 00	
21		Depreciation Expense—			
22		Office Equipment	528	257 00	
23		Depreciation Expense—Building	529	80 00	
24		Uncollectible Accounts Expense	531	75 00	
25		To close temporary accounts with			
26		debit balances.			
27	30	Income Summary	399	2084 00	
28		Ross Maddalon, Capital	301		2084 00
29		To transfer net income to the owner's			
30		capital account.			
31					
32	30	Ross Maddalon, Capital	301	1000 00	
33		Ross Maddalon, Withdrawals	302		1000 00
34		To close the withdrawals account.			
35				35 380 00	35 380 00

- The first step is to close the revenue and other temporary accounts with credit balances. The worksheet provides the necessary information. The amounts to be debited in the journal entry are taken from the Income Statement Credit column of the worksheet. The total of these amounts is credited to the Income Summary account. Study the worksheet on pages 186 and 187 and the first closing entry on page 194.

- The second step is to close the cost, expense, and other temporary accounts with debit balances. The worksheet again provides the necessary information. The accounts to be credited in this journal entry are obtained from the Income Statement Debit column of the worksheet. The total of these amounts is debited to the Income Summary account. Study the worksheet on pages 186 and 187 and the second closing entry on page 194.

- The third step is to close the Income Summary account and transfer the net income to the capital account. The worksheet shows the net income for the period. The Income Summary account is debited for this amount. The offsetting credit is to the capital account. Study the third closing entry above. (If there is a net loss, this entry must be made differently. It is necessary to debit the capital account and credit the Income Summary account.)

- The fourth step is to close the drawing account and transfer its balance to the capital account. The capital account is debited and the drawing account is credited. Study the fourth closing entry above.

After the closing entries are posted, the revenue, cost, expense, summary, and drawing accounts have no balances. Only the permanent accounts are still open. (Refer to the general ledger accounts below and on pages 196 through 201.)

WWW Inquiry
Find the URL address for Kodak. What was the balance in the interest expense account closed out at the end of the most recent year?

Posting the Closing Entries

ACCOUNT Cash   ACCOUNT NO. 101

Date		Description	Post. Ref.	Debit	Credit	Balance Debit	Balance Credit
20 XX							
Apr.	1		J1	1100 00		1100 00	
	30		CR1	1648 4 00		2748 4 00	
	30		CP1		15158 00	12326 00	

Posting the Closing Entries (continued)

ACCOUNT Accounts Receivable   **ACCOUNT NO.** 112

Date	Description	Post. Ref.	Debit	Credit	Balance Debit	Balance Credit
20XX Apr. 1		J1	2400 00		2400 00	
28		J1		106 00	2294 00	
30		S1	4558 00		6852 00	
30		CR1		3126 00	3726 00	

ACCOUNT Allowance for Uncollectible Accounts   **ACCOUNT NO.** 113

Date	Description	Post. Ref.	Debit	Credit	Balance Debit	Balance Credit
20XX Apr. 30	Adjusting	J2		75 00		75 00

ACCOUNT Merchandise Inventory   **ACCOUNT NO.** 114

Date	Description	Post. Ref.	Debit	Credit	Balance Debit	Balance Credit
20XX Apr. 1		J1	8000 00		8000 00	
30	Adjusting	J2		8000 00	-0-	
30	Adjusting	J2	12000 00		12000 00	

ACCOUNT Supplies   **ACCOUNT NO.** 115

Date	Description	Post. Ref.	Debit	Credit	Balance Debit	Balance Credit
20XX Apr. 1		J1	600 00		600 00	
3		CP1	320 00		920 00	
6		CR1		60 00	860 00	
30	Adjusting	J2		240 00	620 00	

ACCOUNT Prepaid Insurance   **ACCOUNT NO.** 116

Date	Description	Post. Ref.	Debit	Credit	Balance Debit	Balance Credit
20XX Apr. 2		CP1	2400 00		2400 00	
30	Adjusting	J2		100 00	2300 00	

ACCOUNT Store Equipment   **ACCOUNT NO.** 126

Date	Description	Post. Ref.	Debit	Credit	Balance Debit	Balance Credit
20XX Apr. 1		J1	6000 00		6000 00	
17		CP1	600 00		6600 00	

Posting the Closing Entries (continued)

ACCOUNT	Accumulated Depreciation—Store Equipment				ACCOUNT NO. 127	
Date	Description	Post. Ref.	Debit	Credit	Balance Debit	Balance Credit
20XX Apr. 30	Adjusting	J2		63 00		63 00

ACCOUNT	Office Equipment				ACCOUNT NO. 128	
Date	Description	Post. Ref.	Debit	Credit	Balance Debit	Balance Credit
20XX Apr. 1		J1	12 000 00		12 000 00	
2		J1	4 200 00		16 200 00	

ACCOUNT	Accumulated Depreciation—Office Equipment				ACCOUNT NO. 129	
Date	Description	Post. Ref.	Debit	Credit	Balance Debit	Balance Credit
20XX Apr. 30	Adjusting	J2		257 00		257 00

ACCOUNT	Building				ACCOUNT NO. 132	
Date	Description	Post. Ref.	Debit	Credit	Balance Debit	Balance Credit
20XX Apr. 1		J1	30 000 00		30 000 00	

ACCOUNT	Accumulated Depreciation—Building				ACCOUNT NO. 133	
Date	Description	Post. Ref.	Debit	Credit	Balance Debit	Balance Credit
20XX Apr. 30	Adjusting	J2		80 00		80 00

ACCOUNT	Land				ACCOUNT NO. 134	
Date	Description	Post. Ref.	Debit	Credit	Balance Debit	Balance Credit
20XX Apr. 1		J1	10 000 00		10 000 00	

Posting the Closing Entries (continued)

ACCOUNT	Accounts Payable				ACCOUNT NO. 202
Date	Description	Post. Ref.	Debit	Credit	Balance Debit / Credit
20XX					
Apr. 1		J1		5 000 00	5 000 00
2		J1		4 200 00	9 200 00
30		J1	150 00		9 050 00
30		P1		12 550 00	21 600 00
30		CP1	7 275 00		14 325 00

ACCOUNT	Sales Tax Payable				ACCOUNT NO. 203
Date	Description	Post. Ref.	Debit	Credit	Balance Debit / Credit
20XX					
Apr. 9		CP1	3 00		3 00
28		J1	6 00		9 00
30		S1		258 00	249 00
30		CR1		639 00	888 00

ACCOUNT	Ross Maddalon, Capital				ACCOUNT NO. 301
Date	Description	Post. Ref.	Debit	Credit	Balance Debit / Credit
20XX					
Apr. 1		J1			75 000 00
16		CR1		2 000 00	77 000 00
30	Net Income	J3		2 084 00	79 084 00
30	Withdrawals	J3	1 000 00		78 084 00

ACCOUNT	Ross Maddalon, Withdrawals				ACCOUNT NO. 302
Date	Description	Post. Ref.	Debit	Credit	Balance Debit / Credit
20XX					
Apr. 30		CP1	1 000 00		1 000 00
30	Closing	J3		1 000 00	–0–

ACCOUNT	Income Summary				ACCOUNT NO. 399
Date	Description	Post. Ref.	Debit	Credit	Balance Debit / Credit
20XX					
Apr. 30	Adjusting	J2	800 00		800 00
30	Adjusting	J2		1 200 00	400 00
30	Closing	J3		15 190 00	19 190 00
30	Closing	J3	17 106 00		2 084 00
30	Net Income	J3	2 084 00		–0–

Posting the Closing Entries (continued)

ACCOUNT Sales   ACCOUNT NO. 401

Date		Description	Post. Ref.	Debit	Credit	Balance Debit	Balance Credit
20XX							
Apr.	30		S1		4 300 00		4 300 00
	30		CR1		10 650 00		14 950 00
	30	Closing	J3	14 950 00			–0–

ACCOUNT Sales Returns and Allowances   ACCOUNT NO. 402

Date		Description	Post. Ref.	Debit	Credit	Balance Debit	Balance Credit
20XX							
Apr.	9		CP1	50 00		50 00	
	28		J1	100 00		150 00	
	30	Closing	J3		150 00	–0–	

ACCOUNT Sales Discount   ACCOUNT NO. 403

Date		Description	Post. Ref.	Debit	Credit	Balance Debit	Balance Credit
20XX							
Apr.	30		CR1	21 00		21 00	
	30	Closing	J3		21 00	–0–	

ACCOUNT Merchandise Purchases   ACCOUNT NO. 501

Date		Description	Post. Ref.	Debit	Credit	Balance Debit	Balance Credit
20XX							
Apr.	30		P1	12 350 00		12 350 00	
	30		CP1	450 00		12 800 00	
	30	Closing	J3		12 800 00	–0–	

ACCOUNT Freight In   ACCOUNT NO. 502

Date		Description	Post. Ref.	Debit	Credit	Balance Debit	Balance Credit
20XX							
Apr.	25		CP1	85 00		85 00	
	30		P1	200 00		285 00	
	30	Closing	J3		285 00	–0–	

Posting the Closing Entries (continued)

ACCOUNT	Purchases Returns and Allowances				ACCOUNT NO. 503
Date	Description	Post. Ref.	Debit	Credit	Balance Debit / Credit
20XX Apr. 16		CR1		30 00	30 00
30		J1		150 00	180 00
30	Closing	J3	180 00		–0–

ACCOUNT	Purchases Discount				ACCOUNT NO. 504
Date	Description	Post. Ref.	Debit	Credit	Balance Debit / Credit
20XX Apr. 30		CP1		60 00	60 00
30	Closing	J3	60 00		–0–

ACCOUNT	Salaries Expense				ACCOUNT NO. 511
Date	Description	Post. Ref.	Debit	Credit	Balance Debit / Credit
20XX Apr. 14		CP1	1 275 00		1 275 00
30		CP1	1 275 00		2 550 00
30	Closing	J3		2 550 00	–0–

ACCOUNT	Telephone Expense				ACCOUNT NO. 512
Date	Description	Post. Ref.	Debit	Credit	Balance Debit / Credit
20XX Apr. 14		CP1	135 00		135 00
30	Closing	J3		135 00	–0–

ACCOUNT	Electricity Expense				ACCOUNT NO. 513
Date	Description	Post. Ref.	Debit	Credit	Balance Debit / Credit
20XX Apr. 14		CP1	350 00		350 00
30	Closing	J3		350 00	–0–

Posting the Closing Entries (continued)

ACCOUNT __Supplies Expense__ ACCOUNT NO. __515__

Date	Description	Post. Ref.	Debit	Credit	Balance Debit	Balance Credit
20XX Apr. 30	Adjusting	J2	240 00		240 00	
30	Closing	J3		240 00	–0–	

ACCOUNT __Insurance Expense__ ACCOUNT NO. __517__

Date	Description	Post. Ref.	Debit	Credit	Balance Debit	Balance Credit
20XX Apr. 30	Adjusting	J2	100 00		100 00	
30	Closing	J3		100 00	–0–	

ACCOUNT __Depreciation Expense—Store Equipment__ ACCOUNT NO. __527__

Date	Description	Post. Ref.	Debit	Credit	Balance Debit	Balance Credit
20XX Apr. 30	Adjusting	J2	63 00		63 00	
30	Closing	J3		63 00	–0–	

ACCOUNT __Depreciation Expense—Office Equipment__ ACCOUNT NO. __528__

Date	Description	Post. Ref.	Debit	Credit	Balance Debit	Balance Credit
20XX Apr. 30	Adjusting	J2	257 00		257 00	
30	Closing	J3		257 00	–0–	

ACCOUNT __Depreciation Expense—Building__ ACCOUNT NO. __529__

Date	Description	Post. Ref.	Debit	Credit	Balance Debit	Balance Credit
20XX Apr. 30	Adjusting	J2	80 00		80 00	
30	Closing	J3		80 00	–0–	

ACCOUNT __Uncollectible Accounts Expense__ ACCOUNT NO. __531__

Date	Description	Post. Ref.	Debit	Credit	Balance Debit	Balance Credit
20XX Apr. 30	Adjusting	J2	75 00		75 00	
30	Closing	J3		75 00	–0–	

PREPARING THE POSTCLOSING TRIAL BALANCE

Before work is started for the next period, it is necessary to check the equality of the debits and credits in the open accounts. For this reason, the following postclosing trial balance was prepared at Maddalon Office Supply on April 30. The accounts that appear on the postclosing trial balance are the asset, liability, and owner's capital accounts.

MADDALON OFFICE SUPPLY
POSTCLOSING TRIAL BALANCE
APRIL 30, 20XX

Acct. No.	Account Name	Debit	Credit
101	Cash	12,326.00	
112	Accounts Receivable	3,726.00	
113	Allowance for Uncollectible Accounts		75.00
114	Merchandise Inventory	12,000.00	
115	Supplies	620.00	
116	Prepaid Insurance	2,300.00	
126	Store Equipment	6,600.00	
127	Accumulated Depreciation—Store Equipment		63.00
128	Office Equipment	16,200.00	
129	Accumulated Depreciation—Office Equipment		257.00
132	Building	30,000.00	
133	Accumulated Depreciation—Building		80.00
134	Land	10,000.00	
202	Accounts Payable		14,325.00
203	Sales Tax Payable		888.00
301	Ross Maddalon, Capital		78,084.00
	Totals	93,772.00	93,772.00

> **WWW Inquiry**
> Return to the URL address for Kodak. What was the balance in the sales account closed out in the most recent year?

CHAPTER 23 SUMMARY

- Adjusting entries must be journalized and posted so that the amounts in the general ledger will agree with the amounts reported on the financial statements.
- Adjusting entries are recorded in the general journal and then posted to the proper general ledger accounts. The information for these entries comes from the Adjustments section of the worksheet.
- After the adjusting entries are completed, it is necessary to journalize and post closing entries. These entries make the general ledger ready to receive transactions for the next period.
- The first closing entry is used to close the temporary accounts with credit balances. The necessary information comes from the Income Statement Credit column of the worksheet.
- The second closing entry is used to close the temporary accounts with debit balances. The necessary information comes from the Income Statement Debit column of the worksheet.
- The third closing entry is used to close the Income Summary account and transfer the net income or net loss to the capital account.
- The fourth closing entry is used to close the drawing account and transfer its balance to the capital account.
- After the closing entries are posted, a postclosing trial balance is prepared to check the equality of the debits and credits in the accounts that remain open.

CHAPTER APPLICATIONS

EXERCISES

Complete the following assignments on the forms provided in your workbook.

EXERCISE 23-1

Recording adjusting entries. The following adjustments are taken from a worksheet prepared at Centurian Hardware.

Instructions:
Use the accounts and amounts shown to record the adjusting entries that would appear in the general journal on April 30 of the current year.

	Adjustments	
	Debit	Credit
Allowance for Uncollectible Accounts		(c) 150
Merchandise Inventory	(b) 3,000	(a) 2,000
Prepaid Insurance		(d) 120
Supplies		(e) 80
Accumulated Depreciation—Office Equipment		(f) 75
Accumulated Depreciation—Store Equipment		(g) 100
Income Summary	(a) 2,000	(b) 3,000
Supplies Expense	(e) 80	
Insurance Expense	(d) 120	
Depreciation Expense—Office Equipment	(f) 75	
Depreciation Expense—Store Equipment	(g) 100	
Uncollectible Accounts Expense	(c) 150	

EXERCISE 23-2

Recording closing entries. The worksheet prepared at the Lesher Furniture Store for the year ended May 31 contains the following information.

Instructions:
Use the accounts and amounts shown to record the closing entries that would appear in the general journal.

	Income Statement		Balance Sheet	
	Debit	Credit	Debit	Credit
Merchandise Inventory			12,000	
Edward Lesher, Capital				60,000
Edward Lesher, Withdrawals			15,000	
Income Summary	10,000	12,000		
Sales		96,000		

(continued)

(continued)

	Income Statement		Balance Sheet	
	Debit	Credit	Debit	Credit
Sales Returns and Allowances	4,000			
Merchandise Purchases	50,000			
Freight In	3,000			
Purchases Returns and Allowances		2,000		
Supplies Expense	1,500			
Insurance Expense	2,200			
Wages Expense	12,000			
Depreciation Expense	1,400			
Office Expense	6,000			
	90,100	110,000	265,000	245,100
Net Income	19,900			19,900
	110,000	110,000	265,000	265,000

EXERCISE 23-3

Recording closing entries. After the revenue, cost, and expense accounts of the Watson Company have been closed, the Income Summary account has a credit balance of $50,000. Alice Watson's withdrawal account has a debit balance of $40,000, and her capital account has a credit balance of $70,000.

Instructions:

1. Record the March 31 closing entries that would be made in the general journal to transfer the net income and the drawing account balance to the capital account.

2. Compute the balance of the capital account at the end of the accounting period.

EXERCISE 23-4

Recording closing entries. The worksheet prepared at the Richards Pharmacy for the year ended June 30 shows the following information.

Jordan Richards, Capital	$60,000
Jordan Richards, Withdrawals	12,000
Net Loss	8,000

Instructions:

1. Record the June 30 entries that would be made in the general journal to transfer the net loss and the drawing account balance to the capital account.

2. Compute the balance of the capital account at the end of the accounting period.

EXERCISE 23-5

Recording adjusting and closing entries. Refer to Exercises 21-4 and 22-4.

Instructions:
Use the information from the worksheet to record the April 30 adjusting and closing entries that would be made in the general journal of Midtown Sportswear.

PROBLEMS

Complete all assigned problems on the forms provided in your workbook.

PROBLEM 23-1

Recording adjusting and closing entries. Use the worksheet for Bucks Furniture Wholesalers from Problems 21-1 and 22-1.

Instructions:
1. Record the adjusting entries.
2. Record the closing entries.

PROBLEM 23-2

Recording adjusting entries and closing entries and preparing a postclosing trial balance. Use the worksheet for Rancocas Toy Distributors from Problems 21-2 and 22-2.

Instructions:
1. Record the adjusting entries. Use 2 as the journal page number.
2. Post the adjusting entries to the general ledger accounts.
3. Record the closing entries. Use 3 as the journal page number.
4. Post the closing entries to the general ledger accounts.
5. Prepare a postclosing trial balance.

CASE STUDY

Write the answer to the case study on the form provided in your workbook.

Postclosing Trial Balance
After the closing entries are posted, a postclosing trial balance is prepared to check the equality of debits and credits in the accounts that remain open.

> **Critical Thinking**
>
> ■ *If total debits equal total credits, does it mean that the entire accounting cycle has been correctly completed?*
> ■ *Is it possible for debits to equal credits on the postclosing trial balance, yet accounts may still be incorrect? How?*

Chapters 21–23

PROJECT 4

Accounting for a Merchandising Business (continued)

This is a continuation of Project 3. Complete the following end-of-period activities for the Jenkins Lumber Company. Use the general ledger accounts from Project 3 and the forms in the workbook.

INSTRUCTIONS:

1. Complete the Trial Balance section of the worksheet. The account names are preprinted. (Obtain the amounts from the trial balance that you prepared in Project 3.)
2. Record the following adjustments on the worksheet. Then complete the Adjustments section and the Adjusted Trial Balance section.
   a. Record the ending merchandise inventory on the worksheet. The adjustment for merchandise inventory is done in two adjusting entries. The amount of inventory on February 28 is $17,000.
   b. Supplies used during February amounted to $107.50.
   c. Expired insurance for the month is $55.
   d. Depreciation on the office equipment is $50.
   e. Depreciation on the warehouse equipment is $65.
   f. Estimated uncollectible accounts expense is $70.
3. Complete the Income Statement and Balance Sheet sections of the worksheet.
4. Prepare an income statement for the month ended February 28 of the current year.
5. Prepare a statement of owner's equity for the month ended February 28.
6. Prepare a classified balance sheet dated February 28.
7. Record the adjusting entries in the general journal. Use 2 as the journal page number.
8. Post the adjusting entries to the general ledger accounts.
9. Record the closing entries in the general journal. Use 3 as the journal page number.
10. Post the closing entries to the general ledger accounts.
11. Prepare a postclosing trial balance.

PART FIVE

Accounting for Special Procedures

- **Chapter 24**
  Banking Procedures
- **Chapter 25**
  Petty Cash and Other Special Cash Procedures
- **Chapter 26**
  Payroll Procedures
- **Chapter 27**
  The Combined Journal
- **Practice Set**

The underlying theme in Part Five is that the money of a business must be managed and controlled. How you work with your bank will certainly have an influence in the operation of your business. You will learn how correct management of cash can keep employees honest and also provide an actual picture of the finances of a business. You will also study how a combination journal can be used in certain businesses that don't have large numbers of transactions. Finally, you will study the correct payroll procedures to follow for the payment of wages and how to account for payroll taxes.

Accounting Careers

Money Management

■ DOES THIS HAPPEN TO YOU?

- Does your money run out before the month does?
- Do you stockpile receipts in a paper bag for future reference?
- Do you adjust your checkbook records by subtracting $50 per month from your records knowing you have forgotten to record a check or two?
- Do you wonder why your paycheck is so much less than your total earnings?

■ MONEY MANAGEMENT TIPS

- Prepare a budget and stick to it.
- Resist impulse buying using credit cards.
- Save a percentage of your take-home pay each pay period, regardless of how small.

ACTIVITY

- Find the website for the Internal Revenue Service—to see how your federal tax deductions are computed.
- Search the internet for information on salary expectations for accountants.
- Prepare a sample budget based on an entry-level accounting position.

CHAPTER TWENTY-FOUR

Banking Procedures

OBJECTIVES

Upon completion of this chapter, you should be able to:

1. Open and use a checking account.
2. Endorse checks.
3. Prepare deposit slips.
4. Complete check stubs and write checks.
5. Reconcile the bank statement.

Accounting Terminology

- Bank reconciliation
- Bank statement
- Blank endorsement
- Canceled checks
- Certified check
- Check
- Check register
- Check stub
- Credit memorandum
- Debit memorandum
- Deposit slip
- Deposits in transit
- Drawer
- Endorsement
- Full endorsement
- Night depository
- Outstanding checks
- Payee
- Restrictive endorsement
- Service charge
- Signature card
- Stop payment order

INTRODUCTION

A bank account is one of the most important tools of a business. Building a strong relationship with a reliable bank is part of a successful business. The business owner must carefully decide which bank to use. In addition to the cost of the services, the owner must also weigh-in factors such as the bank's dependability and courteousness.

Once a bank is selected, the owner will choose among a range of offered services. A variety of services are available. One service provides automatic transfers of funds above a certain amount to another account that may pay more interest. Another service allows a business to move money around easily via the Internet or telephone to different accounts so that interest is maximized.

Appropriate cash control is very important to a business. Cash transactions of a business are handled through the business's checking account. To achieve the best internal control and safety, a business should deposit all cash receipts in the bank at least once a day, if not more often. Then, when the business needs to make a payment, it pays by check from its checking account with the bank. ■

■ OPENING A CHECKING ACCOUNT

One of the first things that the owner of a new business must do is open a checking account. The owner fills out various bank forms and deposits some money. The bank requires that the owner and any other persons who will be signing checks for the business write their names on a *signature card*. This card is kept on file at the bank to verify signatures on checks whenever necessary.

The bank assigns a number to each checking account. This number is printed on the checks and deposit slips that the business receives. Most firms request that their name and address also be printed for easy identification.

Signature Card: Form containing the depositor's signature, which is used by the bank to verify signatures on checks.

■ MAKING BANK DEPOSITS

Bank deposits should be made often to protect cash receipts. For this reason, many businesses deposit their cash receipts daily.

Cash receipts usually include coins, currency (paper money), and cash substitutes such as checks and money orders. The following procedure is used to prepare these items for deposit.

Endorsements: Signature or stamp on the back of a check or money order, which legally transfers the right to collect payment.

- The coins and currency are counted and placed in coin wrappers and currency bands supplied by the bank.

- All checks and money orders are endorsed. An **endorsement** legally transfers the right to collect payment on a check or money order. Endorsements are written or stamped on the back of these items. (Many businesses use a rubber stamp to speed up the process of making endorsements.) Three types of endorsements are shown below. A **blank endorsement** consists of only the name of the endorser. The check or money order is then payable to anyone holding it. A **full endorsement** includes the name of the person or business to whom the check or money order is being transferred. A **restrictive endorsement** limits the use of the check or money order to the purpose stated in the endorsement. This is the safest type of endorsement.

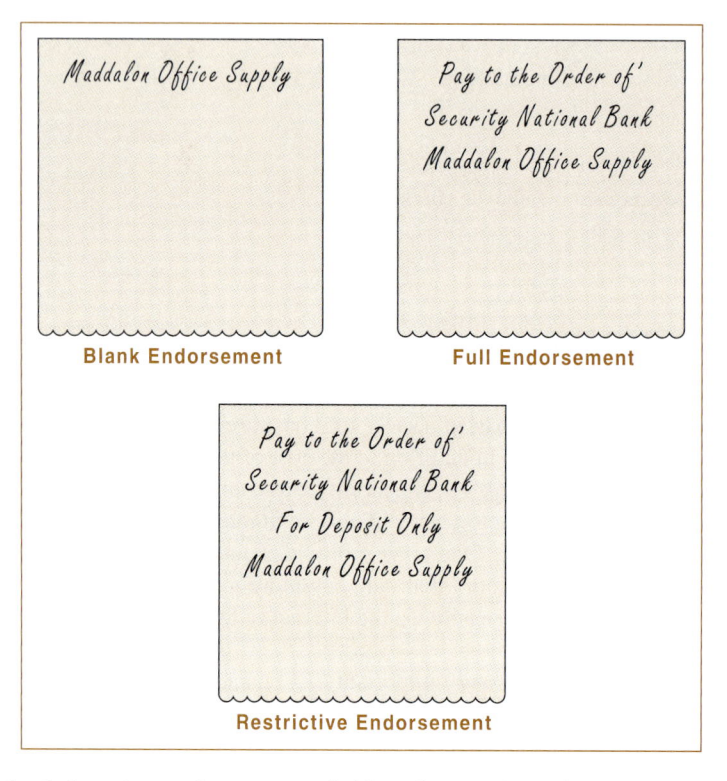

Maddalon Office Supply

Blank Endorsement

*Pay to the Order of
Security National Bank
Maddalon Office Supply*

Full Endorsement

*Pay to the Order of
Security National Bank
For Deposit Only
Maddalon Office Supply*

Restrictive Endorsement

Deposit Slip: Form used to list items to be deposited in the bank.

Every bank deposit must be accompanied by a form called a **deposit slip.** The following deposit slip was prepared at Maddalon Office Supply on April 8. Notice that the amount of each check being deposited is listed separately. (If the checks are too numerous to enter on the deposit slip, they can be recorded on an adding machine tape. The total of the checks is written on the deposit slip, and the adding machine tape is attached to provide a detailed listing.)

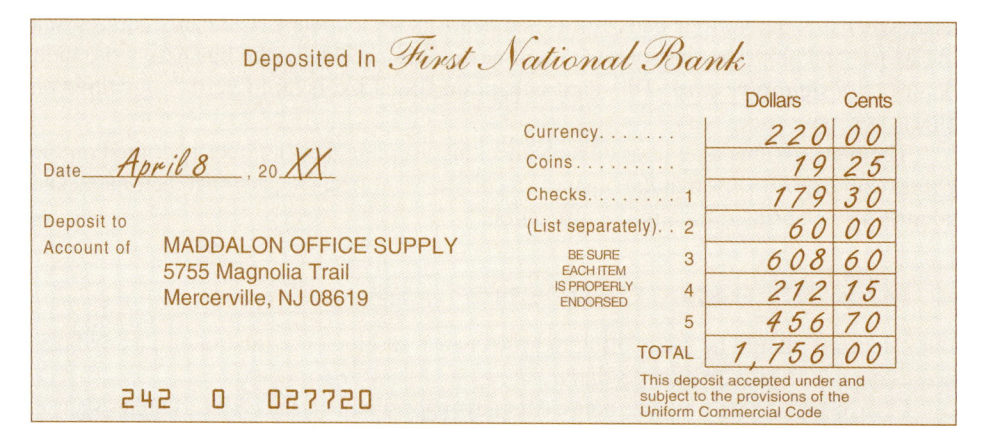

Deposited In *First National Bank*

Date: April 8, 20XX

Deposit to Account of: MADDALON OFFICE SUPPLY
5755 Magnolia Trail
Mercerville, NJ 08619

242 0 027720

	Dollars	Cents
Currency	220	00
Coins	19	25
Checks 1	179	30
(List separately) 2	60	00
3	608	60
4	212	15
5	456	70
TOTAL	1,756	00

This deposit accepted under and subject to the provisions of the Uniform Commercial Code

The deposit slip, along with the coins, currency, and checks, is given to a bank teller, who provides a receipt for the deposit. This receipt is often a copy of the deposit slip, which the bank teller has stamped or initialed. (Many deposit slip forms consist of an original and one or more copies.)

The bank adds the amount of the deposit to the balance of the checking account.

■ WRITING CHECKS

After a business opens a checking account, it may withdraw money by issuing checks. A *check* gives written authorization for the bank to pay a stated amount of money from the business's account.

It is essential that the account contain sufficient funds to cover all checks issued. To make sure of this, the business must have an up-to-date record of the account balance. Every deposit must be added to the balance, and every check must be subtracted. This information is usually shown on *check stubs* or in a *check register.*

The following procedures should be used when issuing checks. Refer to the check stub and check below as you study these procedures.

- Checks should be numbered consecutively to make it easier to keep track of them. (Checks are typically preprinted with consecutive numbers.)
- The check stub or check register entry should be completed before the check is written. All the important facts about the payment must be recorded. Preparing the check stub or check register entry first makes it less likely that this task will be forgotten.
- Checks should be prepared in ink, typewritten, or printed by a computer. Pencil should never be used in writing a check.
- There must be no alterations or erasures on a check. If an error is made, the word VOID is written in large letters across the face of the check and also on the check stub. The check is then placed in a check file. (This file is discussed in the next section.)
- Checks must be carefully prepared to prevent later changes in the amount or the name of the party being paid (the payee). It is a good practice to use a line to fill any space after the name and after the amount in words. It is also a good practice to write the amount in figures close to the dollar sign.
- Checks must have an authorized signature. Only a signature shown on the signature card is valid.

The person or business that issues (draws) a check is known as the *drawer.* The person or business that will receive payment is called the *payee.*

Check 105 issued by Maddalon Office Supply is shown below. The check stub remains in the business's checkbook and is used to record the transaction in the cash payments journal.

Check: Written authorization for the bank to pay a stated amount of money from an account.

Check Stubs or Check Register: Record of deposits, checks, and the account balance.

Drawer: Person or business that issues a check.

Payee: Person or business that will receive payment.

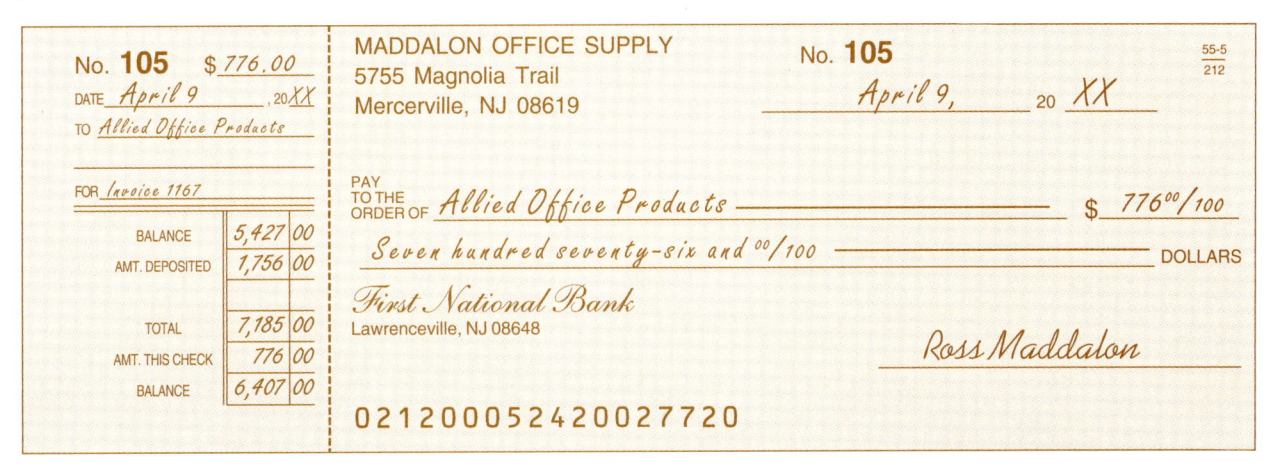

The payee (Allied Office Products) deposits the check in its own bank account. The check is then forwarded to the bank where Maddalon Office Supply has its account. This bank deducts the money from the account of Maddalon Office Supply.

Bank Statement: Form provided by the bank at regular intervals to report checking account transactions.

Canceled Checks: Checks that the bank has paid.

Debit Memorandum: Form issued by the bank to explain a deduction from a depositor's account.

Service Charge: The charge a bank makes for maintaining a depositor's checking account.

■ RECONCILING THE BUSINESS'S RECORDS WITH THE BANK STATEMENT

The owner of Maddalon Office Supply receives a ***bank statement*** every month. This form shows the business's transactions with the bank. For example, the bank statement below reports the deposits and checks that the bank processed for Maddalon Office Supply in April. ***Canceled checks*** accompany the bank statement. Some banks send copies of the checks instead of the actual checks, or make them available to the issuer on request. These are the checks paid from the business's account during the month.

Examine the bank statement for Maddalon Office Supply. The first two columns list all the items deducted from the account balance—paid checks, a ***debit memorandum,*** and a ***service charge.*** The third column of the bank statement shows the deposits, which were added to the account balance. The fourth column gives the dates of the transactions. The fifth column lists the account balance after the completion of each day's transactions. Notice that the balance on April 30 is $9,622 according to the bank statement.

A code at the bottom of the bank statement explains transactions that do not involve checks or deposits. Notice that the letters ***DM*** are used to identify a debit memorandum and the letters ***SC*** are used to identify a service charge.

First National Bank
Lawrenceville, New Jersey 08648

Maddalon Office Supply
5755 Magnolia Trail
Mercerville, NJ 08619

Account Number 242-0-027720

Period Ending April 30, 20XX

Checks	Checks	Deposits	Date	Balance
		11,000.00	April 1	11,000.00
2,400.00			4	8,600.00
2,800.00	320.00	1,756.00	8	7,236.00
		900.00	9	8,136.00
53.00			14	8,083.00
776.00	1,275.00	2,385.00	15	8,417.00
450.00	350.00	2,000.00	17	9,617.00
		870.00	18	10,487.00
135.00	600.00	2,279.00	22	12,031.00
		1,365.00	25	13,396.00
3,639.00	85.00		28	9,672.00
35.00DM	15.00SC		30	9,622.00

Beginning Balance	Total Amount of Deposits	Total Amount of Checks Paid	Total Charges	Total Charges
.00	22,555.00	12,883.00	50.00	9,622.00

Number of Deposits Made	Number of Checks Paid	Number of Other Charges
8	12	2

Codes: CC Certified Check   OD Overdrawn
        DM Debit Memorandum   RI Returned Item
        EC Error Correction   SC Service Charge

Please examine this statement upon receipt and report at once if you find any difference. If no error is reported in ten days, the account will be considered correct. All terms are subject to final payment.

It is necessary to compare the bank statement with the business's own records. In most cases, the final balances will differ. For example, the checkbook of Maddalon Office Supply shows a balance of $12,326 on April 30. This amount agrees with the balance of the Cash account in the general ledger.

The factors causing the difference between the bank statement balance and the checkbook balance must be determined. Then the two balances can be brought into agreement. This procedure is known as *reconciling the bank statement.*

The reconciliation form on page 214 was prepared at Maddalon Office Supply. This form is printed on the back of the bank statement. (Many bank statements contain similar forms.)

The steps needed to reconcile the bank statement are as follows:

1. List the bank statement balance and the checkbook balance on the reconciliation form.
2. Identify any deposits not recorded on the bank statement. The deposits shown on the bank statement must be compared with the deposits shown in the checkbook. Any unrecorded deposits, known as *deposits in transit,* are then listed on the reconciliation form. Maddalon Office Supply made a deposit of $4,929 on April 28. This deposit appears in the checkbook. However, the bank did not complete the processing of the deposit in time to enter it on the April 30 bank statement. The amount of this unrecorded deposit must be added to the bank statement balance.
3. Compare the canceled checks with the amounts of the paid checks shown on the bank statement. It is necessary to make sure that the bank recorded these checks correctly and returned all the canceled checks.
4. Identify any *outstanding checks*—checks that the drawer has issued but the bank has not yet paid. The canceled checks must be arranged in numeric order and compared with the information in the checkbook. Any outstanding checks are then listed on the reconciliation form. Maddalon Office Supply had two outstanding checks on April 30: Check 113 for $1,275 and Check 114 for $1,000. The total of these checks must be subtracted from the bank statement balance.
5. Identify any service charge or other bank charges not yet recorded in the checkbook. The bank statement must be examined for such charges. These charges are explained in debit memorandums that are issued by the bank. The bank statement shown on page 212 lists two charges on April 30. The first covers a $35 debit memorandum for an NSF (nonsufficient funds) check received from John Warren, a customer. Because John Warren did not have sufficient funds in his account, the bank charged the previously deposited check back to Maddalon Office Supply's account. On the reconciliation form, $35 is deducted from the checkbook balance. The second debit memorandum covers a $15 service charge that the bank imposed for handling the firm's account during April. On the reconciliation form, the service charge is also subtracted from the checkbook balance.
6. Compare the adjusted bank statement balance and the adjusted checkbook balance. As a result of the previous steps, each side of the reconciliation form contains an adjusted balance. The two amounts should be the same.

After the bank statement is reconciled, it may be necessary to update the Cash account and the checkbook. For example, at Maddalon Office Supply, the Cash account and the checkbook do not show the NSF check and the service charge. Therefore, the entries shown on page 214 are recorded in the general journal and in the checkbook.

Notice that Miscellaneous Expense is debited for the service charge and Accounts Receivable/John Warren is debited for the NSF check. This is to indicate that he still owes this amount. The total of both charges, $50, is credited to Cash. The entry for the NSF check is posted to Accounts Receivable in the general ledger and to John Warren's subsidiary ledger account.

The NSF check and the service charge are also deducted from the checkbook balance. The checkbook entry is made on the latest check stub. After subtracting the NSF check and

Reconciling the Bank Statement: Finding the factors that cause the bank statement balance and the checkbook balance to differ.

Deposits in Transit: Deposits that have been made but have not yet been entered in the bank's records.

Outstanding Checks: Checks that the drawer has issued but that the bank has not yet paid.

WWW Inquiry
Find the URL address for the American Banking Association. Write a short report on the history of the American Banking Association.

the service charge, the check stub shows a balance of $12,276, which agrees with the adjusted checkbook balance on the reconciliation form and with the Cash account balance.

The procedure for reconciling the bank statement is sometimes more complex. For example, the business may need to list errors as well as bank charges on the reconciliation form. Examine the reconciliation shown on page 215, which was prepared at Video Stores.

THIS FORM IS PROVIDED TO HELP YOU RECONCILE YOUR BANK STATEMENT

April 30, 20 XX

BALANCE SHOWN ON BANK STATEMENT $ 9,622.00

Add: Deposits Not on Statement

Date	Amount
4/28	4,929.00

Total $4,929.00

SUBTOTAL $14,551.00

Subtract: Checks Issued But Not on Statement

Number	Amount
113	1,275.00
114	1,000.00

Total $2,275.00

ADJUSTED BANK BALANCE $12,276.00

BALANCE SHOWN IN CHECKBOOK $ 12,326.00

Add: Corrections

Description	Amount

Total

SUBTOTAL $12,326.00

Subtract: Bank Charges Not in Checkbook and Corrections

Description	Amount
Service Charge	15.00
NSF Check	35.00

Total $50.00

ADJUSTED CHECKBOOK BALANCE $12,276.00

Recording the NSF Check and Bank Service Charge

GENERAL JOURNAL — Page 4

Date	Description	Post Ref.	Debit	Credit
20XX				
Apr. 30	Accounts Receivable/John Warren		35 00	
	Miscellaneous Expense		15 00	
	Cash			50 00
	NSF check from John Warren and			
	bank service charge for April.			

No. 115 $_____

DATE _____, 20____
TO _____
FOR _____

BALANCE	12,326	00
AMT. DEPOSITED	(35)	00
NSF Check Service Charge	(15)	00
TOTAL	12,276	00
AMT. THIS CHECK		
BALANCE		

VIDEO STORES
BANK RECONCILIATION
MARCH 31, 20XX

Balance on bank statement			$22,922.37
Add: Deposit of March 31 in transit		$1,725.62	
Check 440 for $149 incorrectly charged as $194 by the bank		45.00	
Check issued by Video Shop incorrectly charged to Video Stores		300.00	2,070.62
			$24,992.99
Deduct: Outstanding checks			
No. 452	$1,793.47		
No. 453	526.85	$2,320.32	
Deposit of March 24 for $1,560.27 incorrectly recorded by the bank as $1,650.27		90.00	2,410.32
Adjusted bank balance			$22,582.67
Balance in books			$22,621.92
Add: Check 450 for supplies recorded twice in cash payments journal		$500.00	
March 20 deposit for cash sales omitted from cash receipts journal		892.75	
Check 426 to Sound Waves, a creditor for $259 incorrectly recorded in the cash payments journal as $295		36.00	1,428.75
			$24,050.67
Deduct: NSF check from Frank Mason		$125.00	
Bank service charge		17.50	
March 15 deposit of cash sales recorded twice in the cash receipts journal		1,125.50	
Check 445 to Ace Video, a creditor, omitted from the cash payments journal		200.00	1,468.00
Adjusted book balance			$22,582.67

Bank errors must be brought to the attention of the bank and then corrected by the bank. In this example, the bank will issue *credit memorandums* for $45 and $300 to show that the account has been credited for the errors in recording Check 440 and the Video Shop's check. The bank will also issue a $90 debit memorandum to show that the March 24 deposit has been corrected. The next bank statement must be checked to verify that the correction has been made.

Book errors and other items listed in the section of the bank reconciliation form that begins with "Balance in books" must be journalized and posted to the ledger accounts. The entries required for Video Stores appear on page 216. If the same errors were made in the checkbook, then the balance shown on the last stub is corrected by subtracting $39.25 (a total of $1,428.75 for items to be added—a total of $1,468 for items to be deducted) to arrive at the adjusted book balance of $22,582.67. A notation to refer to the March 31 reconciliation form would also be written on the check stub.

Credit Memorandum: Form issued by a bank that explains an addition to a depositor's account.

WWW Inquiry
Find the URL address for Bank of America. Write a short synopsis on the corporate profile of Bank of America.

Bank Reconciliation Entries

GENERAL JOURNAL   Page 3

	Date		Description	Post Ref.	Debit	Credit	
1	20XX						1
2	Apr.	2	Cash		1 428 75		2
3			Supplies			500 00	3
4			Sales			892 75	4
5			Accounts Payable/Sound Waves			36 00	5
6			Correction of errors in recording				6
7			Check 450, the March 20 deposit,				7
8			and Check 426 as shown on the				8
9			March 31 bank reconciliation.				9
10							10
11		2	Accounts Receivable/Frank Mason		125 00		11
12			Miscellaneous Expense		17 50		12
13			Sales		1 125 50		13
14			Accounts Payable/Ace Video		200 00		14
15			Cash			1 468 00	15
16			NSF Check, service charge, and				16
17			correction of errors in recording				17
18			the March 15 deposit and Check				18
19			445 as shown on the March 31				19
20			bank reconciliation.				20

■ OTHER BANK SERVICES

Banks provide a variety of services besides the ones already discussed. For example, some banks lend money to businesses. A firm that has established a good reputation with its bank may be able to arrange short-term loans. Another service offered by some banks is the processing of sales that the businesses make with bank credit cards such as Visa, MasterCard, Discover, and American Express.

Many retail businesses need to make deposits after the bank is closed so that they can safeguard their cash receipts. Banks often provide a **night depository** for this purpose.

If a check is lost or stolen, the drawer can ask the bank to stop payment on the check. It is necessary to notify the bank quickly and fill out a bank form called a **stop payment order**.

In certain transactions, a business may be required to use a **certified check**. The drawer writes a check in the usual way and then takes it to the bank. A bank teller stamps the word **Certified** on the face of the check. The amount is immediately deducted from the account and set aside for payment of the check. Thus the payee has a guarantee that the necessary funds are available to cover the check.

Banks usually charge a fee for services such as stopping payment on checks and certifying checks.

Night Depository: Vault located in an outside wall of the bank, which can be used to make deposits when the bank is closed.

Stop Payment Order: Form instructing the bank not to pay a check.

Certified Check: Check for which the bank guarantees payment.

CHAPTER 24 SUMMARY

- A well-run business deposits all its cash receipts in a bank and makes all cash payments by check.
- Bank deposits should be made often to protect cash receipts. A deposit slip must accompany the coins, currency, and checks that are deposited.
- Every check must be endorsed before it is deposited. An endorsement legally transfers the right to collect payment on the check.
- A business must have a record of its checks, deposits, and account balance. This information is

usually shown on check stubs or in a check register. The check stub or check register entry should be completed before a check is written.
- It is important that all checks be prepared with care and accuracy.
- At regular intervals, the bank provides information about the checking account transactions it has processed. This information is given on the bank statement. The bank sends canceled checks along with the bank statement.
- It is necessary to reconcile the business's records with the bank statement. The factors causing the difference between the bank statement balance and the checkbook balance must be determined. Then the two balances can be brought into agreement.
- After the reconciliation procedure is completed, any unrecorded bank charges or credit memorandums must be entered in the accounting records and the checkbook.
- The canceled checks should be stored in a check file.
- Banks provide a variety of services that are useful to businesses.

CHAPTER APPLICATIONS

EXERCISES

Complete the following assignments on the forms provided in your workbook.

EXERCISE 24-1

Preparing a bank reconciliation.

Instructions:
Use the following information to prepare a bank reconciliation for the Academy Nursery School.

a. The checkbook balance on May 31 is $15,000.
b. The bank statement balance on May 31 is $14,000.
c. A May 31 deposit for $2,000 is in transit.
d. Check 942 for $1,000 is outstanding.

EXERCISE 24-2

Preparing a bank reconciliation. After comparing the Riverside Restaurant's checkbook to the deposits, canceled checks, and debit memorandums listed on its bank statement, the firm's accountant found that the items listed below were causing a difference.

Instructions:
Use this information to prepare a bank reconciliation.

a. The bank statement balance on June 30 is $7,185.
b. A deposit of $472.80 made on June 30 and a deposit of $624.56 made on June 30 do not appear on the bank statement.
c. A $15.60 service charge has not been recorded in the books.
d. A $47 debit memorandum for an NSF check from Juan Gomez has not been recorded in the book.
e. Check 657 for $198.79 and Check 658 for $927.66 are outstanding.
f. The Cash account balance on June 30 is $7,218.51.

EXERCISE 24-3

Preparing a bank reconciliation.

Instructions:
Use the following information to reconcile the Brandon Department Store's bank statement.

a. The checkbook balance on July 31 is $11,723.43.
b. The bank statement balance on July 31 is $10,956.31.
c. A deposit of $1,276.42 made on July 31 does not appear on the bank statement.
d. The following checks were issued but have not yet been paid by the bank: Check 357, $144.32; Check 359, $217.60; and Check 360, $135.88.
e. A $29 debit memorandum for an NSF check from Duke Farmer has not been recorded in the books.
f. A $13.50 service charge has not been recorded in the books.
g. Cash sales of $895 were incorrectly recorded as $859 in the books.
h. Check 352 drawn by the Brandon Department Store for $97 was incorrectly recorded as $79 on the bank statement.

PROBLEMS

Complete all assigned problems on the forms provided in your workbook.

PROBLEM 24-1

Preparing endorsements and a deposit slip. Miguel's Music Center is a retail store that sells stereo records and tapes. On March 15 of the current year, the business had the following items to be deposited in its account at the Mountain National Bank.

a. Four $20 bills, nine $10 bills, six $5 bills, seventeen $1 bills, seven half-dollars, fifteen quarters, eighteen dimes, twenty-one nickels, and eleven pennies.

b. Checks for $48.95, $24.72, and $56.40.

Instructions:

1. Show the various ways that the checks could be endorsed. Prepare a blank endorsement, a full endorsement, and a restrictive endorsement. Use the partial checks in the workbook.
2. Prepare the deposit slip needed to accompany the bank deposit.
3. Record the deposit on the stub of the check in the workbook.

PROBLEM 24-2

Writing a check. On March 16 of the current year, Miguel's Music Center bought some store equipment from Apex Corporation.

Instructions:
Issue Check 514 for $1,026.80 to pay the bill. Leave the signature line blank. The owner will sign the check. Remember to prepare the check stub first.

PROBLEM 24-3

Preparing a bank reconciliation; correcting the Cash account. On August 3 of the current year, the Delmuth Garden Supply Store received its bank statement and canceled checks for July.

Instructions:

1. Use the following information to prepare the bank reconciliation. The necessary form is in the workbook.
2. Record a general journal entry to correct the Cash account. Use 4 as the journal page number.
    a. The bank statement balance on July 31 is $1,228.68.
    b. The checkbook balance on July 31 is $1,573.63.
    c. The checkbook balance shows a deposit of $422.60, dated July 30, that does not appear on the bank statement.
    d. The following checks are outstanding: Check 868 for $18.76, Check 870 for $45.97, Check 872 for $12.30, and Check 873 for $64.82.
    e. The bank statement shows a service charge of $14.20 that has not been recorded in the books.
    f. The bank statement shows a $50 NSF check received from Benjamin Ferello that has not been recorded in the books.

PROBLEM 24-4

Preparing a bank reconciliation; correcting the Cash account. On May 2 of the current year, Elmer E. Mears, M.D., received the bank statement and canceled checks for his medical practice for April.

Instructions:

1. Use the following information to prepare a bank reconciliation.
2. Record a general journal entry to correct the Cash account. Use 5 as the journal page number. Refer to the format of the bank reconciliation for Video Stores on page 215.
    a. The bank statement balance on April 30 is $9,184.62.
    b. The checkbook balance on April 30 is $10,103.12.
    c. A deposit of $1,457 made on April 30 is not recorded on the bank statement.
    d. The following checks are outstanding: Check 453 for $274.20, Check 454 for $87.50, and Check 455 for $156.80.
    e. A deposit of $1,560 made on April 25 was incorrectly recorded as $1,650 on the bank statement.
    f. A $75 NSF check received from Vince Vendetti has not been recorded in the books.
    g. Check 440 drawn by Elmer E. Mears for $153 was incorrectly recorded as $53 on the bank statement.
    h. A $15 service charge has not been recorded in the books.
    i. Check 425 for $187 to purchase supplies was incorrectly recorded as $107 in the checkbook.

CASE STUDY

Write the answer to the case study on the form provided in your workbook.

Endorsements

You own a small business. When your customers pay you for your goods, they pay cash, use charge cards, or write checks. As you learned in accounting class, cash and checks should be deposited at least daily. You never bother to write "For Deposit Only" on the checks because the bank employees have always just accepted your checks along with the deposit slip.

One day the manager, a friend, asks to speak with you. He indicates to you that it might be wiser to endorse the checks you are depositing.

Critical Thinking

■ *Why would the bank manager make this suggestion?*

CHAPTER TWENTY-FIVE

Petty Cash and Other Special Cash Procedures

OBJECTIVES

Upon completion of this chapter, you should be able to:

1. Set up and use a petty cash fund.
2. Prove and replenish a petty cash fund.
3. Use a change fund and provide travel advances.
4. Account for cash shortages and overages.

INTRODUCTION

A well-run business pays all bills by check. However, most businesses need a small amount of money on hand to take care of items that cannot conveniently be paid by check. Examples of such items are carfare for messengers, purchases of postage stamps, supper money for employees who work overtime, and purchases of minor amounts of supplies. A *petty cash fund* provides a way of handling small cash payments. ■

■ SETTING UP THE PETTY CASH FUND

The size of the petty cash fund is determined by the needs of each business. Usually, the amount chosen is large enough to take care of petty cash needs for several weeks or a month. The fund is set up by issuing a check payable to Petty Cash for the required amount. The bank will cash such a check for any authorized person after the check is endorsed. The money is taken in various denominations of currency and coins.

On May 1, Ross Maddalon decided to set up a $50 petty cash fund for Maddalon Office Supply. He issued Check 115 for this amount. The entry for the transaction is made in the cash payments journal as shown below.

Accounting Terminology

- Cash over
- Cash short
- Change fund
- Petty cash fund
- Petty cash voucher
- Proving petty cash
- Replenishing petty cash
- Travel advances

Petty Cash Fund: Money kept on hand to make small cash payments.

CASH PAYMENTS JOURNAL
FOR MONTH OF MAY, 20XX   Page 2

Date	Ck. No.	Explanation	Accounts Payable Debit	Merch. Purchase Debit	Other Accounts Debit Account Name	Post. Ref.	Amount	Purchase Discount Credit	Cash Credit	
20XX										1
May 1	115	Set up petty			Petty Cash	102	50 00		50 00	2
		cash fund								3

219

A new asset account called Petty Cash is debited, and Cash is credited. Now, the business has two cash accounts: Cash (in the form of a checking account in the bank) and Petty Cash (in the form of currency and coins in a petty cash box at the office).

The balance of the Petty Cash account should always reflect the original amount of the fund ($50) unless the fund is permanently increased or decreased to meet operating needs. No further entries are made in this account unless the amount of the fund is changed.

■ USING THE PETTY CASH FUND

The petty cash fund is put into the care of a responsible office employee who usually keeps it in a locked box. This employee must make sure that no unauthorized person has access to the money and that it is safely locked away at night. In a large business, there may be many petty cash funds. Each fund will be under the care of a different employee such as a department secretary.

Petty Cash Voucher: Form that explains and authorizes a petty cash payment.

To obtain a payment from the fund, it is necessary to fill out a form called a *petty cash voucher*. This form should be prepared in ink or typewritten to prevent later changes. The petty cash voucher used by Maddalon Office Supply is shown below. Notice that it has space for writing the name of the account to be charged. Spaces are also provided for the signature of the person to whom payment is made and the signature of the person who approves the payment.

Any bill or receipt that verifies the payment is stapled to the petty cash voucher. After the voucher is paid, it is placed in the petty cash box.

PETTY CASH VOUCHER			NO. 1
DESCRIPTION OF EXPENDITURE	CHARGE TO ACCOUNT		AMOUNT
Supper money	Miscellaneous Expense		7 50
		TOTAL	7 50
RECEIVED Paul Sanchez DATE 5/2/XX	APPROVED BY Ross Maddalon		DATE 5/2/XX

■ PROVING THE PETTY CASH FUND

Proving Petty Cash: Making sure that the total of the money and the vouchers in the petty cash box equals the amount of the fund.

At any time, the person who is in charge of the petty cash fund should be able to account for the amount of the fund. This is done by *proving petty cash.* The money in the petty cash box is counted. Then the amounts of the petty cash vouchers in the box are added to find out how much was spent. The total cash on hand and the total of the vouchers should equal the original amount of the fund.

On May 31, the petty cash box at Maddalon Office Supply contained $14.20 in cash and five vouchers. The form at the top of page 221 shows how the amounts were proved.

■ REPLENISHING THE PETTY CASH FUND

Replenishing Petty Cash: Restoring the petty cash fund to its original amount.

The petty cash fund is restored to its original amount at the end of each month and at any other time when the money in the box is low. This procedure is known as *replenishing petty cash.* The steps to be followed are listed on page 221.

PROOF OF PETTY CASH FUND
MAY 31, 20XX

Cash on hand						
$5 bills		×	2	=	$10.00	
1 bills		×	3	=	3.00	
Quarters	0.25	×	2	=	0.50	
Dimes	0.10	×	4	=	0.40	
Nickels	0.05	×	5	=	0.25	
Pennies	0.01	×	5	=	0.05	
Total cash						$14.20

Vouchers on hand
1. Supper money (Miscellaneous Expense) — $7.50
2. Carfare (Miscellaneous Expense) — 2.00
3. Telephone calls (Telephone Expense) — 5.30
4. Stamps (Miscellaneous Expense) — 4.00
5. Withdrawal (Ross Maddalon, Withdrawals) — 17.00

Total vouchers	35.80
Total cash and vouchers	$50.00
Amount of fund	50.00
Cash short or over	—

1. The petty cash fund is proved.
2. The vouchers are sorted according to the nature of the expenses. The amount spent for each kind of expense is then listed on a memorandum or some other type of form. (See the form above.)
3. The proof of the fund, the vouchers, and the supporting bills and receipts are given to the accounting clerk along with a request for replenishment.
4. The accounting clerk cancels the vouchers by writing the word *PAID* across each of them or by perforating them. This is done to make sure that the vouchers are not used again. The accounting clerk then gives a check to the person in charge of the petty cash fund. This check is for the total amount spent (which is the total of all the vouchers submitted). The person in charge of the fund cashes the check and puts the money in the petty cash box.
5. The accounting clerk makes an entry in the cash payments journal to record the replenishment of the petty cash fund.

On May 31, the person in charge of the petty cash fund at Maddalon Office Supply prepared the following request for replenishment of the fund.

WWW Inquiry
Find the URL address for General Motors. What was the increase in total net sales and revenues over the last two years?

REQUEST FOR REPLENISHMENT OF PETTY CASH FUND
MAY 31, 20XX

Original amount of fund	$50.00
Vouchers 1–5 (attached):	
Miscellaneous Expense	$13.50
Telephone Expense	5.30
Ross Maddalon, Withdrawals	17.00
Total spent	$35.80
Cash on hand	14.20
Total accounted for	$50.00
Amount requested	$35.80

The journal entry shown below was made when the petty cash fund was replenished on May 31. After the amounts in this entry are posted, there is a record of all expenses paid from the fund during May.

CASH PAYMENTS JOURNAL FOR MONTH OF MAY, 20XX — Page 2

Date	Ck. No.	Explanation	Accounts Payable Debit	Merch. Purchase Debit	Other Accounts Debit — Account Name	Post. Ref.	Amount	Purchase Discount Credit	Cash Credit
20XX May 31	138	Replenish petty cash fund			Miscellaneous Expense	519	13 50		
					Telephone Expense	512	5 30		
					Ross Maddalon, Withdrawals	302	17 00		35 80

It is important to replenish the petty cash fund at the end of each month. In this way, the expenses can be recorded in the month they are incurred, and the money in the petty cash box can be brought into agreement with the balance of the Petty Cash account.

■ OTHER CASH FUNDS

Petty cash is one type of cash fund. Cash funds can be set up for other uses besides providing money for small office expenses. For example, some firms set up a cash fund to provide *travel advances* to employees who must go on out-of-town business trips.

Many retail stores have a *change fund.* This fund consists of currency and coins that are always kept on hand to make change when customers pay cash. The change fund is placed in the cash register every morning. At the end of the day, the fund is separated from the cash receipts and placed in an office safe. The cash receipts are deposited in the bank. The amount of the fund is shown in an asset account called Change Fund.

Travel Advances: Cash given to employees for business trips.

Change Fund: Money kept on hand to make change when customers pay cash.

■ CASH SHORTAGES AND OVERAGES

Because dishonesty or errors are always possible in the handling of cash, all cash funds should be proved often. Petty cash funds are proved as described earlier in this chapter. When there are cash sales, the money in the cash register must be proved against the audit tape prepared by the register.

Sometimes the amount of money in the cash register will not agree with the amount that should be there. If less cash is on hand than there should be, cash is *short.* If more cash is on hand than there should be, cash is *over.* In businesses that have cash sales, some shortages and overages can be expected because of errors in making change. However, large or frequent shortages or overages should be investigated. They may be a sign of poor cash-handling procedures or dishonesty.

For proper control of cash, amounts short and over must be recorded. An account called Cash Short or Over is used. This account is debited for cash shortages and credited for cash overages. Entries for cash shortages or overages are recorded in the cash receipts journal.

The Cash Short or Over account may be considered either as an expense or as revenue according to its balance at the end of the accounting period. If the account has a debit balance (shortages exceed overages), it appears on the income statement as an expense. If the account has a credit balance (overages exceed shortages), it appears on the income statement as revenue.

Cash Short: Less cash on hand than there should be.

Cash Over: More cash on hand than there should be.

> **WWW Inquiry**
> Find the URL address for Hewlett Packard. On the last available balance sheet, what percentage of total assets does net property and equipment represent?

CHAPTER 25 SUMMARY

- The petty cash fund is used for small cash payments. A petty cash voucher must be prepared to explain each payment.

- When the petty cash fund is set up, an asset account called Petty Cash is debited. The balance of this account always reflects the original amount of the fund unless the fund is permanently increased or decreased.

- The petty cash fund is replenished at the end of each month and at any other time when the money is low. A check is issued for the total amount spent. Then an entry is made in the cash payments journal. This entry involves debits to the various expense accounts affected by the petty cash payments. The Cash account is credited for the total amount.

- The petty cash fund is one common type of cash fund. Other types used by many businesses are funds for giving travel advances and funds for making change.

- All cash funds should be proved often. It is also necessary to prove the cash receipts in a cash register.

- Cash shortages and overages must be recorded. The Cash Short or Over account is used for this purpose.

CHAPTER APPLICATIONS

EXERCISES

Complete the following assignments on the forms provided in your workbook.

EXERCISE 25-1
Handling petty cash.

Instructions:

1. Set up T accounts, and enter the following balances in the accounts.

Cash	$5,000	Kevin Atkinson,	–0–
Petty Cash	–0–	Withdrawals	
Kevin Atkinson, Capital	5,000	Delivery Expense	–0–
		Miscellaneous Expense	–0–

2. Analyze each of the following transactions, and record the effects in the T accounts.
3. Compute the balance of each account.
4. Add the debit balances and the credit balances to prove that they are equal.

Transactions:

a. Issued Check 101 for $50 to set up a petty cash fund.
b. Issued Check 127 to replenish the petty cash fund for the following: a withdrawal by the owner, $35; messenger fees, $7 (Delivery Expense); and a plant for the office, $6 (Miscellaneous Expense).
c. Issued Check 128 for $50 to increase the petty cash fund to $100.

EXERCISE 25-2
Handling the change fund and recording cash shortages and overages.

Instructions:

1. Set up T accounts, and enter the following balances in the accounts.

Cash	$7,000	Sales	–0–
Change Fund	–0–	Cash Short or Over	–0–
Cheryl Carr, Capital	7,000		

2. Analyze each of the following transactions, and record the effects in the T accounts.
3. Compute the balance of each account.
4. Add the debit balances and the credit balances to prove that they are equal.

Transactions:

a. Issued Check 146 for $50 to establish a change fund.
b. Cash on hand at the end of June 28 totaled $747. The cash register tape shows sales of $750.
c. Cash on hand at the end of June 29 totaled $752. The cash register tape shows sales of $751.
d. Cash on hand at the end of June 30 totaled $549. The cash register tape shows sales of $550.

PROBLEMS

Complete all assigned problems on the forms provided in your workbook.

PROBLEM 25-1

Handling petty cash. On June 1 the owner of the Fantasy Gift Shoppe issued Check 134 to establish a $75 petty cash fund. During June, the payments listed below were made from the fund.

Petty Cash Payments:

a. Voucher 1, $6.78 for pens and pencils (Supplies).
b. Voucher 2, $12.22 for mailing packages (Delivery Expense).
c. Voucher 3, $5.80 for file folders (Supplies).
d. Voucher 4, $11.92 for supper money (Miscellaneous Expense).
e. Voucher 5, $10 to Eileen McDonald, as a withdrawal for personal use.

At the end of the month, the currency and coins in the petty cash box consisted of one $10 bill, one $5 bill, ten $1 bills, nine quarters, eight dimes, three nickels, and eight pennies.

Instructions:

1. Record an entry in the cash payments journal to establish the fund. Use *1* as the journal page number.
2. Prove the petty cash fund as of June 30 of the current year.
3. Prepare a request for replenishment of the petty cash fund.
4. Record the entry to replenish the petty cash fund in the cash payments journal. Check 154 for $46.72 was issued.
5. Record an entry in the cash payments journal to increase the petty cash fund to $100. Check 155 was issued on June 30.

PROBLEM 25-2

Handling cash short and over. Chan's Restaurant opened for business on May 25. The money in the cash register is counted and deposited daily. Each day's sales and sales tax totals are printed on the cash register tape. At the end of the day, the total cash in the register is compared to the total sales plus sales tax on the tape to determine whether the cash is short or over.

Instructions:

Use the information below to complete the following activities.

1. Determine whether each day's cash is short or over.
2. Record each transaction in the cash receipts journal. If cash is over, place the amount in parentheses in the Cash Short or Over Debit column. Use *1* as the journal page number.
3. Foot and cross-foot to prove the accuracy of the journal.
4. Enter the totals and rule the journal.

Date	Money in Cash Register	Sales	Sales Tax	Total
May 25	$366.87	$350.20	$17.51	$367.71
26	313.12	298.40	14.92	313.32
27	326.16	310.50	15.53	326.03
28	289.21	275.25	13.76	289.01
29	274.90	262.65	13.13	275.78
30	318.64	304.30	15.22	319.52
31	270.93	257.55	12.88	270.43

CASE STUDY

Write the answer to the case study on the form provided in your workbook.

Internal Control

You learned in accounting class that wherever cash is used in a business it should be proven often and accurately. The Petty Cash Fund has been consistently short.

Critical Thinking

- What are the methods you would employ to assure that cash would be handled appropriately?

CHAPTER TWENTY-SIX

Payroll Procedures

OBJECTIVES

Upon completion of this chapter, you should be able to:

1. Compute gross earnings using different pay plans.
2. Read a time card and compute regular hours and overtime hours.
3. Compute deductions and net pay.
4. Prepare a payroll register and employee earnings record.
5. Journalize the payroll and payroll taxes.

INTRODUCTION

Most businesses have employees. By law, these businesses must keep accurate, complete payroll records and perform certain payroll procedures. For example, they are required to compute employee earnings, deduct taxes from these earnings, compute their own tax contributions, send all taxes to the proper government agencies, and prepare payroll tax reports for the government. Businesses are also responsible for providing employees with information about earnings and deductions. The employees need this information in order to file income tax returns. ■

■ PAY PLANS

The total amount an employee earns is known as **gross earnings**. This amount can be determined in various ways, depending on the type of pay plan used for the employee. The most common pay plans are explained in this section.

Salary Plan. Under the *salary plan,* employees earn a fixed amount for each pay period. [Pay periods vary from business to business. However, they are usually on a weekly, biweekly (every two weeks), semimonthly (twice a month), or monthly basis]. Most office employees, supervisors, and managers are paid according to the salary plan.

Hourly-Rate Plan. When the *hourly-rate plan* is used, employees earn a fixed amount for each hour they work. The number of hours an employee worked during a pay period is multiplied by the employee's hourly rate to find the gross earnings. Production employees in factories and service employees in retail businesses are often paid according to the hourly-rate plan.

Piece-Rate Plan. Under the *piece-rate plan,* employees earn a fixed amount for each item they produce. At the end of the pay period, the number of items completed is multiplied by the rate per item to determine the employee's gross earnings. The piece-rate plan is referred to as an *incentive plan* because employees can increase their earnings by producing more. Some factories use the piece-rate plan.

Commission Plan. The *commission plan* is an incentive plan for salespeople. In some businesses, the amount that such employees earn is based on the amount of goods they sell. At the end of the pay period, the amount of goods sold is multiplied by the commission rate to find the gross earnings. The commission rate is a percentage.

Accounting Terminology

- Direct deposit
- Employee earnings record
- Gross earnings
- Hourly-rate plan
- Net pay
- Overtime
- Pay statement
- Payroll register
- Piece-rate plan
- Salary plan
- Time cards
- Time clock
- Time sheets
- Year-to-date earnings

Gross Earnings: Total amount an employee earns.

Salary Plan:
Salary = Gross Earnings
$425 = $425

Hourly-Rate Plan:
Hours × Rate = Gross Earnings
40 × $8 = $320

Piece-Rate Plan:
Items × Rate = Gross Earnings
2,900 × $0.10 = $290

Commission Plan:
Sales × Rate (%) = Gross Earnings
$15,000 × 0.03 = $450

Salary-Commission Plan. In the *salary-commission plan,* salespeople receive a salary as well as a commission on the goods they sell. The salary and the commission are added to determine the gross earnings for a pay period.

Salary-Commission Plan				
Salary	+	Commission (Sales × Rate)	=	Gross Earnings
$200	+	($12,000 × 0.01)	=	$320
$200	+	$120	=	$320

■ COMPUTING GROSS EARNINGS

Gross earnings may include both regular earnings and overtime earnings. Many employees are subject to the federal Fair Labor Standards Act. One section of this law specifies that employees must receive extra pay for *overtime*—all time worked beyond 40 hours a week. The rate paid for overtime hours must be at least 1½ times the regular rate.

There are a number of methods for keeping track of the hours that employees work. Some businesses use a form called a *time sheet.* Daily arrival and departure times are recorded on this sheet by the employees or by their supervisor, depending on the policy of the firm. Other businesses use a *time clock* and *time cards.* When employees enter or leave their work area, they place the cards in the time clock. This device prints the time on each card. Some companies use the employee ID card linked to a computer for electronic control.

At the end of the pay period, it is necessary to total the hours recorded on the time sheet or time cards. Then the gross earnings of each employee can be computed. Study the time card shown below. (No deductions were made for lateness because the firm allows lateness of up to 5 minutes without penalty.)

Overtime: All time worked beyond 40 hours a week.

Time Sheets and Time Cards: Records showing hours worked by employees.

Time Clock: Device used to print arrival and departure times on time cards.

Notice how the gross earnings are computed on the time card.

1. The regular hours worked are multiplied by the employee's hourly rate to find the regular earnings (40 hours × $8 = $320).

2. The overtime hours worked are multiplied by the employee's overtime rate to find the overtime earnings (4 hours × $12 = $48). The overtime rate is 1½ times the regular rate of $8.
3. The regular earnings and the overtime earnings are added to find the gross earnings ($320 + $48 = $368).

■ DETERMINING EMPLOYEE DEDUCTIONS

The amount of pay that employees actually receive is usually less than their gross earnings. Most employees are subject to deductions for federal income tax, social security (FICA) tax, and the Medicare tax. These deductions are required by law. Other required deductions in some areas are state income tax, city income tax, state disability tax, and state unemployment tax. If employees belong to a union, they may have a required deduction for union dues. Many employees also have voluntary deductions for items such as medical insurance, savings bonds, and pension plan contributions.

The procedures for determining the deductions for federal income tax, social security (FICA) tax, and the Medicare tax are discussed in this section.

Federal Income Tax Withholding.
At the end of each pay period, a business must withhold federal income tax from the earnings of its employees. The amount to be withheld for any employee depends on three factors: the employee's gross earnings, marital status, and withholding allowances.

When employees are hired, the business must obtain information about the number of withholding allowances they are claiming. Each employee is therefore asked to fill out a government form called an *Employee's Withholding Allowance Certificate* (*Form W-4*). This form is placed in the business's payroll files after the employee completes it.

The easiest way to find the proper amount of federal income tax withholding for an employee is to use the tax tables in the *Employer's Tax Guide,* which is published by the Internal Revenue Service (IRS). (This booklet is also known as *Circular E.*) There are separate tax tables for different pay periods. For example, the tax tables given on pages 228 through 231 cover a weekly pay period. Notice that one of these tables is for single persons, and the other is for married persons. The IRS publishes the form on their website.

To use an income tax withholding table, look at the first two columns and select the line that covers the employee's gross earnings. Then follow the line across the table until you reach the column for the number of withholding allowances the employee claims. The figure shown at this point in the table is the amount of income tax to be withheld.

According to the time card on page 226, John Christopher earned $368 during the week ended May 22. Christopher is married and claims two withholding allowances. The table for married persons given on page 230 shows that $9 should be deducted from his gross earnings for federal income tax withholding.

States and cities that have an income tax provide tables similar to those for federal income tax.

Social Security (FICA) Tax and Medicare Tax.
The Federal Insurance Contributions Act (FICA) specifies that taxes must be deducted from the earnings of most employees to support the social security program. This program provides retirement, survivors, and disability benefits, and health insurance for the aged (Medicare). The rates of tax change periodically. They are revised by Congress.

At the end of a pay period, the amount of social security tax and Medicare tax for each employee can be found by multiplying the employee's gross earnings by the current tax rates. For example, with assumed rates of 6.2 percent for social security tax and 1.45 percent for Medicare tax, John Christopher's deductions for the week would be computed as follows:

$368 × 0.062 = $22.82 social security tax

$368 × 0.0145 = $5.34 Medicare tax

WWW Inquiry
Use a search engine to find information on the Fair Labor Standards Act. Write a short report on the act.

SINGLE Persons—WEEKLY Payroll Period
(For Wages Paid Through December 2004)

If the wages are—		And the number of withholding allowances claimed is—									
At least	But less than	0	1	2	3	4	5	6	7	8	9	10
		The amount of income tax to be withheld is—										
$0	$55	$0	$0	$0	$0	$0	$0	$0	$0	$0	$0	$0
55	60	1	0	0	0	0	0	0	0	0	0	0
60	65	1	0	0	0	0	0	0	0	0	0	0
65	70	2	0	0	0	0	0	0	0	0	0	0
70	75	2	0	0	0	0	0	0	0	0	0	0
75	80	3	0	0	0	0	0	0	0	0	0	0
80	85	3	0	0	0	0	0	0	0	0	0	0
85	90	4	0	0	0	0	0	0	0	0	0	0
90	95	4	0	0	0	0	0	0	0	0	0	0
95	100	5	0	0	0	0	0	0	0	0	0	0
100	105	5	0	0	0	0	0	0	0	0	0	0
105	110	6	0	0	0	0	0	0	0	0	0	0
110	115	6	0	0	0	0	0	0	0	0	0	0
115	120	7	1	0	0	0	0	0	0	0	0	0
120	125	7	1	0	0	0	0	0	0	0	0	0
125	130	8	2	0	0	0	0	0	0	0	0	0
130	135	8	2	0	0	0	0	0	0	0	0	0
135	140	9	3	0	0	0	0	0	0	0	0	0
140	145	9	3	0	0	0	0	0	0	0	0	0
145	150	10	4	0	0	0	0	0	0	0	0	0
150	155	10	4	0	0	0	0	0	0	0	0	0
155	160	11	5	0	0	0	0	0	0	0	0	0
160	165	11	5	0	0	0	0	0	0	0	0	0
165	170	12	6	0	0	0	0	0	0	0	0	0
170	175	12	6	0	0	0	0	0	0	0	0	0
175	180	13	7	1	0	0	0	0	0	0	0	0
180	185	13	7	1	0	0	0	0	0	0	0	0
185	190	14	8	2	0	0	0	0	0	0	0	0
190	195	14	8	2	0	0	0	0	0	0	0	0
195	200	15	9	3	0	0	0	0	0	0	0	0
200	210	16	9	3	0	0	0	0	0	0	0	0
210	220	18	10	4	0	0	0	0	0	0	0	0
220	230	19	11	5	0	0	0	0	0	0	0	0
230	240	21	12	6	1	0	0	0	0	0	0	0
240	250	22	13	7	2	0	0	0	0	0	0	0
250	260	24	15	8	3	0	0	0	0	0	0	0
260	270	25	16	9	4	0	0	0	0	0	0	0
270	280	27	18	10	5	0	0	0	0	0	0	0
280	290	28	19	11	6	0	0	0	0	0	0	0
290	300	30	21	12	7	1	0	0	0	0	0	0
300	310	31	22	13	8	2	0	0	0	0	0	0
310	320	33	24	15	9	3	0	0	0	0	0	0
320	330	34	25	16	10	4	0	0	0	0	0	0
330	340	36	27	18	11	5	0	0	0	0	0	0
340	350	37	28	19	12	6	0	0	0	0	0	0
350	360	39	30	21	13	7	1	0	0	0	0	0
360	370	40	31	22	14	8	2	0	0	0	0	0
370	380	42	33	24	15	9	3	0	0	0	0	0
380	390	43	34	25	17	10	4	0	0	0	0	0
390	400	45	36	27	18	11	5	0	0	0	0	0
400	410	46	37	28	20	12	6	0	0	0	0	0
410	420	48	39	30	21	13	7	1	0	0	0	0
420	430	49	40	31	23	14	8	2	0	0	0	0
430	440	51	42	33	24	15	9	3	0	0	0	0
440	450	52	43	34	26	17	10	4	0	0	0	0
450	460	54	45	36	27	18	11	5	0	0	0	0
460	470	55	46	37	29	20	12	6	0	0	0	0
470	480	57	48	39	30	21	13	7	1	0	0	0
480	490	58	49	40	32	23	14	8	2	0	0	0
490	500	60	51	42	33	24	15	9	3	0	0	0
500	510	61	52	43	35	26	17	10	4	0	0	0
510	520	63	54	45	36	27	18	11	5	0	0	0
520	530	64	55	46	38	29	20	12	6	0	0	0
530	540	66	57	48	39	30	21	13	7	1	0	0
540	550	67	58	49	41	32	23	14	8	2	0	0
550	560	69	60	51	42	33	24	15	9	3	0	0
560	570	70	61	52	44	35	26	17	10	4	0	0
570	580	72	63	54	45	36	27	18	11	5	0	0
580	590	73	64	55	47	38	29	20	12	6	0	0
590	600	75	66	57	48	39	30	21	13	7	1	0

SINGLE Persons—WEEKLY Payroll Period
(For Wages Paid Through December 2004)

If the wages are—		And the number of withholding allowances claimed is—									
At least	But less than	0	1	2	3	4	5	6	7	8	9	10
		The amount of income tax to be withheld is—									
$600	$610	$78	$67	$58	$50	$41	$32	$23	$14	$8	$2	$0
610	620	80	69	60	51	42	33	24	15	9	3	0
620	630	83	70	61	53	44	35	26	17	10	4	0
630	640	85	72	63	54	45	36	27	18	11	5	0
640	650	88	73	64	56	47	38	29	20	12	6	0
650	660	90	75	66	57	48	39	30	21	13	7	1
660	670	93	78	67	59	50	41	32	23	14	8	2
670	680	95	80	69	60	51	42	33	24	15	9	3
680	690	98	83	70	62	53	44	35	26	17	10	4
690	700	100	85	72	63	54	45	36	27	18	11	5
700	710	103	88	73	65	56	47	38	29	20	12	6
710	720	105	90	75	66	57	48	39	30	21	13	7
720	730	108	93	78	68	59	50	41	32	23	14	8
730	740	110	95	80	69	60	51	42	33	24	15	9
740	750	113	98	83	71	62	53	44	35	26	17	10
750	760	115	100	85	72	63	54	45	36	27	18	11
760	770	118	103	88	74	65	56	47	38	29	20	12
770	780	120	105	90	75	66	57	48	39	30	21	13
780	790	123	108	93	78	68	59	50	41	32	23	14
790	800	125	110	95	80	69	60	51	42	33	24	15
800	810	128	113	98	83	71	62	53	44	35	26	17
810	820	130	115	100	85	72	63	54	45	36	27	18
820	830	133	118	103	88	74	65	56	47	38	29	20
830	840	135	120	105	90	75	66	57	48	39	30	21
840	850	138	123	108	93	78	68	59	50	41	32	23
850	860	140	125	110	95	80	69	60	51	42	33	24
860	870	143	128	113	98	83	71	62	53	44	35	26
870	880	145	130	115	100	85	72	63	54	45	36	27
880	890	148	133	118	103	88	74	65	56	47	38	29
890	900	150	135	120	105	90	76	66	57	48	39	30
900	910	153	138	123	108	93	78	68	59	50	41	32
910	920	155	140	125	110	95	81	69	60	51	42	33
920	930	158	143	128	113	98	83	71	62	53	44	35
930	940	160	145	130	115	100	86	72	63	54	45	36
940	950	163	148	133	118	103	88	74	65	56	47	38
950	960	165	150	135	120	105	91	76	66	57	48	39
960	970	168	153	138	123	108	93	78	68	59	50	41
970	980	170	155	140	125	110	96	81	69	60	51	42
980	990	173	158	143	128	113	98	83	71	62	53	44
990	1,000	175	160	145	130	115	101	86	72	63	54	45
1,000	1,010	178	163	148	133	118	103	88	74	65	56	47
1,010	1,020	180	165	150	135	120	106	91	76	66	57	48
1,020	1,030	183	168	153	138	123	108	93	78	68	59	50
1,030	1,040	185	170	155	140	125	111	96	81	69	60	51
1,040	1,050	188	173	158	143	128	113	98	83	71	62	53
1,050	1,060	190	175	160	145	130	116	101	86	72	63	54
1,060	1,070	193	178	163	148	133	118	103	88	74	65	56
1,070	1,080	195	180	165	150	135	121	106	91	76	66	57
1,080	1,090	198	183	168	153	138	123	108	93	78	68	59
1,090	1,100	200	185	170	155	140	126	111	96	81	69	60
1,100	1,110	203	188	173	158	143	128	113	98	83	71	62
1,110	1,120	205	190	175	160	145	131	116	101	86	72	63
1,120	1,130	208	193	178	163	148	133	118	103	88	74	65
1,130	1,140	210	195	180	165	150	136	121	106	91	76	66
1,140	1,150	213	198	183	168	153	138	123	108	93	78	68
1,150	1,160	215	200	185	170	155	141	126	111	96	81	69
1,160	1,170	218	203	188	173	158	143	128	113	98	83	71
1,170	1,180	220	205	190	175	160	146	131	116	101	86	72
1,180	1,190	223	208	193	178	163	148	133	118	103	88	74
1,190	1,200	225	210	195	180	165	151	136	121	106	91	76
1,200	1,210	228	213	198	183	168	153	138	123	108	93	79
1,210	1,220	230	215	200	185	170	156	141	126	111	96	81
1,220	1,230	233	218	203	188	173	158	143	128	113	98	84
1,230	1,240	235	220	205	190	175	161	146	131	116	101	86
1,240	1,250	238	223	208	193	178	163	148	133	118	103	89

$1,250 and over   Use Table 1(a) for a **SINGLE person** on page 3. Also see the instructions on page 2.

MARRIED Persons—WEEKLY Payroll Period
(For Wages Paid Through December 2004)

If the wages are—		And the number of withholding allowances claimed is—									
At least	But less than	0	1	2	3	4	5	6	7	8	9	10
		The amount of income tax to be withheld is—									
$0	$125	$0	$0	$0	$0	$0	$0	$0	$0	$0	$0	$0
125	130	0	0	0	0	0	0	0	0	0	0	0
130	135	0	0	0	0	0	0	0	0	0	0	0
135	140	0	0	0	0	0	0	0	0	0	0	0
140	145	0	0	0	0	0	0	0	0	0	0	0
145	150	0	0	0	0	0	0	0	0	0	0	0
150	155	0	0	0	0	0	0	0	0	0	0	0
155	160	0	0	0	0	0	0	0	0	0	0	0
160	165	1	0	0	0	0	0	0	0	0	0	0
165	170	1	0	0	0	0	0	0	0	0	0	0
170	175	2	0	0	0	0	0	0	0	0	0	0
175	180	2	0	0	0	0	0	0	0	0	0	0
180	185	3	0	0	0	0	0	0	0	0	0	0
185	190	3	0	0	0	0	0	0	0	0	0	0
190	195	4	0	0	0	0	0	0	0	0	0	0
195	200	4	0	0	0	0	0	0	0	0	0	0
200	210	5	0	0	0	0	0	0	0	0	0	0
210	220	6	0	0	0	0	0	0	0	0	0	0
220	230	7	1	0	0	0	0	0	0	0	0	0
230	240	8	2	0	0	0	0	0	0	0	0	0
240	250	9	3	0	0	0	0	0	0	0	0	0
250	260	10	4	0	0	0	0	0	0	0	0	0
260	270	11	5	0	0	0	0	0	0	0	0	0
270	280	12	6	0	0	0	0	0	0	0	0	0
280	290	13	7	1	0	0	0	0	0	0	0	0
290	300	14	8	2	0	0	0	0	0	0	0	0
300	310	15	9	3	0	0	0	0	0	0	0	0
310	320	16	10	4	0	0	0	0	0	0	0	0
320	330	17	11	5	0	0	0	0	0	0	0	0
330	340	18	12	6	0	0	0	0	0	0	0	0
340	350	19	13	7	1	0	0	0	0	0	0	0
350	360	20	14	8	2	0	0	0	0	0	0	0
360	370	21	15	9	3	0	0	0	0	0	0	0
370	380	22	16	10	4	0	0	0	0	0	0	0
380	390	23	17	11	5	0	0	0	0	0	0	0
390	400	24	18	12	6	0	0	0	0	0	0	0
400	410	25	19	13	7	1	0	0	0	0	0	0
410	420	26	20	14	8	2	0	0	0	0	0	0
420	430	27	21	15	9	3	0	0	0	0	0	0
430	440	28	22	16	10	4	0	0	0	0	0	0
440	450	30	23	17	11	5	0	0	0	0	0	0
450	460	31	24	18	12	6	0	0	0	0	0	0
460	470	33	25	19	13	7	1	0	0	0	0	0
470	480	34	26	20	14	8	2	0	0	0	0	0
480	490	36	27	21	15	9	3	0	0	0	0	0
490	500	37	28	22	16	10	4	0	0	0	0	0
500	510	39	30	23	17	11	5	0	0	0	0	0
510	520	40	31	24	18	12	6	0	0	0	0	0
520	530	42	33	25	19	13	7	1	0	0	0	0
530	540	43	34	26	20	14	8	2	0	0	0	0
540	550	45	36	27	21	15	9	3	0	0	0	0
550	560	46	37	29	22	16	10	4	0	0	0	0
560	570	48	39	30	23	17	11	5	0	0	0	0
570	580	49	40	32	24	18	12	6	0	0	0	0
580	590	51	42	33	25	19	13	7	1	0	0	0
590	600	52	43	35	26	20	14	8	2	0	0	0
600	610	54	45	36	27	21	15	9	3	0	0	0
610	620	55	46	38	29	22	16	10	4	0	0	0
620	630	57	48	39	30	23	17	11	5	0	0	0
630	640	58	49	41	32	24	18	12	6	0	0	0
640	650	60	51	42	33	25	19	13	7	1	0	0
650	660	61	52	44	35	26	20	14	8	2	0	0
660	670	63	54	45	36	27	21	15	9	3	0	0
670	680	64	55	47	38	29	22	16	10	4	0	0
680	690	66	57	48	39	30	23	17	11	5	0	0
690	700	67	58	50	41	32	24	18	12	6	0	0
700	710	69	60	51	42	33	25	19	13	7	1	0
710	720	70	61	53	44	35	26	20	14	8	2	0
720	730	72	63	54	45	36	27	21	15	9	3	0
730	740	73	64	56	47	38	29	22	16	10	4	0

MARRIED Persons—WEEKLY Payroll Period
(For Wages Paid Through December 2004)

If the wages are—		And the number of withholding allowances claimed is—										
At least	But less than	0	1	2	3	4	5	6	7	8	9	10
		The amount of income tax to be withheld is—										
$740	$750	$75	$66	$57	$48	$39	$30	$23	$17	$11	$5	$0
750	760	76	67	59	50	41	32	24	18	12	6	1
760	770	78	69	60	51	42	33	25	19	13	7	2
770	780	79	70	62	53	44	35	26	20	14	8	3
780	790	81	72	63	54	45	36	27	21	15	9	4
790	800	82	73	65	56	47	38	29	22	16	10	5
800	810	84	75	66	57	48	39	30	23	17	11	6
810	820	85	76	68	59	50	41	32	24	18	12	7
820	830	87	78	69	60	51	42	33	25	19	13	8
830	840	88	79	71	62	53	44	35	26	20	14	9
840	850	90	81	72	63	54	45	36	27	21	15	10
850	860	91	82	74	65	56	47	38	29	22	16	11
860	870	93	84	75	66	57	48	39	30	23	17	12
870	880	94	85	77	68	59	50	41	32	24	18	13
880	890	96	87	78	69	60	51	42	33	25	19	14
890	900	97	88	80	71	62	53	44	35	26	20	15
900	910	99	90	81	72	63	54	45	36	27	21	16
910	920	100	91	83	74	65	56	47	38	29	22	17
920	930	102	93	84	75	66	57	48	39	30	23	18
930	940	103	94	86	77	68	59	50	41	32	24	19
940	950	105	96	87	78	69	60	51	42	33	25	20
950	960	106	97	89	80	71	62	53	44	35	26	21
960	970	108	99	90	81	72	63	54	45	36	27	22
970	980	109	100	92	83	74	65	56	47	38	29	23
980	990	111	102	93	84	75	66	57	48	39	30	24
990	1,000	112	103	95	86	77	68	59	50	41	32	25
1,000	1,010	114	105	96	87	78	69	60	51	42	33	26
1,010	1,020	115	106	98	89	80	71	62	53	44	35	27
1,020	1,030	117	108	99	90	81	72	63	54	45	36	28
1,030	1,040	118	109	101	92	83	74	65	56	47	38	29
1,040	1,050	120	111	102	93	84	75	66	57	48	39	31
1,050	1,060	121	112	104	95	86	77	68	59	50	41	32
1,060	1,070	123	114	105	96	87	78	69	60	51	42	34
1,070	1,080	124	115	107	98	89	80	71	62	53	44	35
1,080	1,090	126	117	108	99	90	81	72	63	54	45	37
1,090	1,100	127	118	110	101	92	83	74	65	56	47	38
1,100	1,110	129	120	111	102	93	84	75	66	57	48	40
1,110	1,120	130	121	113	104	95	86	77	68	59	50	41
1,120	1,130	132	123	114	105	96	87	78	69	60	51	43
1,130	1,140	133	124	116	107	98	89	80	71	62	53	44
1,140	1,150	135	126	117	108	99	90	81	72	63	54	46
1,150	1,160	136	127	119	110	101	92	83	74	65	56	47
1,160	1,170	138	129	120	111	102	93	84	75	66	57	49
1,170	1,180	139	130	122	113	104	95	86	77	68	59	50
1,180	1,190	141	132	123	114	105	96	87	78	69	60	52
1,190	1,200	142	133	125	116	107	98	89	80	71	62	53
1,200	1,210	144	135	126	117	108	99	90	81	72	63	55
1,210	1,220	145	136	128	119	110	101	92	83	74	65	56
1,220	1,230	147	138	129	120	111	102	93	84	75	66	58
1,230	1,240	148	139	131	122	113	104	95	86	77	68	59
1,240	1,250	150	141	132	123	114	105	96	87	78	69	61
1,250	1,260	152	142	134	125	116	107	98	89	80	71	62
1,260	1,270	155	144	135	126	117	108	99	90	81	72	64
1,270	1,280	157	145	137	128	119	110	101	92	83	74	65
1,280	1,290	160	147	138	129	120	111	102	93	84	75	67
1,290	1,300	162	148	140	131	122	113	104	95	86	77	68
1,300	1,310	165	150	141	132	123	114	105	96	87	78	70
1,310	1,320	167	153	143	134	125	116	107	98	89	80	71
1,320	1,330	170	155	144	135	126	117	108	99	90	81	73
1,330	1,340	172	158	146	137	128	119	110	101	92	83	74
1,340	1,350	175	160	147	138	129	120	111	102	93	84	76
1,350	1,360	177	163	149	140	131	122	113	104	95	86	77
1,360	1,370	180	165	150	141	132	123	114	105	96	87	79
1,370	1,380	182	168	153	143	134	125	116	107	98	89	80
1,380	1,390	185	170	155	144	135	126	117	108	99	90	82
1,390	1,400	187	173	158	146	137	128	119	110	101	92	83

$1,400 and over Use Table 1(b) for a **MARRIED person** on page 3. Also see the instructions on page 2.

To simplify the process of determining these deductions, many businesses use a tax table. The *Employer's Tax Guide* (*Circular E*) contains such a table.

In any calendar year (January 1 to December 31), only a certain amount of gross earnings is subject to tax. When an employee's earnings reach the maximum amount (called the *tax base*), no further deductions are made during that year. Like the tax rates, the tax bases change periodically.

Businesses must contribute to the social security program by paying an employer's tax. This tax is equal to the amount of tax deducted from the earnings of the employees.

■ COMPUTING NET PAY

After all deductions for an employee have been determined, the amounts are added. The total of the deductions is then subtracted from the employee's gross earnings for the period. The resulting figure is the employee's ***net pay,*** or ***take-home pay.*** This is the amount that the employee actually receives.

Net Pay: Amount that an employee receives after deductions are subtracted from gross earnings.

John Christopher had three deductions for the week ended May 22. The total of these deductions is $48.16. Thus, Christopher's net pay for the period is $319.84 ($368 − $48.16 = $319.84).

■ PREPARING PAYROLL RECORDS

Government regulations make it necessary for businesses to keep records showing detailed information about payroll. Many firms use a payroll register and employee earnings records to satisfy these regulations.

Payroll Register: Record showing hours worked, gross earnings, deductions, and net pay of all employees for a pay period.

Payroll Register. At the end of the pay period, the hours worked, gross earnings, deductions, and net pay of all employees is entered in the ***payroll register.*** For employees on the hourly-rate plan, this information is taken from the time cards. An example of a payroll register is given below. Notice that the beginning and ending dates of the pay period are shown at the top of the payroll register sheet.

PAYROLL REGISTER

WEEK BEGINNING May 16, 20XX   AND ENDING May 22, 20XX   PAID May 25, 20XX

No.	Name	With. All.	Mar. Status	Hours Worked Reg.	Hours Worked OT	Reg. Hrly. Rate	Over-Time Rate	Earnings Regular	Earnings Over-Time	Earnings Total	Inc. Tax	Soc. Sec.	Medi-care	Deductions Total	Net Pay Amount	Ck. No.
1	Christopher, John	2	M	40	4	8 00	12 00	320 00	48 00	368 00	9 00	22 82	5 34	37 16	330 84	752
2	Kinney, David Chapman	1	S	40	5	8 50	12 75	340 00	63 75	403 75	37 00	25 03	5 85	67 89	335 86	753
3	Pfeffenberger, Doug	2	S	40	2	8 40	12 60	336 00	25 20	361 20	22 00	22 39	5 24	49 63	311 57	754
4	Rudy, John	4	M	40	3	7 50	11 25	300 00	33 75	333 75	0	20 69	4 84	25 53	308 22	755
5	Saleha, Begum	3	M	40	1	8 00	12 00	320 00	12 00	332 00	0	20 58	4 81	25 39	306 61	756
	Totals							1,616 00	182 70	1,798 70	68 00	111 52	26 08	205 60	1,593 10	

The payroll register should be totaled and proved before the employees are paid. The cross-footing method is used to verify the accuracy of the amounts.

1. The totals of the Regular Earnings column and the Overtime Earnings column are added. The sum of these amounts must equal the total of the Total Earnings column.
2. The totals of the Income Tax, the Social Security, and the Medicare columns are added. The sum of these amounts must equal the total of the Total Deductions column.
3. The total of the Total Deductions column is subtracted from the total of the Total Earnings column. The resulting figure must equal the total of the Net Pay column.

When the payroll checks are issued, the date of payment and the check numbers are entered in the payroll register.

Employee Earnings Record. The information in the payroll register is transferred to *employee earnings records.* A separate earnings record is set up for each employee at the beginning of the year. Entries are made in this record throughout the year as each pay period ends. Thus the earnings record contains complete payroll information for the employee. An example of this type of record is shown below.

Notice that there is a column for entering the *year-to-date earnings*—the employee's gross earnings from the beginning of the year to the current date. This column makes it easy to see whether the employee has reached the maximum amount of yearly earnings subject to social security tax.

> **Employee Earnings Record:** Record showing complete payroll information for an employee during a year.
>
> **Year-to-Date Earnings:** An employee's gross earnings from the beginning of the year to the current date.

■ PAYING THE EMPLOYEES

There are several different methods for paying employees. The most common practice is to prepare a check for each employee. However, some businesses make cash payments. In this case, each employee is given a pay envelope containing currency and coins. Other businesses have their bank place each employee's net pay in his or her checking account. This method is called *direct deposit* because the money is transferred from the firm's account directly into each employee's account.

> **Direct Deposit:** Net pay earned by the employee is transferred directly to the employee's bank account.

EMPLOYEE EARNINGS RECORD FOR THE YEAR 20XX

NAME: John Christopher
ADDRESS: 2761 Pinewood Avenue
Houston, Texas 77047

SOCIAL SECURITY NO. 424-08-9572
MARITAL STATUS: Married
POSITION: Delivery Truck Driver

WITHHOLDING EXEMPTIONS: 2

Period Ending	Rate Reg.	Rate OT.	Hours Reg.	Hours OT.	Earnings Regular	Earnings Overtime	Earnings Total	Year-To-Date Earnings	Income Tax	Deductions Soc. Sec.	Deductions Medicare	Deductions Total	Net Pay
Jan. 7	8	12	40		320 00		320 00		14 00	19 84	4 64	38 48	281 52
May 22	8	12	40	4	320 00	48 00	368 00	6,780 00	9 00	22 82	5 34	37 16	330 84

Many businesses provide each employee with a *pay statement* listing the hours worked, gross earnings, deductions, and net pay. This statement is usually attached to the payroll check, or it appears on the front of the pay envelope. The necessary information is obtained from the payroll register.

> **Pay Statement:** A form listing payroll information, which is given to an employee at the end of a pay period.

■ RECORDING THE PAYROLL

After the payroll is computed, it must be recorded in the general journal. The amounts needed for this entry come from the payroll register.

GENERAL JOURNAL Page 10

	Date	Description	Post. Ref.	Debit	Credit	
1	20 XX					1
2	May 22	Salaries and Wages Expense	511	1 798 70		2
3		Employee Income Tax Payable	221		68 00	3
4		Social Security Tax Payable	222		111 52	4
5		Medicare Tax Payable	226		26 08	5
6		Salaries and Wages Payable	225		1 593 10	6
7		Payroll for the week ended May 22.				7

The total of the employee earnings represents an expense for the business and is debited to the Salaries and Wages Expense account. The taxes deducted from employee earnings are liabilities until the money is sent to the government. The totals of these taxes are credited to the Employee Income Tax Payable account, the Social Security Tax Payable account, and the Medicare Tax Payable account. The total of the net pay is a liability until the employees are paid. It is therefore credited to the Salaries and Wages Payable account.

When the payroll checks are issued, an entry must be made in the cash payments journal. The total of the net pay is debited to the Salaries and Wages Payable account, and the amount of each check is credited to the Cash account.

CASH PAYMENTS JOURNAL
FOR MONTH OF MAY, 20XX
Page 5

	Date	Ck. No.	Explanation	✓	Accounts Receivable Debit	Merch. Purchase Debit	Other Accounts Debit Account Name	Post. Ref.	Amount	Purchase Discount Credit	Cash Credit	
1	20XX											1
2	May											2
5	25	752	Christopher, John				Salaries and Wages				330 84	5
6		753	Kinney, David				Payable	225	1 593 10			6
7			Chapman								335 86	7
8		754	Pfeffenberger, Doug								311 57	8
9		755	Rudy, John								308 22	9
10		756	Saleha, Begum								306 61	10

If the employees are paid in cash, a single check is drawn in order to obtain the necessary currency and coins for the pay envelopes. The entry recorded in the cash payments journal is the same as the one shown above except that only one check number is listed.

■ RECORDING THE EMPLOYER'S PAYROLL TAXES

> **WWW Inquiry**
> Find the URL address for the Internal Revenue Service. What is Publ 225?

Most businesses are subject to several payroll taxes—the employer's social security tax, Medicare tax, federal unemployment tax, and state unemployment tax. Remember that businesses must contribute to the social security program by paying taxes equal to the amounts deducted from employee earnings. In addition, the federal and state governments impose unemployment taxes on businesses. The money from these taxes is used to provide benefits for jobless workers.

Unemployment tax rates and regulations vary somewhat among the states. Also, the federal and state governments increase their rates from time to time. Another factor that determines the state tax to be paid is the merit-rating system. Under this system, businesses that give steady employment pay a reduced rate. Most states have such a system.

The payroll register on page 232 lists total employee earnings of $1,798.70 for the weekly pay period ended May 22. Let's assume that the business has the following payroll taxes: employer's social security tax of 6.2 percent on a base of $72,600, Medicare tax on all wages, federal unemployment tax of 0.8 percent on a base of $7,000, and state unemployment tax of 4.7 percent on a base of $7,000. (Remember that the tax base is the maximum amount of each employee's yearly earnings on which tax is paid.) If all earnings from the May 22 pay period are taxable, the business's payroll taxes would be computed as follows:

Employer's Social Security Tax	$1,798.70	×	0.062	=	$111.52
Employer's Medicare Tax	1,798.70	×	0.0145	=	26.08
Federal Unemployment Tax	1,798.70	×	0.008	=	14.39
State Unemployment Tax	1,798.70	×	0.047	=	84.54
Total					$236.53

After these payroll taxes are computed, they must be recorded in the general journal as shown on page 235.

Payroll taxes represent an expense for the business and are therefore debited to the Payroll Taxes Expense account. The amount owed for each type of tax is a liability until it is paid to the proper government agency. Thus four liability accounts are credited: Social Security Tax Payable, Medicare Tax Payable, Federal Unemployment Tax Payable, and State Unemployment Tax Payable.

GENERAL JOURNAL Page 10

	Date	Description	Post Ref.	Debit	Credit
1	20XX				
2	May				
3	22	Payroll Taxes Expense	518	236 53	
4		Social Security Tax Payable	222		111 52
5		Medicare Tax Payable	226		26 08
6		Federal Unemployment Tax Payable	223		14 39
7		State Unemployment Tax Payable	224		84 54
8		Employer's taxes on May 22 payroll.			

Federal and state laws specify when a business must pay taxes. The dates for submitting federal income tax withholdings, social security and Medicare taxes and federal unemployment taxes vary according to the amounts owed. State unemployment taxes are usually paid quarterly. When the taxes are paid, the following entries are recorded in the cash payments journal. Notice that the tax liability accounts are debited and the Cash account is credited.

CASH PAYMENTS JOURNAL FOR MONTH OF JULY, 20XX Page 7

	Date	Ck. No.	Explanation	✓	Accounts Receivable Debit	Merch. Purchase Debit	Other Accounts Debit Account Name	Post. Ref.	Amount	Purchase Discount Credit	Cash Credit
1	20XX										
2	July 25	809	Deposit of				Empl. Inc Tax Pay.	221	1032 50		
3			employee inc.				Soc. Sec. Tax Pay.	222	916 01		
4			tax, soc. sec. tax,				Medicare Tax Pay.	226	211 39		2159 90
5			and Medicare tax				State Unemployment				
6	25	810	Deposit of sec.				Tax Payable	224	1044 34		1044 34
7			quarter state				Fed. Unemployment				
8			unempl. tax				Tax Payable	223	182 33		182 33
9	25	811	Deposit of sec.								
10			quarter federal								
11			unempl. tax								

■ PAYROLL TAX FORMS

The federal government requires businesses to prepare a number of payroll tax forms. For example, at the end of each quarter, it is necessary to submit an *Employer's Quarterly Federal Tax Return* (*Form 941*) to the Internal Revenue Service. This form reports the federal income tax withholdings and the social security and Medicare taxes for the quarter.

In January of each year, the business must prepare a *Wage and Tax Statement* (*Form W-2*) for each employee, showing the employee's earnings, federal income tax withheld, and social security and Medicare tax withheld during the previous year. If there are state and city income taxes, these amounts are also shown on Form W-2. The employee receives two or more copies of this form. The business also sends a copy of each employee's Form W-2 to the Social Security Administration along with a *Transmittal of Income and Tax Statements* (*Form W-3*).

Another tax form that must be filed in January of each year is the Employer's *Annual Federal Unemployment Tax Return* (*Form 940*). This form reports the business's federal unemployment tax for the previous year.

Businesses usually pay federal income tax withholdings and social security and Medicare taxes (both the employee's and employer's contributions) by depositing them in a bank that the Internal Revenue Service has authorized to receive these taxes. Each payment must be accompanied by a *Federal Tax Deposit* (*Form 8109*). These forms are available on the IRS website.

State and city tax agencies may also require that employers prepare a variety of payroll tax forms.

CHAPTER 26 SUMMARY

- The total amount an employee earns is known as gross earnings. This amount can be computed in various ways according to the pay plan used. There are a number of different pay plans.

- Gross earnings may include both regular earnings and overtime earnings. By law, many employees are entitled to receive overtime pay for all time worked in excess of 40 hours a week. The overtime rate must be at least 1½ times the regular rate. Businesses must keep records such as time sheets or time cards in order to determine the number of regular hours and overtime hours.

- Net pay is usually less than gross earnings because most employees have deductions. Some deductions such as federal income tax withholding, social security, and Medicare tax are required. Other deductions are voluntary.

- The amount of federal income tax withheld for each employee depends on the employee's gross earnings, marital status, and number of withholding allowances. The social security and Medicare taxes are a percentage of the employee's gross earnings. When the earnings reach a certain maximum amount in any year, no further deductions are made during that year for social security.

- By law, businesses must keep detailed records of the hours worked, gross earnings, deductions, and net pay of their employees. For this reason, many businesses prepare a payroll register and employee earnings records.

- After the payroll is computed, it must be recorded in the general journal. When the employees are paid, an entry is made in the cash payments journal.

- Most businesses are subject to several payroll taxes—the employer's social security and Medicare tax, federal unemployment tax, and state unemployment tax. After the payroll amounts are determined, these taxes are computed and recorded in the general journal. As checks are issued to send the payroll taxes to the proper agencies, entries are made in the cash payments journal.

- Businesses must prepare a number of payroll tax forms for the federal government. Other payroll tax forms may be required by state and city tax agencies.

CHAPTER APPLICATIONS

EXERCISES

Complete the following assignments on the forms provided in your workbook.

EXERCISE 26-1

Computing gross earnings under the salary plan.

Instructions:
On the form in your workbook compute the salary for each pay period.

	Pay Period				
	Yearly	Monthly	Semi-monthly	Biweekly	Weekly
Example	$18,480	$1,540	$770	$711	$355
1	17,600				
2	19,654				
3	22,450				
4	28,900				

EXERCISE 26-2

Computing gross earnings under the hourly-rate plan. Reilly Transport pays its employees 1½ times the regular rate of pay for all time worked beyond 40 hours in a week.

Instructions:
Compute the regular earnings, overtime earnings, and gross earnings for each employee.

Employee	Rate per Hour	Hours Total	Hours Reg.	Hours OT.	Earnings Reg.	Earnings OT.	Earnings Gross
J. Burke	$9.00	48					
M. Casciola	10.75	44					
A. Elyse	10.20	46					
Z. Evans	10.50	49					

EXERCISE 26-3

Computing gross earnings under the piece-rate plan. Cajobi Manufacturing pays its employees $0.50 for each unit produced. Listed below are the employees and the number of units they produced during the week ended May 17.

Instructions:
Compute the total number of units produced and the gross earnings for each employee.

Employee	Monday	Tuesday	Wednesday	Thursday	Friday	Total Units	Gross Earnings
D. Kinney	148	145	162	138	150		
D. Pfeffenberger	152	155	158	140	153		
J. Rudy	156	149	152	158	155		
B. Seleha	146	148	152	145	149		

EXERCISE 26-4

Computing gross earnings under the commission plan. Casertano's Department Store pays its salespeople a 10 percent commission on their weekly sales. The employees and their sales for the week ended August 9 are listed below.

Instructions:
Compute the total sales and the gross earnings for each employee.

Employee	Monday	Tuesday	Wednesday	Thursday	Friday	Saturday	Total Sales	Gross Earnings
J. Bossone	$700	$690		$850	$490	$810		
B. Cannuli	520		$410	660	905	750		
S. Leacy		752	694	558	625	807		
L. McGovern	650	590		942	639	825		

EXERCISE 26-5

Computing gross earnings under the salary-commission plan. Seltzer Products pays its salespeople a salary of $150 a week plus a commission of 5 percent of their weekly sales. Listed below are the employees and their total sales for the week ended March 15.

Instructions:
Compute the commission and gross earnings for each employee.

Employee	Total Sales	Salary	Commission	Gross Earnings
B. Shirley	$3946.00			
J. Smith	4013.00			
G. Spano	4575.00			
B. Wallace	4196.00			

EXERCISE 26-6

Computing payroll deductions and net pay, and recording the payroll. Sternberg Distributing pays its employees on a weekly basis. The employees and their withholding allowances, marital status, and gross earnings for the week ended January 7 are listed below.

Instructions:

1. Refer to the tax tables on pages 228 through 231 to determine the federal income tax withholding for each employee.

2. Use 6.2 percent to compute each employee's social security tax and 1.45 percent for each employee's Medicare tax.

3. Subtract the deductions from the gross earnings to compute the net pay for each employee.

4. Show the general journal entry that would be made to record the payroll.

Employee	Withholding Allowance	Marital Status	Gross Earnings	Income Tax	Social Security	Medicare	Total Deduction	Net Pay
S. Alverez	1	S	$560					
D. Oliver	2	M	640					
A. Russomano	3	M	650					
J. Warner	4	M	510					

EXERCISE 26-7

Computing and recording the employer's payroll taxes.

Instructions:

1. Refer to Exercise 26-6, and compute Sternberg Distributing's payroll taxes for the week ended January 7. The rates are as follows: social security tax, 6.2 percent; Medicare tax, 1.45 percent; federal unemployment tax, 0.8 percent; and state unemployment tax, 4.7 percent.

2. Show the general journal entry that would be made to record the employer's payroll taxes.

EXERCISE 26-8

Recording payroll entries. Allen Marcus, D.D.S., pays his dental assistant a weekly salary of $420. For the week ended January 12, this employee had the following earnings, deductions, and net pay.

Gross earnings		$420.00
Federal income tax	$50.00	
Social security tax	26.04	
Medicare tax	6.09	82.13
Net pay		$337.87

The employer's payroll taxes were computed as follows.

Social security tax	$26.04
Medicare tax	6.09
Federal unemployment tax	3.36
State unemployment tax	19.74

Instructions:
In general journal form, record (1) the payroll on January 12, (2) the employer's payroll taxes on January 12, and (3) the issuance of the payroll check.

EXERCISE 26-9

Recording payroll tax payments. On July 26, Surati Ceramics paid the following taxes to federal and state agencies.

Instructions:
Record the payments in general journal form.

1. Check 149 for $206 in payment of state unemployment tax.

2. Check 150 for $122 in payment of federal unemployment tax.

3. Check 151 for $1,910 in payment of federal income tax withholding of $1,375, social security tax of $434.69, and Medicare tax of $100.31.

PROBLEMS

Complete all assigned problems on the forms provided in your workbook.

PROBLEM 26-1

Completing a time card. Heather DeCosta is employed by the Reliable Electronics Company. She is single and claims one withholding allowance. Her time card for the week ended June 30 of the current year is given in the workbook.

Instructions:
Complete the time card as follows.

1. Determine and enter the number of hours worked each day. Also enter the regular hours, overtime hours, and total hours for the week. (The normal workday is from 8 A.M. to 12 noon and from 1 to 5 P.M. Don't count differences of 5 minutes or less from these times.)

2. Determine and enter the regular earnings, overtime earnings, and gross earnings. The hourly rates are shown on the time card.

3. Determine and enter the deductions. Use the tax table on page 228 of the text to find the amount of federal income tax to be withheld. Compute the social security tax and Medicare tax at the assumed rates of 6.2 percent and 1.45 percent respectively. This employee also has voluntary deductions of $5.50 for medical insurance and $10 for savings bonds. Be sure to record the total deductions.

4. Determine and enter the net pay.

PROBLEM 26-2

Completing a payroll register. Payroll information for the Felton Auto Parts Company is shown below. The hours worked cover the week of March 24–30 of the current year.

Instructions:

1. Determine the earnings, deductions, and net pay for each employee. Use the income tax tables on pages 228 through 231 of the text. Assume a social security tax rate of 6.2 percent and a Medicare tax rate of 1.45 percent.

2. Complete the payroll register given in the workbook. Cross-foot to prove the totals.

Employee No.	Name	Withholding Allowances	Marital Status
1	Del Rocco, Dawn	4	M
2	Galloway, Edna	2	S
3	Gilmour, James	5	M
4	McGrath, Daniel	1	S
5	Walsh, John	6	M
6	Yarrow, Jean Marie	3	M

Employee No.	Hours Worked Regular	Hours Worked Overtime	Hourly Rate Regular	Hourly Rate Overtime
1	40	5	$10.00	$15.00
2	40	7	9.50	14.25
3	40	3	9.00	13.50
4	40	2	10.60	15.90
5	40	4	9.40	14.10
6	40	9	10.20	15.30

PROBLEM 26-3

Recording payroll entries. The following information comes from the payroll register of Funk Tool Distributors. This information is for the week of June 22–28 of the current year.

Total Earnings	$1,976.80
Total Income Tax Deduction	327.70
Total Social Security Tax Deductions	122.56
Total Medicare Tax Deductions	28.66
Total Net Pay	1,497.88

Instructions:

1. Record the payroll in the general journal. Use 6 as the page number.

2. Determine the business's payroll taxes. Assume a rate of 6.2 percent for social security tax, a rate of 1.45 percent for Medicare tax, a rate of 0.8 percent for federal unemployment tax, and a rate of 4.7 for state unemployment tax.

3. Record the payroll taxes in the general journal.

PROBLEM 26-4

Recording payroll and tax payments.

Instructions:

Complete the following tasks for the Brower Office Supply Store. Use page 3 for the cash payments journal for this work.

1. Record the payment of the payroll for the biweekly period ended March 31 of the current year. Check 594 for $917.80 was issued to obtain the necessary cash on April 2.

2. Record the payment of state unemployment tax for the quarter ended March 31 of the current year. Check 595 for $191.30 was issued on April 26.

3. Record the payment of federal income tax, social security tax, and Medicare tax for March. The general ledger showed the following balances:

Employee Income Tax Payable	$483.45
Social Security Tax Payable	218.73
Medicare Tax Payable	50.48

Check 596 for the total taxes owed was issued on April 26.

4. Record the payment of federal unemployment tax for the quarter ended March 31 of the current year. Check 597 for $105.36 was issued on April 27.

CASE STUDY

Write the answer to the case study on the form provided in your workbook.

Payroll Processing

After working for three months in the office of Mark Casciola, you recognize that it costs the business time and money to accurately compute and record payroll transactions. You have learned about federal withholding, FICA tax, Medicare tax, state tax, local tax, and miscellaneous other accounts affecting payroll.

In addition to the regular employees, many workers are employed by Mr. Casciola on a free-lance basis as contractors. Taxes are not withheld for these contract workers.

Critical Thinking

■ *From your study of payroll records and procedures, what advantages and disadvantages do you see to the employer and employee of each method of payment?*

CHAPTER TWENTY-SEVEN

The Combined Journal

OBJECTIVES

Upon completion of this chapter, you should be able to:

1. Record transactions in a combined journal.
2. Total, prove, and rule the combined journal.
3. Post from the combined journal.

Accounting Terminology

- Combined journal
- Posting reference *C*

INTRODUCTION

Special journals provide an efficient way of recording transactions. However, some small businesses prefer to use a single multicolumn journal known as the *combined journal*. ■

■ RECORDING TRANSACTIONS IN THE COMBINED JOURNAL

The combined journal is suitable for a business that has a limited number of entries each month. The combined journal shown on pages 242 and 243 has special columns for Cash, Accounts Receivable, Accounts Payable, Merchandise Purchases, and Sales. All other transactions are recorded in the Other Accounts section of the journal.

The advantages and disadvantages of the combined journal can be seen by examining the entries made at the Bowen Paint Shop during June.

Cash Balance. At the beginning of each month, a memorandum entry is recorded in the combined journal to show the cash balance. Notice how this entry was made on June 1. A line was drawn through the Cash section, and "Cash balance, $9,187" was written in the Explanation column.

Payment of Expenses. The Bowen Paint Shop made several cash payments for expenses during June. For example, Check 413 for $800 was issued on June 2 to pay the rent. Because the business's combined journal does not have any special columns for expense accounts, the name of the account to be debited (Rent Expense) must be written in the Other Accounts section. The amount is recorded in the Other Accounts Debit column and the Cash Credit column. Additional examples of cash payments for expenses appear on lines 7, 8, and 26. The entries on lines 39 and 40 show the expenses that were recorded when the petty cash fund was replenished. The entry on line 43 is for the expense incurred when the bank deducted a service charge from the business's checking account.

Purchases of Merchandise on Credit. On June 3, the Bowen Paint Shop purchased merchandise for $1,700 on credit from the Durable Paint Company. The amount is recorded in the Merchandise Purchases Debit column and the Accounts Payable Credit column. Other entries for purchases of merchandise on credit appear on lines 12 and 20.

COMBINED JOURNAL

Line	Date	Check No.	Explanation	Cash Debit	Cash Credit	✓	A/R Debit	A/R Credit
1								
2	June 1		Cash balance, $9,187					
3	2	413	Rent for June		800 00			
4	3		Durable Paint Co.—Inv. 931; 6/1; 2/10, n/30					
5	4	414	Purchase of electronic calculator		165 00			
6	5		Perez Decorating Service—Sales Slip 689			✓	420 00	
7	6	415	Electric bill		107 40			
8	6	416	Telephone bill		89 60			
9	6		Cash sales for June 1–6	2875 00				
10	8		Hudson Painters—Sales Slip 690			✓	380 00	
11	9	417	Durable Paint Co.—Inv. 931		1666 00			
12	10	418	Cash purchase of merchandise		440 00			
13	11		Ideal Paint Corp.—Inv. 1233; 6/9; 2/20, n/60					
14	13		Perez Decorating Service—Sales Slip 689	411 60		✓		420 00
15	13		Cash sales for June 8–13	2790 00				
16	15	419	Withdrawal by owner		900 00			
17	17		Hudson Painters—Sales Slip 690	372 40		✓		380 00
18	19		Ideal Paint Corp.—CM95 on Inv. 1233					
19	20		Cash sales for June 15–20	1947 00				
20	22		Bell Contracting Co.—Sales Slip 691			✓	445 00	
21	23		Variety Paints, Inc.—Inv. A468; 6/20; n/30					
22	27	420	Ideal Paint Corp.—Inv. 1233 less CM95		1862 00			
23	27		Cash sales for June 22–27	2231 00				
24	29		Bell Contracting Co.—CM37 on					
25			Sales Slip 691			✓		25 00
26	30	421	Delivery service for June		67 00			
27	30		Payroll for June					
32	30		Employer's payroll taxes for June					
39	30	422	Payment of payroll		3015 66			
40	30		Cash sales for June 29 and 30	463 00				
41	30	423	Replenish petty cash fund		39 00			
43	30	—	Bank service charge for June		5 00			
44			Totals	11 090 00	9 156 66		1 245 00	825 00
45				(101)	(101)		(112)	(112)

Combined Journal:
Multicolumn journal that combines features of the general journal and several specific journals.

FOR MONTH OF JUNE, 20XX — Page 6

✓	Accounts Payable Debit	Accounts Payable Credit	Merch. Purch. Debit	Sales Credit	Other Accounts — Account Title	Post. Ref.	Debit	Credit	
									1
					Rent Expense	517	80 00		2
✓		1 70 00	1 70 00						3
					Office Equipment	123	1 65 00		4
				42 00					5
					Utilities Expense	519	1 07 40		6
					Telephone Expense	518	89 60		7
				2 87 50					8
				38 00					9
✓	1 70 00				Purchases Discount	504		34 00	10
			44 00						11
✓		1 98 00	1 98 00						12
					Sales Discount	403	8 40		13
				2 79 00					14
					Russell Owen, Withdrawals	302	90 00		15
					Sales Discount	403	7 60		16
✓	80 00				Purchases Ret. and Allow.	503		80 00	17
				1 94 70					18
				44 50					19
✓		63 00	63 00						20
✓	1 90 00				Purchases Discount	504		38 00	21
				2 23 10					22
					Sales Returns and				23
					Allowances	402	25 00		24
					Delivery Expense	512	67 00		25
					Wages Expense	520	3 72 6 00		26
					Employee Income Tax				27
					Payable	221		4 25 30	28
					Social Security Tax Payable	222		2 31 01	29
					Medicare Tax Payable	226		54 03	30
					Wages Payable	225		3 01 5 66	31
					Payroll Taxes Expense	516	4 15 45		32
					Social Security Tax Payable	222		2 31 01	33
					Medicare Tax Payable	226		54 03	34
					Federal Unemployment				35
					Tax Pay.	223		29 81	36
					State Unemployment Tax				37
					Payable	224		1 00 60	38
					Wages Payable	225	3 01 5 66		39
				4 63 00					40
					Miscellaneous Expense	515	18 70		41
					Office Expense	521	20 30		42
					Miscellaneous Expense	515	5 00		43
	3 6 8 0 00	4 3 1 0 00	4 7 5 0 00	11 5 5 1 00			9 3 7 1 11	4 2 9 3 45	44
	(202)	(202)	(501)	(401)			(X)	(X)	45

Purchases of Long-Term Assets. On June 4, the Bowen Paint Shop purchased an electronic calculator for use in the office. Check 414 for $165 was issued to pay for this purchase. The account to be debited (Office Equipment) is written in the Other Accounts section. The amount is recorded in the Other Accounts Debit column and the Cash Credit column.

Sales of Merchandise on Credit. The Bowen Paint Shop makes most of its sales for cash to individuals. However, the business sells on credit to several firms that paint houses, apartments, and offices. The terms for all credit customers are 2/10, n/30. On June 5, the Bowen Paint Shop sold merchandise for $420 on credit to the Perez Decorating Service. The amount is recorded in the Accounts Receivable Debit column and the Sales Credit column. Other entries for sales on credit appear on lines 9 and 19.

Sales of Merchandise for Cash. During the week of June 1–6, the Bowen Paint Shop had cash sales of $2,875. These sales were entered on June 6 by recording the total amount in the Cash Debit column and the Sales Credit column. Other entries for cash sales appear on lines 14, 18, 22, and 39.

Payments to Creditors. On June 9, the Bowen Paint Shop issued Check 417 for $1,666 to the Durable Paint Company for Invoice 931 ($1,700) less discount ($34). The total of the invoice is recorded in the Accounts Payable Debit column. Because there is no special column for purchases discount, the name of this account must be written in the Other Accounts section. The amount of the discount is entered in the Other Accounts Credit column. The amount of the cash payment is recorded in the Cash Credit column. Another entry for a payment to a creditor appears on line 21.

Cash Purchases of Merchandise. On June 10, the Bowen Paint Shop purchased merchandise for $440 in cash. Check 418 was issued for this purchase. The amount is recorded in the Merchandise Purchases Debit column and the Cash Credit column.

> **WWW Inquiry**
> Return to the URL address for Kellogg's. What is the percentage of current assets to total assets on its current balance sheet?

Cash Received From Credit Customers. On June 13, the Bowen Paint Shop received $411.60 in cash from the Perez Decorating Service for Sales Slip 689 ($420) less discount ($8.40). The amount of cash received is recorded in the Cash Debit column. Because there is no special column for sales discount, the name of this account must be written in the Other Accounts section. The amount of the discount is entered in the Other Accounts Debit column. The total of the sales slip is recorded in the Accounts Receivable Credit column. Another entry for cash received from a credit customer appears on line 16.

Withdrawals by the Owner. On June 15, the owner of the Bowen Paint Shop wanted to make a cash withdrawal of $900. Check 419 was issued for this purpose. The account to be debited (Russell Owen, Withdrawals) must be written in the Other Accounts section. The amount is recorded in the Other Accounts Debit column and the Cash Credit column.

Returns and Allowances on Credit Purchases. The Bowen Paint Shop returned some merchandise to the Ideal Paint Corporation and received Credit Memorandum 95 for $80 on June 19. The name of the account to be credited (Purchases Returns and Allowances) is written in the Other Accounts section. The amount is recorded in the Accounts Payable Debit column and the Other Accounts Credit column.

Returns and Allowances on Credit Sales. On June 29, the Bowen Paint Shop issued Credit Memorandum 37 for $25 to the Bell Contracting Company. This credit memorandum is for a return of merchandise that was sold on credit. The name of the account to be debited (Sales Returns and Allowances) is written in the Other Accounts section. The amount is recorded in the Other Accounts Debit column and the Accounts Receivable Credit column.

Employee Earnings and Deductions. The Bowen Paint Shop pays its employees at the end of each month. The payroll register prepared on June 30 showed total earnings of $3,726, total income tax deductions of $425.30, total social security tax deductions of $231.01, total Medicare tax deductions of $54.03, and total net pay of $3,015.66. Refer to lines 26–30. Because there are no special columns for the payroll accounts, the Other Accounts section must be used for this type of entry.

Employer's Payroll Taxes. The Bowen Paint Shop had the following taxes on the June payroll: employer's social security tax, $231.01; employer's Medicare tax, $54.03; federal unemployment tax, $29.81; and state unemployment tax, $100.60. These amounts were recorded in the combined journal on June 30. Refer to lines 31–37. Again, the Other Accounts section must be used.

Payment of the Payroll. On June 30, Check 422 for $3,015.66 was issued to obtain the cash needed to pay the employees of the Bowen Paint Shop. The account to be debited (Wages Payable) is written in the Other Accounts section. The amount is recorded in the Other Accounts Debit column and the Cash Credit column.

■ POSTING FROM THE COMBINED JOURNAL

During the month, the amounts in the Other Accounts section of the combined journal are posted individually to the general ledger accounts listed. As each amount is posted, the account number is written in the Posting Reference column of the journal. The abbreviation C and the journal page number are recorded in the ledger accounts to identify the source of the entry.

The amounts in the Accounts Receivable section and the Accounts Payable section are posted individually to the subsidiary ledger accounts shown in the Explanation column. As each amount is posted, a check mark is placed in the journal.

At the end of the month, the money columns of the combined journal are pencil-footed. Then a proof is prepared to check the equality of the debits and credits recorded in the journal.

Posting from the Combined Journal:
- During the month, post individual entries in Other Accounts section to general ledger. Post individual entries in Accounts Receivable section and Accounts Payable section to subsidiary ledgers.
- At end of month, post all column totals to general ledger except totals in Other Accounts section.

BOWEN PAINT SHOP
PROOF OF COMBINED JOURNAL
MONTH ENDED JUNE 30, 20XX

	Debit	Credit
Cash	$11,090.00	$9,156.66
Accounts Receivable	1,245.00	825.00
Accounts Payable	3,680.00	4,310.00
Merchandise Purchases	4,750.00	
Sales		11,551.00
Other Accounts	9,371.11	4,293.45
Totals	$30,136.11	$30,136.11

After the proof is completed, the column totals are entered in ink and the journal is ruled. The totals are posted to the general ledger accounts named in the column headings. As these postings are made, the account numbers are recorded below the totals in the journal. The letter X is entered below the totals of the Other Accounts section to show that they are not posted. (Remember that the amounts in the Other Accounts section are posted individually during the month.)

The combined journal is convenient for the Bowen Paint Shop. However, it would present problems for a business that had more transactions to record. The large number of

WWW Inquiry
Return to the URL address for Kellogg's. Refer to the notes to the financial statements to determine how Kellogg's depreciates fixed assets.

CHAPTER 27 SUMMARY

- Some small businesses use a combined journal. These businesses find it more convenient to have a single multicolumn journal than a general journal and several special journals.
- In the combined journal, special columns are provided for recording the types of transactions that occur most often, such as those involving cash, accounts receivable, accounts payable, merchandise purchases, and sales.
- During the month, the amounts in the Other Accounts section are posted individually to the general ledger. The amounts in the Accounts Receivable section and the Accounts Payable section are posted individually to the subsidiary ledgers.
- At the end of the month, the money columns of the combined journal are pencil-footed. Then the equality of the debits and credits is proved.
- After the combined journal is totaled and ruled, the totals of the special columns are posted to the general ledger.

columns increases the likelihood of making errors when entering amounts. Also, only one person at a time can journalize or post transactions. In contrast, when special journals are used, several employees can do accounting work at the same time.

CHAPTER APPLICATIONS

EXERCISES

Complete the following assignments on the forms provided in your workbook.

EXERCISE 27-1

Using a combined journal. The Pilot Store uses a combined journal that provides the following column headings.

a. Cash Debit
b. Cash Credit
c. Accounts Receivable Debit
d. Accounts Receivable Credit
e. Accounts Payable Debit
f. Accounts Payable Credit
g. Merchandise Purchases Debit
h. Sales Credit
i. Other Accounts Debit
j. Other Accounts Credit

Instructions:
1. Decide which columns should be used to record each of the following transactions.
2. List the number of the transaction.
3. Write the identifying letters of the columns next to the number of the transaction.

Transactions:

Example: *Issued Check 81 to pay the electric bill.*

Debit	Credit
i	b

1. Issued Check 82 for $100 to establish a petty cash fund.
2. Purchased merchandise for $800 on credit from Ace Distributing, Invoice 631, terms 2/10, n/30.
3. Purchased office supplies for $370 on credit from Office Forms.
4. Issued Invoice 824 for $560 for the sale of merchandise on credit to Lauren Van Hook.
5. Issued Check 83 for $784 to Ace Distributing in payment of Invoice 631; $800 less a discount of $16.
6. Issued Check 84 for $500 to Sam McDonough as a withdrawal for personal use.
7. Returned damaged office supplies to Office Forms and received Credit Memorandum 98 for $37.
8. Issued Credit Memorandum 39 for $60 to Lauren Van Hook for the return of defective merchandise sold on Invoice 824.
9. Received $525 for cash sales.
10. Received $500 from Lauren Van Hook in payment of the balance due on Invoice 824.

EXERCISE 27-2

Recording payroll entries in a combined journal.
Jackson Advertising records its payroll entries in the combined journal columns that follow.

Date	Check No.	Cash Debit	Cash Credit	Account Name	Other Accounts Debit	Other Accounts Credit

Instructions:
Record the following transactions.

July 18 payroll:
Gross earnings		$ 3,000
Federal income tax withheld	$ 540	
Social security tax	186	
Medicare tax	43.50	769.50
Net pay		$2,230.50

July 18 employer's payroll taxes:
Social security tax	$ 186
Medicare tax	43.50
Federal unemployment tax	24
State unemployment tax	141

July 20 payroll checks:
No. 264 Ann Bronski	$ 560
No. 265 Robert Ming	550
No. 266 Stanley Preston	485
No. 267 Judith Sanchez	635.50

PROBLEMS

Complete all assigned problems on the forms provided in your workbook.

PROBLEM 27-1

Using a combined journal. The transactions that took place at the Russell Carpet Store during May of the current year are listed below. This business makes most of its sales for cash to individuals. However, some merchandise is sold on credit to decorators and various organizations. The terms for such sales are 2/10, n/30.

Instructions:

1. Record each of the May transactions in the combined journal. Before you begin, make a memorandum entry for the cash balance of $4,327.85 on May 1.
2. Pencil-foot the money columns. Then prepare a proof of the combined journal as of May 31.
3. Enter the column totals, and rule the combined journal.

Transactions:

May 1 Issued Check 323 for $550 to pay the monthly rent for the store.
2 Sold merchandise for $685 on credit to Pat Lutz; Sales Slip 220.
3 Issued Check 324 for $142.50 to pay for newspaper advertisements.
4 Purchased merchandise for $3,218 on credit from the Gosling Carpet Company; Invoice 2417, dated 5/1, terms 2/10, n/30.
6 Sold merchandise for $1,892.75 in cash during May 1–6.
8 Issued Check 325 for $3,153.64 to the Gosling Carpet Company for Invoice 2417; $3,218 less a discount of $64.36.
10 Sold merchandise for $2,186 on credit to the Frederick Motel; Sales Slip 221.
11 Received $671.30 in cash from Pat Lutz for Sales Slip 220; $685 less a discount of $13.70.
13 Sold merchandise for $1,327.92 in cash during May 8–13.
15 Purchased merchandise for $2,280 on credit from Lighthouse Rugs, Inc.; Invoice 961, dated 5/12, terms 1/20, n/60.
17 Issued Check 326 for $999.99 to purchase a computer for use in the office.
19 Received $2,142.28 in cash from the Frederick Motel for Sales Slip 221; $2,186 less a discount of $43.72.
20 Sold merchandise for $1,594.68 in cash during May 15–20.
22 Returned some damaged merchandise that was purchased from Lighthouse Rugs, Inc. (Invoice 961). Received Credit Memorandum 72 for $130.
24 Issued Check 327 for $129.67 to pay the electric bill.
25 Sold merchandise for $346 on credit to Harry Snyder; Sales Slip 222.
27 Sold merchandise for $1,721.40 in cash during May 22–27.
29 Issued Check 328 for $1,200 for a cash withdrawal by Phyllis Elitsky, the owner.
31 Issued Check 329 for $189.70 to pay for delivery service during May.
31 Computed the payroll for May. The amounts are as follows: total earnings, $1,950; total income tax deductions, $256.50; total social security tax deductions, $120.90; total Medicare tax deductions, $28.28; total net pay, $1,544.32.
31 Computed the business's payroll taxes for May. The amounts are as follows: employer's social security tax, $120.90; employer's Medicare tax, $28.28; federal unemployment tax, $15.60; state unemployment tax, $91.65.
31 Issued Check 330 for $1,544.32 to obtain the cash needed for payment of the payroll.
31 Sold merchandise for $789.65 in cash during May 29–31.

CASE STUDY

Write the answer to the case study on the form provided in your workbook.

The Combination Journal

Your brother would like you to help him create and organize the books for a garden supply business he is creating on the World Wide Web. He anticipates the following accounts in the beginning:

    Cash
    Accounts Receivable
    Accounts Payable
    Sales
    Purchases
    Capital
    Drawing
    Expenses

Critical Thinking

- *Since he expects a few sales per week, he thinks he should use a combination journal but would like your opinion. What do you think? Why?*

PRACTICE SET

This practice set provides you with a practical application of the accounting procedures that have been explained in the text. In this set, you will complete the accounting work for Brennan Lighting for the month of May.

The Business

Brennan Lighting sells interior, exterior, and security lighting fixtures and electrical supplies for cash and on credit. Credit sales are made to electrical contractors, lighting consultants, and interior decorators. Cash sales are made to individuals who need flood or track lighting, lamps, fixtures, switches, and bulbs. A 6 percent sales tax is charged on all sales. A one percent discount is allowed on credit sales if payment is received within 10 days from the date of sale.

Tricia Brennan owns and operates the business. She is assisted by seven employees. The employees are paid semimonthly.

The Accounting System

The Accounting system includes special journals for sales, purchase, cash receipts, and cash payments. The business also uses a general journal, a general ledger, and subsidiary ledgers for accounts receivable and accounts payable. The chart of accounts follows.

General Instructions

The journals, ledger accounts, worksheet, and other accounting forms are provided in the workbook. The May 1 balances have been recorded in the accounts.

Record each of the transactions in the proper journal. Post amounts individually from the general journal and from the Other Accounts section of the cash receipts journal and cash payments journal. Post entries to the subsidiary ledgers on a daily basis.

Remember to record the cash on hand in the cash receipts journal. Refer to the Cash account in the general ledger to obtain the May 1 balance.

Brennan Lighting
Chart of Accounts

Assets
- 101 Cash
- 102 Petty Cash
- 111 Notes Receivable
- 112 Accounts Receivable
- 113 Allowance for Uncollectible Accounts
- 114 Merchandise Inventory
- 115 Supplies
- 116 Prepaid Insurance
- 121 Store Equipment
- 122 Accumulated Depreciation—Store Equipment
- 123 Office Equipment
- 124 Accumulated Depreciation—Office Equipment

Liabilities
- 201 Notes Payable
- 202 Accounts Payable
- 221 Employee Income Tax Payable
- 222 Social Security Tax Payable
- 223 Medicare Tax Payable
- 224 Federal Unemployment Tax Payable
- 225 State Unemployment Tax Payable
- 226 Salaries Payable
- 231 Sales Tax Payable

Owner's Equity
- 301 Tricia Brennan, Capital
- 302 Tricia Brennan, Withdrawals
- 399 Income Summary

Revenue
- 401 Sales
- 402 Sales Returns and Allowances
- 403 Sales Discount

Other Income
- 491 Interest Income

Costs and Expenses
- 501 Merchandise Purchases
- 502 Freight In
- 503 Purchases Returns and Allowances
- 504 Purchases Discount
- 511 Advertising Expense
- 512 Telephone Expense
- 513 Depreciation Expense—Store Equipment
- 514 Depreciation Expense—Office Equipment
- 516 Payroll Taxes Expense
- 517 Rent Expense
- 518 Supplies Expense
- 519 Utilities Expense
- 520 Salaries Expense
- 521 Uncollectible Accounts Expense
- 522 Insurance Expense
- 536 Miscellaneous Expense
- 591 Interest Expense

Transactions for May 1–6

May 1 Issued Check 425 for $2,750 to Hager Realty for monthly rent.

1 Sold merchandise for $1,950 plus $117 sales tax on credit to Botzer Builders; Invoice 507, terms 1/10, n/30.

2 Purchased merchandise for $5,240.72 plus a freight charge of $92.60 on credit from

Grady Transportation Company; Invoice CA74, dated May 1, terms 2/10, n/30.

2 Received $2,574 from Leidy and Gabriel for the balance due on their account.

3 Issued Check 426 for $1,080 to pay the six-month premium for fire and theft insurance.

4 Issued Check 427 for $125 to pay for a newspaper advertisement.

5 Purchased merchandise for $3,800.65 plus a freight charge of $197 from Baskets by Pat; Invoice 264, dated May 2, terms 2/10, n/30.

6 Received $11,299.83 for weekly cash sales of $10,660.22 plus $639.61 sales tax.

Transactions for May 8–13

May 8 Received a 20-day, 12 percent promissory note for $3,750 from Duld Lighting in settlement of its balance due.

8 Received $2,047.50 from Botzer Builders for Invoice 507 of May 1 ($2,067), less a $19.50 discount.

8 Purchased merchandise for $4,596.80 plus a freight charge of $87.56 from Grady Transportation Company; Invoice CA92, dated May 8, terms 2/10, n/30.

9 Purchased merchandise for $2,764.86 from Kennedy Welding Supply; Invoice 247, dated May 8, terms 2/10, n/30.

10 Sold merchandise for $3,690.70 plus $221.44 sales tax to Fagan Contractors; Invoice 508, terms 1/10, n/30.

10 Issued Check 428 for $5,228.51 to Grady Transportation Company for Invoice CA74; $5,333.32 less a $104.81 discount.

12 Issued Check 429 for $3,921.64 to Baskets by Pat for Invoice 264; $3,997.65 less a $76.01 discount.

12 Received Invoice 326 for $325 from Ruth Ann's Service for cleaning services terms net 30.

13 Issued a 30-day, 12 percent promissory note for $7,962 to Brian's Lamp Manufacturing in settlement of its account.

13 Issued Check 430 for $2,747.96 to pay employee income tax withholdings and the employer's and employee's social security and Medicare tax due. The amounts are income tax $874, social security tax $1,518.76, and Medicare tax $355.20.

13 Issued Check 431 for $3,221.36 to pay the sales tax collected in April.

13 Purchased merchandise for $3,790.24 from Gardzinski Electric; Invoice D27, dated May 11, terms 1/15, n/30.

13 Received $12,848.76 for weekly cash sales of $12,121.47 plus $727.29 sales tax.

Transactions for May 15–20

May 15 Issued Check 432 for $1,967.24 to Lamp Outlet for the cash purchase of merchandise.

15 Issued Check 433 for $864.54 to pay the telephone bill.

15 Recorded the payroll for the semimonthly period ended May 15. The payroll register shows the following amounts: total earnings $6,124; total income tax deductions, $437; total employee's social security tax deductions, $379.69; total employee's Medicare tax deductions, $88.80; and total net pay, $5,218.51.

15 Recorded the payroll taxes for the semimonthly period. The amounts are as follows: employer's social security tax $379.69; employer's Medicare tax $88.80; federal unemployment tax $48.99; and state unemployment tax $287.83.

15 Issued Check 434 for $5,218.51 to obtain the cash to pay the May 15 payroll.

15 Issued Check 435 for $1,500 for a cash withdrawal by Tricia Brennan, the owner.

16 Issued Check 436 for $276.52 to Van Lieu Freight Lines to pay for transportation charges on merchandise.

17 Issued Check 437 for $50 to increase the petty cash fund to $100.

17 Issued Check 438 for $4,592.42 to Grady Transportation Company for Invoice CA92; $4,684.36 less a $91.94 discount.

17 Issued Check 439 for $2,709.56 to Kennedy Welding Supply for Invoice 247; $2,764.86 less a $55.30 discount.

18 Issued Check 440 for $4,876 to purchase a new computer for the office.

19 Issued Check 441 for $325 to Ruth Ann's Service to pay the May 1 balance in its account.

20   Received $3,875.23 from Fagan Contractors for Invoice 408 of May 10 ($3,912.14 less a $36.91 discount).

20   Purchased merchandise for $5,927.60 plus a freight charge of $215.82 from Baskets by Pat; Invoice 296, dated May 18, terms 2/10, n/30.

20   Received $13,134.29 for weekly cash sales of $12,390.84 plus $743.45 sales tax.

Transactions for May 22–27

May 22   Returned damaged merchandise purchased from Baskets by Pat (Invoice 296). Received Credit Memorandum 247 for $638.46.

23   Sold merchandise for $3,862.50 plus $231.75 sales tax to Illuminations; Invoice 509, terms 1/10, n/30.

23   Sold merchandise for $2,486.80 plus $149.21 sales tax to Botzer Builders; Invoice 510, terms 1/10, n/30.

24   Issued Check 442 for $3,752.34 to Gardzinski Electric for Invoice D27; $3,790.24 less a $37.90 discount.

24   Purchased merchandise for $3,127.06 from Kennedy Welding Supply Invoice 342, dated May 22, terms 2/10, n/30.

24   Purchased merchandise for $1,560.47 plus a freight charge of $127.50 from Brian's Lamp Manufacturing; Invoice 6-07, dated May 23, terms 2/10, n/30.

24   Sold merchandise for $3,094.26 plus $185.66 sales tax to Leidy and Gabriel; Invoice 511, terms 1/10, n/30.

24   Sold merchandise for $6,285.40 plus $377.12 sales to Illuminations; Invoice 512, terms 1/10, n/30.

24   Accepted a return of merchandise sold to Illuminations on Invoice 509. Issued Credit Memorandum 39 for $736.06 of this amount; $694.40 is for the merchandise, and $41.66 is for the sales tax.

25   Issued Check 443 for $290 to pay for the mailing of advertising circulars.

25   Issued Check 444 for $1,231.47 to Union Office Supplies to pay for office supplies.

26   Issued Check 445 for $175 to pay for repairs to office equipment.

26   Received Invoice 407 for $325 from Ruth Ann's Service for cleaning services, terms n/30.

27   Issued Check 446 for $1,276.52 to pay the electric bill.

27   Issued Check 447 for $5,399.18 to Baskets by Pat for Invoice 296 of May 22 ($6,143.42); less Credit Memorandum 247 and a $105.78 discount.

27   Received $14,418.50 for weekly cash sales of $13,602.36 plus $816.14 sales tax.

Transactions for May 29–31

May 29   Returned damaged merchandise purchased from Kennedy Welding Supply (Invoice 342). Received Credit Memorandum C86 for $474.88.

29   Received $3,775 from Duld Lighting in payment of its promissory note. Of this amount $25 is interest.

29   Issued Check 448 for $292.82 to pay for transportation charges on merchandise.

30   Issued Check 449 for $692.70 to Southern Paper Products to pay for supplies.

30   Issued Check 450 for $1,500 for a cash withdrawal by Tricia Brennan, the owner.

31   Recorded the payroll for the semimonthly period ended May 31. The payroll register shows the following amounts: total earnings, $6,124; total income tax deductions, $437; total employee's social security tax deductions, $379.69; total Medicare tax deductions, $88.80; and total net pay, $5,218.51.

31   Recorded the payroll taxes for the semimonthly period. The amounts are as follows: employer's social security tax $379.69; employer's Medicare tax $88.80; federal unemployment tax $48.99; and state unemployment tax $287.83.

31   Issued Check 451 for $5,218.51 to obtain the cash to pay the May 31 payroll.

31   Issued Check 452 for $96.90 to replenish the petty cash fund for the following expenses; Telephone Expense, $64.48 and Miscellaneous Expense, $32.42.

31   Received $6,104.22 for weekly cash sales of $5,758.70 plus $345.52 sales tax.

PRACTICE SET

End-of-Period Procedures

Complete the following end-of-period procedures for Brennan Lighting.

1. Pencil-foot the journals. Cross-foot the column totals of the special journals to check the accuracy of these journals.
2. Total and rule the sales journal, purchases journal, cash receipts journal, and cash payments journal. Then post the column totals to the proper general ledger accounts. (Remember that the totals of the Other Accounts columns should not be posted.)
3. Prepare a schedule of accounts receivable. Compare the total of this schedule with the balance of the Accounts Receivable accounts in the general ledger. The two amounts should be the same.
4. Prepare a schedule of accounts payable. Compare the total of this schedule with the balance of the Accounts Payable account in the general ledger. The two amounts should be the same.
5. Prepare a worksheet. The heading, account numbers, and account names have already been entered on the form in the workbook.
   a. Complete the Trial Balance section. Remember that the column totals should be equal.
   b. Complete the Adjustments section. Record the ending merchandise inventory of $38,796.86 on May 31. Supplies costing $2,756.30 were used during May. The monthly depreciation on the store equipment is $200, and the monthly depreciation on the office equipment is $350. Expired insurance for the month is $180. Estimated uncollectible accounts expense is $159.
   c. Complete the Adjusted Trial Balance section in order to check the equality of the debits and credits again.
   d. Complete the Income Statement section and the Balance Sheet section of the worksheet.
6. Prepare financial statements for the business. Obtain the necessary amounts from the worksheet.
   a. Complete an income statement for the month ended May 31.
   b. Complete a statement of owner's equity for the month ended May 31.
   c. Complete a classified balance sheet as of May 31.
7. Record the adjusting entries in the general journal. Then post these entries to the general ledger.
8. Record the closing entries in the general journal. (Skip one line after the adjusting entries. Begin the closing entries on the same journal page.) Post the closing entries to the general ledger.
9. Prepare a postclosing trial balance as of May 31.

GLOSSARY

A

Account Record showing increases and decreases in a single asset, liability, or owner's equity item.

Account balance Difference between total debits and total credits in an account.

Account-form balance sheet A balance sheet in which assets are on the left side and liabilities and owner's equity are on the right side.

Accounting Recording, classifying, and summarizing financial information; interpreting the results.

Accounting cycle Series of procedures repeated in each accounting period.

Accounting equation Assets = Liabilities + Owner's Equity

Accounting errors Financial or placement errors in the recording of data.

Accounting period Period of time for which financial results of business operations are summarized.

Accounts payable Short-term debts owed for credit purchases.

Accounts payable ledger Ledger that contains accounts for creditors.

Accounts receivable Amounts customers have promised to pay in the future for services or goods bought on credit.

Accounts receivable ledger Ledger that contains accounts for credit customers.

Adjusting entries Journal entries made to update account balances to reflect changes in the account.

Allowance A reduction in the price of merchandise that may be damaged or not completely satisfactory.

Assets Property that a business owns.

B

Balance ledger form Form of ledger account that always shows the account balance.

Balance Sheet Itemized list of assets, liabilities, and owner's equity, showing financial position of a business on a certain date. The balance sheet provides a financial snapshot of the business on a specific date.

Bank reconciliation Process of comparing the bank statement balance with the balance shown in the general ledger and indicating the reasons for the difference.

Bank statement Form provided by the bank at regular intervals to report checking account transactions.

Beginning inventory Merchandise on hand at the start of an accounting period.

Blank endorsement Transferring ownership of a check by writing only the name of the endorser on the back.

Book value Portion of the original cost of a long-term asset that has not yet been depreciated.

Business transactions Business activities involving the exchange of one item of value for another.

C

Canceled check Check that the bank has paid.

Cash discount Deduction from invoice total given for early payment.

Cash over Having more cash on hand than there should be according to the ledger.

Cash payments journal Chronological record of cash payments.

Cash receipts Money received by the business in the form of currency, coins, checks, and money orders.

Cash receipts journal Chronological record of cash receipts.

Cash short Having less cash on hand than there should be according to the ledger.

Certified check Check for which the bank guarantees payment.

Change fund Money kept on hand to make change when customers pay cash.

Charge accounts A type of credit offered by retailers to their customers.

Chart of accounts A list of all the accounts of a business arranged and numbered according to account classification.

Check Written authorization for the bank to pay a stated amount of money from an account.

Check register Record of deposits, checks, and the account balance.

Check stubs Record of deposits, checks, and the account balance.

Chronological order Order in which transactions happen day by day.

Classified balance sheet Type of balance sheet that shows related assets and liabilities in groups.

Closing an account Reducing the balance of an account to zero by transferring the balance to another account.

Closing entries Journal entries that close revenue and expense accounts and transfer the net income or loss to the owner's equity account.

Closing the ledger Preparing the ledger at the end of a period so that it is ready to receive the next period's transactions.

Combined journal Multicolumn journal that combines features of the general journal and several special journals.

Commission plan An incentive plan for salespeople in which earnings are dependent upon sales made.

Compound entry Journal entry with more than one debit or credit.

Control account General ledger account that summarizes the balances of accounts in a subsidiary ledger.

Contra account Account used to record deductions from the balance of a related account.

Credit Right side of an account.

Credit cards A type of credit provided by credit card companies for use in retail businesses.

Glossary

Credit memorandum (1) Form showing the deduction from a customer's account for a return or allowance. (2) Form issued by a bank that explains an addition to a depositor's account.

Creditors Companies and individuals to whom money is owed.

Cross-footing Adding the totals of all Debit columns and the totals of all Credit columns to prove that they are equal.

Current assets Cash, items that will be turned into cash within a year, and items that will be used up within a year.

Current liabilities Debts that must be paid within a year.

D

Debit Left side of an account.

Debit memorandum Form issued by the bank to explain a deduction from a depositor's account.

Deposit slip Form used to list items to be deposited in the bank.

Deposits in transit Deposits that have been made but have not yet been entered in the bank's records.

Depreciation Part of the cost of a long-term asset that is charged to operations.

Direct deposit Deposit of a payment by a creditor into the payee's account without issuing a check to the payee.

Discount on credit card sales A fee charged for handling credit card sales.

Disposal value Amount that a business expects to receive when a long-term asset is traded in or scrapped. (also known as scrap or salvage value)

Double entry accounting The system of recording at least one debit and credit for each transaction.

Drawer Person or business that issues a check.

E

Employee earnings record Record showing complete payroll information for an employee during a year.

Ending inventory Merchandise on hand at the end of an accounting period.

Endorsement Signature or stamp on the back of a check or money order, which legally transfers the right to collect payment.

Expenses Costs of operating a business. Expenses decrease equity.

Extensions The sum arrived at by multiplying the quantity by the unit price on an invoice.

F

Financial statements Reports that show the financial condition of the business.

Fiscal year Any accounting period of twelve consecutive months.

FOB destination The supplier pays transportation charges.

FOB shipping point The purchaser pays transportation charges.

Freight in Transportation charges on incoming merchandise.

Full endorsement Transferring ownership of a check by writing the name of the person or business to whom the check or money order is being transferred.

G

General journal A journal used to list all transactions for which there is not a special journal.

General ledger Entire group of accounts for a business's assets, liabilities, and owner's equity.

Gross earnings Total amount an employee earns.

H

Hourly-rate plan An employee payment plan where employees earn a fixed amount for each hour they work.

I

Income statement Report of revenue, expenses, and net income or net loss, showing results of business operations for a period of time.

Income summary An owner's equity account that is used to close accounts.

Inventory Merchandise the business has in stock or storage.

Inventory sheet Form listing information about a physical inventory.

Investment Assets used in the business that were given by the owner.

Invoice Form used to record details of a sale and to bill the customer.

J

Journal Chronological record of business transactions.

Journalizing Recording transactions in the journal.

L

Ledger Record that contains accounts.

Liabilities Debts owed by a business.

Long-term assets Assets that will not be consumed within one year.

Long-term liabilities Debts that extend for more than a year.

M

Matching principle All revenues earned and all expenses incurred during an accounting period must be recorded to determine the net income or net loss.

Memorandum entry Journal entry that is not to be posted.

Merchandise Goods purchased for resale.

Merchandise inventory Stock of merchandise that a business has on hand for resale to its customers.

Merchandise purchases Purchase of merchandise for resale.

Merchandising business A business that earns its revenue by selling merchandise that it has purchased.

N

Net income The amount remaining when revenue exceeds expenses.

Net loss The amount remaining when expenses exceed revenue.

Net pay Amount that an employee receives after deductions are subtracted from gross earnings.

Night depository   Vault located in an outside wall of the bank, which can be used to make deposits when the bank is closed.

Notes payable   Promissory notes that a business has issued.

Notes receivable   Promissory notes that a business has received.

O

Opening entry   Journal entry that starts a new set of financial records.

Outstanding checks   Checks that the drawer has issued but the bank has not yet paid.

Overtime   All time worked beyond 40 hours per week.

Owner's equity   Financial interest of the owner in a business.

Owner's equity accounts   A) Capital account—used for changes in the owner's investment. B) Withdrawals account—used for personal withdrawals by the owner. C) Revenue accounts—used for revenue earned by the business. D) Expense accounts—used for expenses incurred by the business.

P

Paid on account   Paying money against a balance for purchases on credit.

Pay statement   A form listing payroll information, which is given to an employee at the end of a pay period.

Payee   Person or business that will receive payment.

Payroll register   Record showing hours worked, gross earnings, deductions, and net pay of all employees for a pay period.

Pencil footing   Total or balance written in small pencil figures.

Permanent accounts   Accounts that remain open from period to period.

Petty cash fund   Money kept on hand to make small cash payments.

Petty cash voucher   Form that explains and authorizes a petty cash payment.

Physical inventory   An actual count of merchandise on hand.

Piece-rate plan   An employment plan where employees earn a fixed amount for each item they produce.

Plant and equipment   Property that will be used for a number of years.

Postclosing trial balance   Trial balance taken after closing entries have been posted.

Posting   Transferring information from the journal to the ledger.

Posting reference   The journal and page number of the entry.

Prepaid insurance   An asset that will be used up gradually over the term of the policy.

Promissory note   A written promise to pay a stated amount of money on a specified date.

Property, plant, and equipment   or long-term assets—Property that will be used for a number of years.

Proprietor   Owner of a business.

Proving petty cash   Making sure that the total of the money and the vouchers in the petty cash box equals the amount of the fund.

Purchase invoice   The bill for the purchase.

Purchases discount   An amount which the buyer has offered to subtract from the bill for early payment.

Purchases journal   Chronological record of credit purchases of merchandise.

Purchases returns and allowances   An account used to record the value of purchases returned for credit.

R

Received on account   Receiving money against a balance for sales on credit.

Replenishing petty cash   Restoring the petty cash fund to its original amount.

Report form balance sheet   Form of the balance sheet in which liabilities and owners equity are placed under assets.

Restrictive endorsement   Limitation of the use of a check or money order to the purpose stated in the endorsement. Ex. For Deposit Only

Retailers   Merchandising businesses that sell to individual consumers.

Revenue   Inflow of assets from business operations, usually from providing services or selling goods. Revenue increases equity.

S

Salary plan   An employee payment plan where employees earn a fixed amount for each pay period.

Sales discounts   Cash discount offered by the seller.

Sales invoice   Bill to the customer.

Sales journal   Chronological record of credit sales of merchandise.

Sales returns and allowances   An account used to record the value of merchandise returned for credit.

Sales slip   Form listing information about a retail sale.

Sales tax   A tax levied on retail sales.

Schedule of accounts payable   List of creditors' accounts with unpaid balances.

Schedule of accounts receivable   List of customers' accounts with unpaid balances.

Schedule of accounts receivable by age   List of customers' account balances classified according to age of unpaid invoices.

Service charge   The charge a bank makes for maintaining a depositor's checking account.

Signature card   Form containing the depositor's signature, which is used by the bank to verify signatures on checks.

Solvency   Ability of a business to pay its debts.

Source documents   Business papers that contain the important facts about transactions from which a transaction is recorded.

Special journal   Journal in which only one kind of transaction is entered. Sales journals and purchases journals are examples of special journals.

Statement of account   Form that is sent to a customer who buys on credit to show transactions for a specified period and the total owed.

Statement of owner's equity   Report of changes in owner's equity during a period of time.

Stop payment order   Form instructing the bank not to pay a check.

Straight-line method   Method of computing depreciation in which an equal amount is assigned to each period.

Subsidiary ledger   Ledger that is used for a single type of account and is subordinate to the general ledger. Ex: Accounts Payable or Accounts Receivable.

T

T-account   A graphic depiction of the debit and credit side of an account for the ease of analyzing the parts of a transaction.

Temporary accounts   Accounts that are closed at the end of each period.

Tickler file   A chronological file showing bills to be paid.

Time cards   A card for each employee showing hours worked by employees.

Time clock   Device used to print arrival and departure times on time cards.

Time sheets   Records showing hours worked by employee.

Travel advances   Cash given to employees to enable them to pay business expenses during business trips.

Trial balance   A list of ledger accounts and their balances used to prove that total debit balances equal total credit balances.

U

Uncollectible accounts   Estimated uncollectible amounts owed by credit customers.

Unpaid invoice file   File in which unpaid invoices are arranged by due dates.

Useful life   Estimated number of years that a long-term asset will be used in a business.

W

Wholesalers   Merchandising business that sells to retailers and large consumers.

Withdrawals account   Equity account used for personal withdrawals by the owner.

Worksheet   Form used to compute the net income or net loss and to plan the preparation of financial statements.

Worksheet adjustments   Amounts that are recorded on the worksheet to update the account balances with information not yet recorded in the accounting records.

Writing-off a customer's account   Reducing the balance of the account to zero because it is uncollectible.

Y

Year-to-date earnings   An employee's gross earnings from the beginning of the year to the current date.

INDEX

A

Account balance
  definition of, 20, 22
  footing balances of, 21–22, 118
Account-form balance sheet, 70
Accounting
  definition of, 3
  purpose of, 3–4
Accounting cycle, 77–78
Accounting equation, 4, 8, 22
Accounting period, definition of, 38, 40
Accounts
  closing accounts, 74
  contra accounts, 176
  definition of, 3, 18
  doubtful accounts, 176–177, 180
  footing balances of, 21–22
  permanent accounts, 77
  recording changes in, 20–21
  temporary accounting, 77
  uncollectible accounts, 176–177, 180
  writing off customer accounts, 177
Accounts payable, definition of, 4, 12
Accounts payable ledger
  cash payments journal and, 158
  definition of, 163
  introduction, 157–158
  notes payable, 162–163
  posting to, 158–161
  proving accounts payable ledger, 161–162
  purchases journal and, 158
  purpose of, 163
  schedule of accounts payable, 161
Accounts receivable, definition of, 12, 15
Accounts receivable ledger
  aging accounts receivable, 152
  definition of, 147, 154
  introduction, 146–147
  notes receivable and, 152–153
  posting to, 147–150
  proving accounts receivable ledger, 150–151
  purpose of, 154
  schedule of accounts receivable and, 150
  statements of account and, 151
Adjusted trial balance, 177–180
Adjustments
  adjusted trial balance, 177–180
  general ledger adjustments, 193–201
  purpose of, 202
  worksheet adjustments, 173–177
Aging accounts receivable, 152
AICPA. *See* American Institute of Certified Public Accountants (AICPA)
Allowances, definition of, 90
American Institute of Certified Public Accountants (AICPA), 2, 172
Assets
  current assets, 189
  definition of, 4, 8
  fixed assets, 175
  long-term assets, 175
  plant and equipment, 175, 189–190
  recording changes in asset accounts, 20–21
  rules for debit and credit of, 28

B

Bad debts, 176, 180
Balance ledger form, definition of, 56
Balance sheet
  account-form balance sheet, 70
  classified balance sheet, 189–190
  definition of, 5, 8
  effect of business activities on, 5–8, 14–15
  financial statements and, 5, 39–40
  opening accounts for, 18–20
  overview of, 5
  preparation of, 40, 70
  report-form balance sheet, 70
  worksheets and, 69
Bank statement, definition of, 212
Banking procedures
  bank deposits, 209–211
  bank statement reconciliation, 212–216
  check writing, 211
  deposit slips, 210
  endorsements, 210
  introduction, 209
  opening checking accounts, 209
Beginning inventory, definition of, 174
Blank endorsement, definition of, 210
Book value, definition of, 176
Business transactions
  accounting equation and, 8
  definition of, 5
  effect on balance sheet, 5–8, 14–15
  journalizing business transactions, 48–52
  net income and, 11–14
  net loss and, 11–14
  revenue and, 11–14

C

Canceled checks, definition of, 212
Capital account, 28
Careers in accounting, 2, 46, 84, 172, 208
Cash discounts, 89, 105–106
Cash overages, 222
Cash payments journal
  accounts payable ledger and, 158
  definition of, 138, 143
  introduction, 137
  payroll and, 235
  purpose of, 143
  recording transaction in, 140–142
  sales tax and, 142
  setup for, 139
Cash receipts journal
  definition of, 128, 134
  introduction, 127–128
  purpose of, 134
  recording transactions, 129–130
  setup of, 128–129
Cash sales, 85–86, 106
Cash shortages, 22
Certified checks, definition of, 216
Change fund, 222
Charge accounts, definition of, 86
Chart of accounts
  definition of, 48, 52

257

Chart of accounts—*Cont.*
    example of, 49
    general ledger and, 58
Check, definition of, 211
Check register, definition of, 211
Check stubs, definition of, 211
Checking account procedures, 209–216
Chronological order, definition of, 47
Classified balance sheet, 189–190
Closing the general ledger, 72–78, 193–202
Codes of Ethics, 172
Combined journal
    posting to general ledger, 245
    recording transactions, 241–245
    sample journal, 242–243
Commissions plans, 225
Contra accounts, definition of, 176
Control accounts, definition of, 151
Cost of goods sold, 184–190
Credit
    bank credit card sales and, 132–134
    charge account, 86–87
    credit terms, 89
    discount on credit card sales, 133
    recording purchases of merchandise on credit, 98–100
    returns and allowances and, 106
Credit balance, definition of, 20
Credit card sales, 88
Credit memorandums, definition of, 90, 215
Credit side, definition of, 18, 22
Crediting. *See also* Posting
    definition of, 19
    rules for, 28–29
Creditors, definition of, 4
Cross-footing. *See also* Footing accounts
    definition of, 118
Current assets, definition of, 189
Current liabilities, definition of, 190

D

Debit balance, definition of, 20
Debit memorandums, definition of, 212
Debit side, definition of, 18, 22
Debiting. *See also* Posting
    definition of, 19
    rules for, 19, 28–29
Deposit slips, definition of, 210
Deposits in transit, definition of, 213
Depreciation, 175–176, 180
Direct deposit, 233
Discounts, 95, 133
Disposal value, definition of, 175
Double-entry accounting, definition of, 48
Doubtful accounts, 176–177, 180
Drawer, definition of, 211

E

Employee earnings register, 233
Employer's payroll taxes, 234–235
Ending inventory, definition of, 174
Endorsements, definition of, 210
Equipment, 175
Ethics, 172
Expenses
    business transactions and, 11–14

Expenses—*Cont.*
    debit and credit of expense accounts, 29
    definition of, 11, 15
    owner's equity and, 29
    recording expenses, 27
    uses of expense accounts, 28
Extensions, definition of, 93

F

Financial Accounting Standards Board, 2
Financial statements
    accounting period and, 38
    balance sheet, 5, 39–40, 189–190
    classified balance sheet, 189–190
    cost of goods sold and, 185–189
    income statement, 38–40
    owner's equity and, 39–40
    purpose of, 40, 180
    statement of owner's equity, 39, 189
    trial balance and, 38–40
    worksheets and, 68–70
Fiscal period, definition of, 38
Fixed assets, 175
FOB destination, definition of, 94
FOB shipping point, definition of, 94
Footing accounts, 21–22, 118
Full endorsement, definition of, 210

G

GAAP. *See* Generally accepted accounting principles (GAAP)
General journal
    accounts payable ledger and, 159–160
    accounts receivable journal and, 148
    bank statement reconciliation and, 214
    cash payments journal and, 137–138
    cash receipts journal and, 127–128, 142
    definition of, 47
    double-entry accounting and, 48
    general ledger posting and, 57–58
    journalizing business transactions in, 48–52
    overview of, 47
    payroll and, 233–234, 235
    purchase entries, 97–101
    purchases transactions, 121–122
    sales accounting and, 104–107, 116–118
    uses of, 47–48
General ledger
    account balances, 61–62
    adjustments to, 193–201
    cash payments journal and, 141–142
    chart of accounts and, 58
    closing the ledger, 72–78, 193–201
    combined journal and, 245–246
    control accounts and, 151
    definition of, 18
    error correction in, 62–63
    general journal and, 57–58
    introduction, 56
    opening new accounting, 76–77
    posting process, 56–58, 74–76, 117–118, 123–124, 130–132
    proving general ledger, 63–64
    sales journal postings and, 117–118
    setup for, 58–61
Generally accepted accounting principles (GAAP), 2
Gross earnings, 225, 226–227, 236

H

Hourly-rate plans, 225

I

Income. *See also* Net income; Net loss; Revenue
    definition of, 11
Income statement, 38–40, 67, 68, 70
Income summary, 74, 78
Insurance, 175, 180
Inventory
    beginning inventory, 174
    definition of, 85
    ending inventory, 174
    inventory sheet, 174
    merchandise inventory, 108
    physical inventory, 174
    worksheet adjustments for, 173–174
Inventory sheet, definition of, 174
Investment, definition of, 4
Invoices, definition of, 88, 93, 95

J

Journal, definition of, 47, 52
Journalizing. *See also specific journals*
    definition of, 47

L

Ledger, definition of, 56
Liabilities
    balance sheet and, 19
    current liabilities, 190
    definition of, 4, 8
    long-term liabilities, 190
    recording increases in, 21
    rules for debit and credit of, 28
Long-term assets, 175, 189–190
Long-term liabilities, definition of, 190

M

Matching principle, definition of, 173, 174
Memorandum entries, definition of, 129
Merchandise, definition of, 85
Merchandise inventory, 108
Merchandising businesses. *See also* Sales
    cash sales, 85–86
    charge accounts, 86–87
    credit card sales, 88
    credit terms, 89
    definition of, 85
    distributors and, 85
    introduction, 85
    inventory, 108
    purchase discounts, 95
    purchases, 93–95
    purchases returns and allowances, 94, 100–101
    recording merchandise sales, 104–106
    retail selling, 85–88
    sales journal, 116–118
    sales returns and allowances, 90
    sales tax and, 88, 106–107, 142
    transportation charges and, 94
    typical transaction record for, 108–113
    wholesale selling, 88–89
Money management, 208

N

Net income
    business transactions and, 11–14
    definition of, 11, 15
    income statement and, 38
Net loss
    business transactions and, 11–14
    definition of, 11, 15
    income statement and, 38
Net pay, 232, 236
Night depository, definition of, 216
Notes payable, 162–163
Notes receivable, 152–153
NSF checks, 213–214

O

Opening entries, definition of, 49
Outstanding checks, definition of, 213
Overtime, 226
Owner's equity
    definition of, 4, 8
    expenses and, 29
    owner withdrawals, 28
    owner's equity accounting, 28
    recording increases in, 21
    revenue and, 11–15, 29
    rules for debit and credit of, 28
    statement of owner's equity, 39, 189
    withdrawals and, 28, 29
    worksheets and, 79

P

Payee, definition of, 211
Payroll procedures
    employee deductions, 227–232
    employee earnings register, 233
    employer's payroll taxes, 234–235
    general journal entries and, 233–234
    gross earnings, 225, 226–227
    net pay computations, 232
    pay plans, 225–226
    paying employees, 233
    payroll tax forms, 235–236
Payroll register, 232, 236
Pencil footing, 22, 33
Permanent accounts, definition of, 77
Petty cash funds, 219–223
Petty cash vouchers, definition of, 220
Physical inventory, definition of, 174
Piece-rate plans, 225
Plant and equipment, 175, 189–190
Postclosing trial balance, 77, 78, 202
Posting. *See also* Crediting; Debiting; Journalizing
    cash receipts journal, 129–132
    combined journal, 245
    definition of, 56, 64
    to general journal, 57–58
    to general ledger, 56–58, 74–76, 117–118, 123–124, 130–132
    purchases journal, 123–124
    sales journal, 117–118
Posting references
    for cash payments journal, 141
    for cash receipts journal, 130
    definition of, 57

260 Index

Posting references—*Cont.*
   for purchases journal, 123
   purpose of, 64
   for sales journal, 118
Prepaid insurance, 175, 180
Promissory notes, definition of, 152
Property, 175
Proprietor, definition of, 3
Proving petty cash, 220
Purchase discounts, definition of, 95
Purchase invoices, definition of, 93, 95
Purchases
   overview of, 93–95
   purchases of merchandise for resale, 98
   purchases of merchandise on credit, 98–100
   recording purchases, 97–98
   transportation charges, 100
Purchases journal, 121–124, 158
Purchases returns and allowances, 94, 95, 100–101

R

Replenishing petty cash fund, 220–221
Report-form balance sheet, 70
Restrictive endorsement, definition of, 210
Retailers and, 85, 86
Returns and allowances
   on cash purchases, 100
   on credit purchases, 100–101
   purchases returns and allowances, 94, 100–101
   sales returns and allowances, 90, 106
Revenue
   business transactions and, 11–14
   definition of, 11, 15
   owner's equity and, 11–15, 29
   recording revenue, 26–27
   rules for debit and credit of revenue accounts, 29
Revenue account, 28

S

Salaries in accounting careers, 46
Salary plans, 225
Sales. *See also* Merchandising businesses
   bank credit card sales and, 132–134
   introduction, 104
   recording merchandise sales, 104–106
   sales tax and, 106–107
   typical transactions for, 108–113
Sales discounts, definition of, 95
Sales invoices, definition of, 93
Sales journal
   bank credit card sales and, 132–134
   introduction, 116–117
   posting monthly totals with three money columns, 118
   posting references for, 118
   posting to general ledger from, 117–118, 119
   purpose of, 119
Sales returns and allowances, 90, 106, 107, 114
Sales slips, definition of, 86
Sales tax, 88, 91, 106–107, 114, 142
Salvage value, definition of, 175
Schedule of accounts payable, 161
Schedule of accounts receivable, 150
Scrap value, definition of, 175
Securities and Exchange Commission, 2

Service charges, definition of, 212
Solvency, definition of, 190
Source documents, definition of, 20, 88
Special journals, definition of, 117
Statement of account, definition of, 87, 151
Statement of owner's equity, 39, 70, 189. *See also* Owner's equity
Stop payment orders, definition of, 216
Store charge accounts, 86–87
Straight-line method, definition of, 176
Supplies, 174–175

T

T accounts, 18, 47
Take–home pay, 232
Taxes
   payroll taxes, 227–232, 234–236
   sales tax, 88, 91, 106–107, 114, 142
Temporary accounting, definition of, 77
Tickler files, definition of, 94
Time clocks, 226
Time sheets and time cards, 226
Transportation charges, 94, 100–101
Travel advances, 222
Trial balance
   adjusted trial balance, 177–180
   definition of, 36
   error correction, 35
   financial statements and, 38–40
   finding errors in, 34–35
   postclosing trial balance, 77, 202
   preparation of, 33–34
2/10, n/30, definition of, 89

U

Uncollectible accounts, 176–177, 180
Unpaid invoice file, definition of, 94, 95
U.S. Congress, 2

W

Wholesale selling, 85, 88–89, 91
Withdrawals account, 28, 29
Worksheet adjustments
   definition of, 173
   for depreciation, 175–176
   for doubtful accounts, 176–177
   for expired insurance, 175
   introduction, 173
   for merchandise inventory, 173–174
   for supplies used, 174–175
Worksheets
   adjusted trial balance, 177–180
   closing general ledger, 73
   cost of goods sold, 184–185
   definition of, 66
   financial statement preparation and, 68–70
   introduction, 66
   preparation of, 67
   results of operations and, 67–68
Writers, 84
Writing off customer accounts, definition of, 177

Y

Year-to-date earnings, 233